Spread Love Like Wildfire

Guitar Tablature

By 3ichael 7ambert

"Spread Love Like Wildfire" is a testament to the power of music to ignite emotions and inspire change. This guitar tablature book is a comprehensive guide to every song on my debut album, meticulously transcribed to capture the essence and energy of each track. Whether you're a seasoned guitarist or a passionate beginner, you'll find detailed tabs, chord diagrams, and performance notes that will bring these songs to life. Dive into the melodies and harmonies that define "Spread Love Like Wildfire," and join me in spreading love, one strum at a time.

Table of Contents

Are You Out There?	7
As The Rain	39
Egypt	45
C Is For Cassie	73
Carnival City	81
Dear Father	103
Fight!	109
Forget Her	145
Hello My Friend, Hello	169
I Never Thought	181
Last Night	205
Anti-Christ	235
OMG We Like To Party	247
The Feeling I Get	257
Tonight's The Night	265

Are You Out There

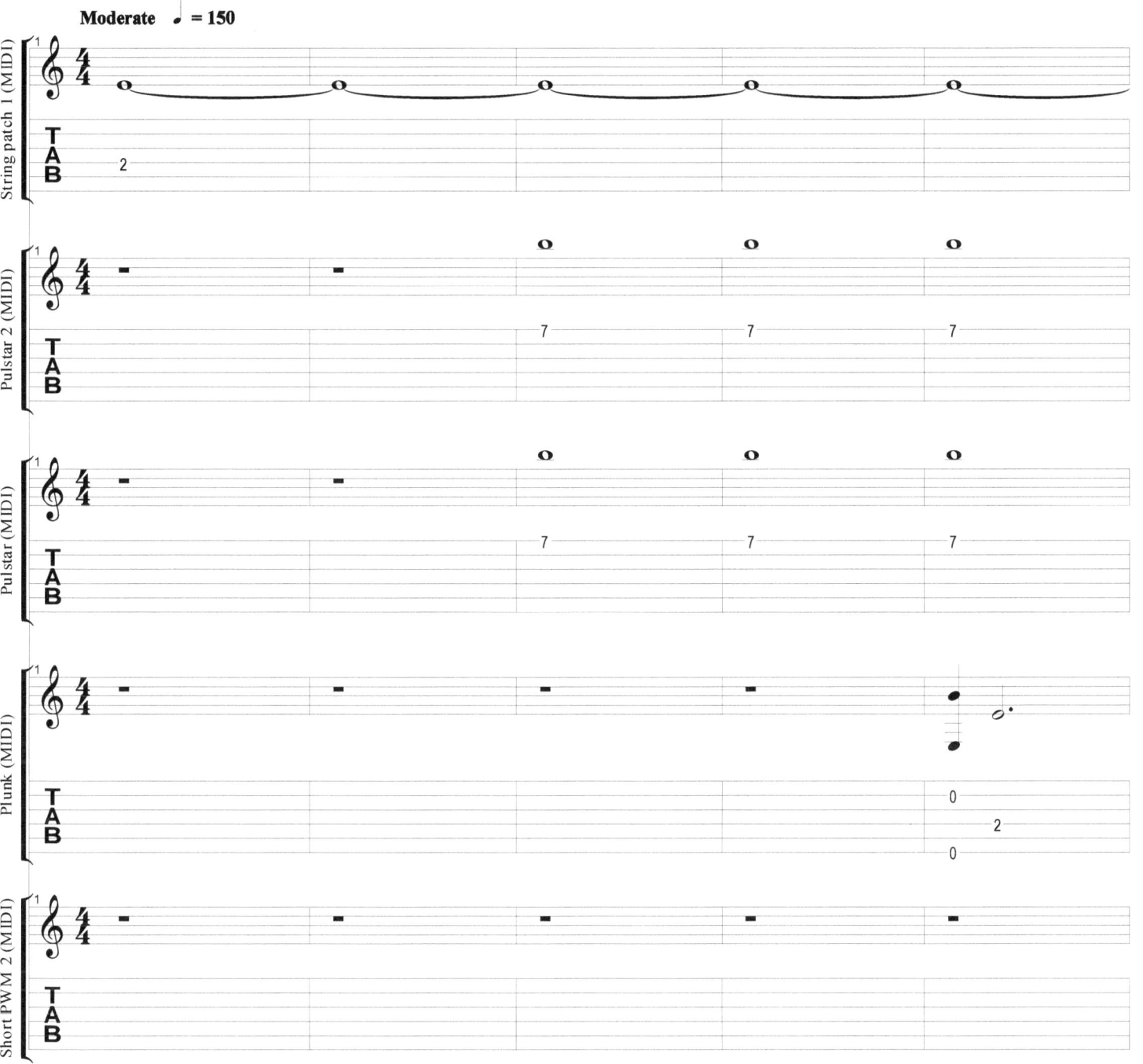

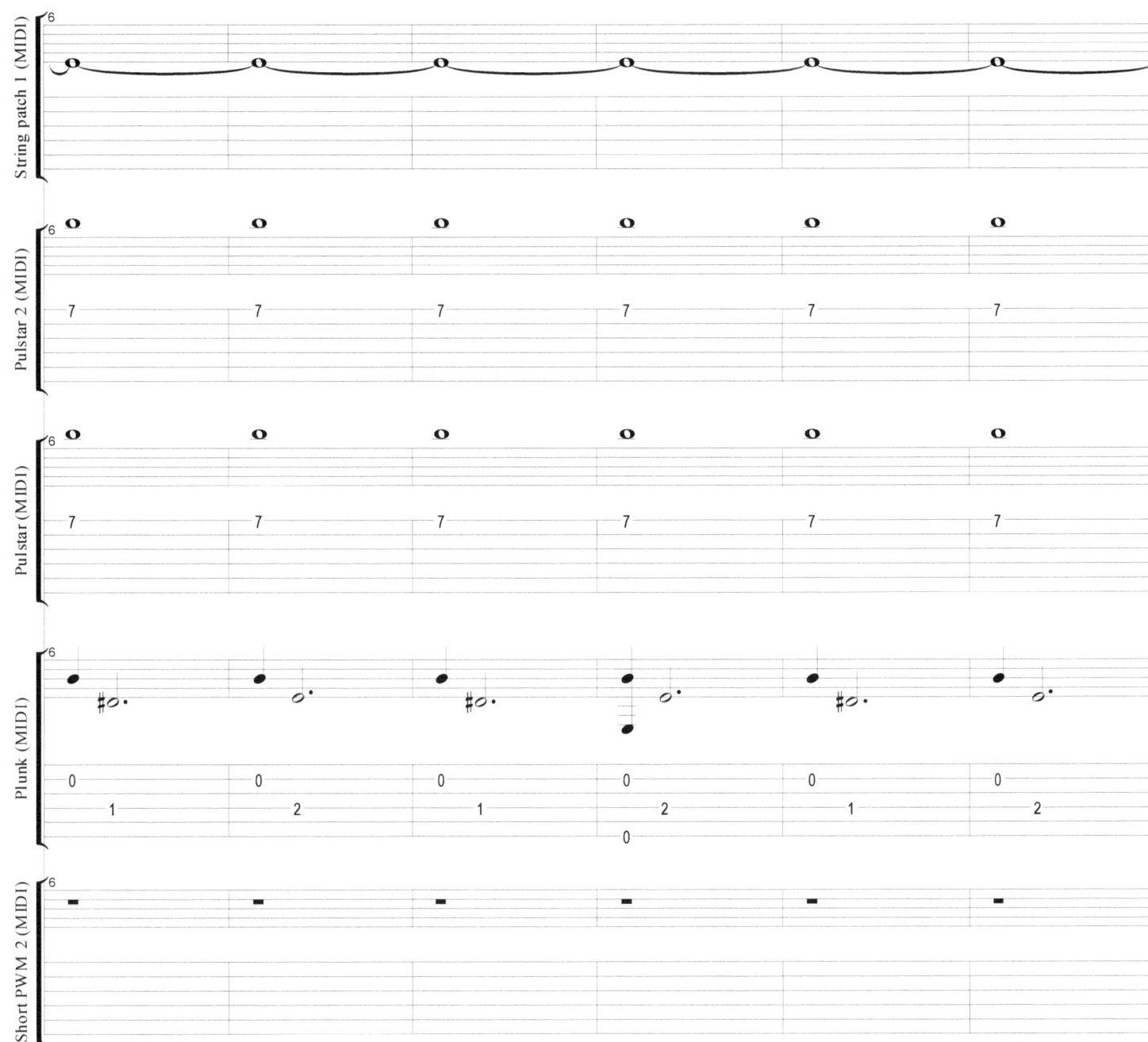

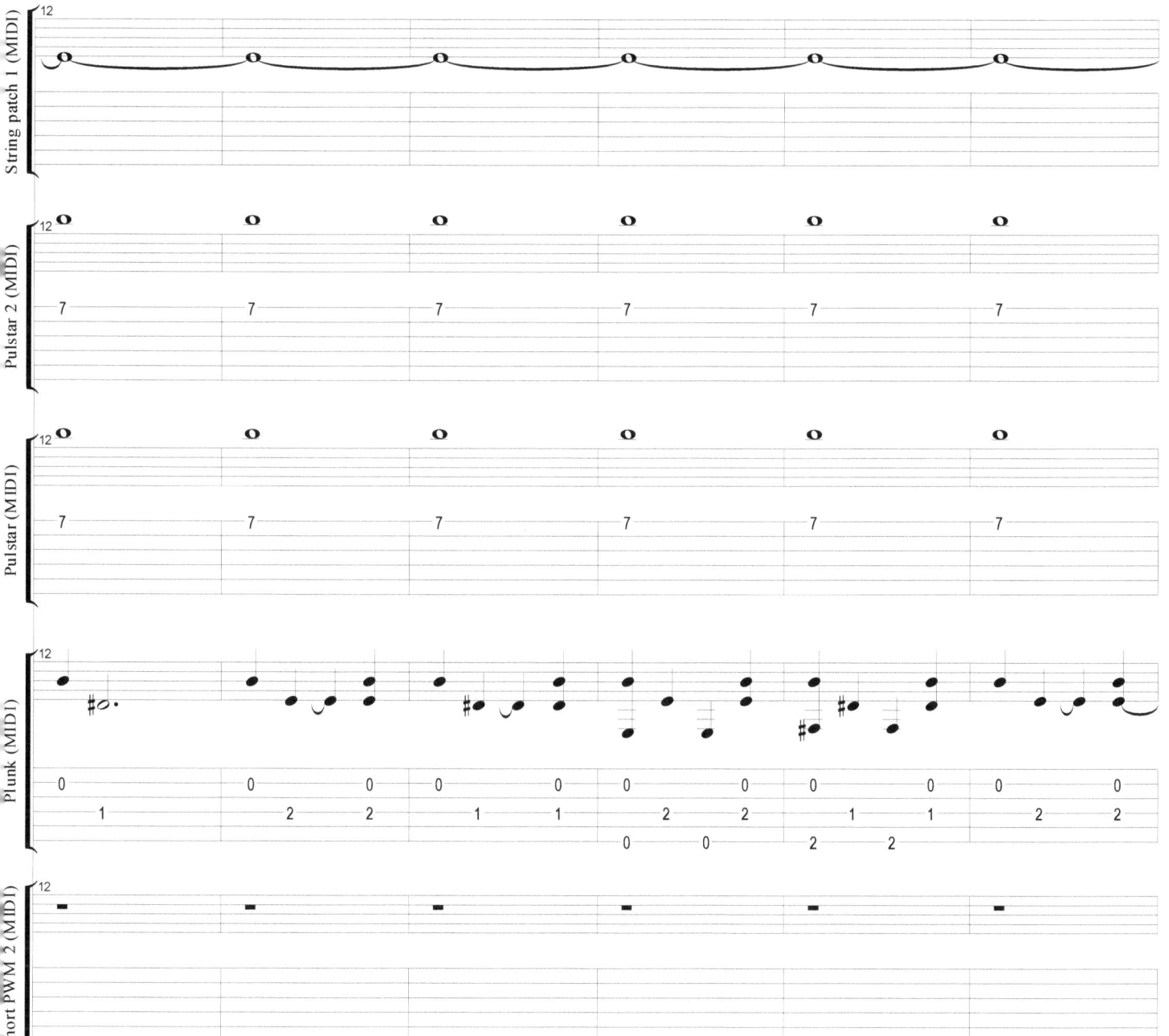

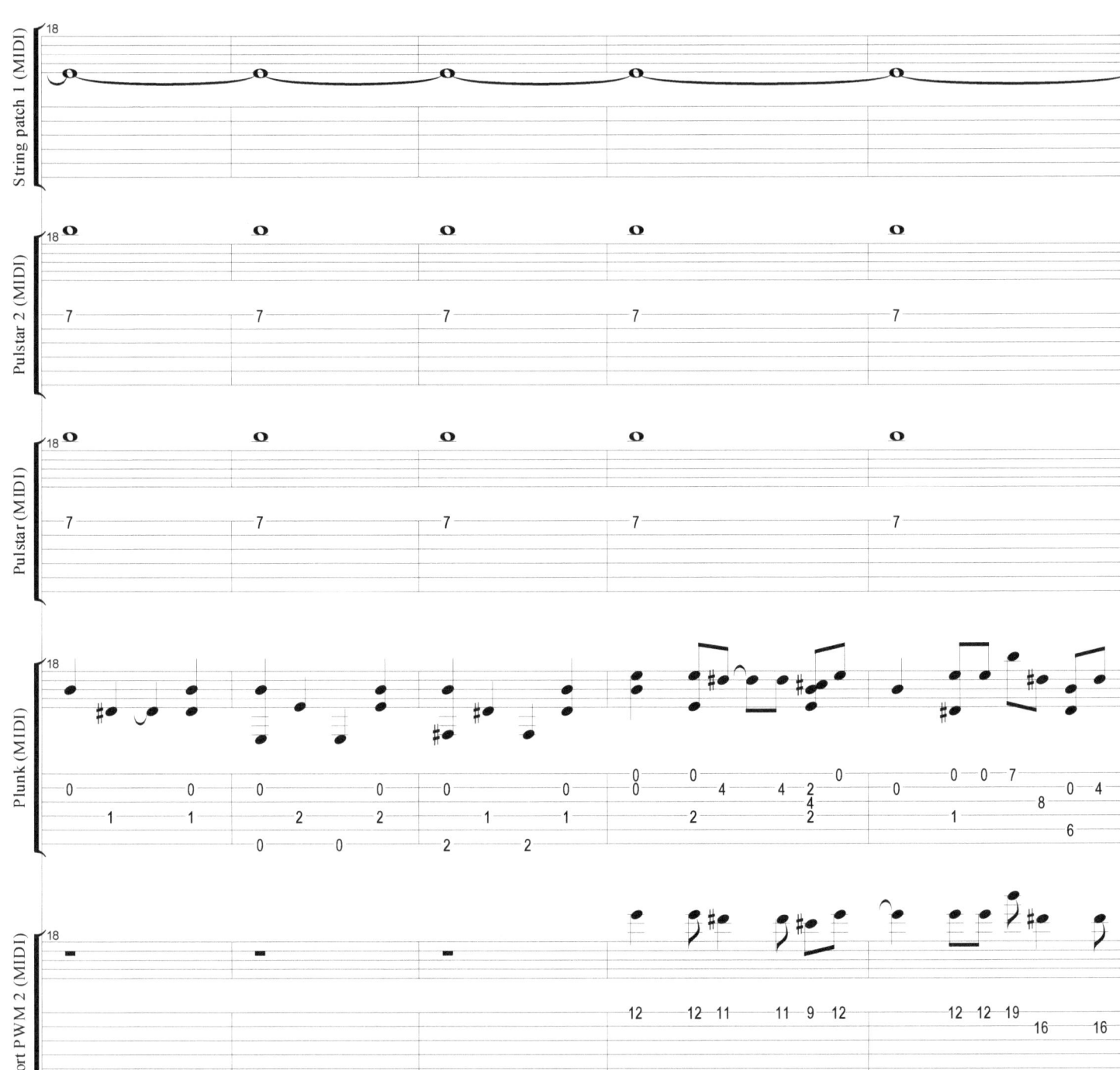

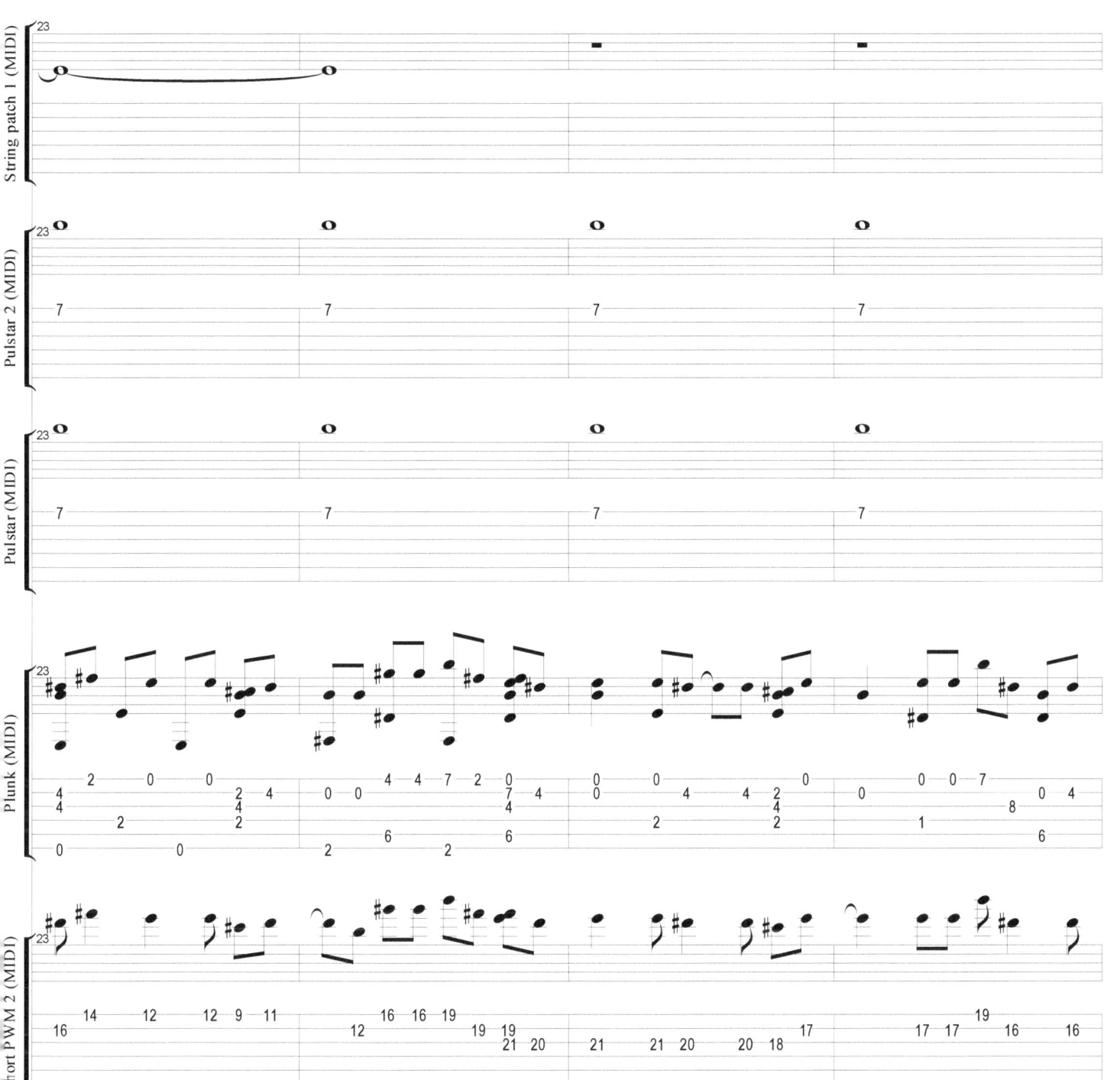

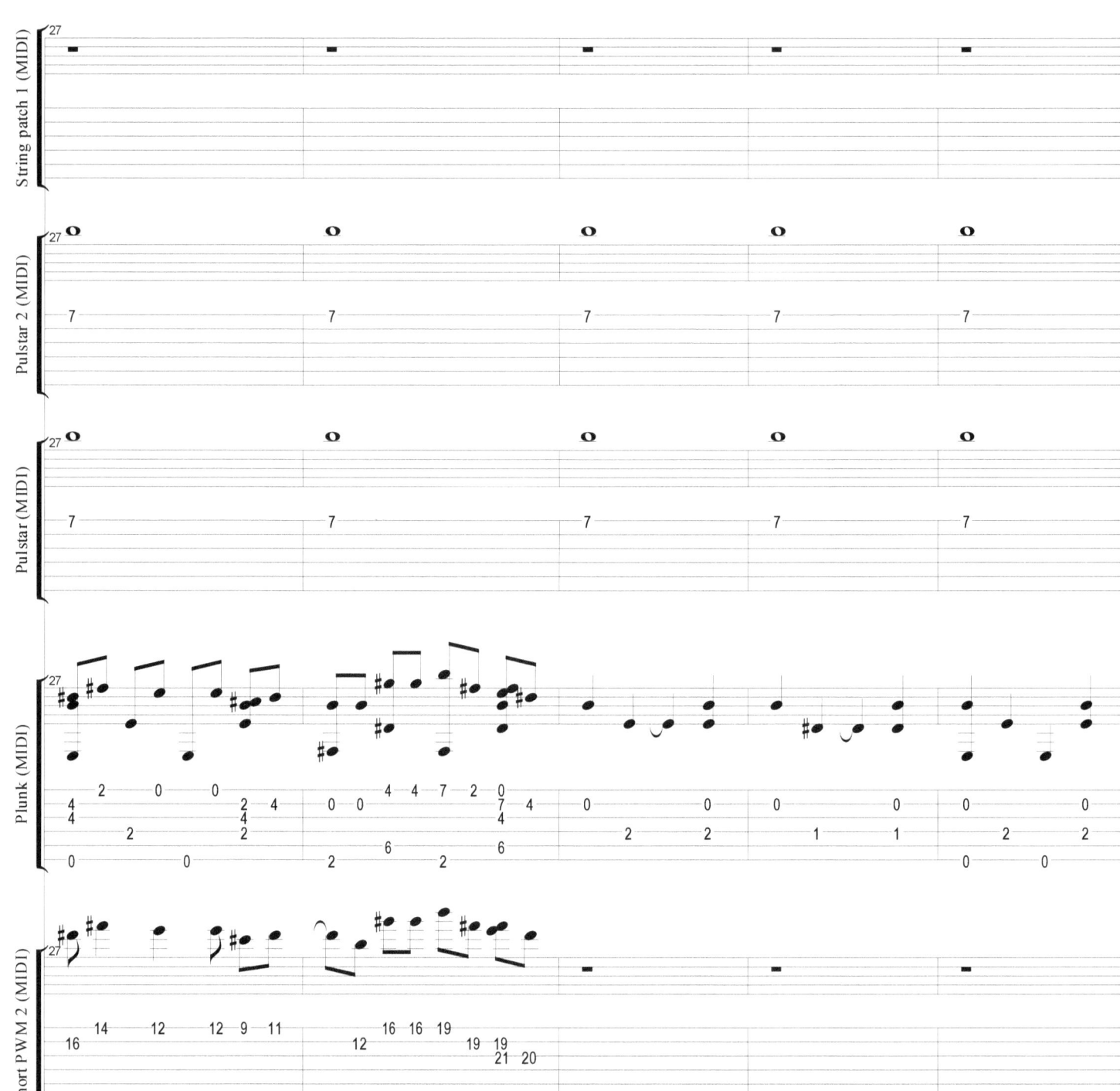

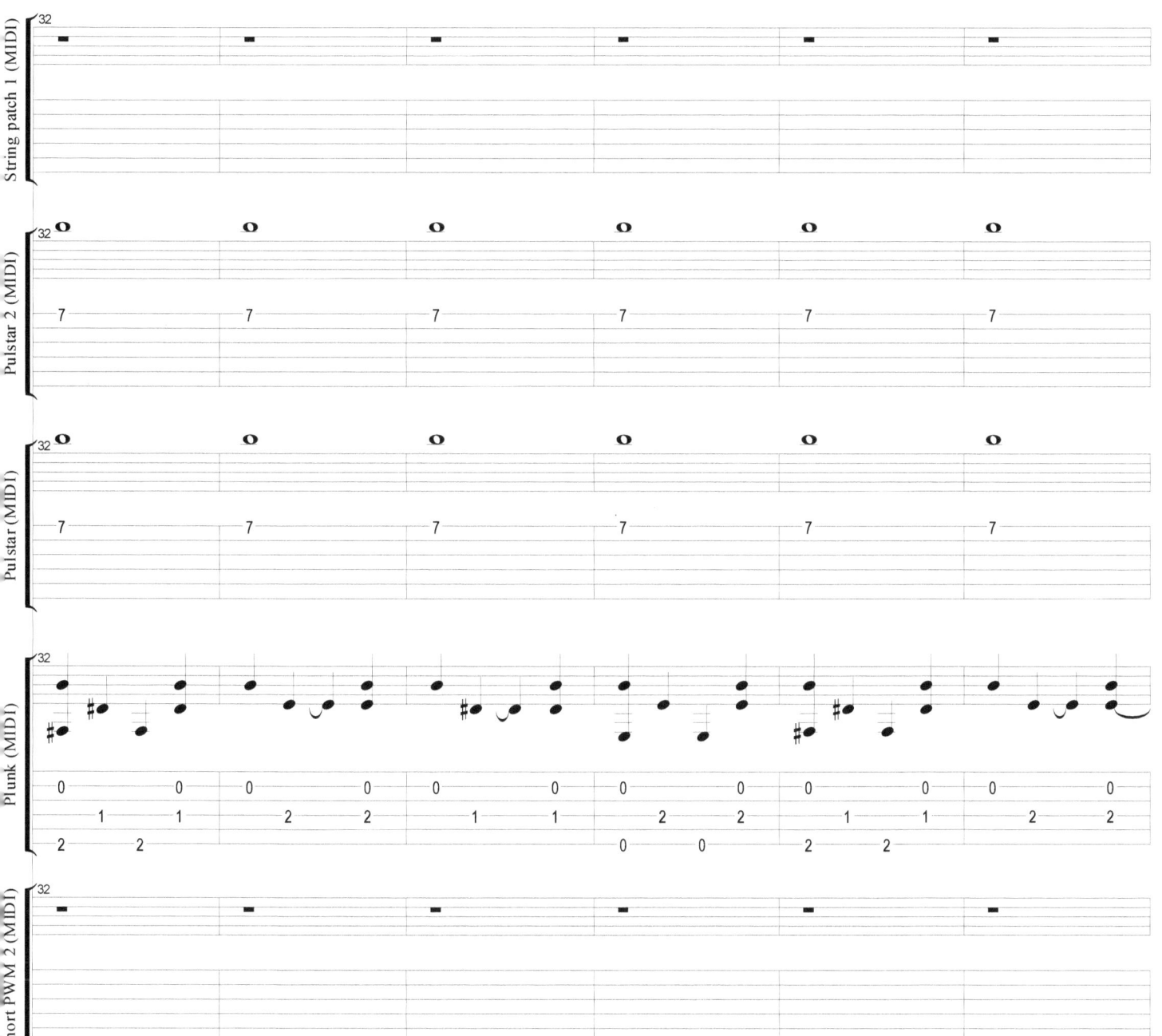

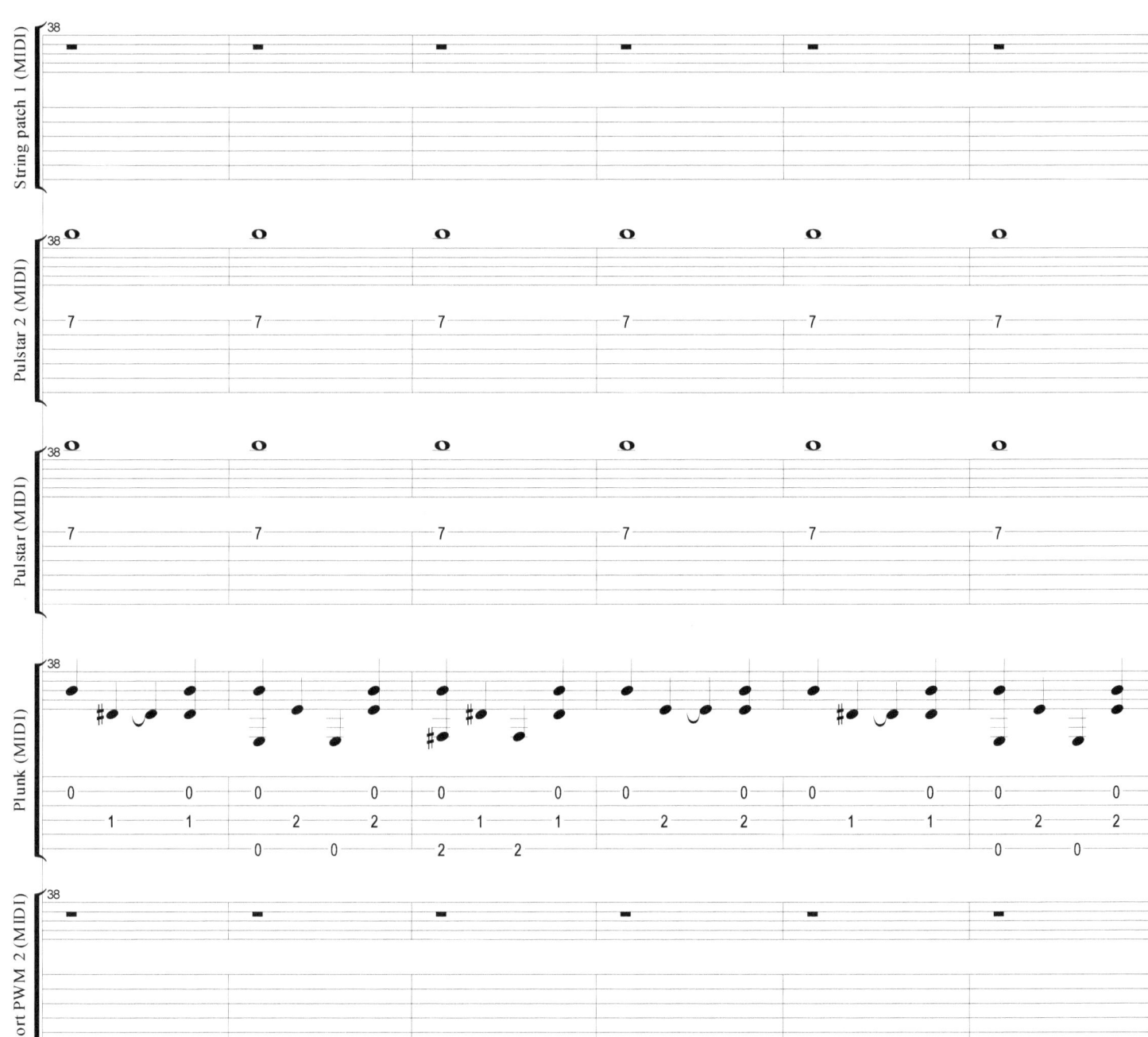

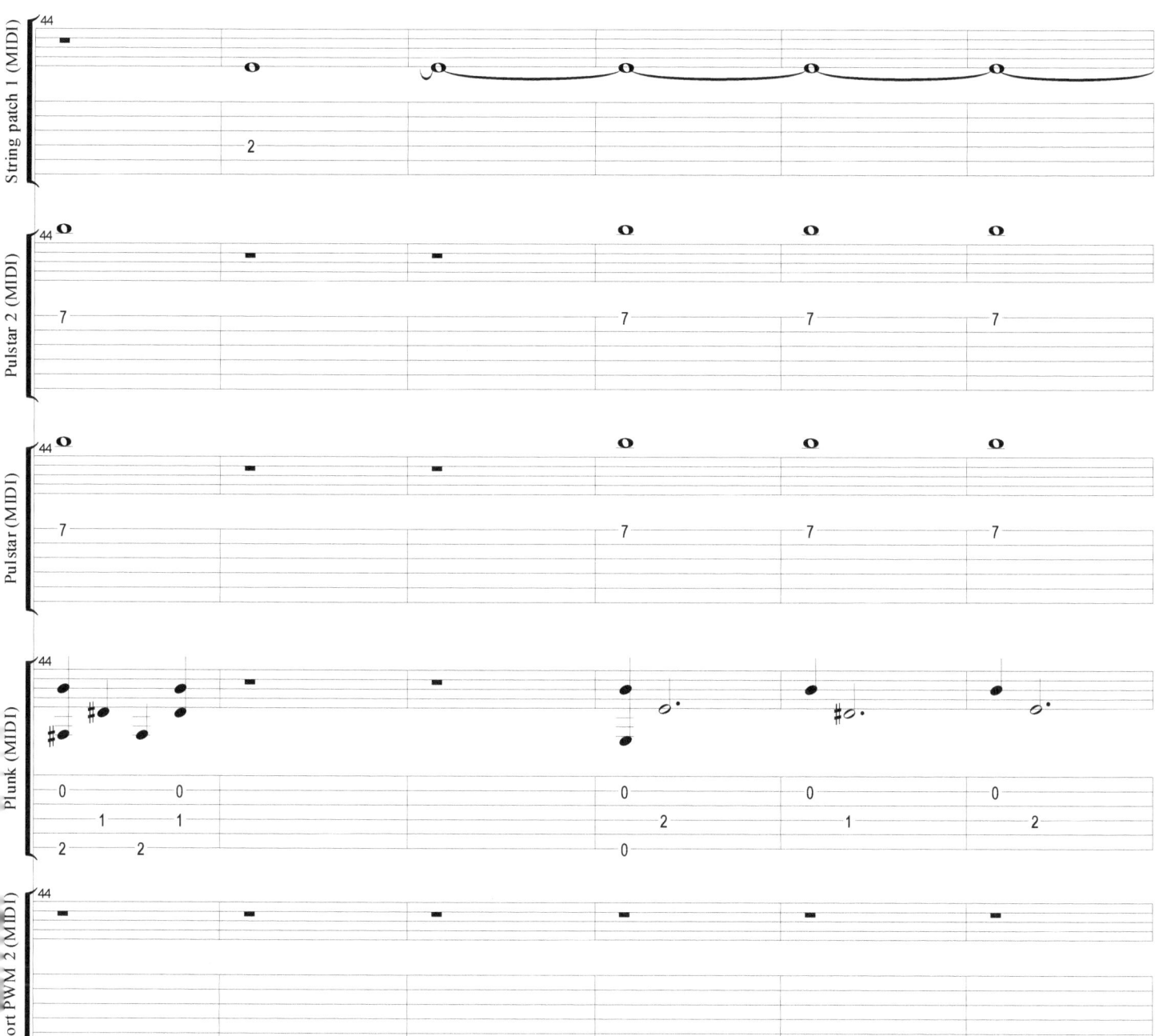

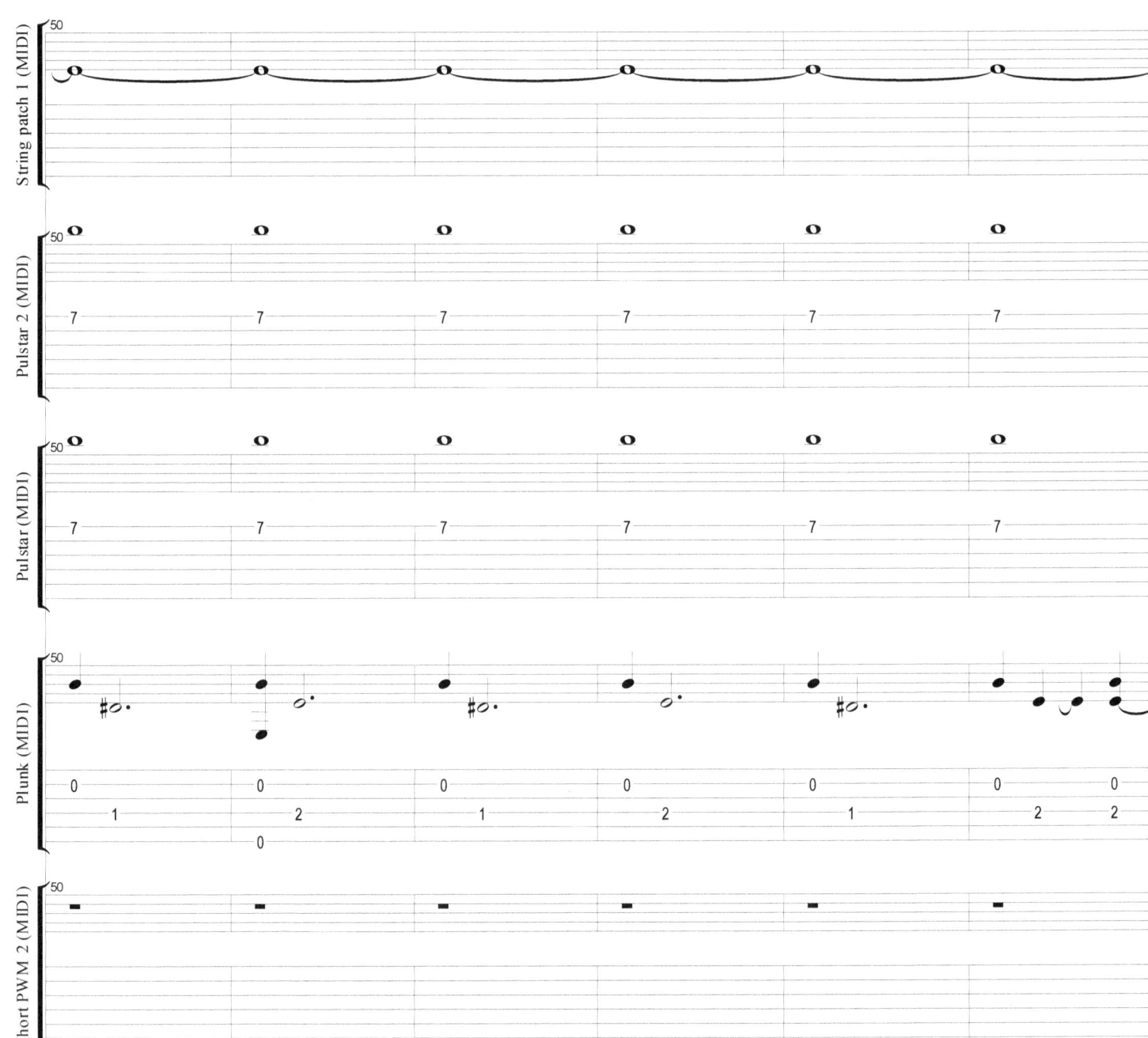

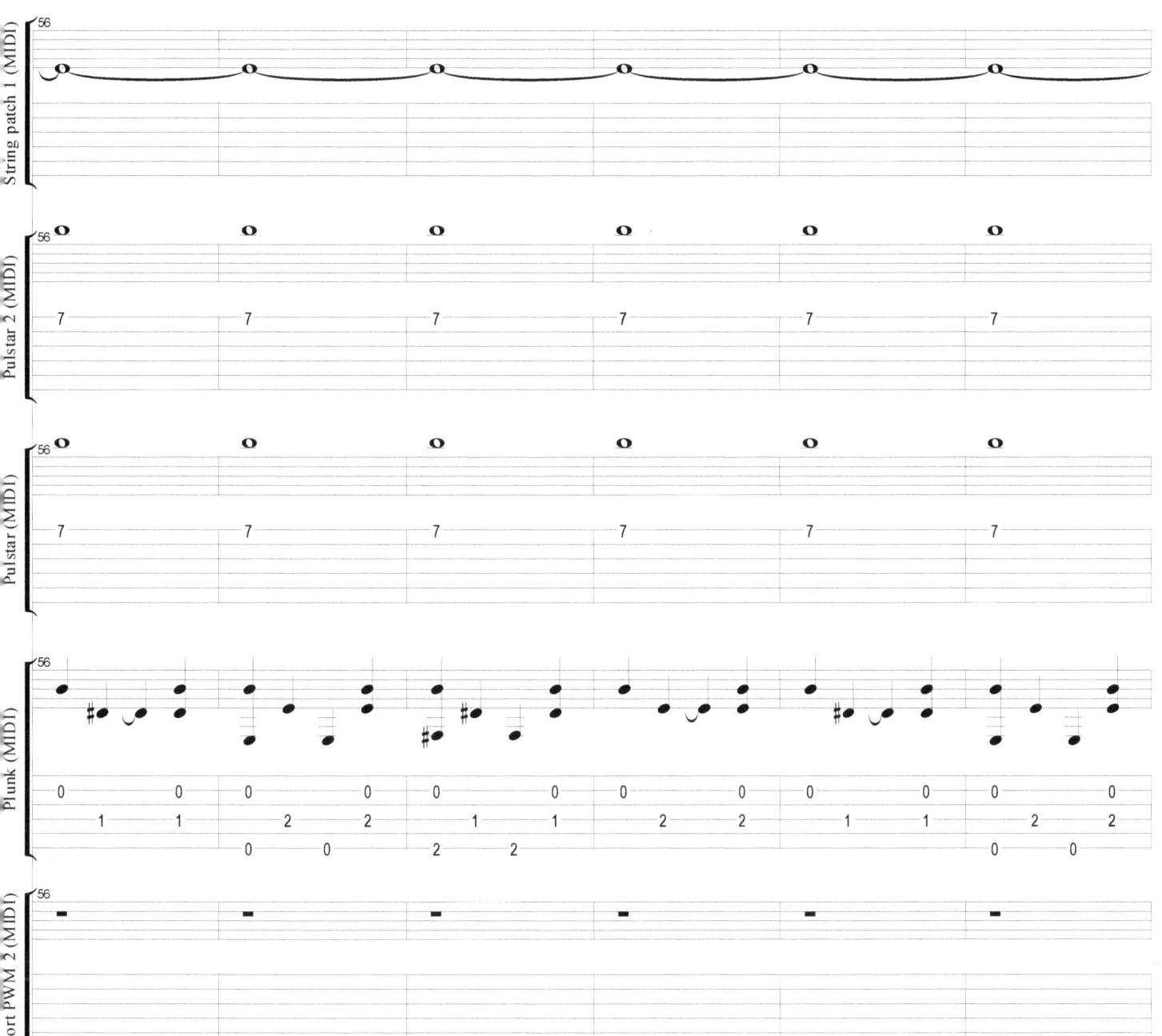

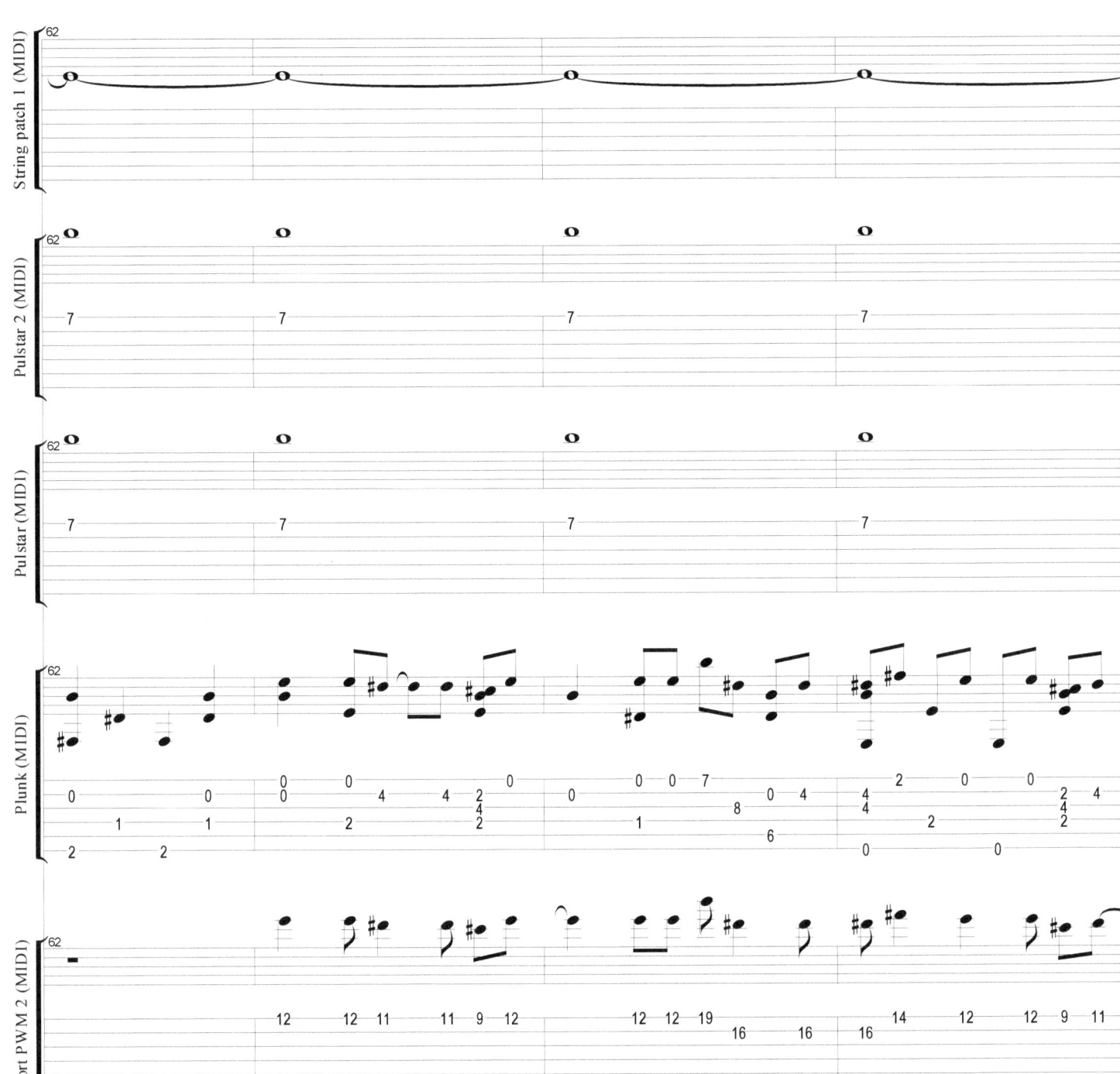

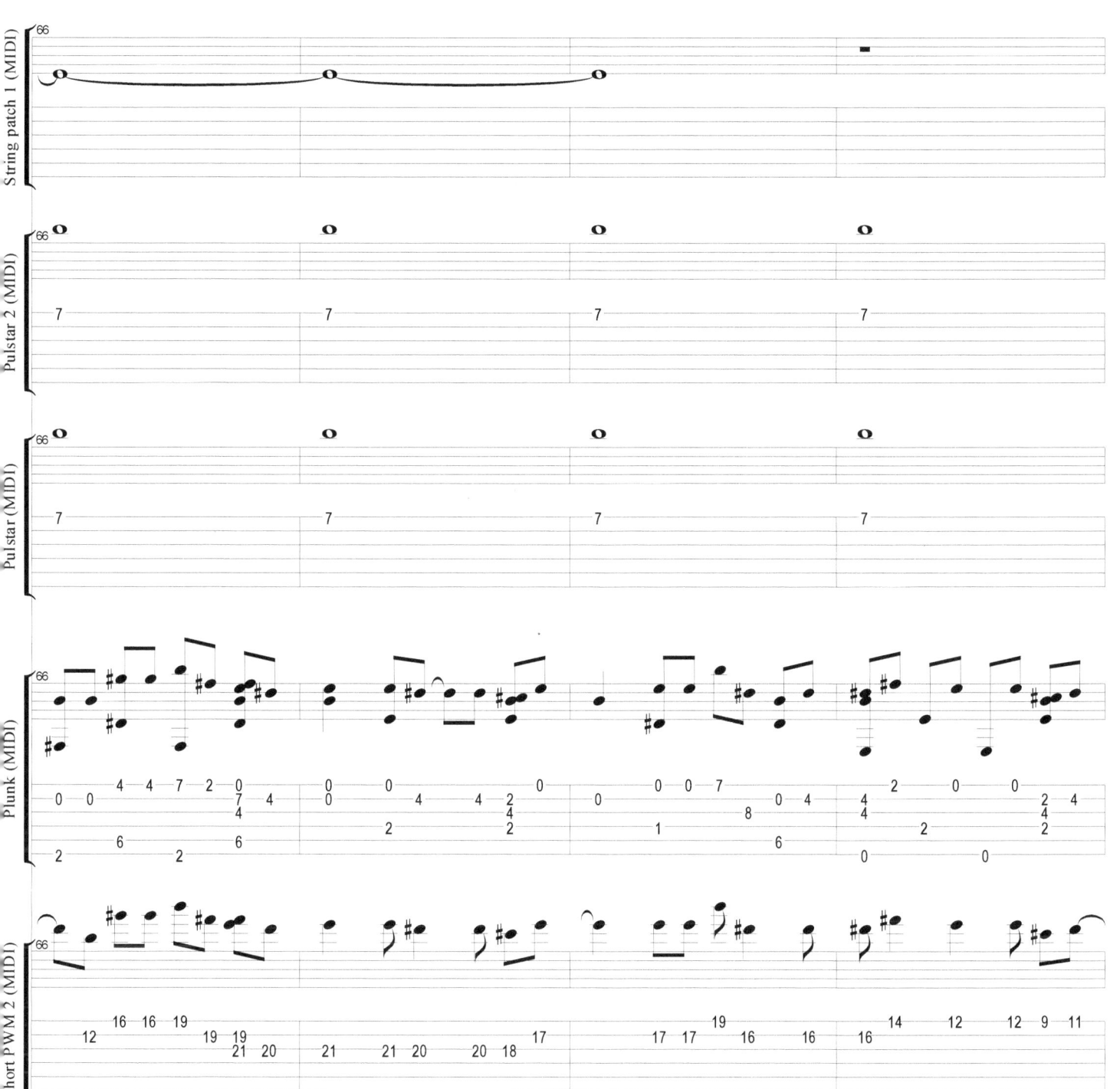

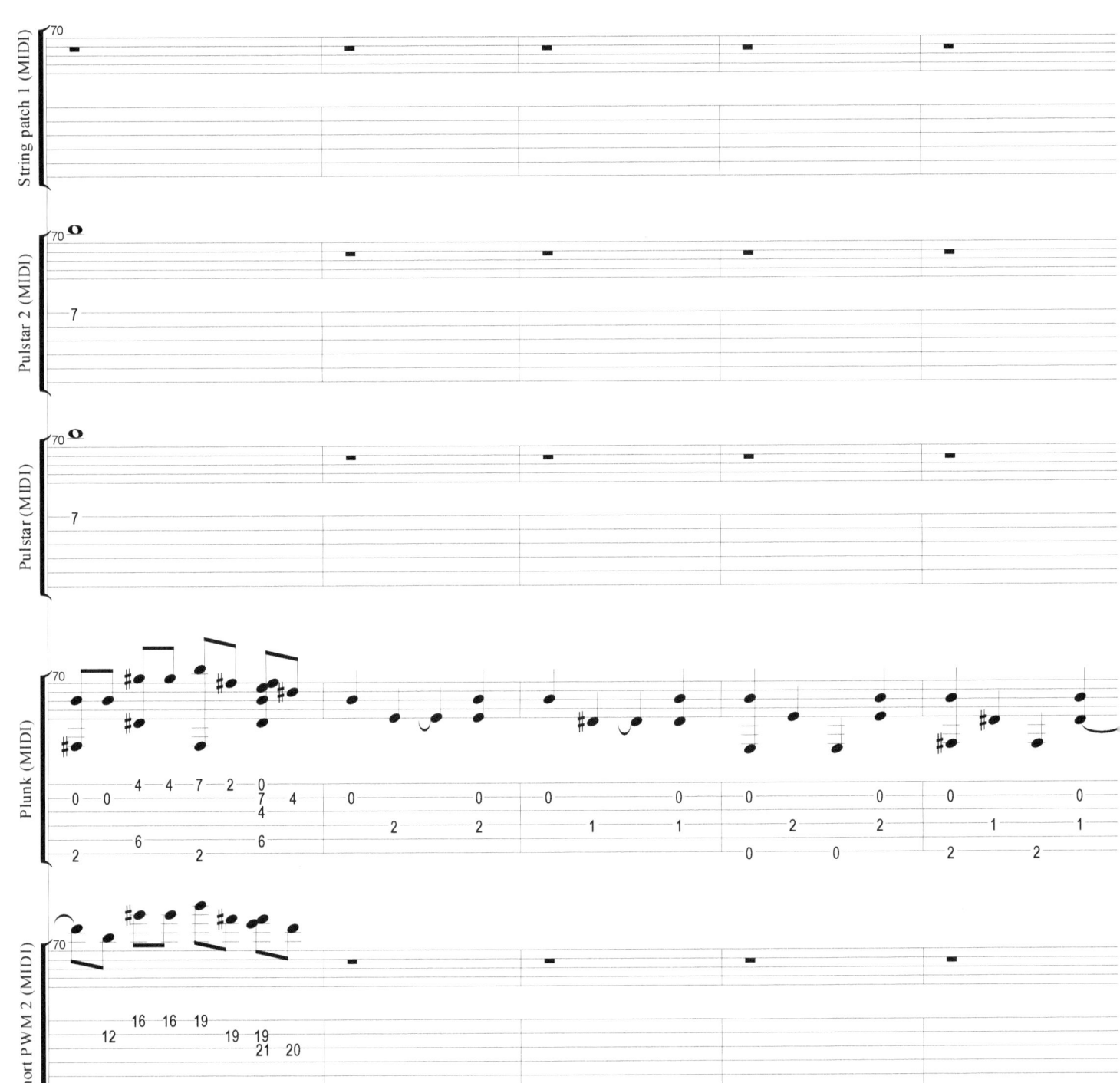

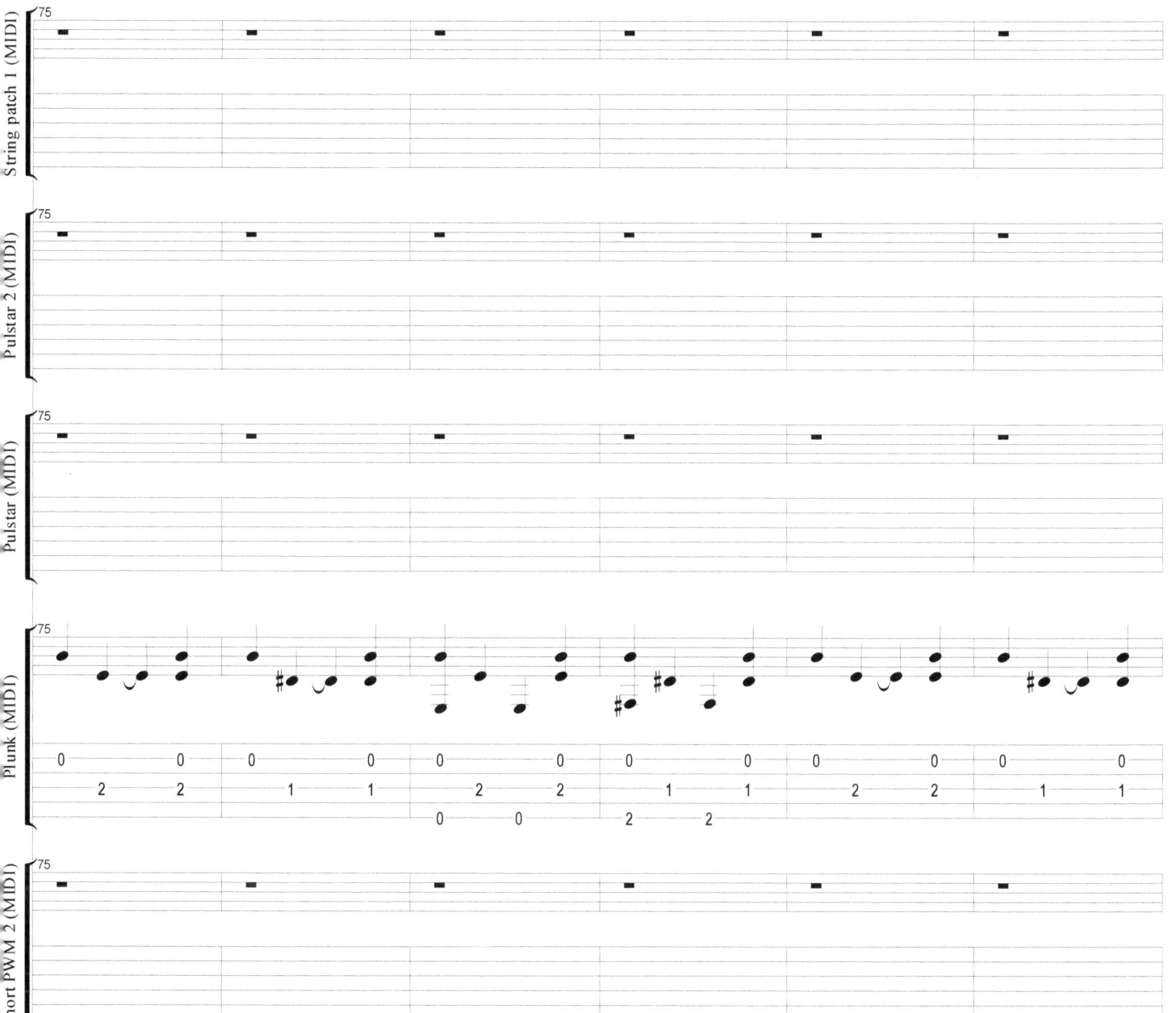

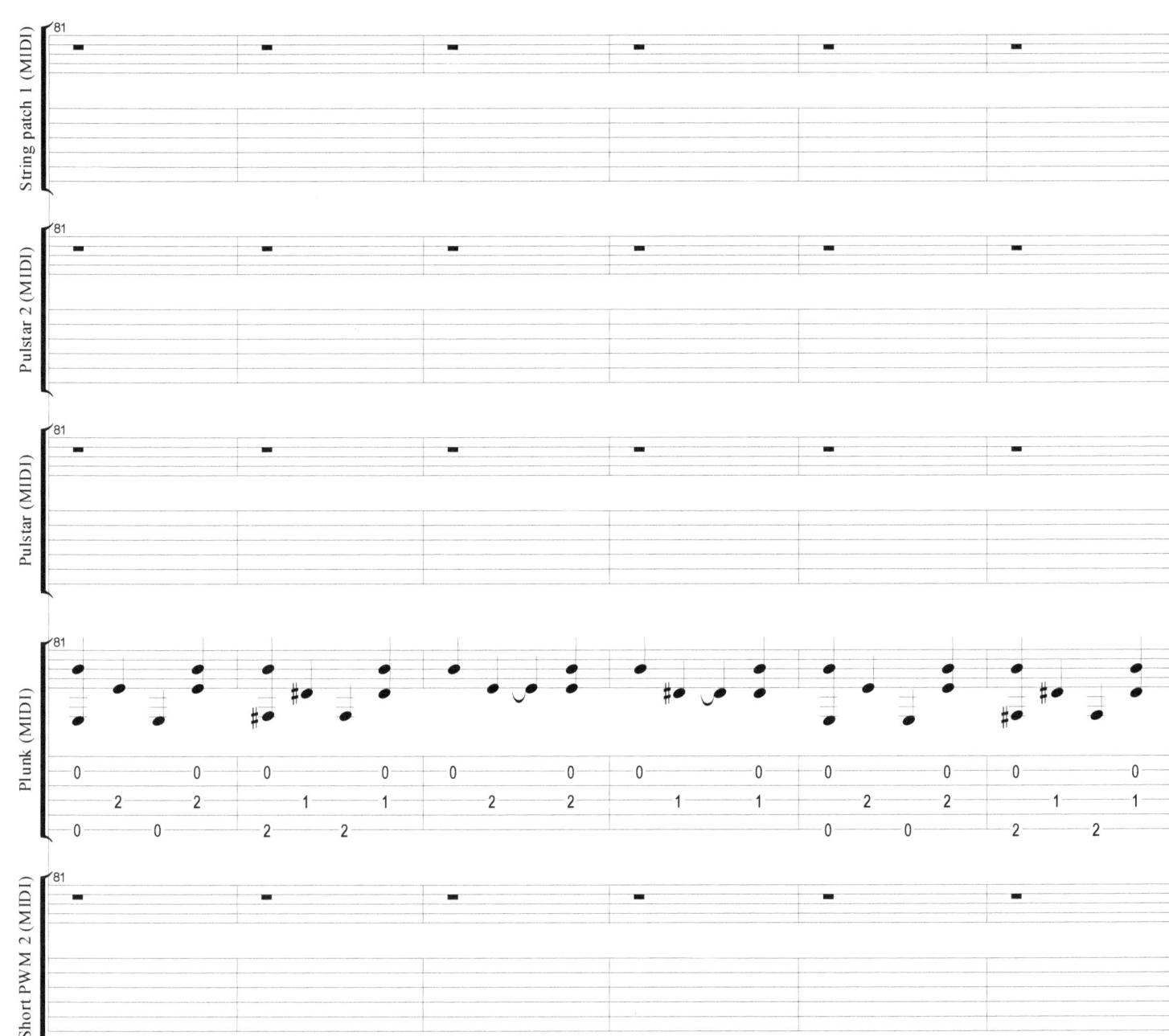

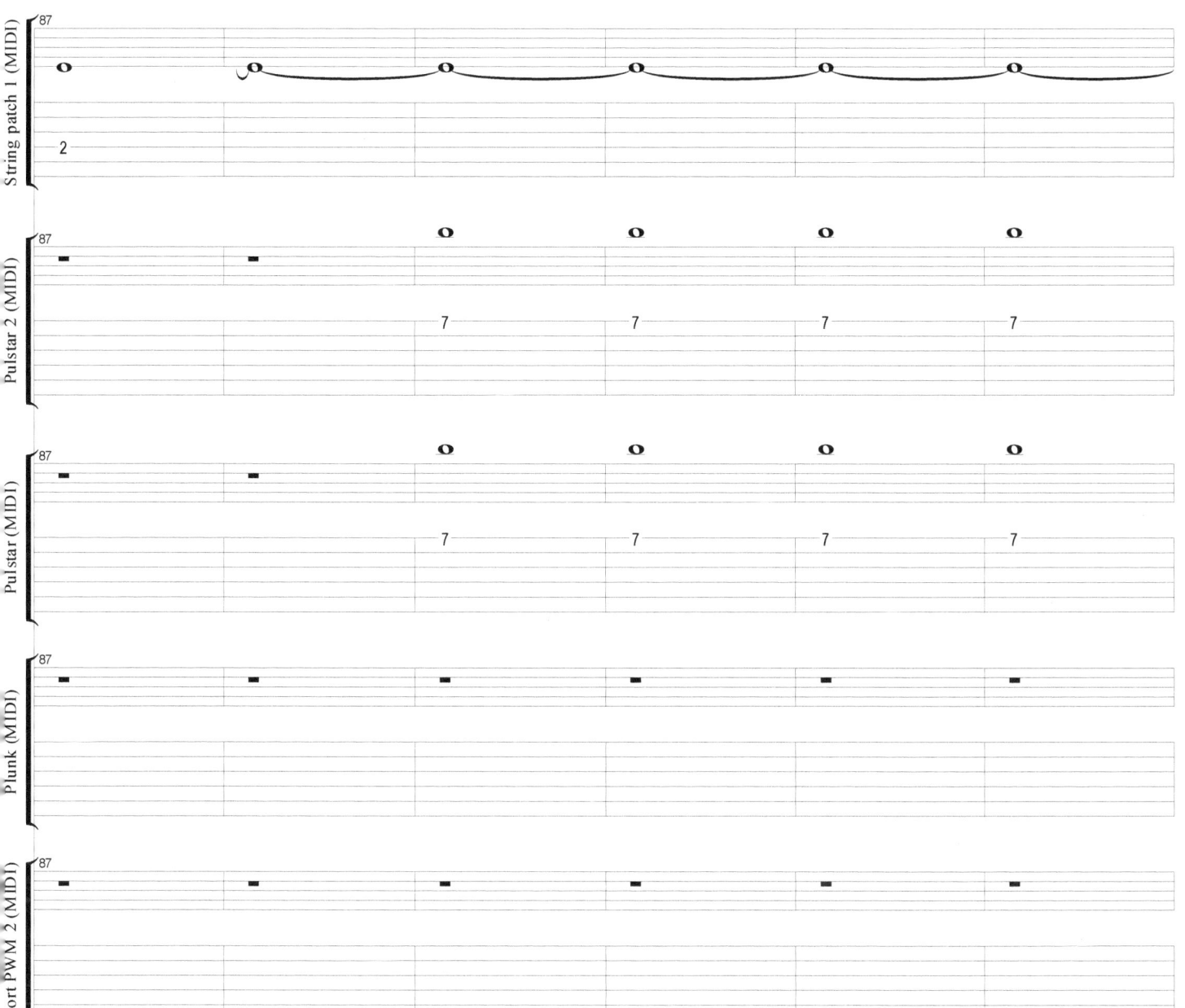

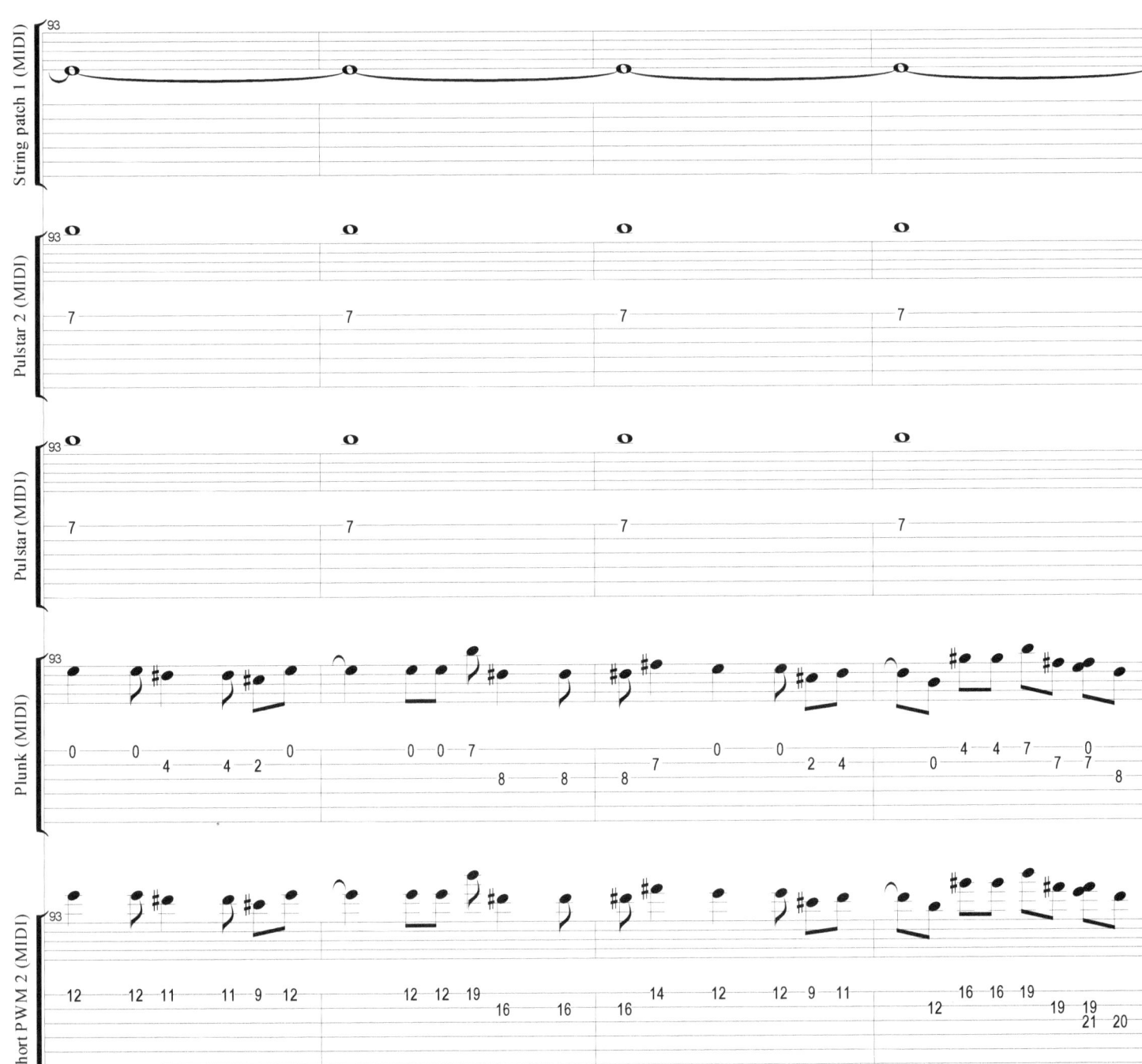

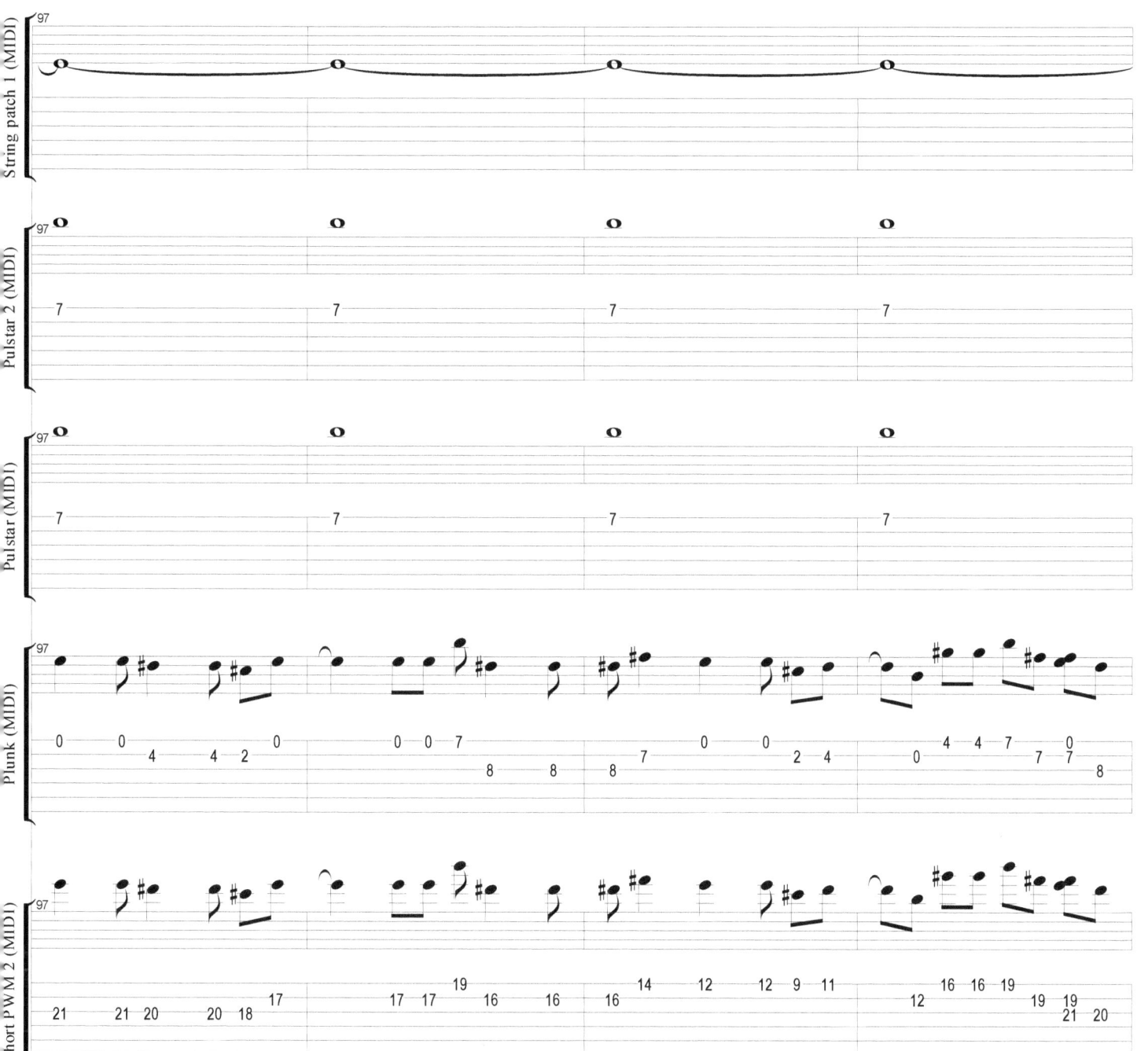

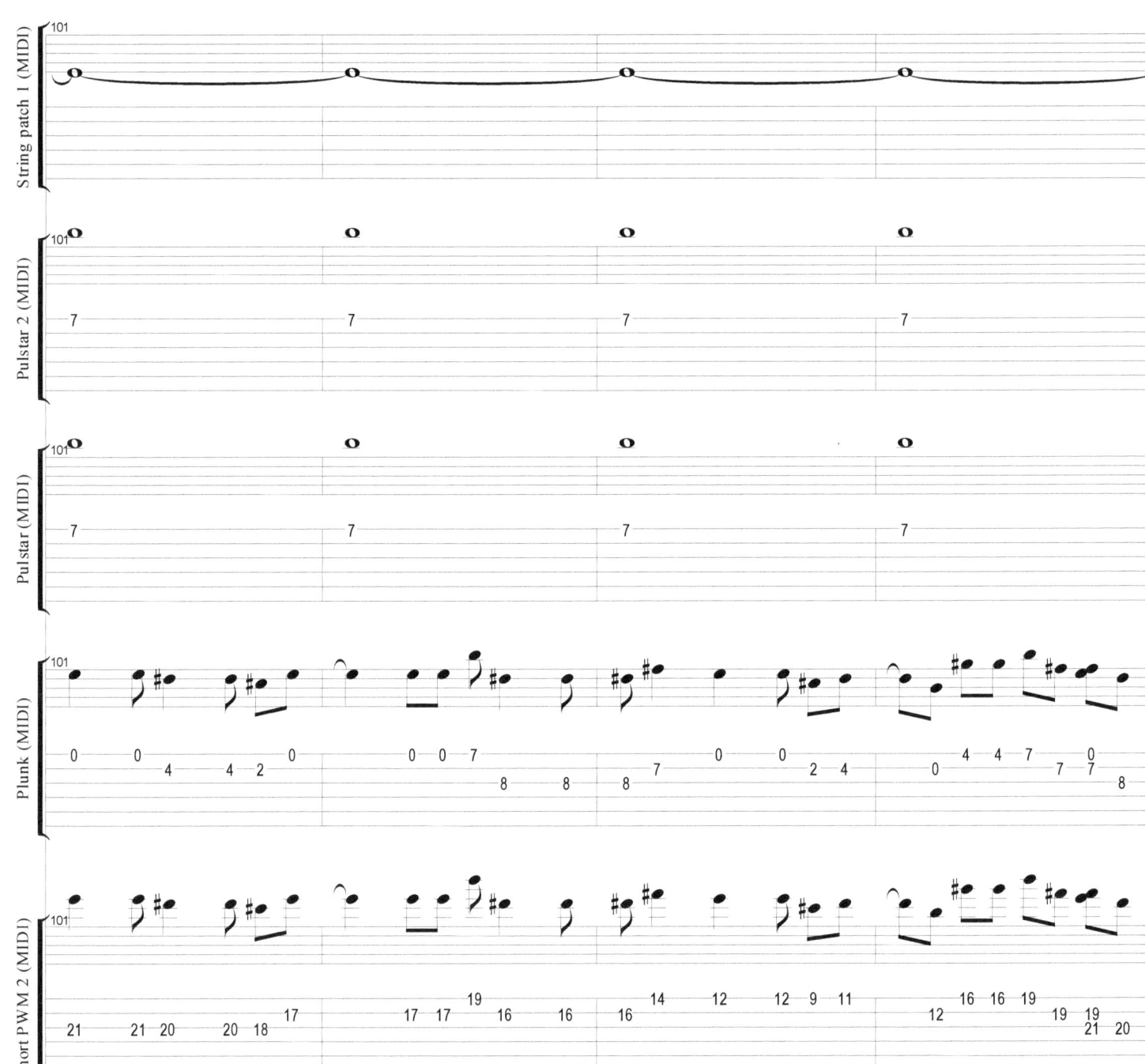

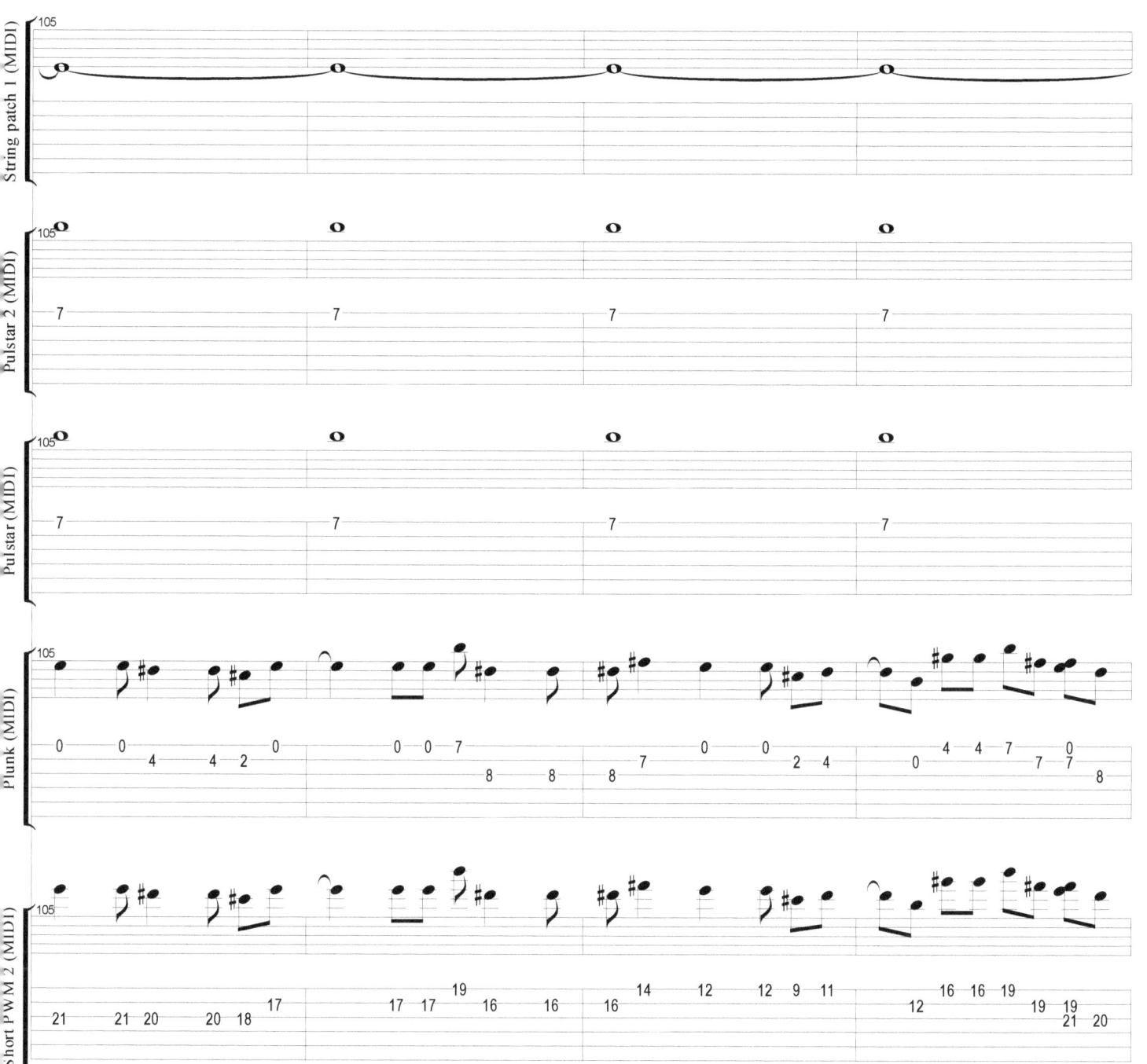

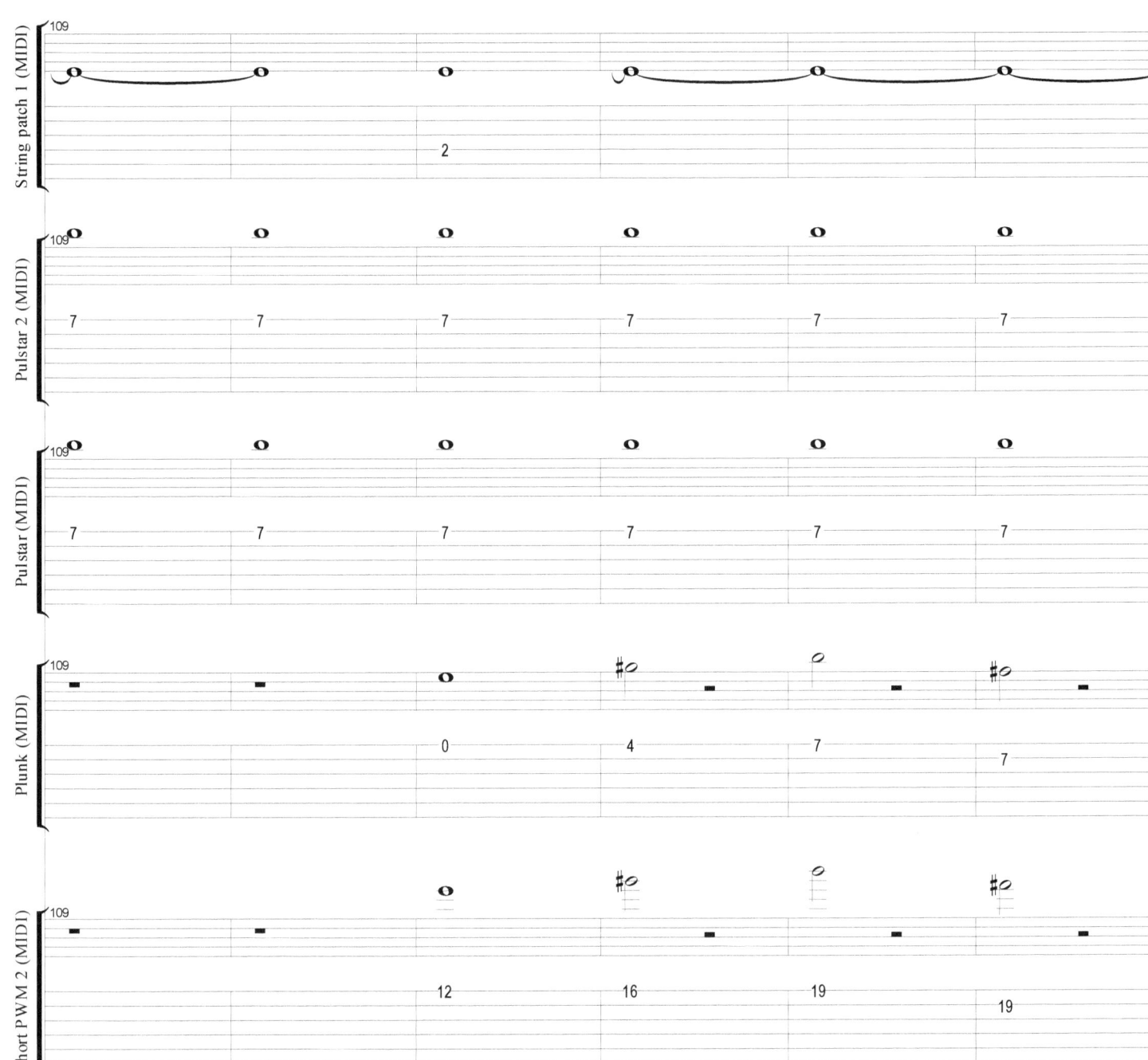

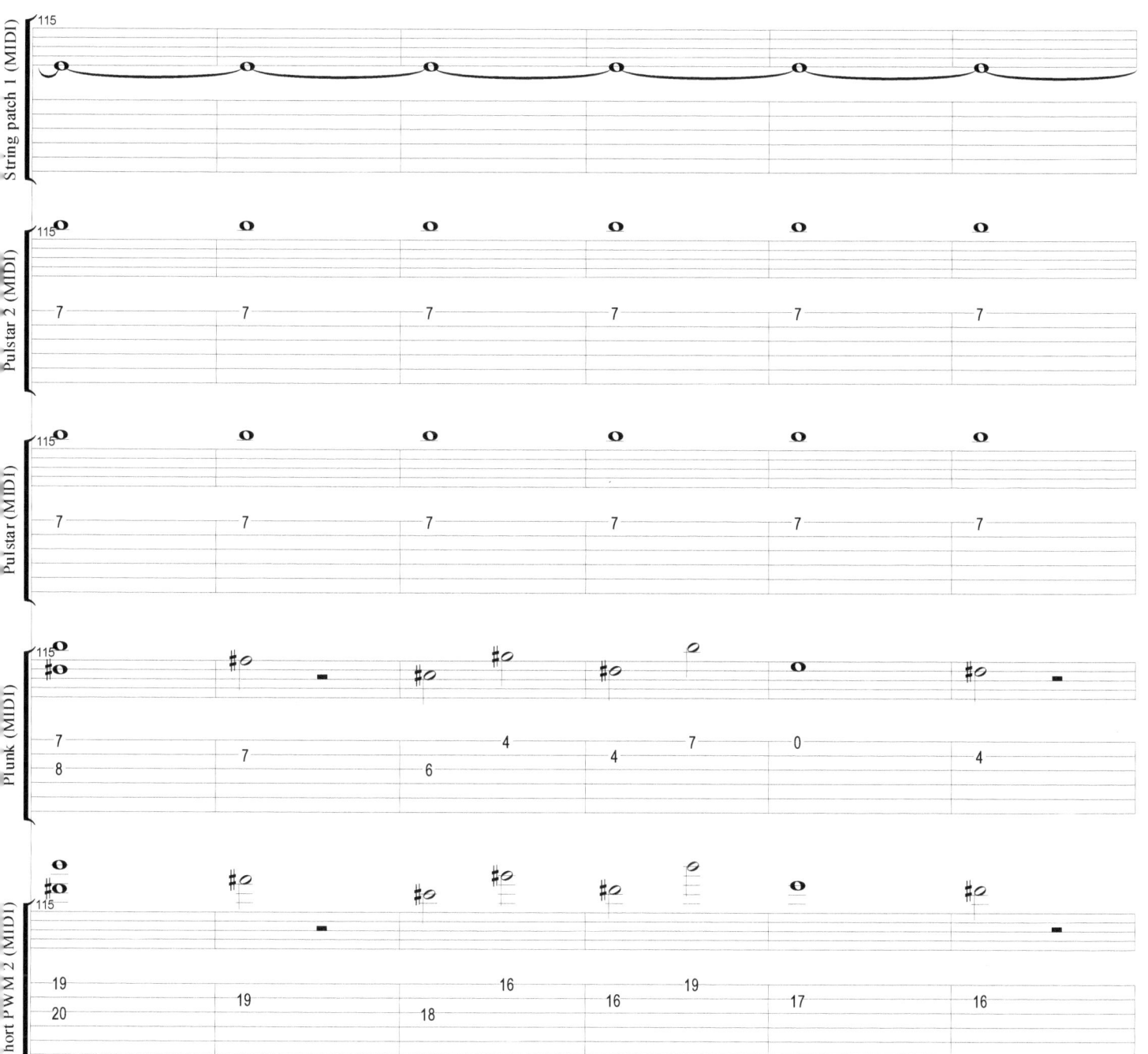

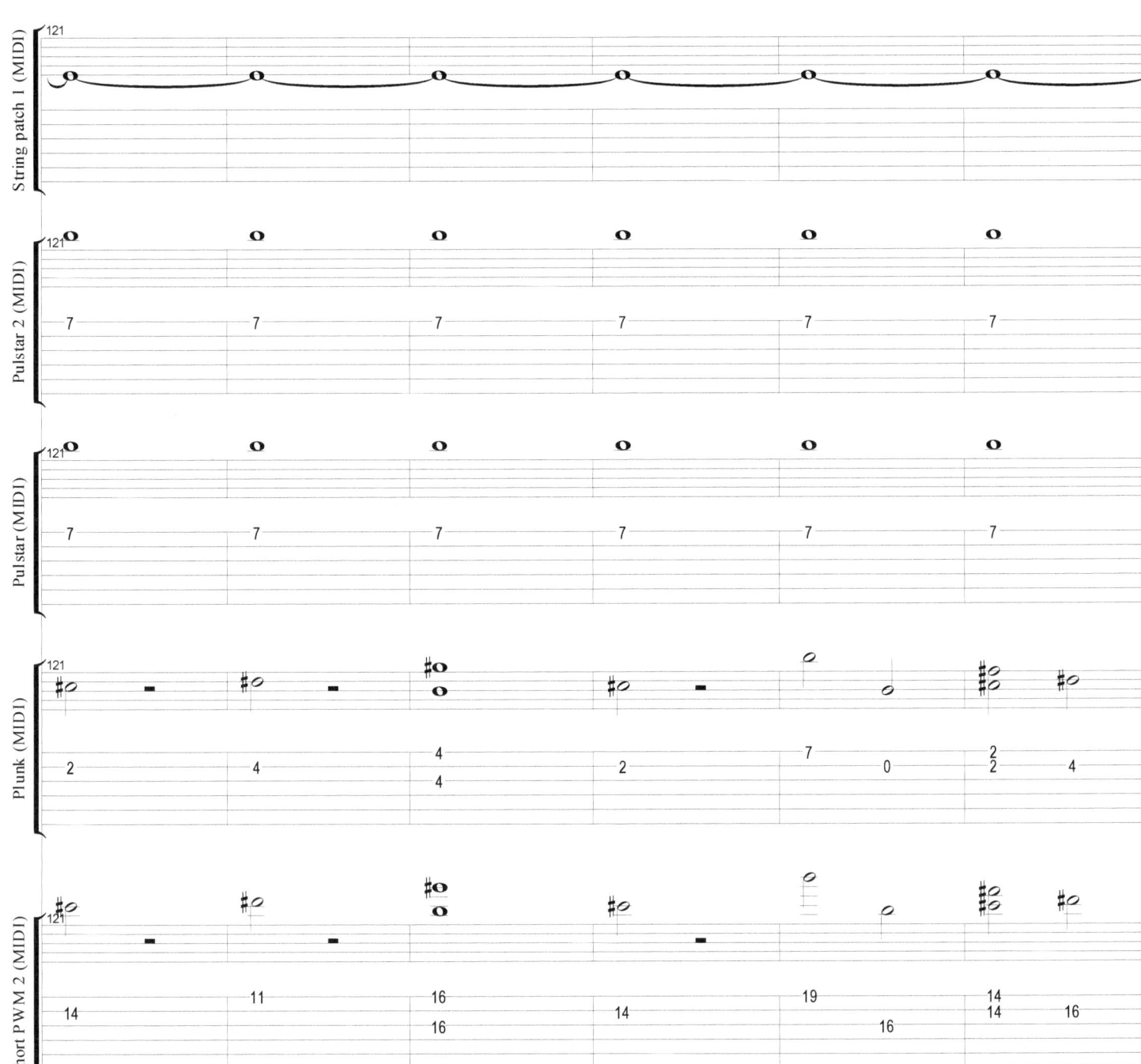

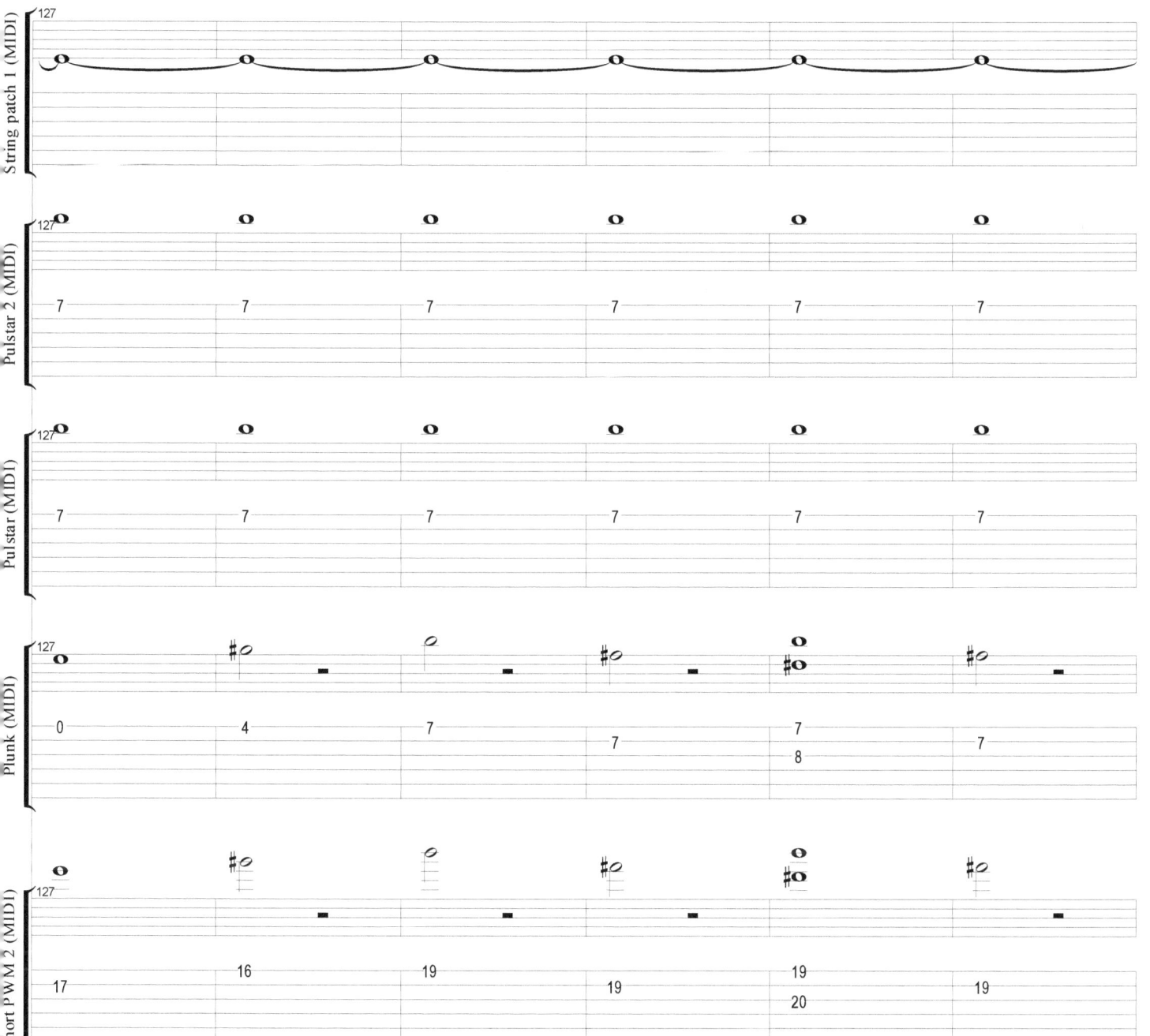

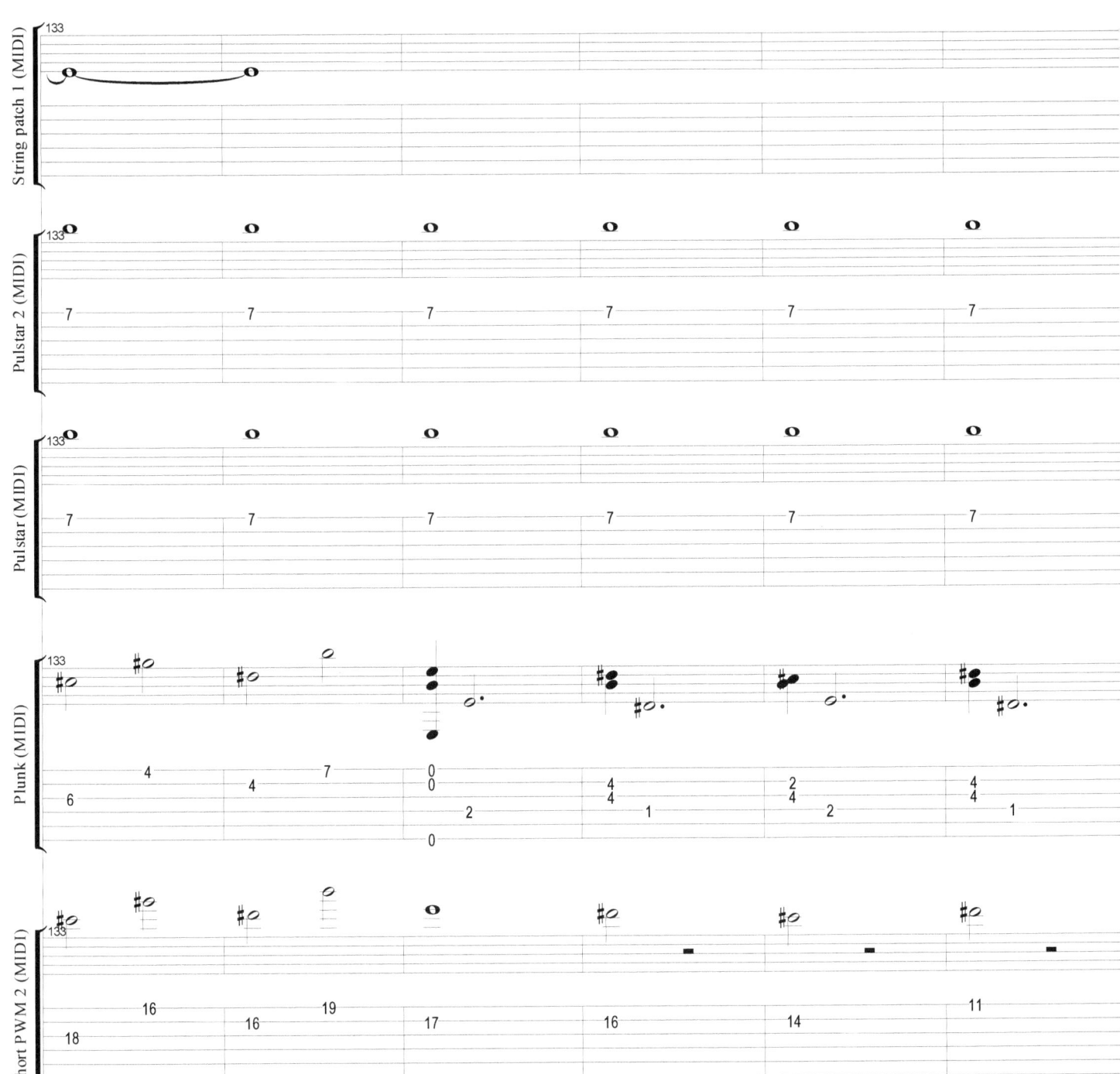

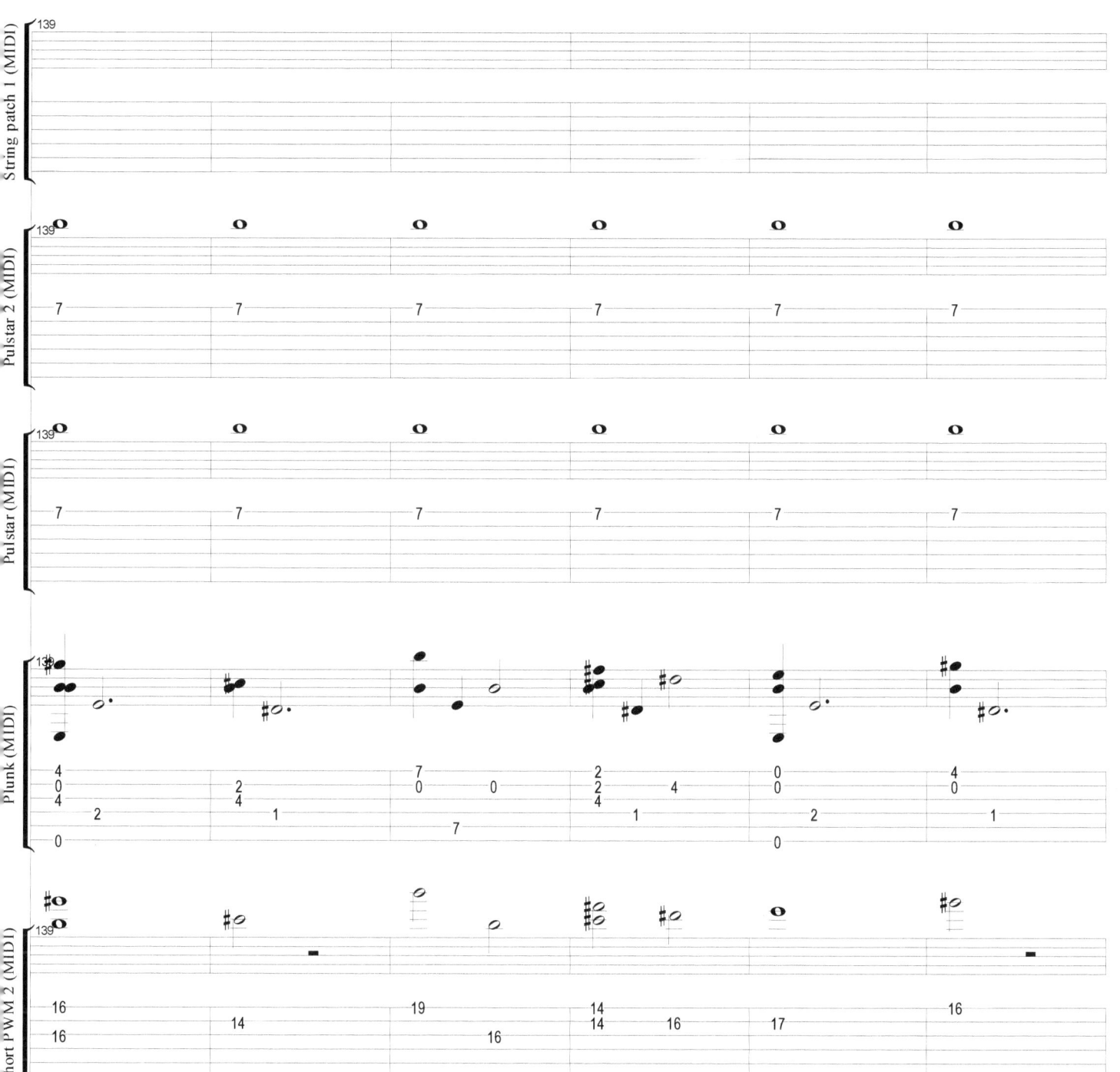

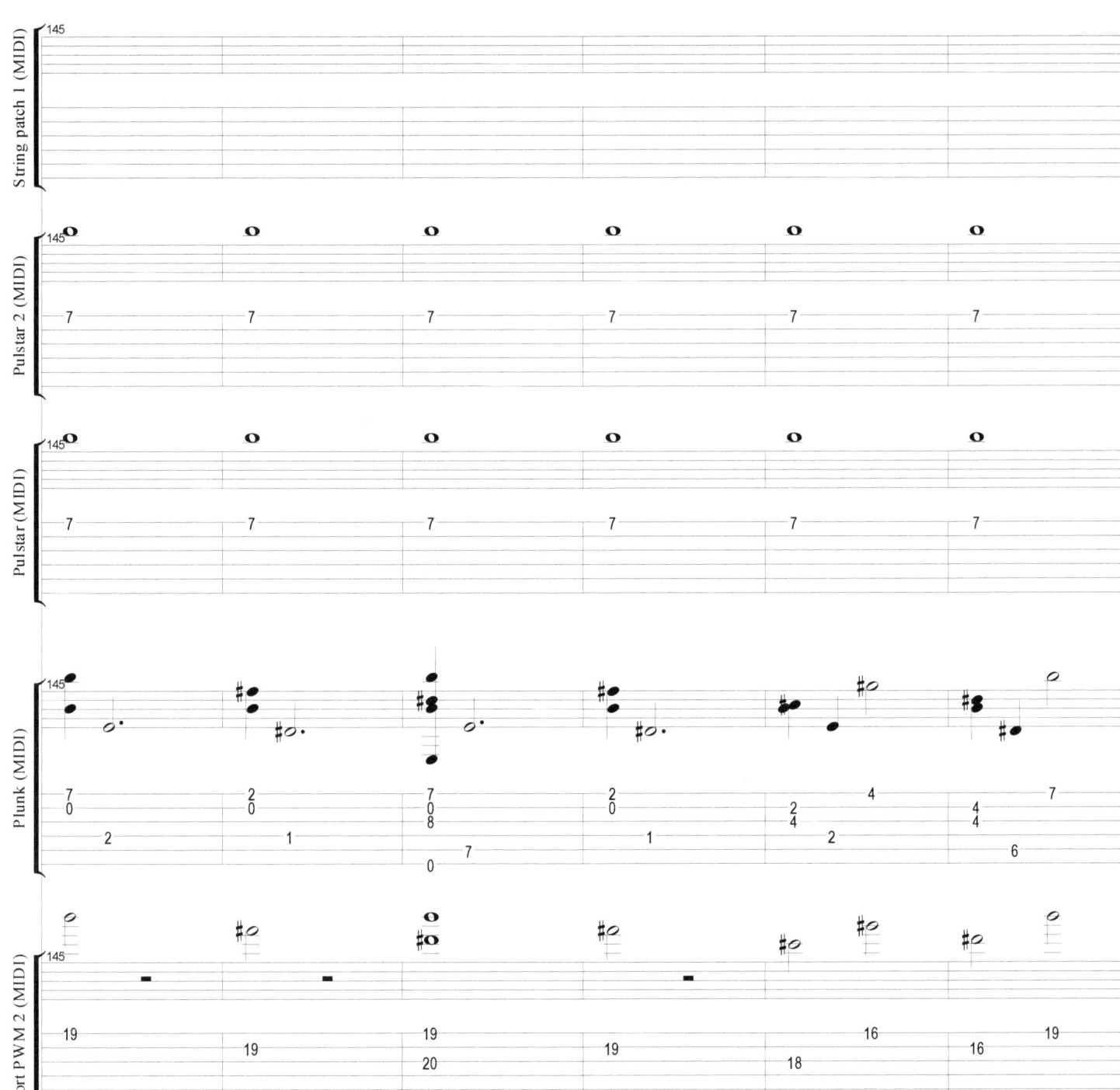

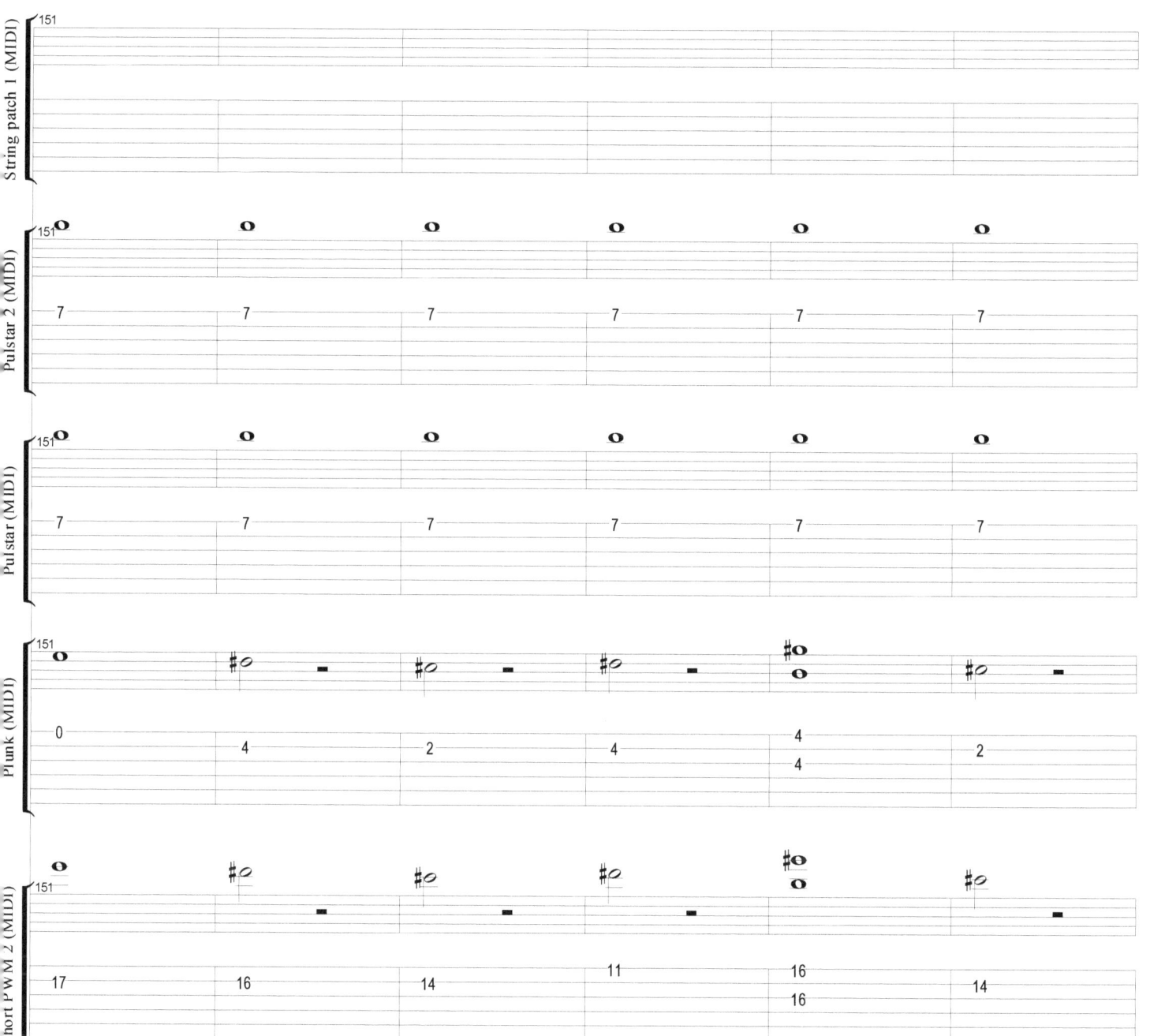

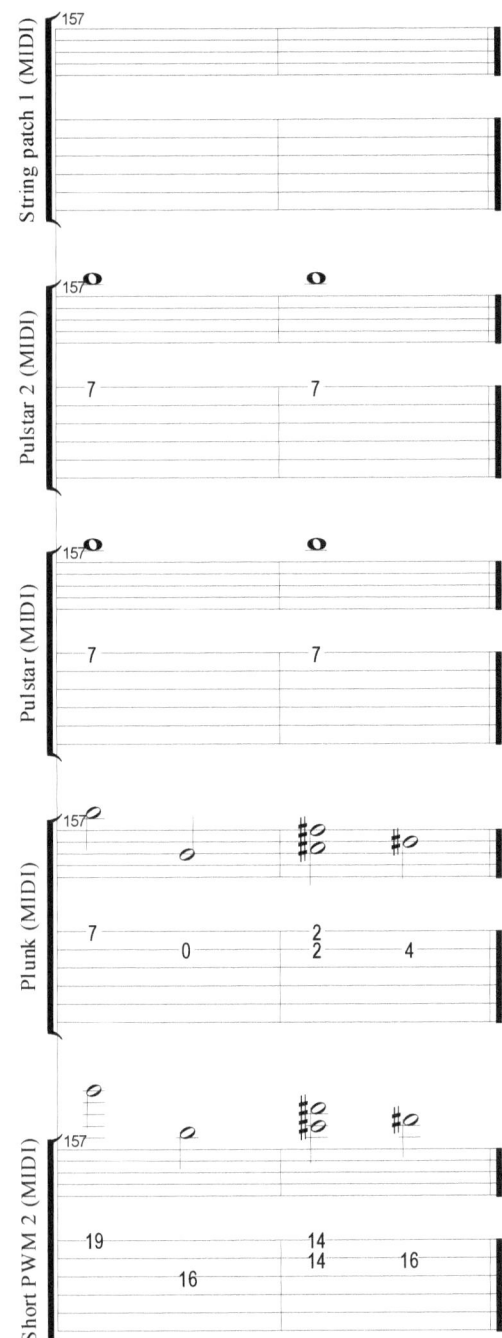

As The Rain

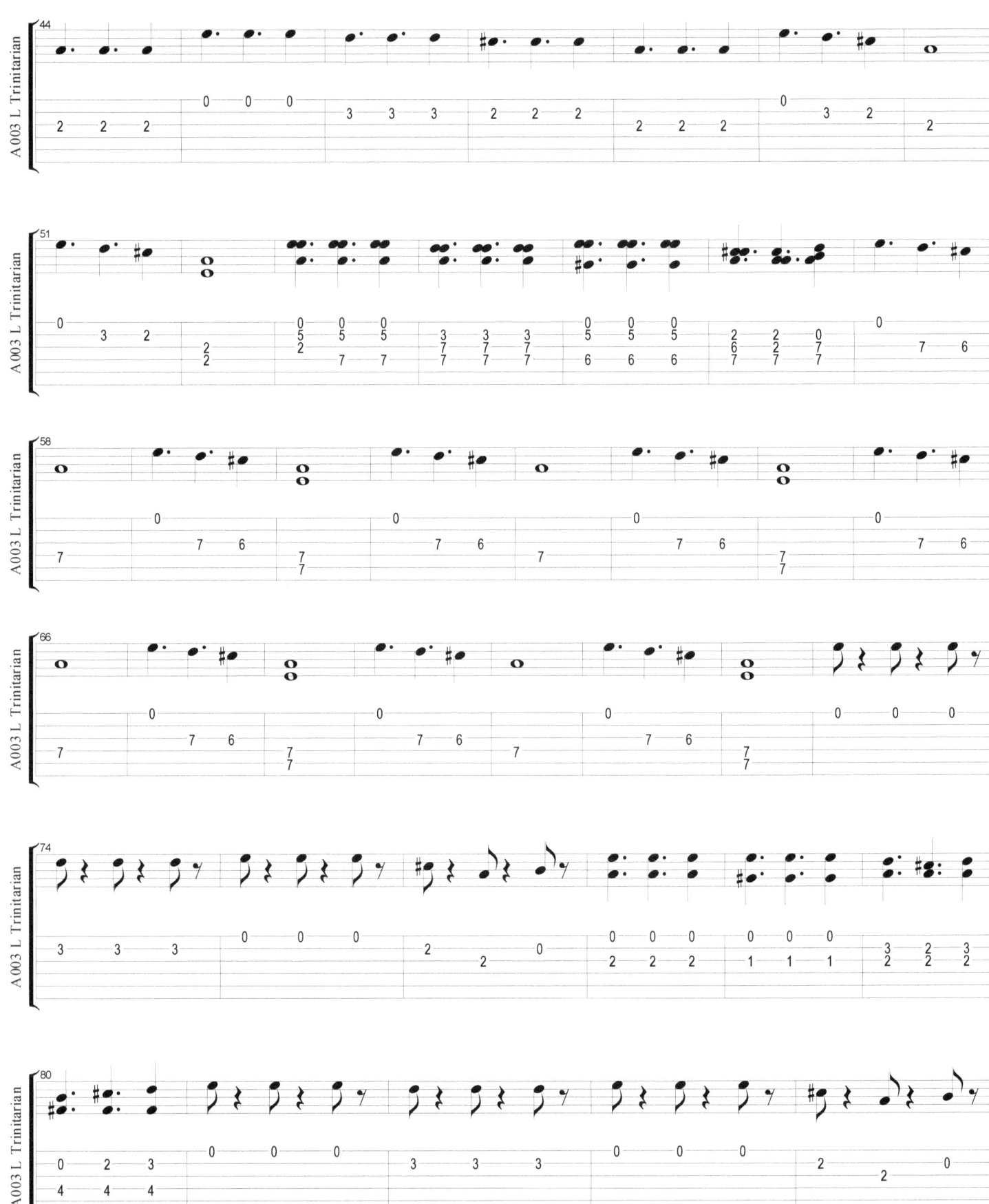

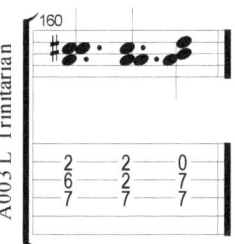

Egypt

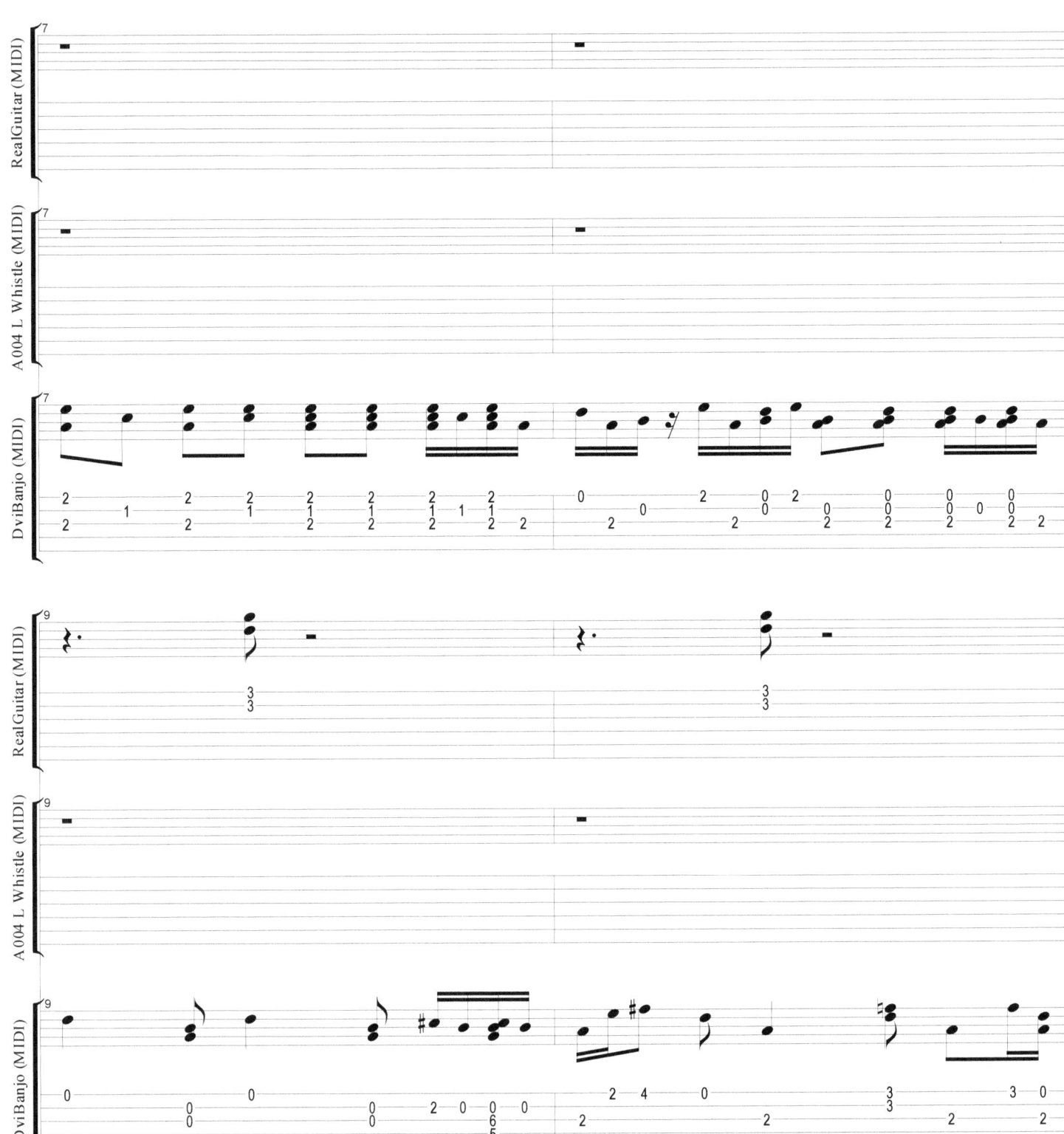

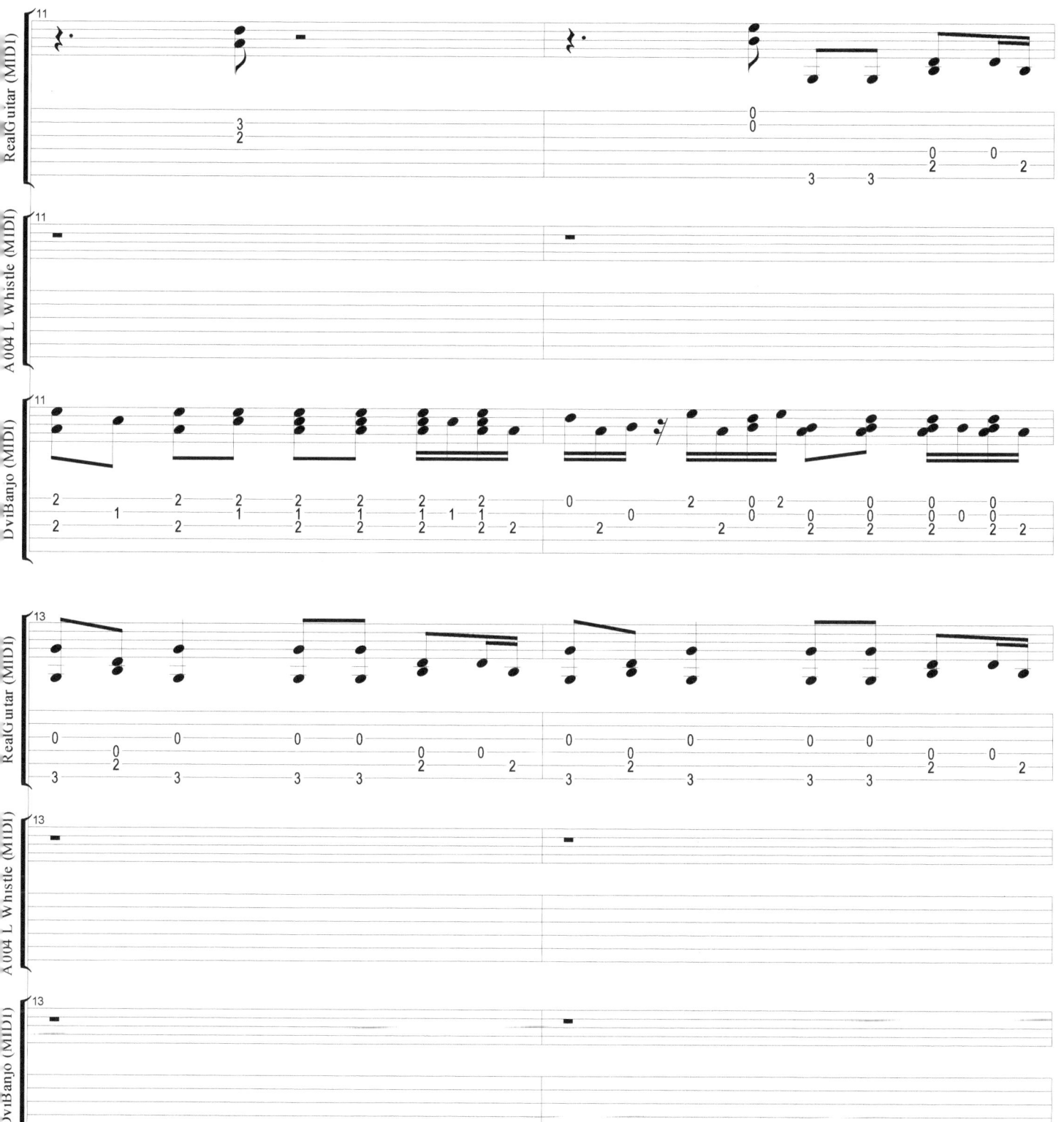

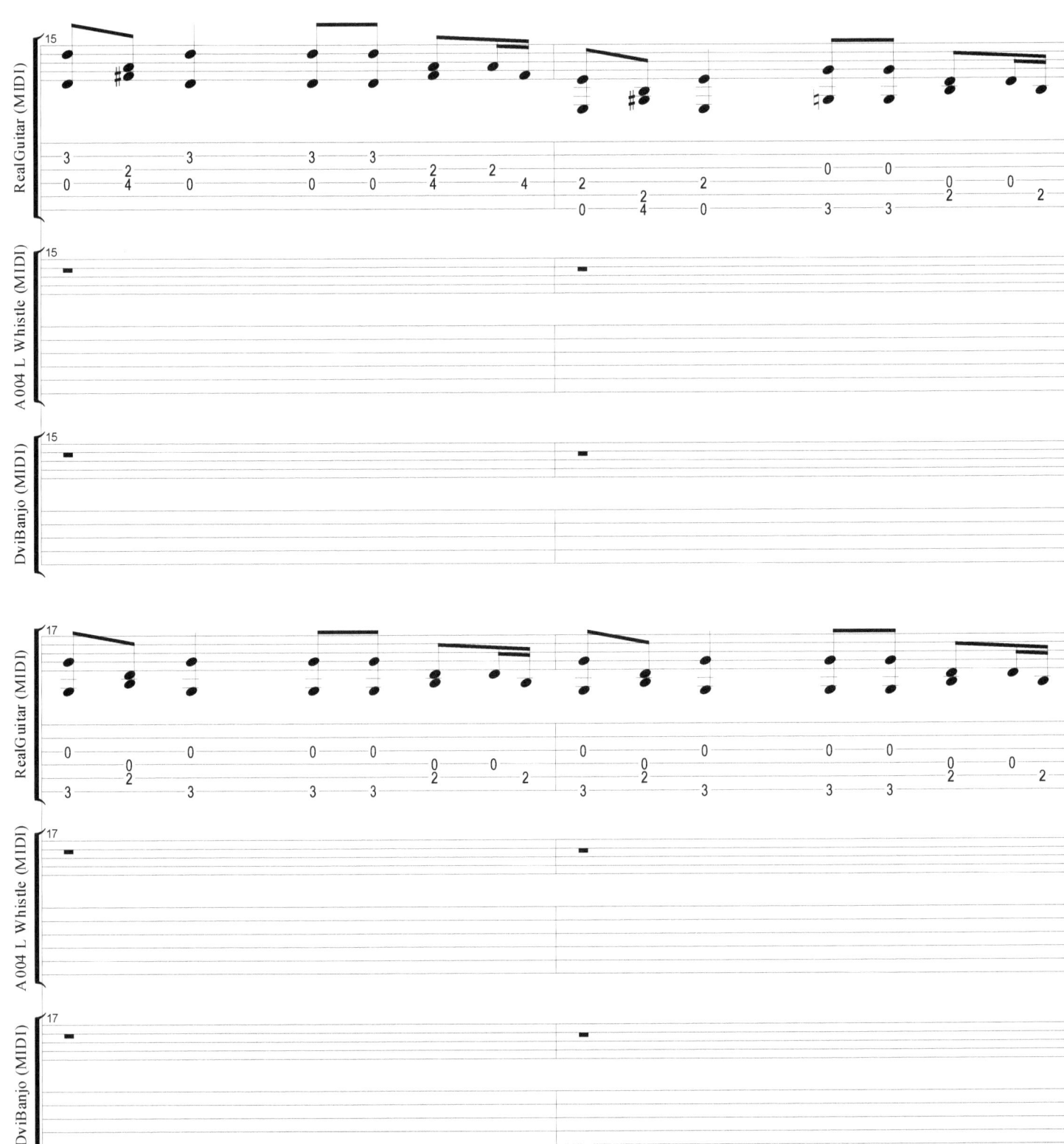

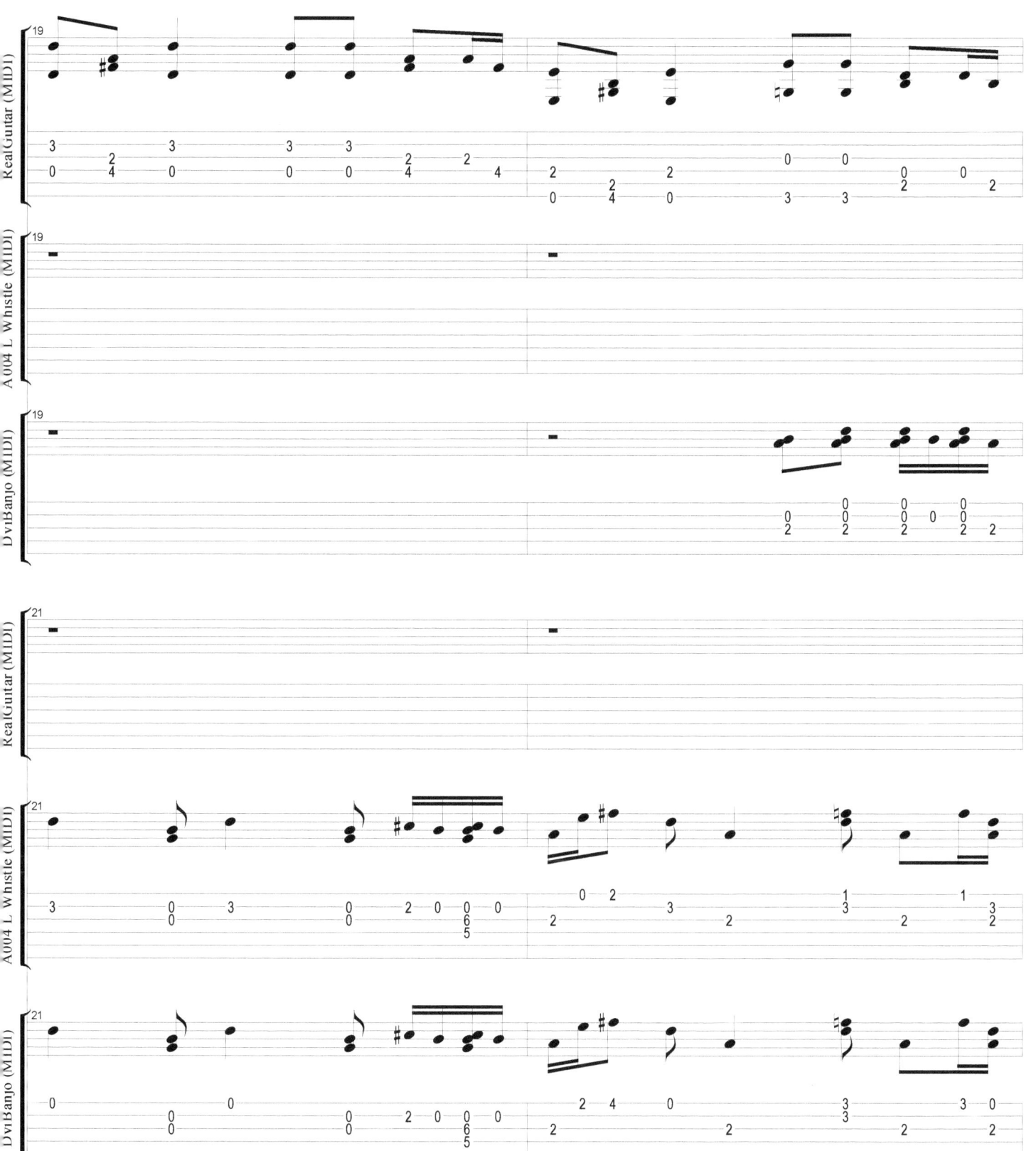

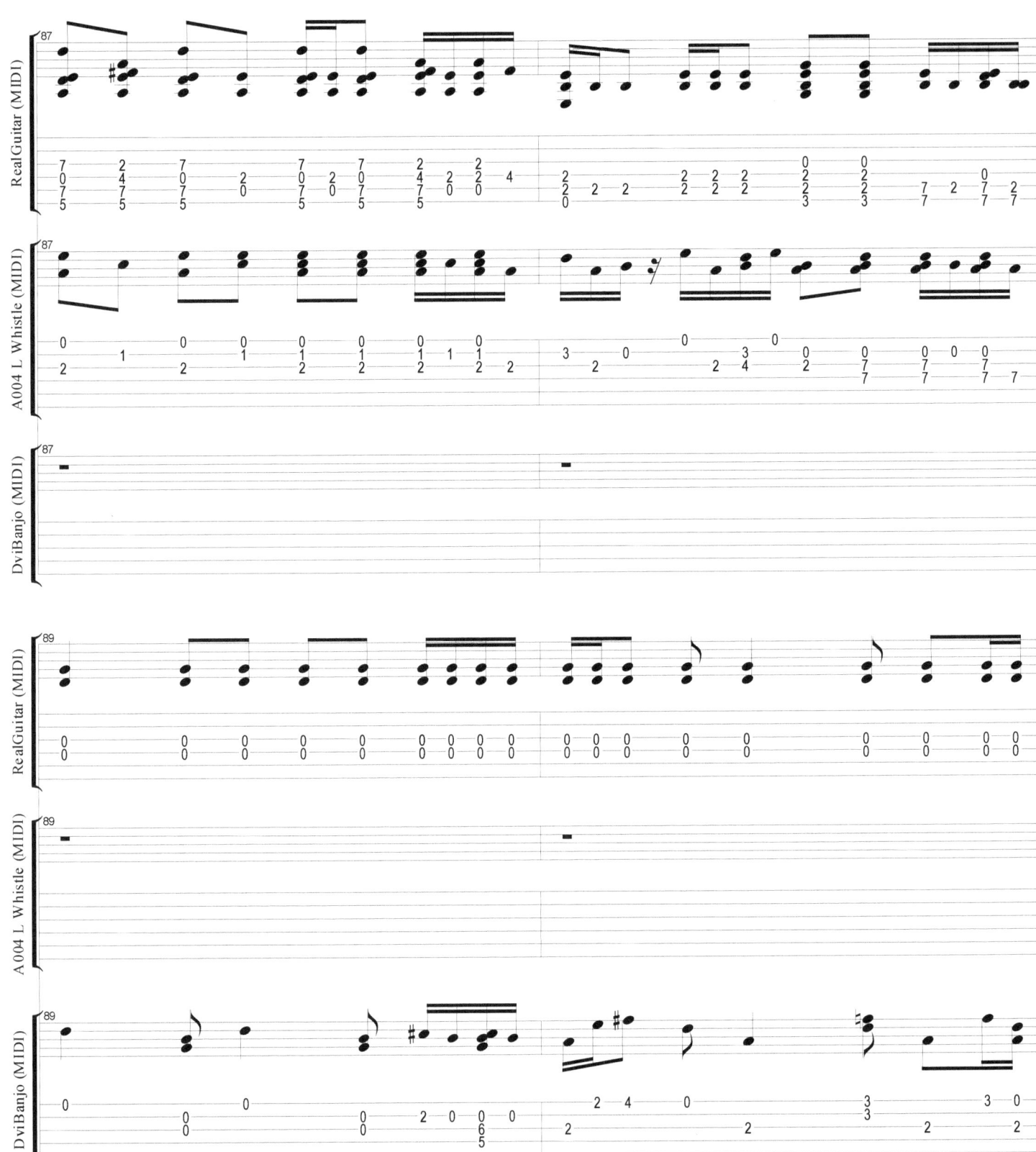

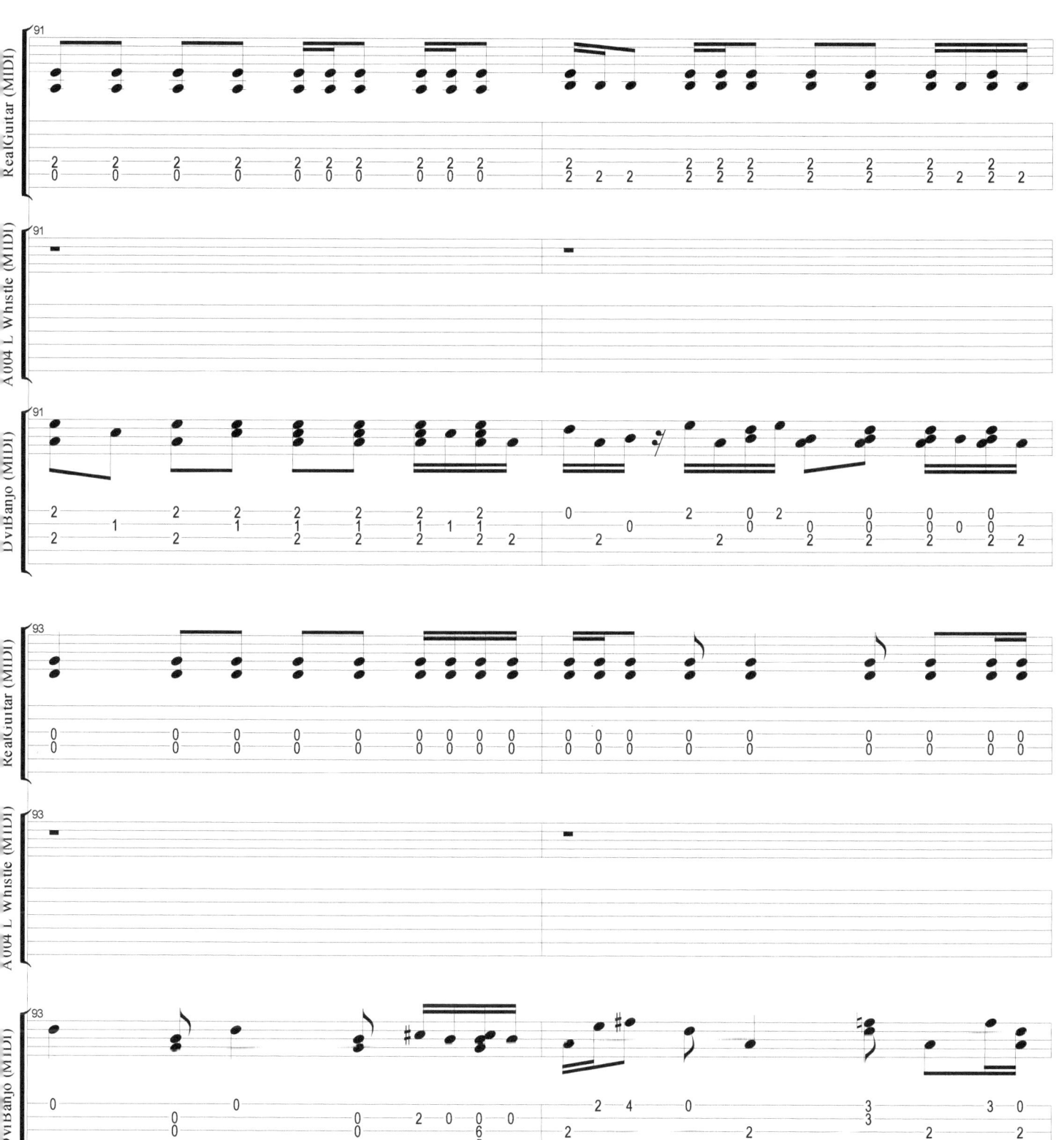

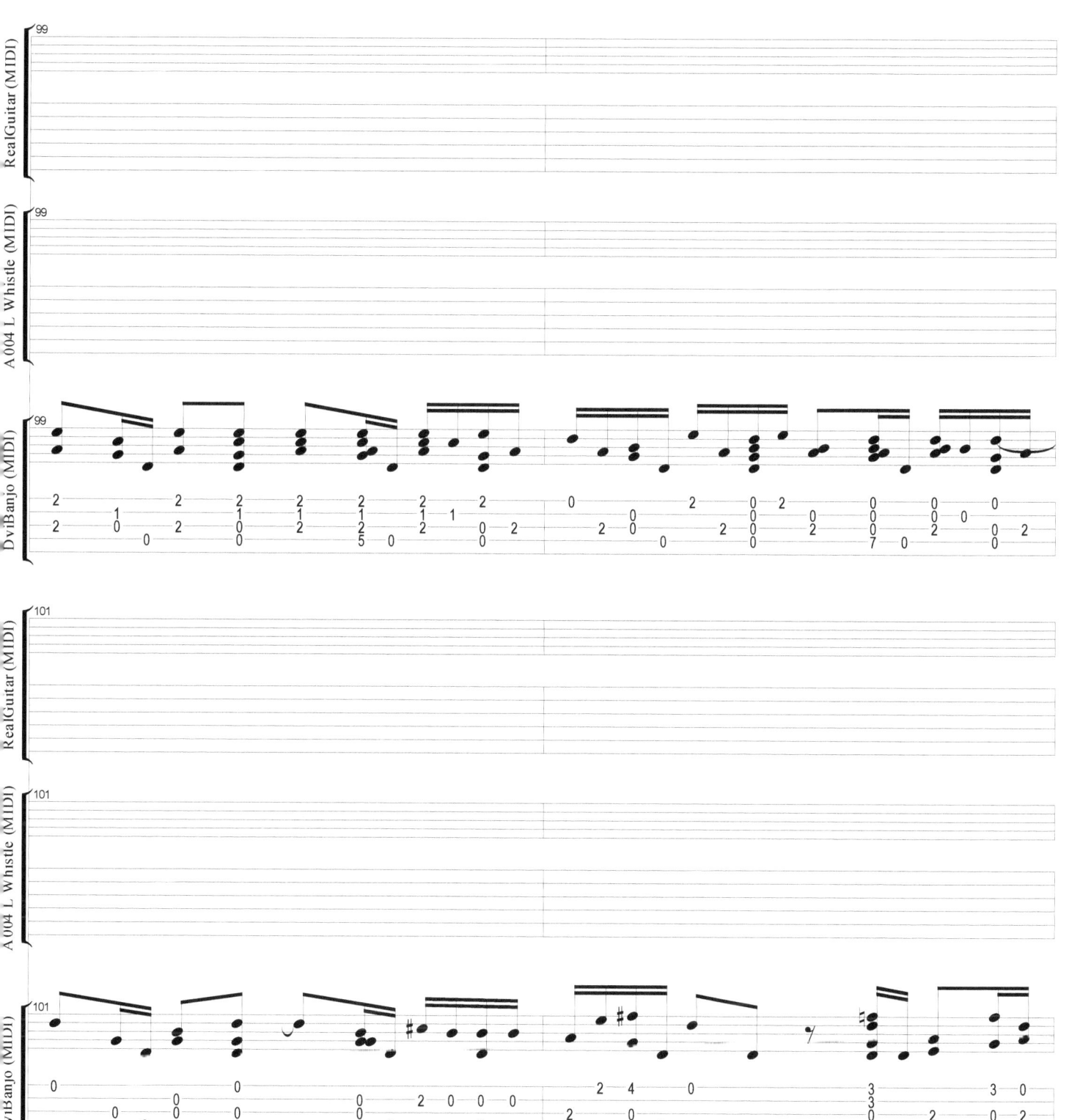

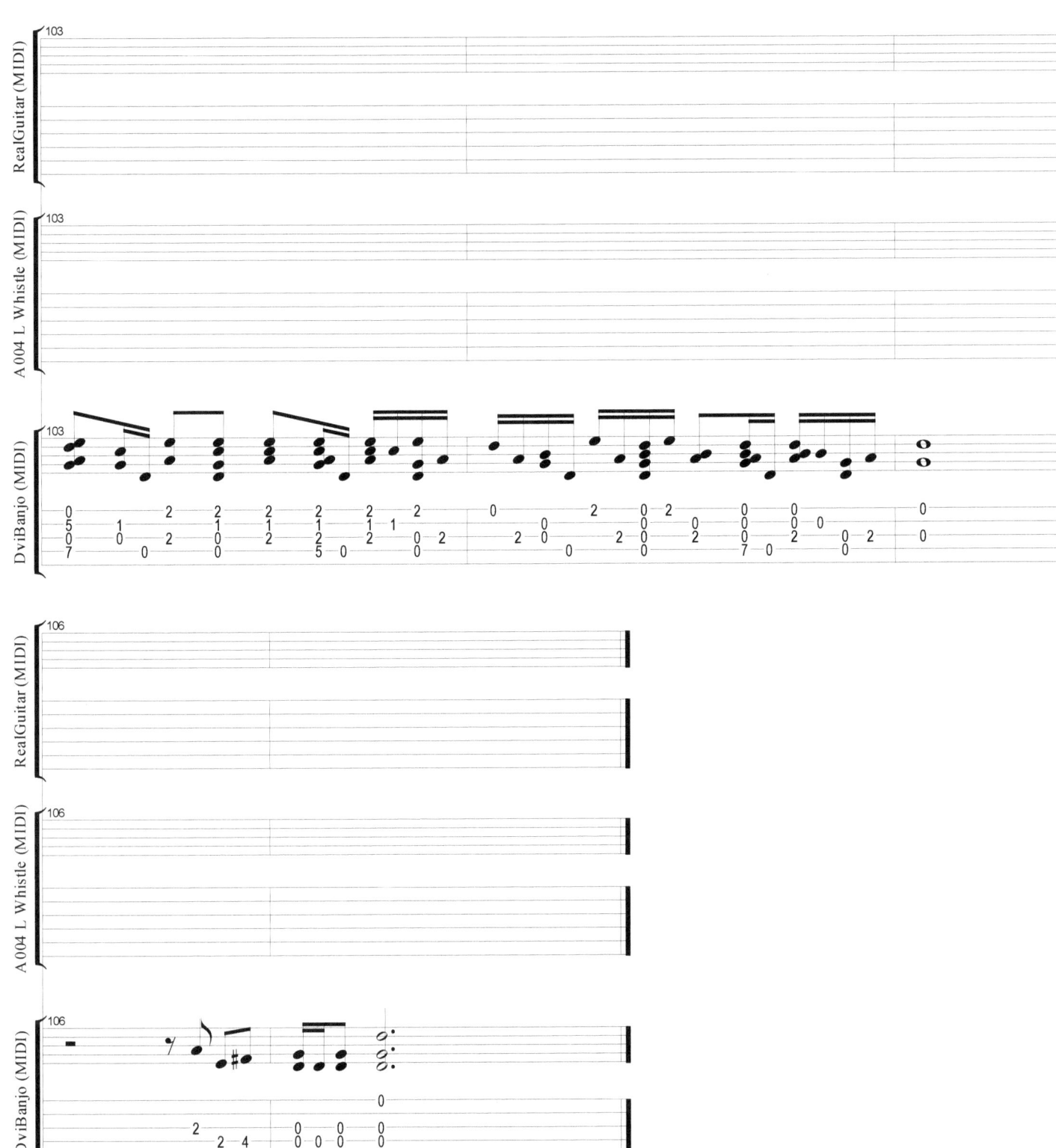

C Is For Cassie

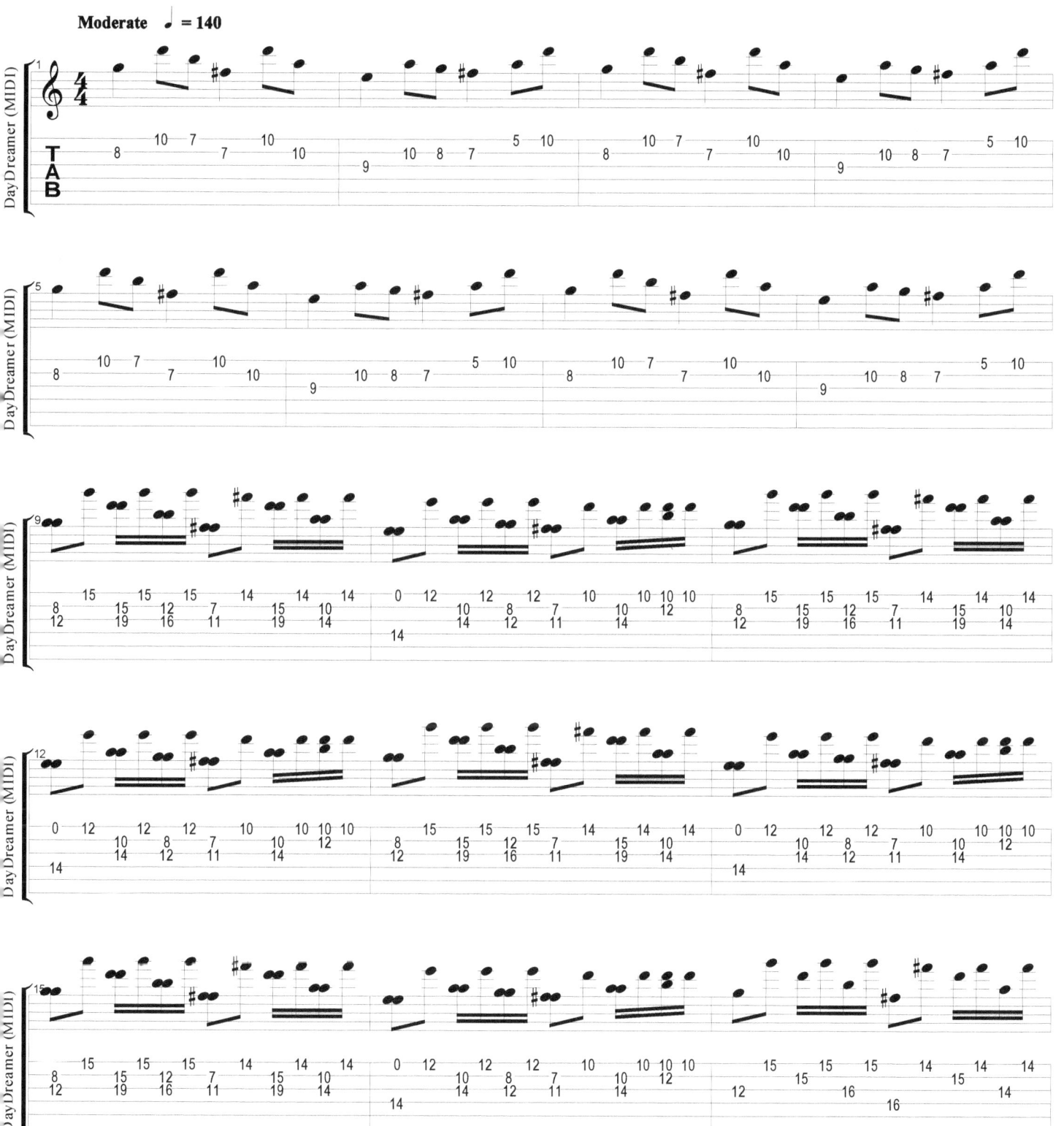

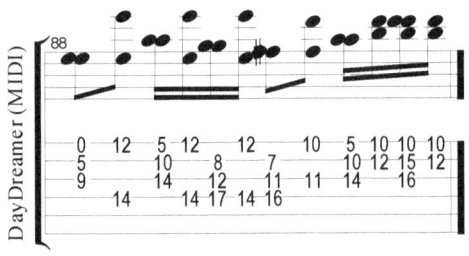

Carnival City

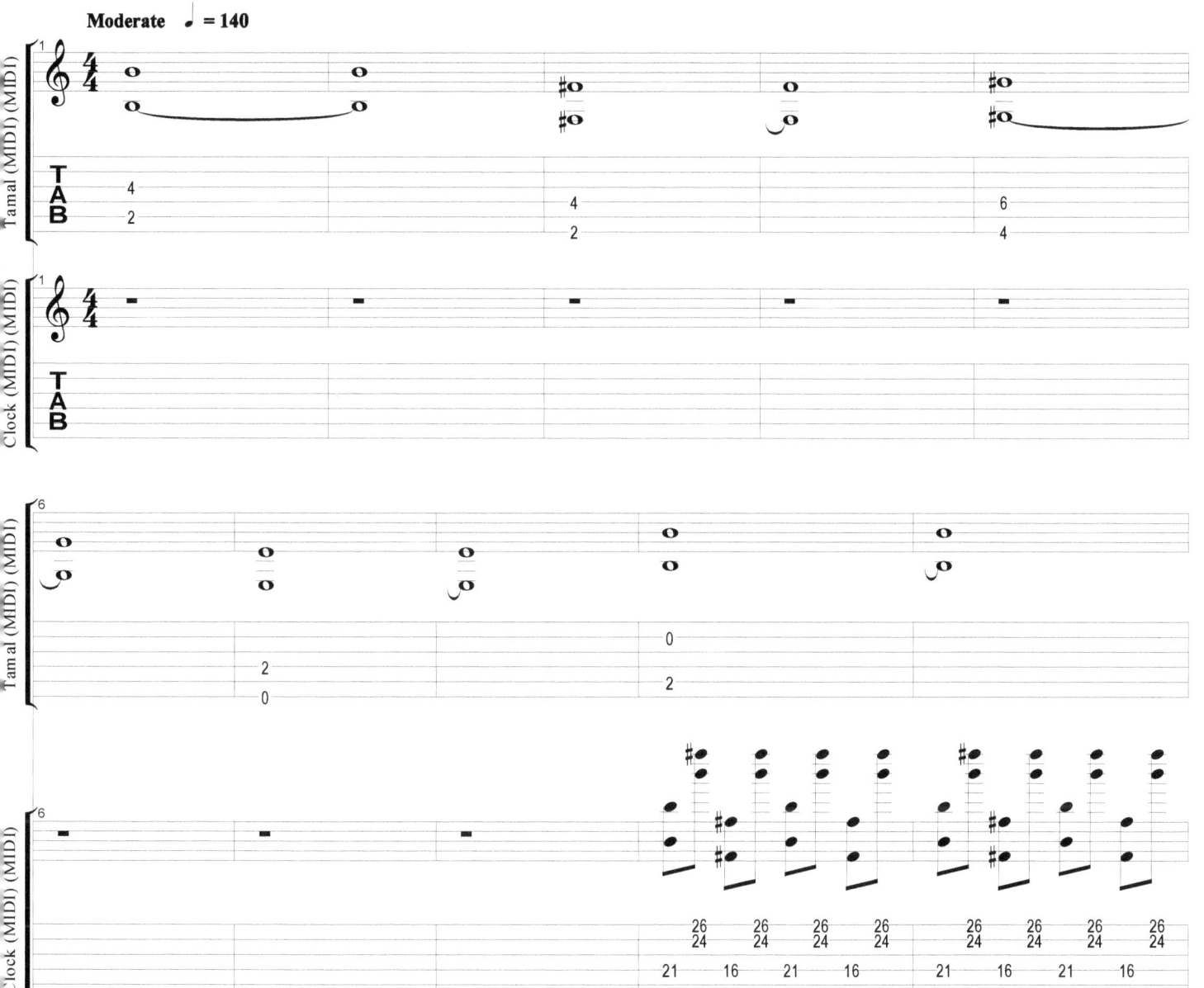

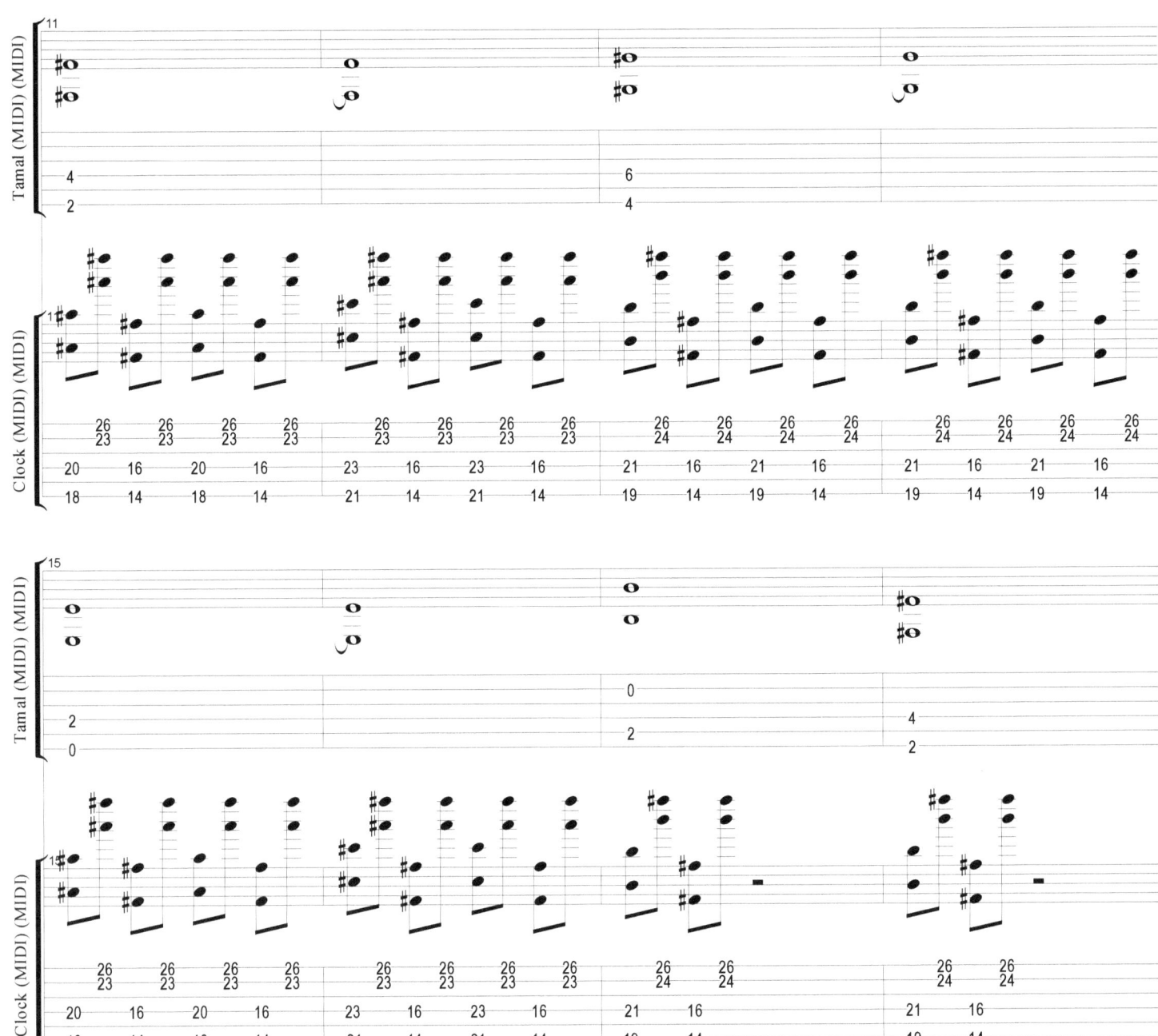

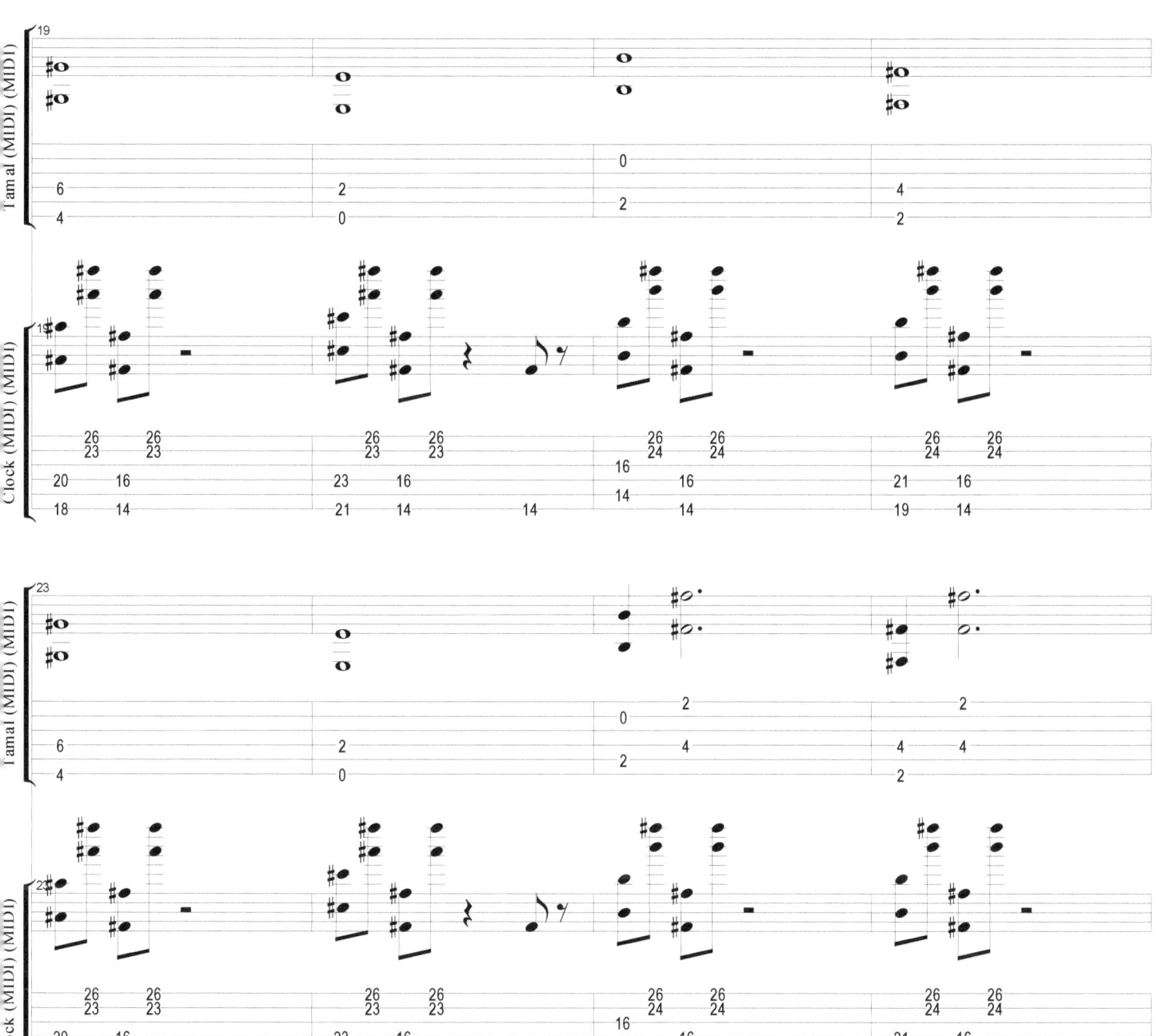

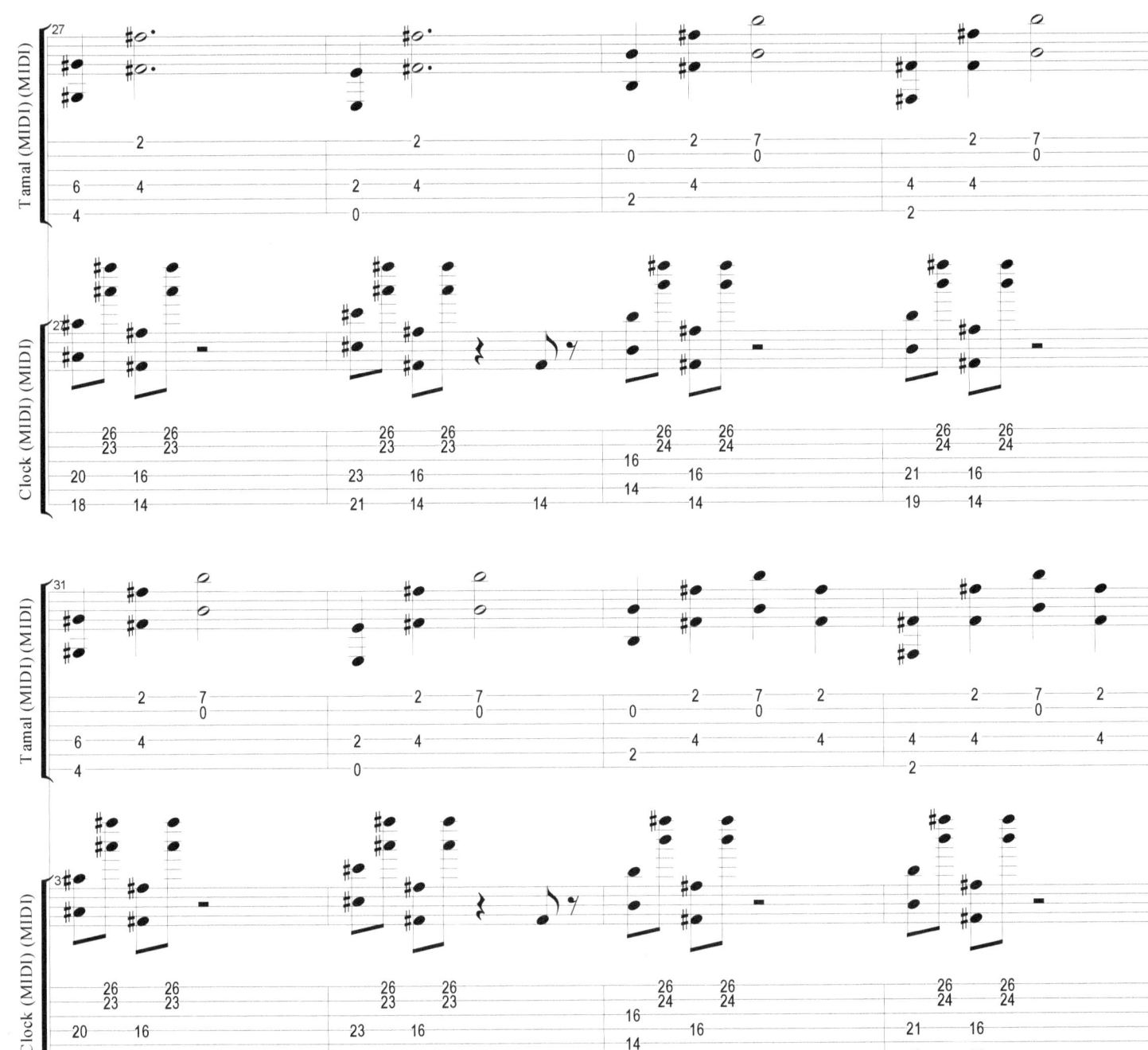

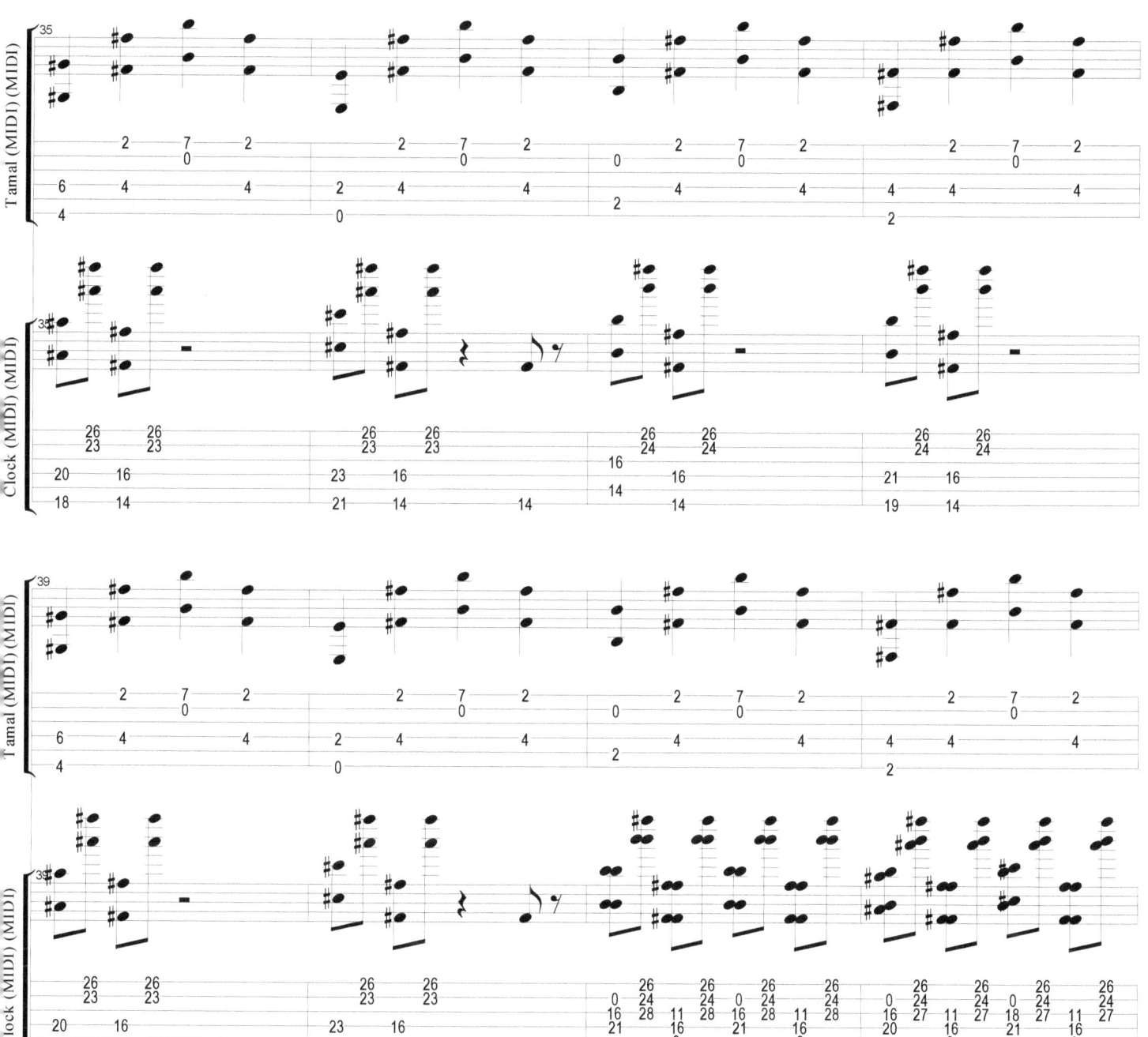

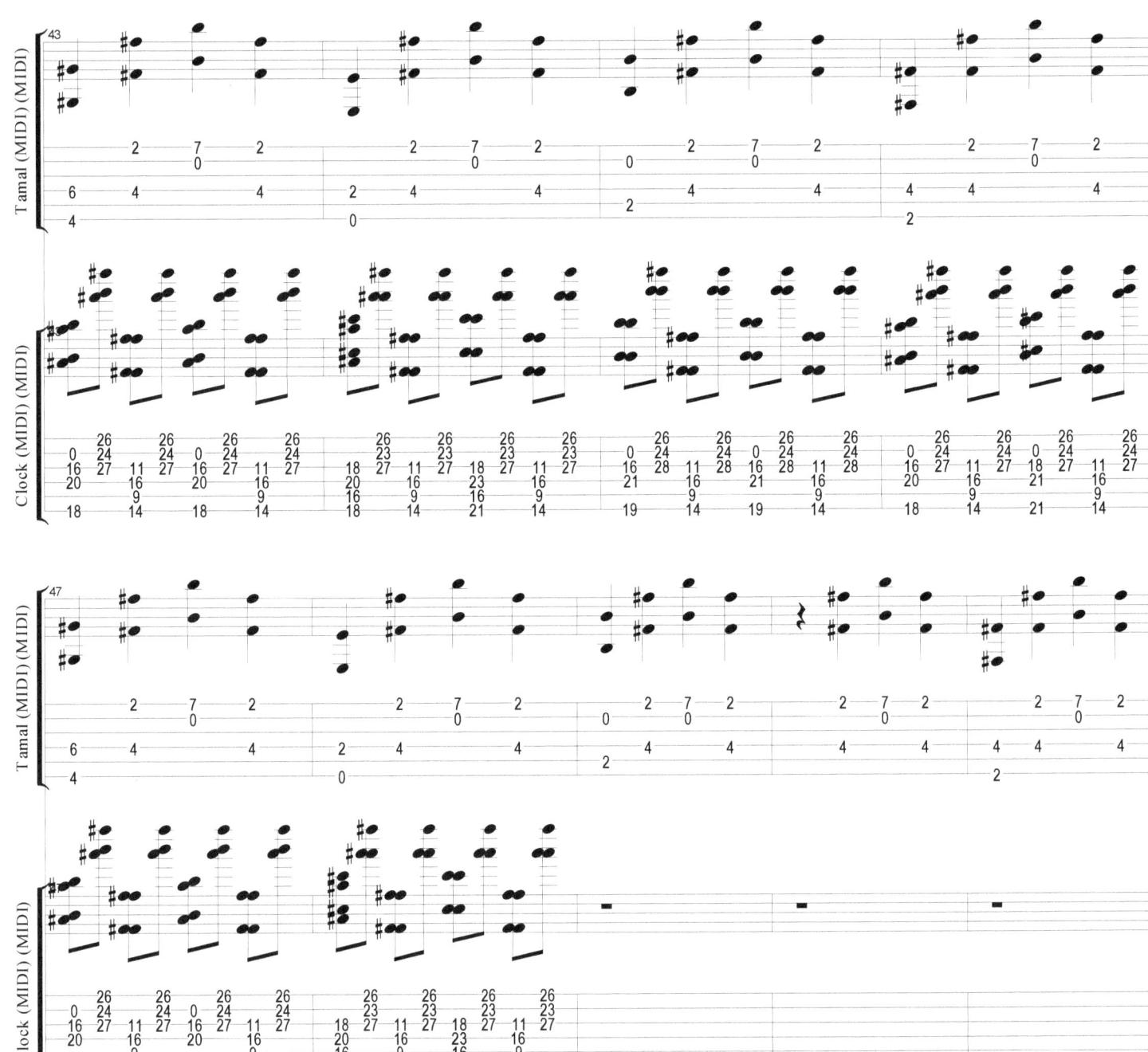

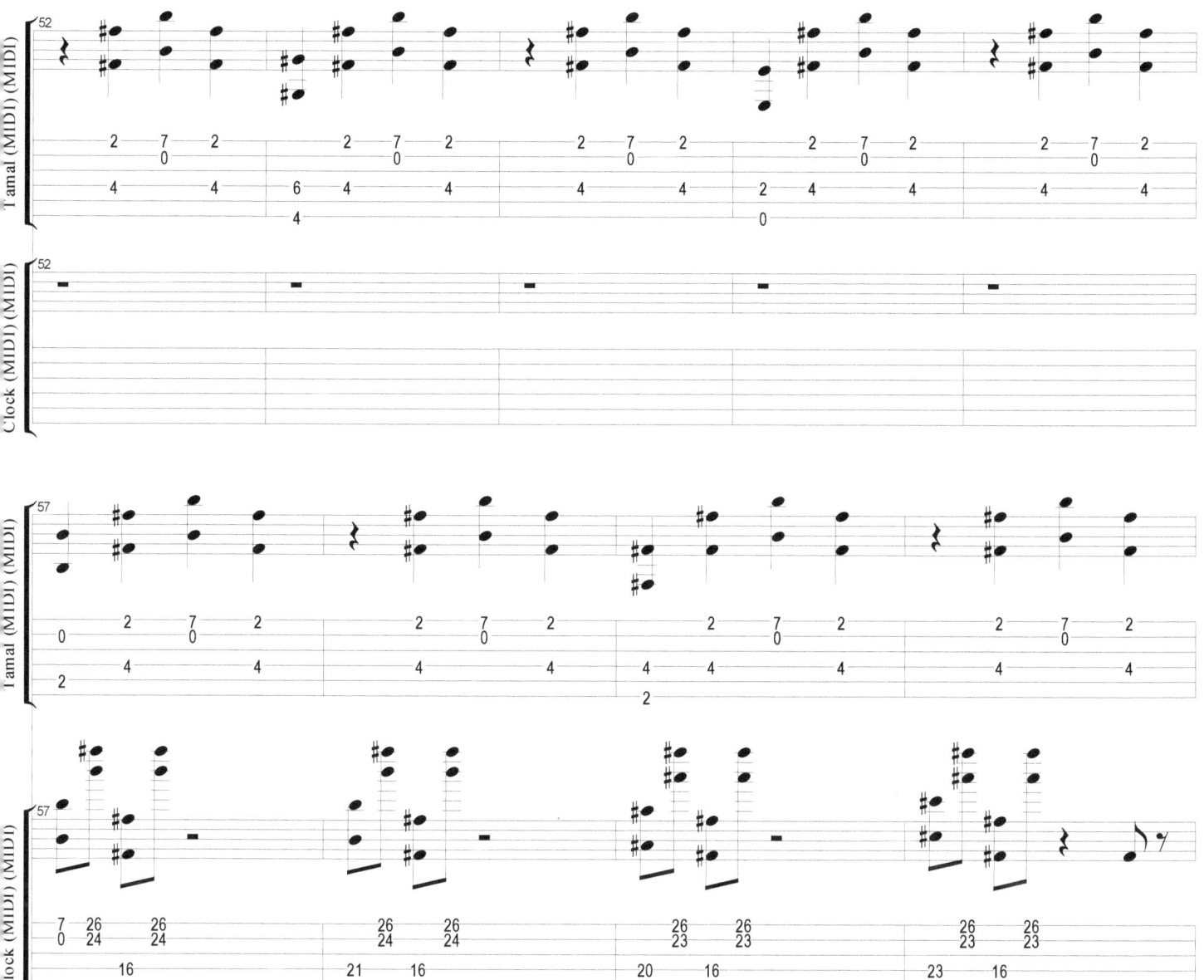

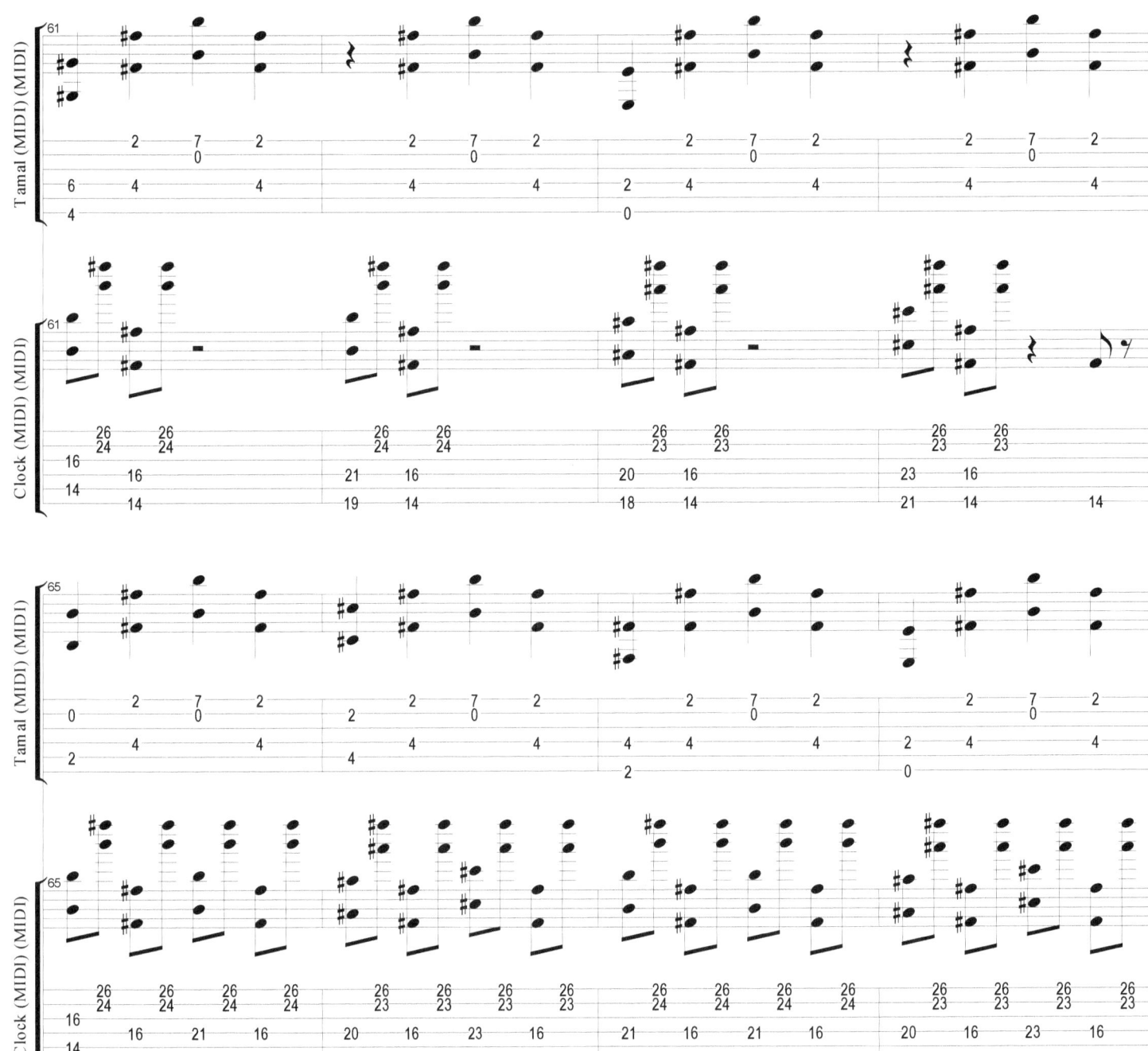

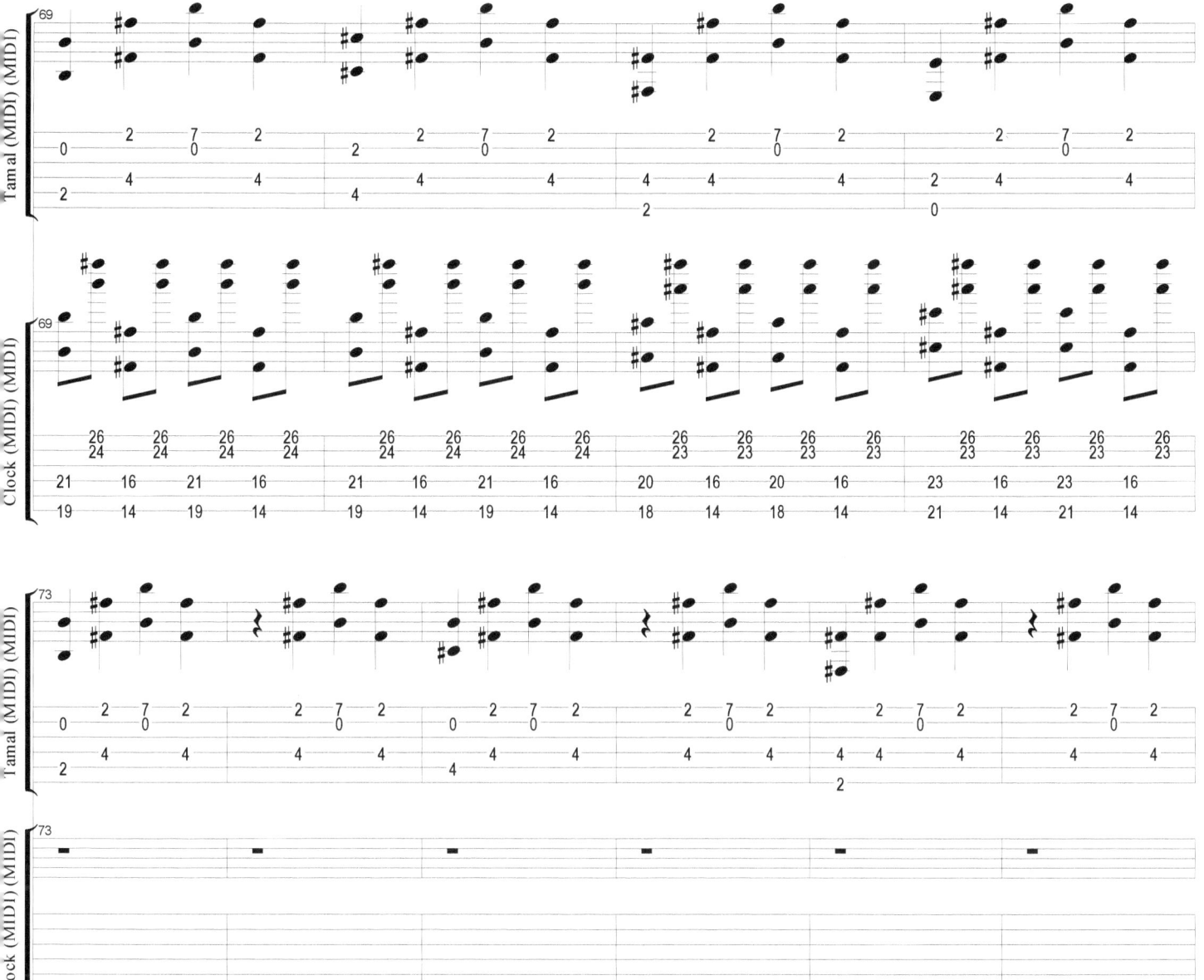

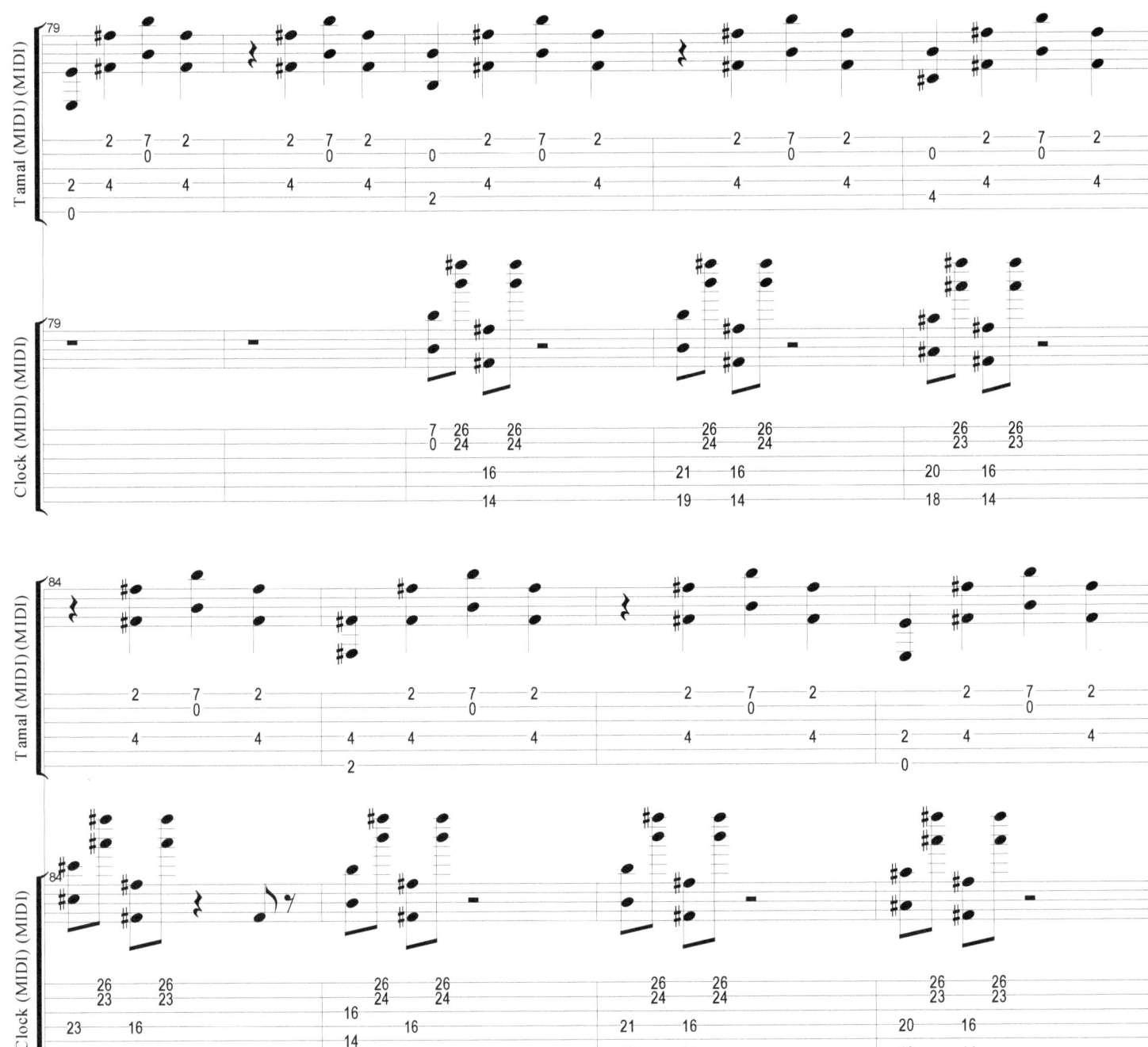

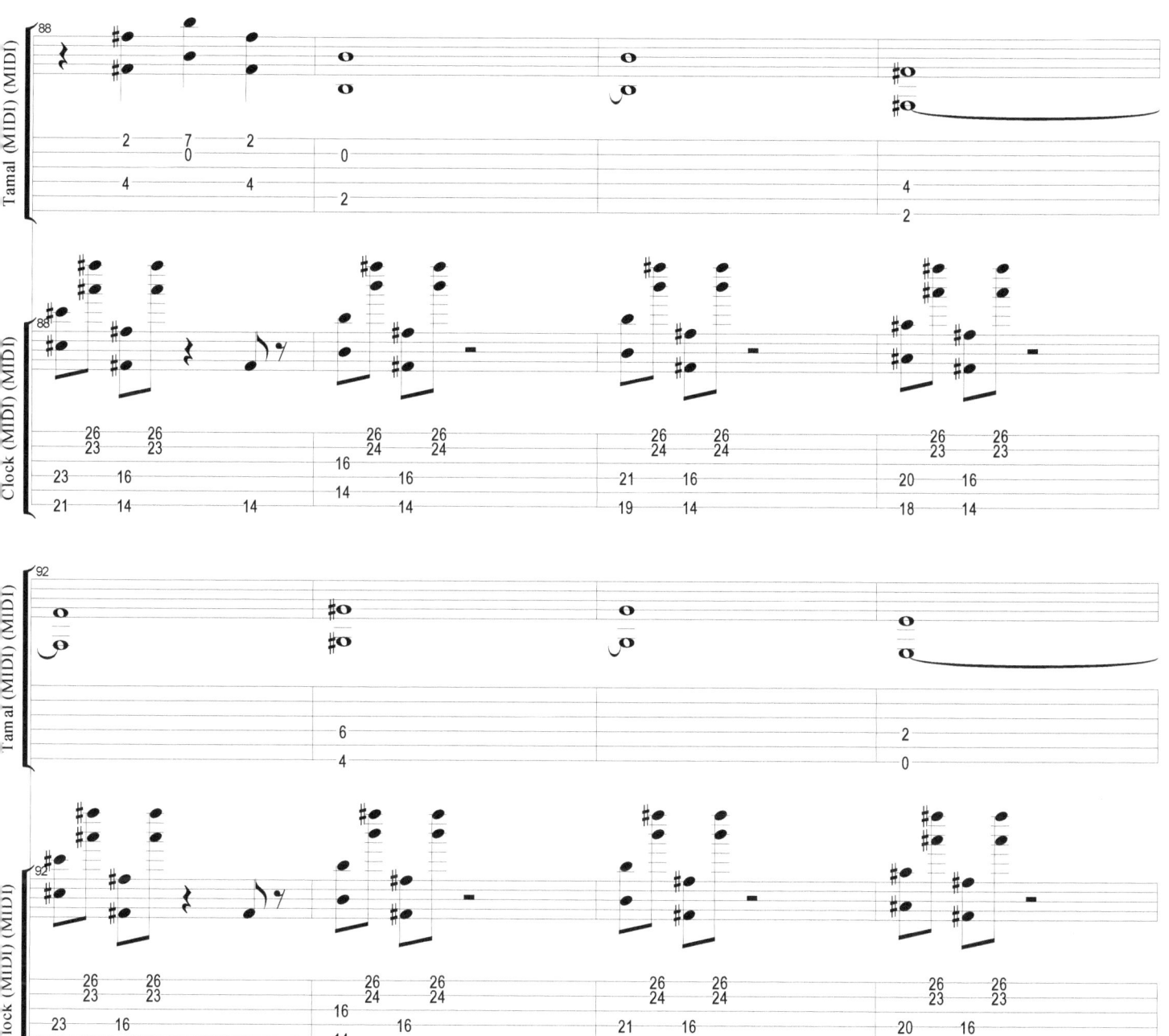

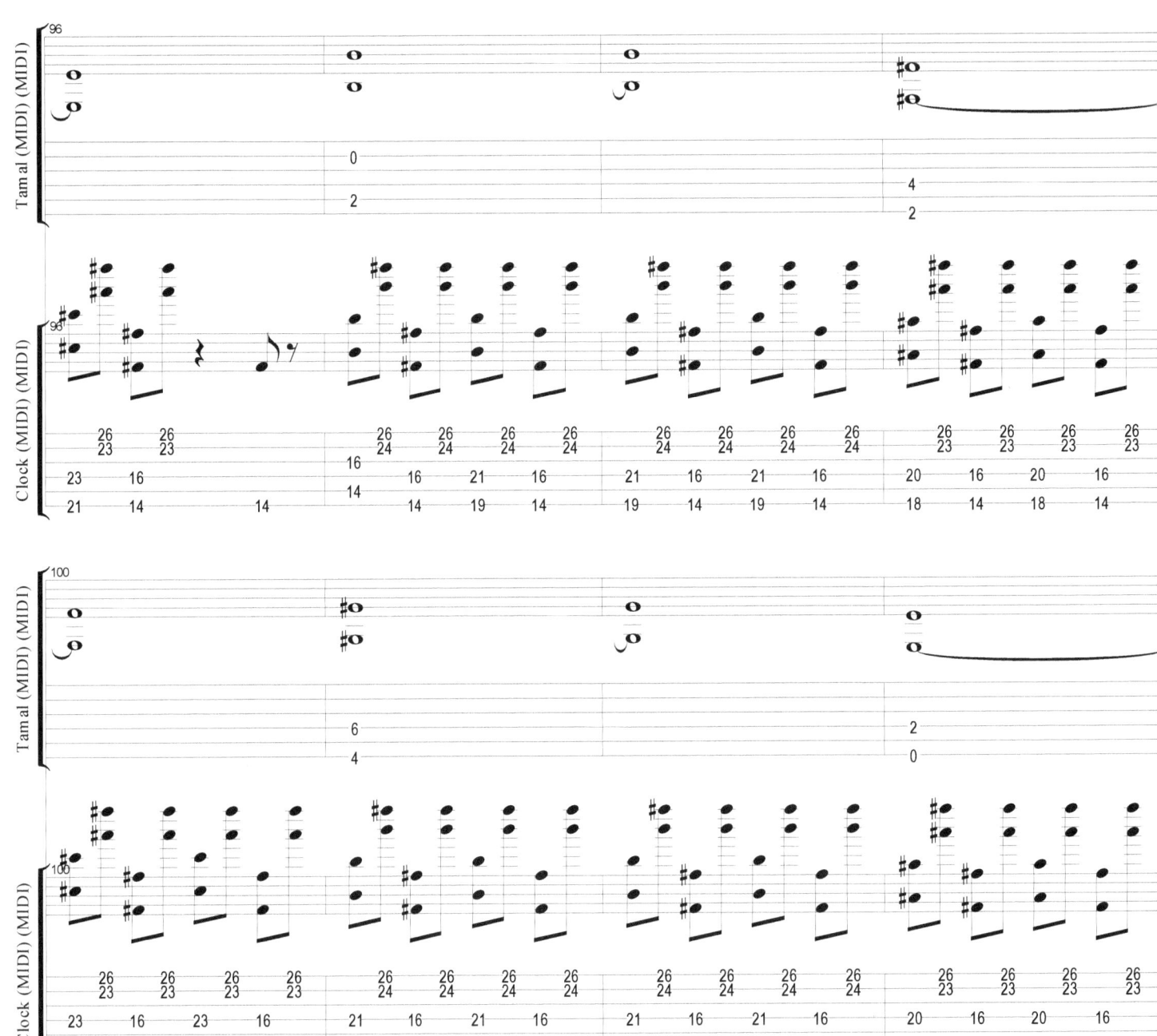

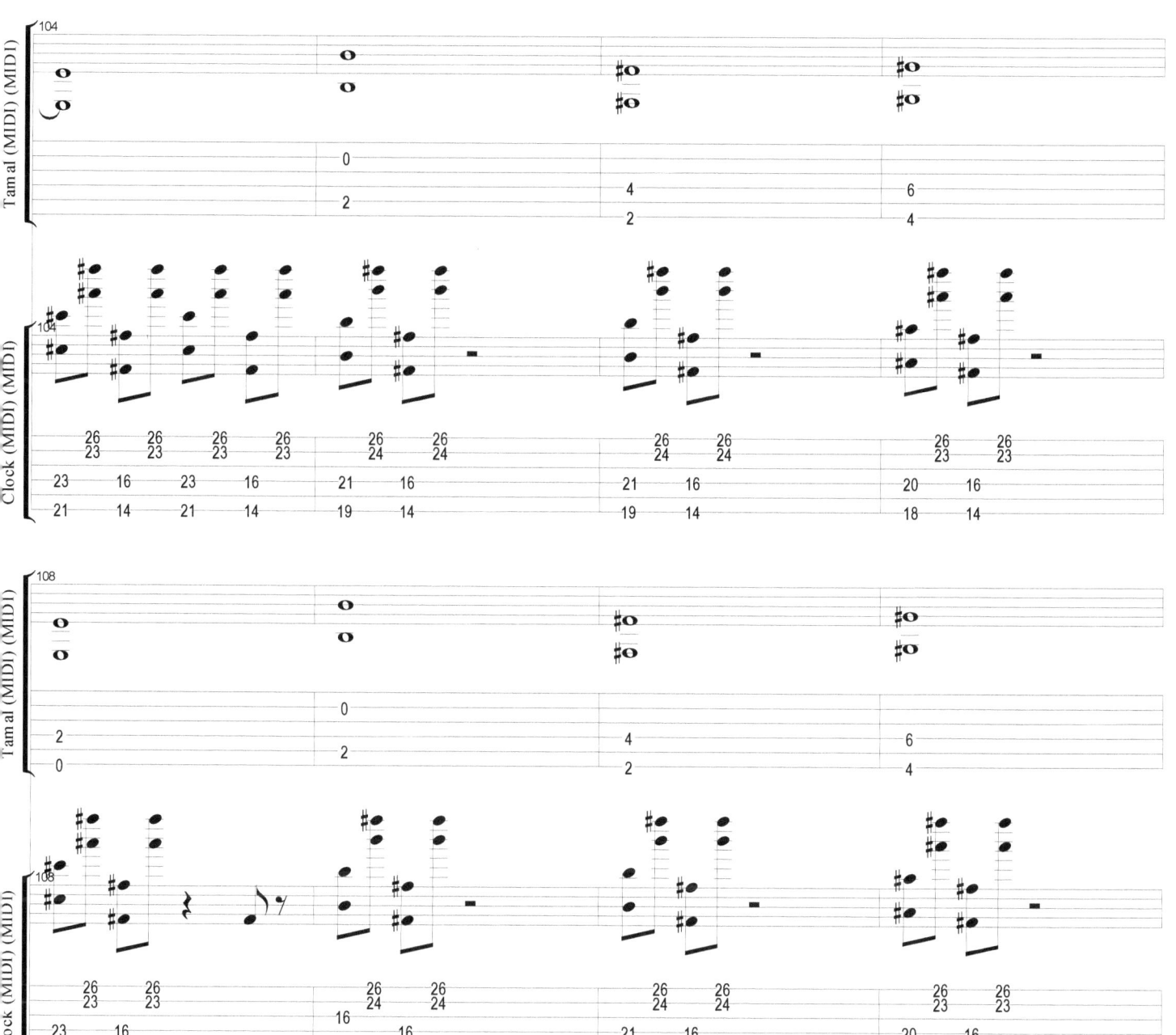

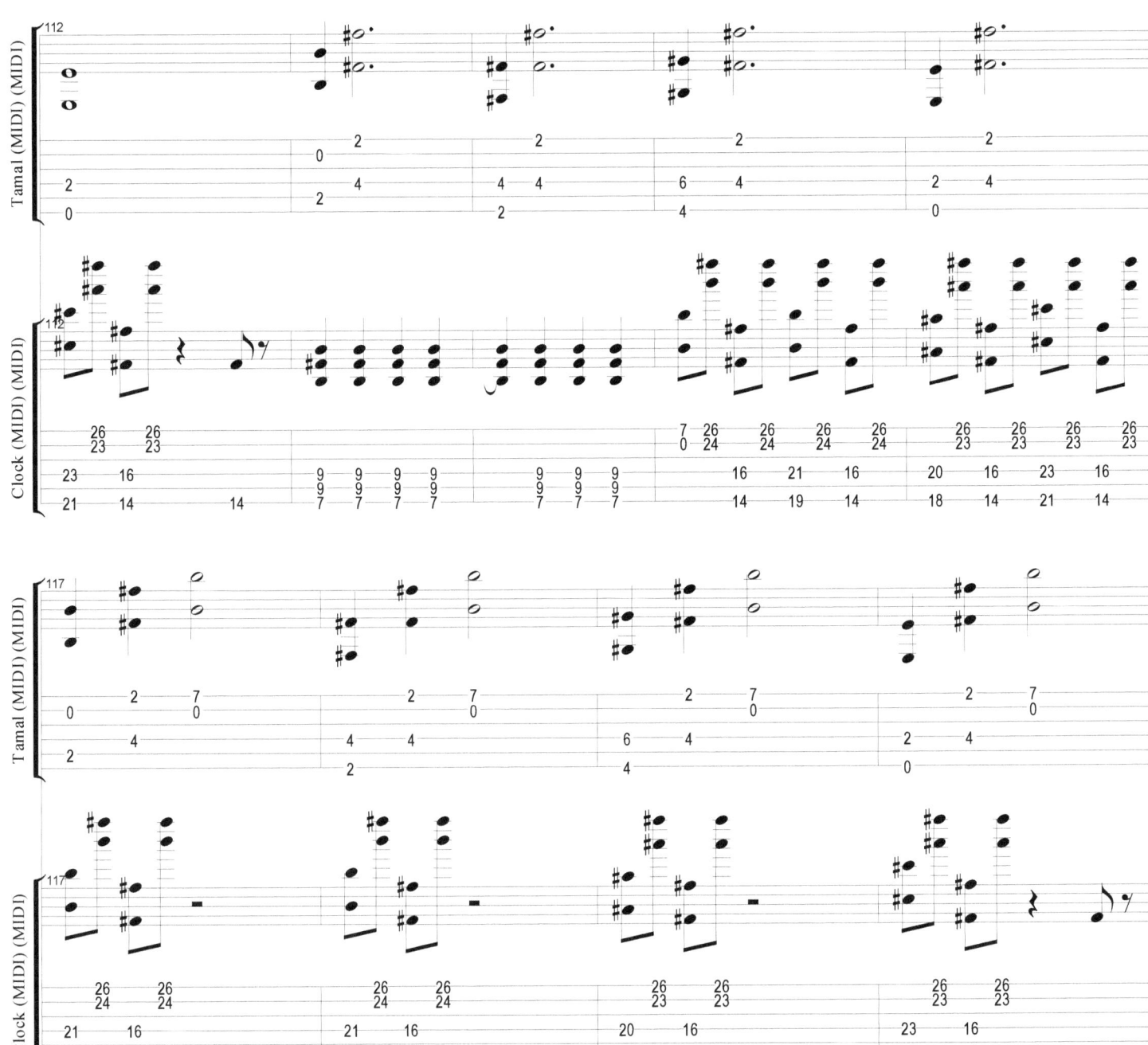

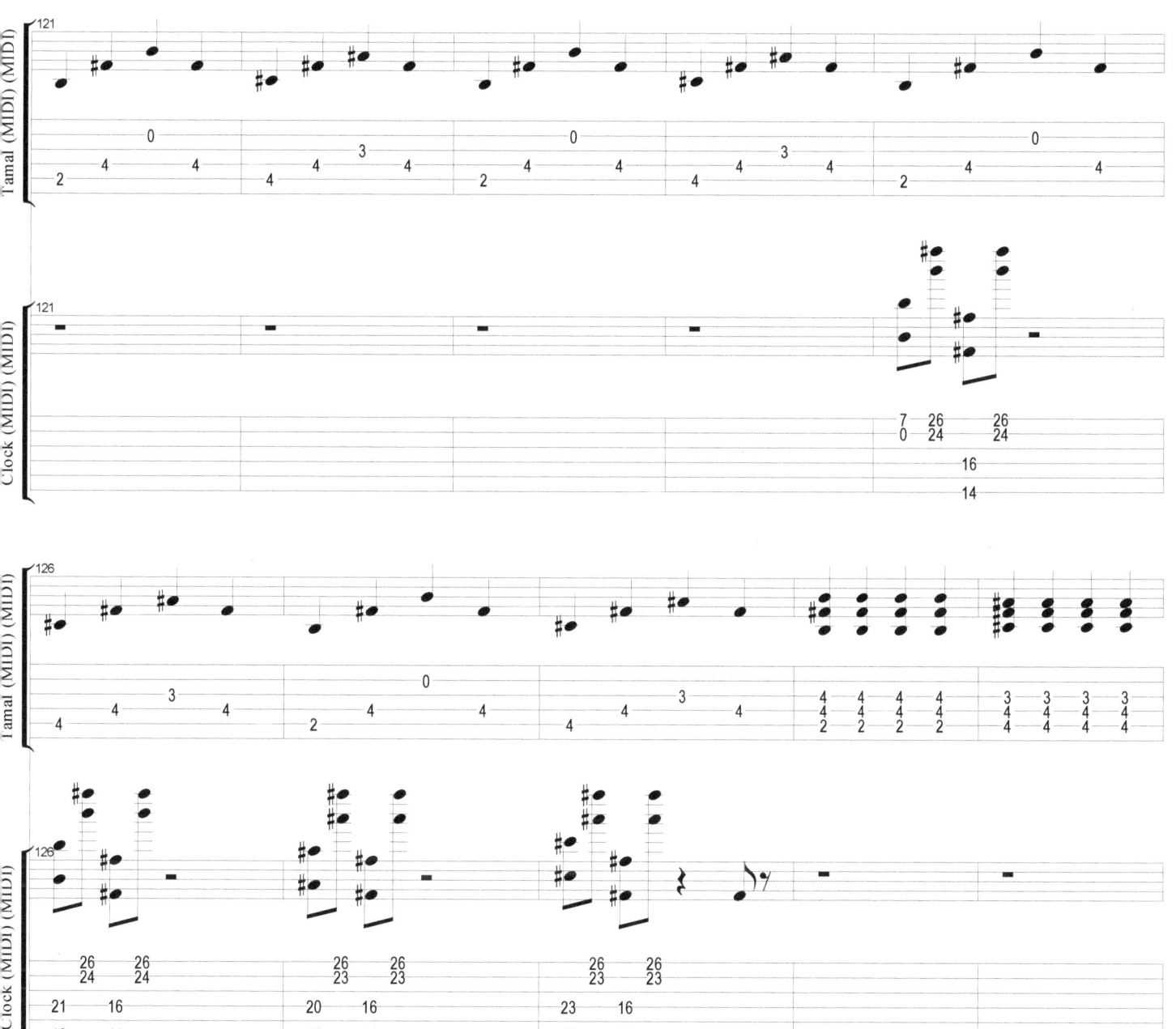

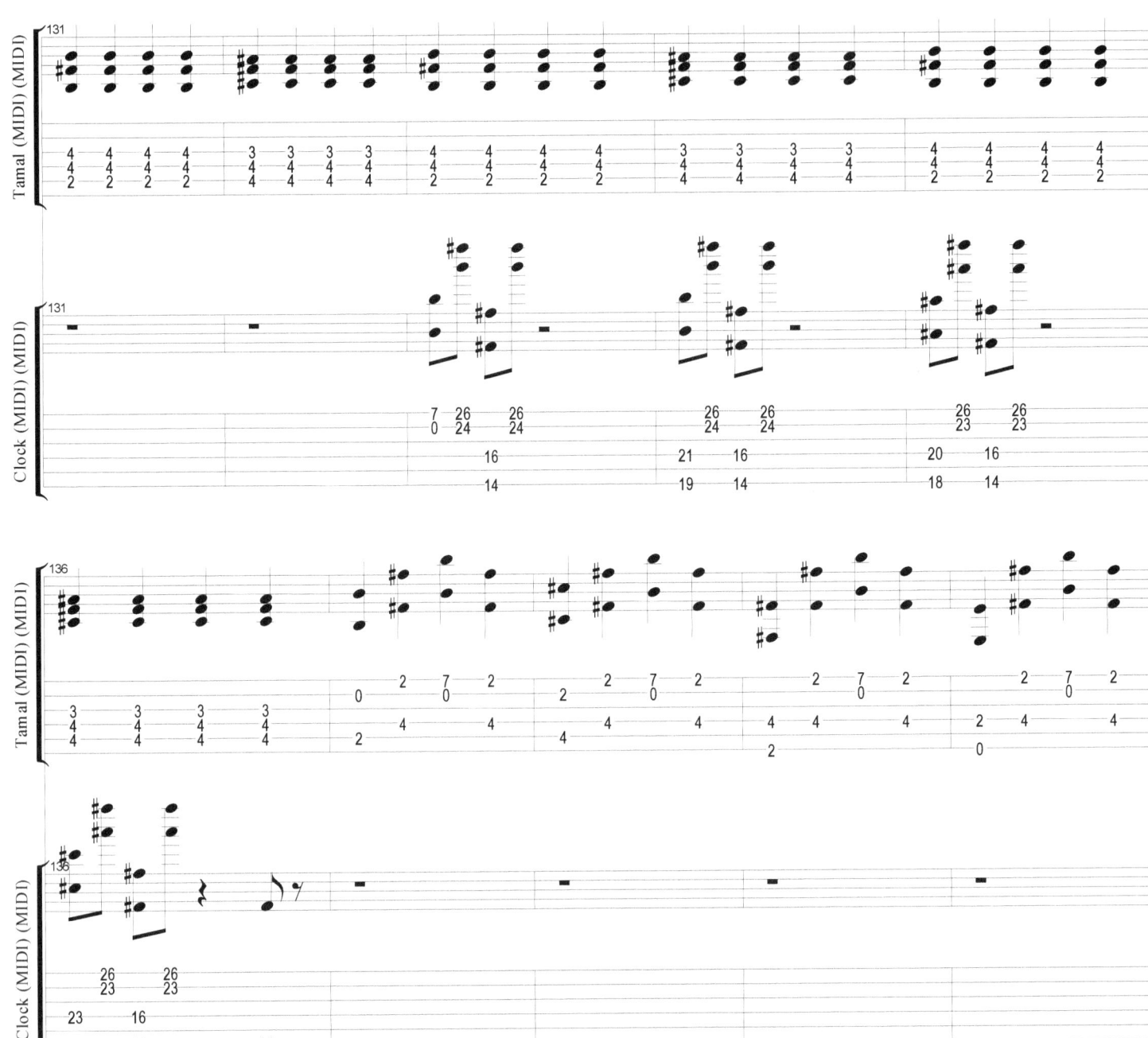

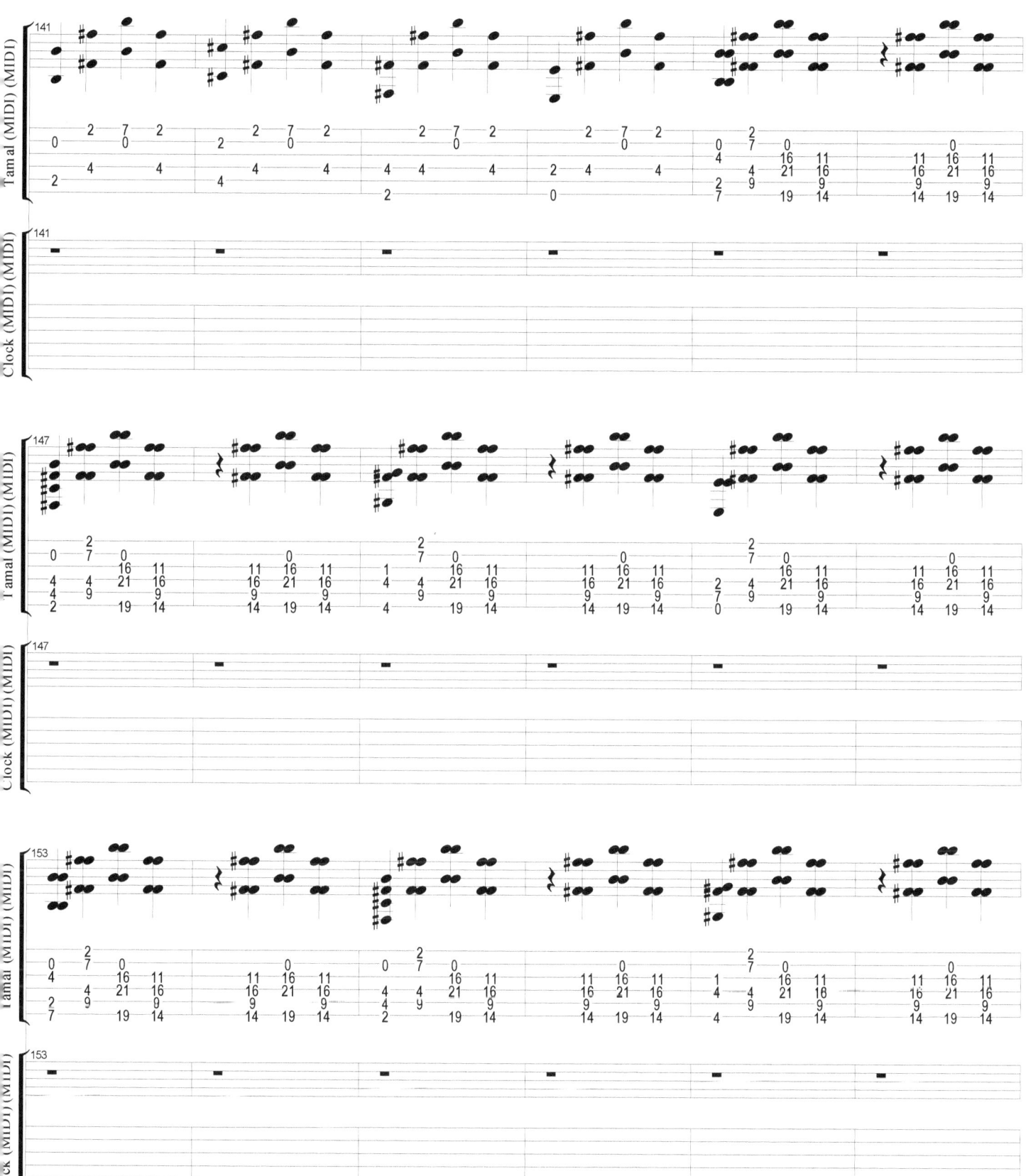

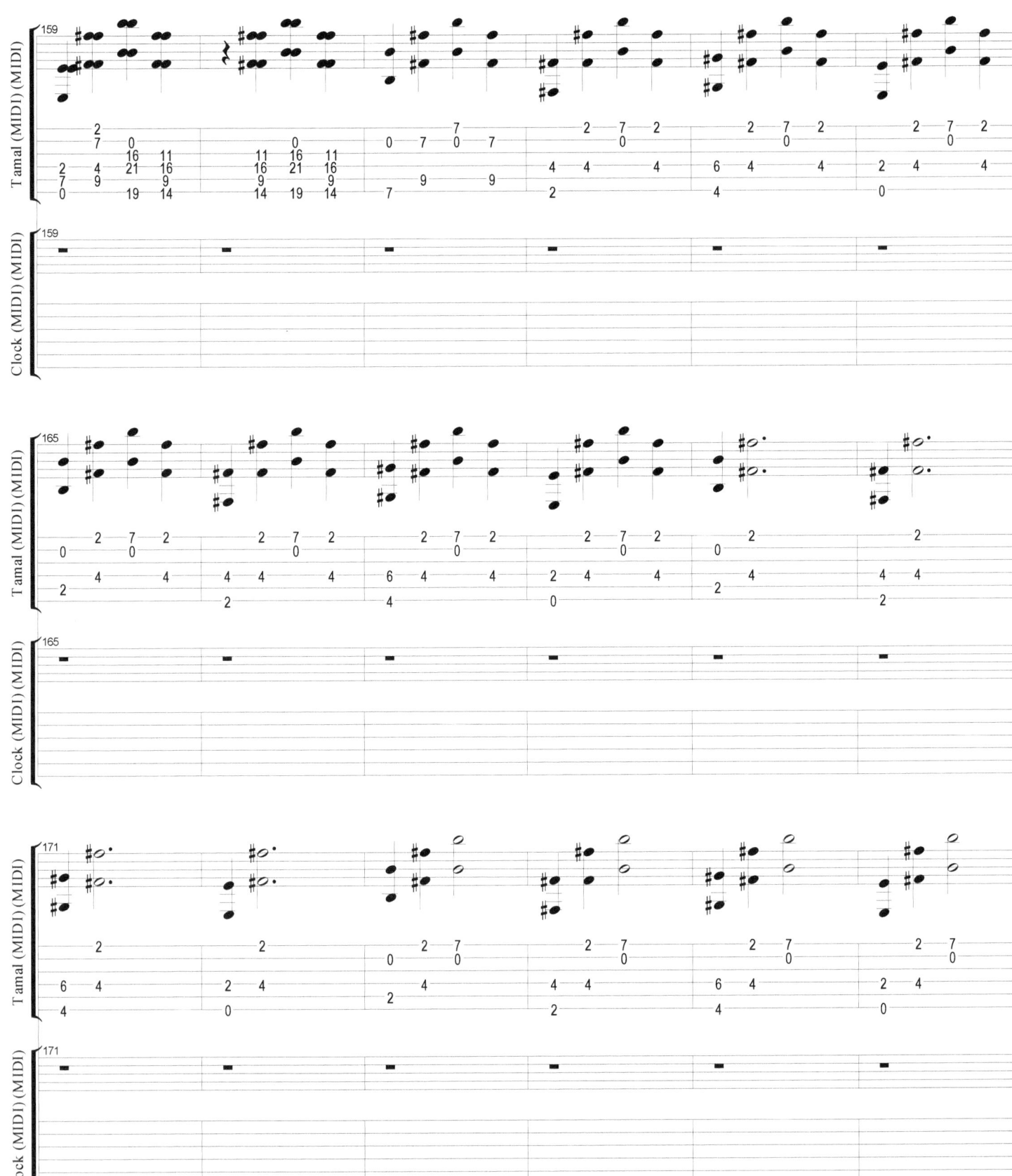

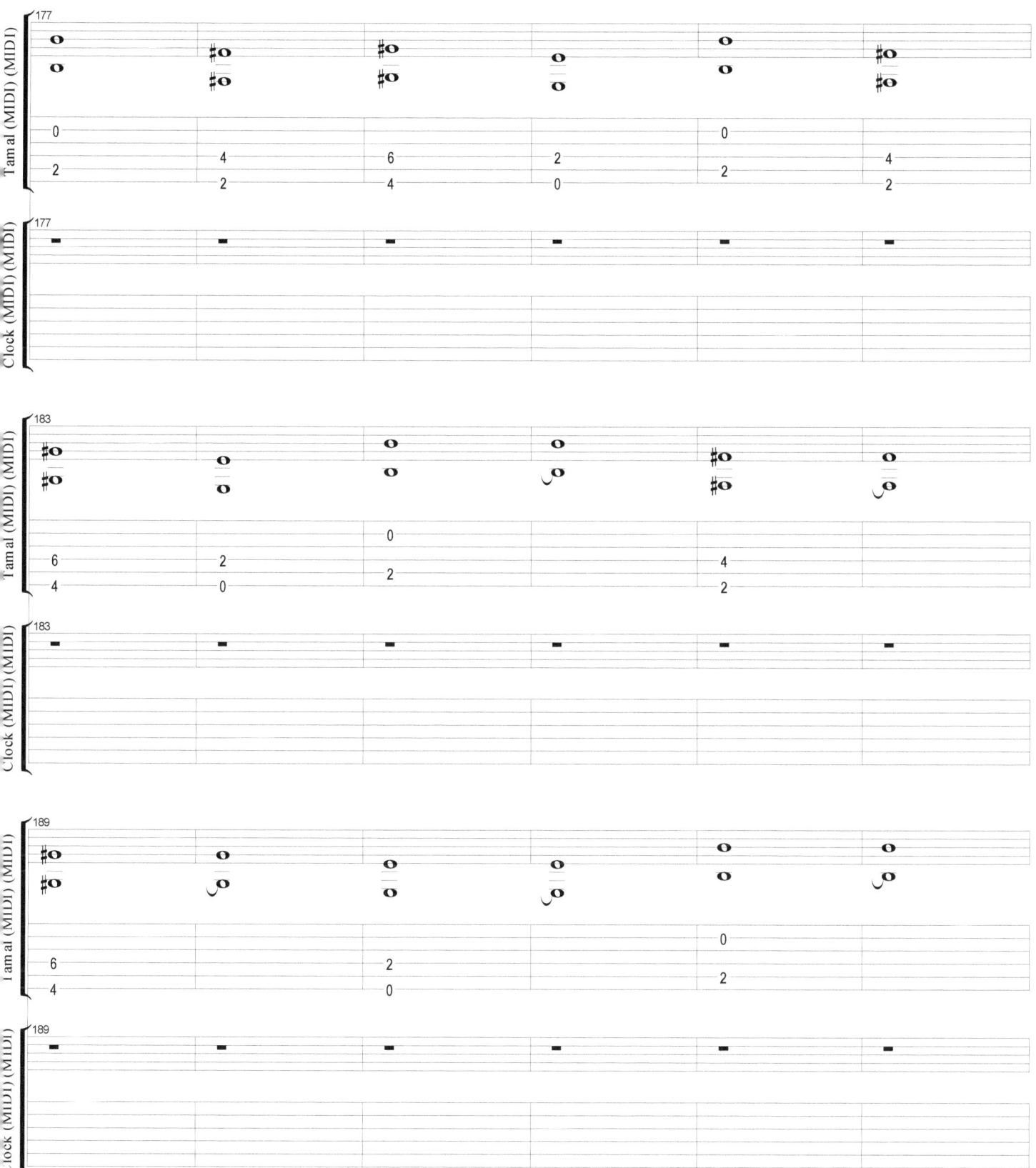

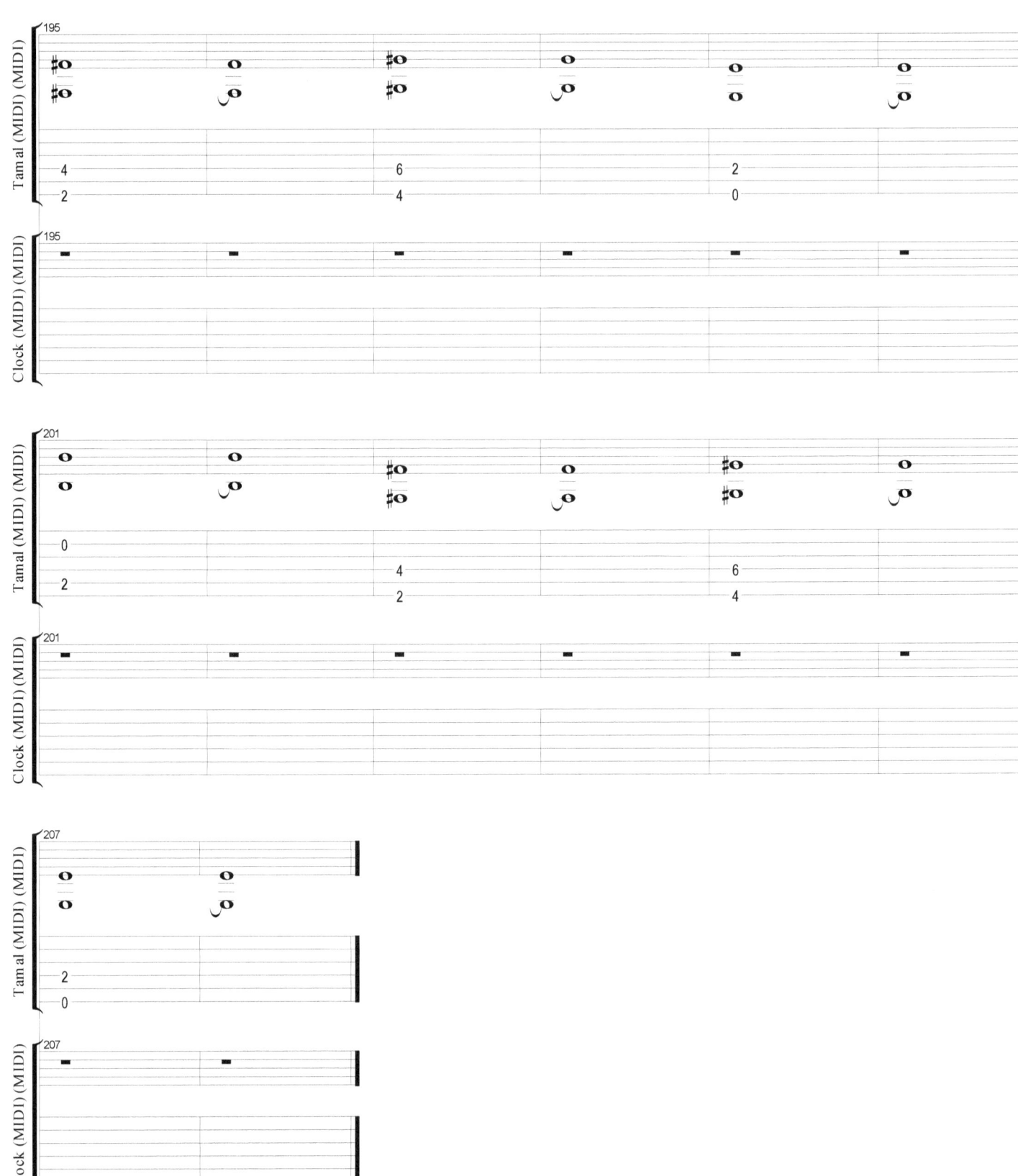

Dear Father

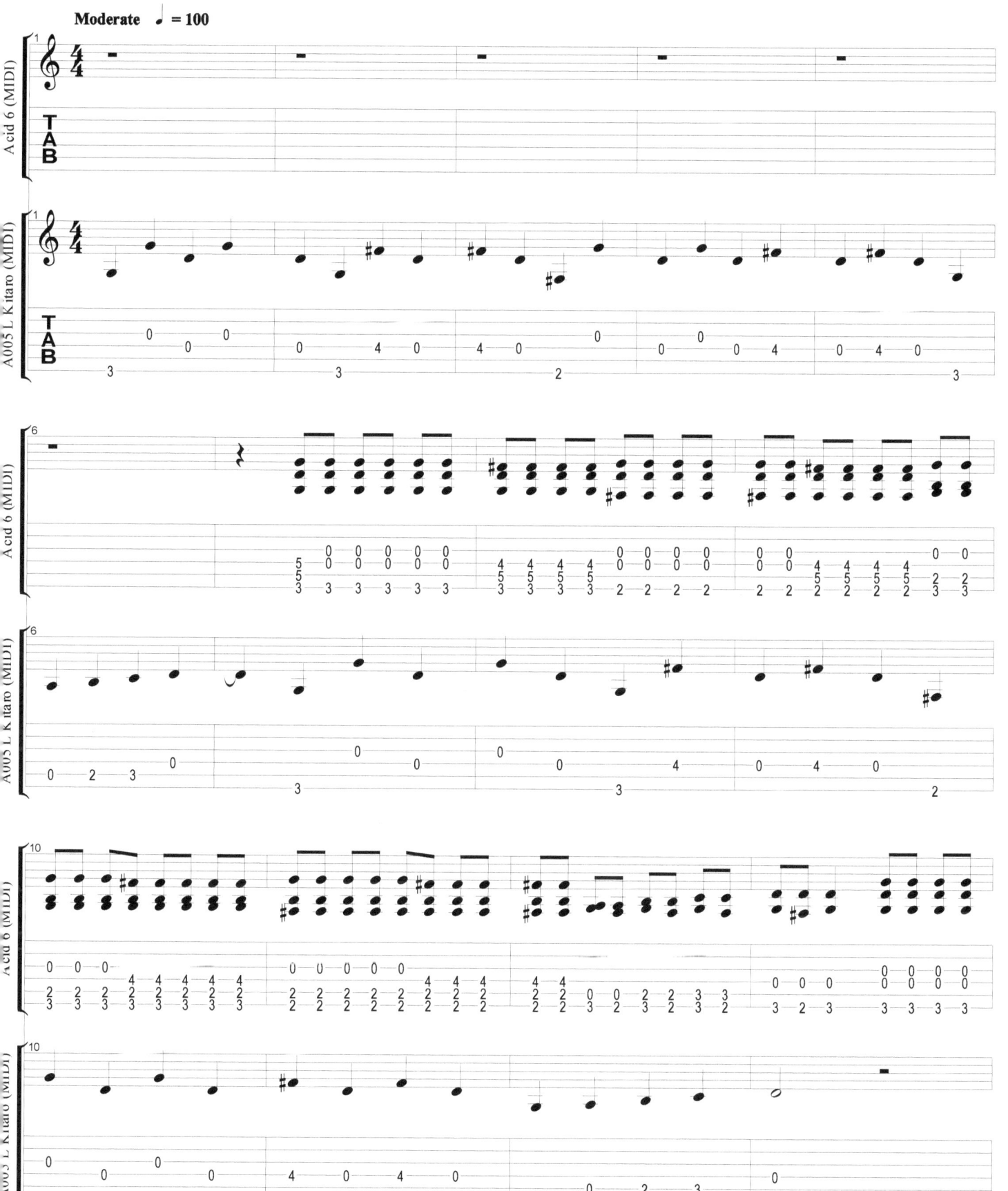

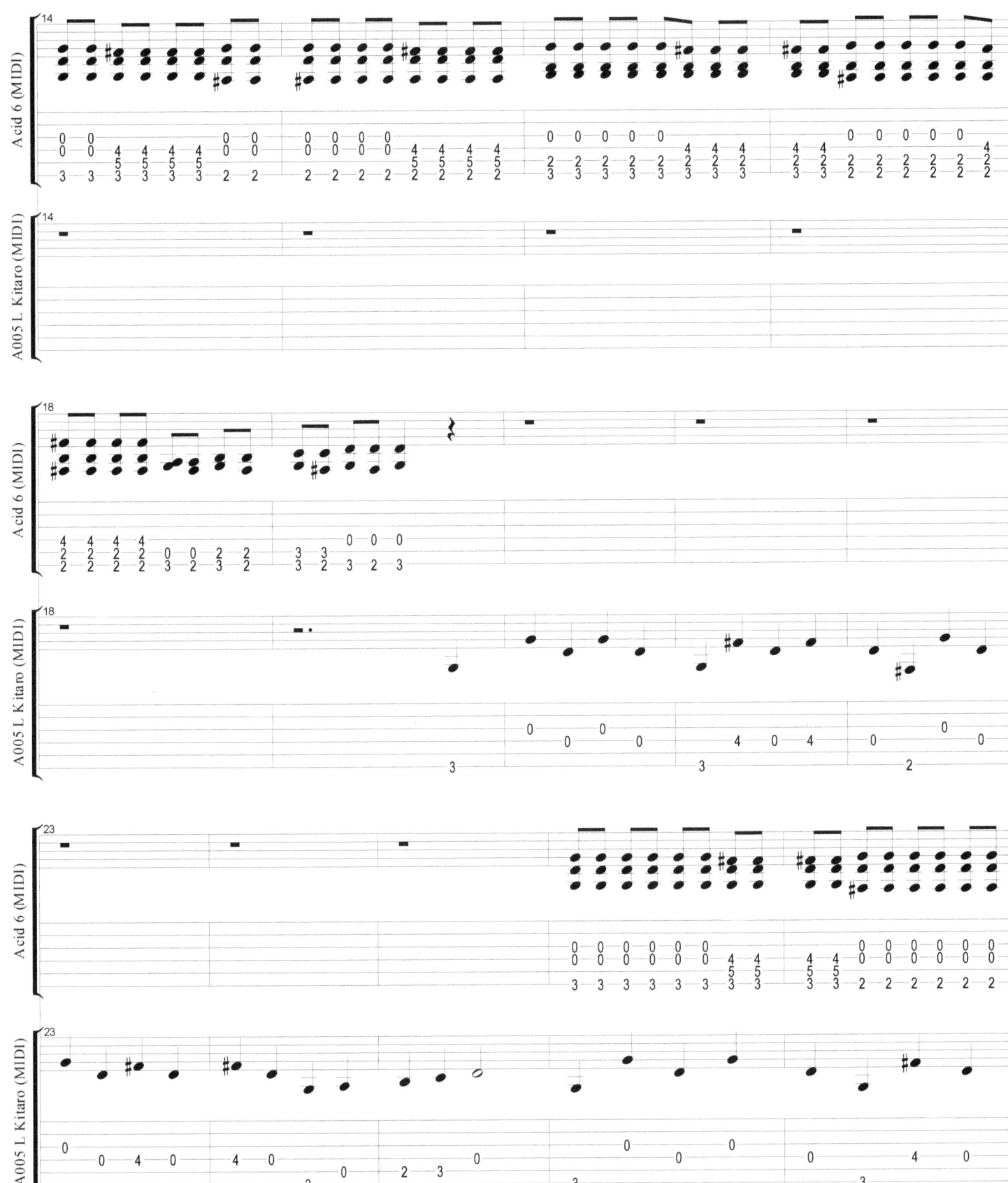

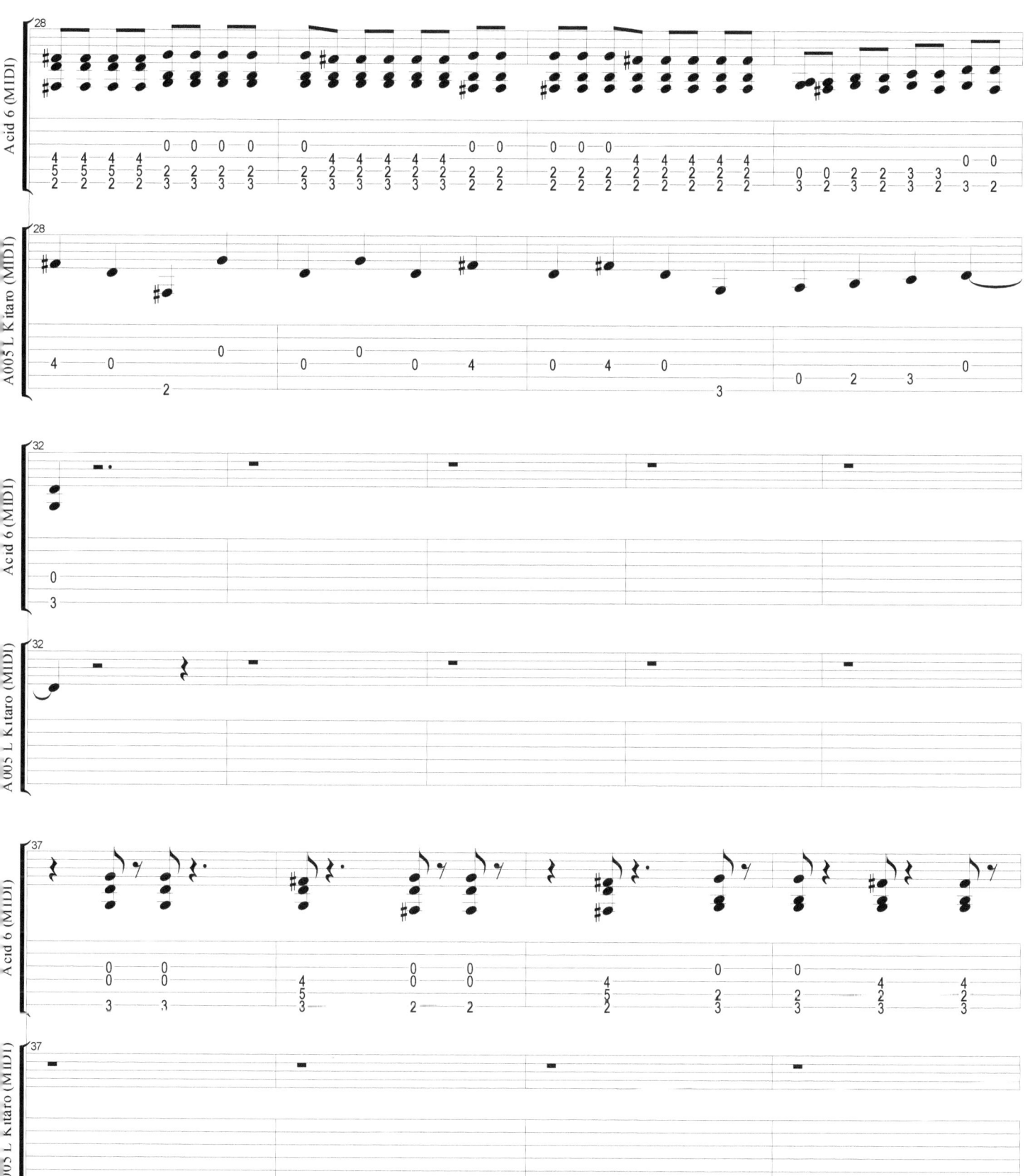

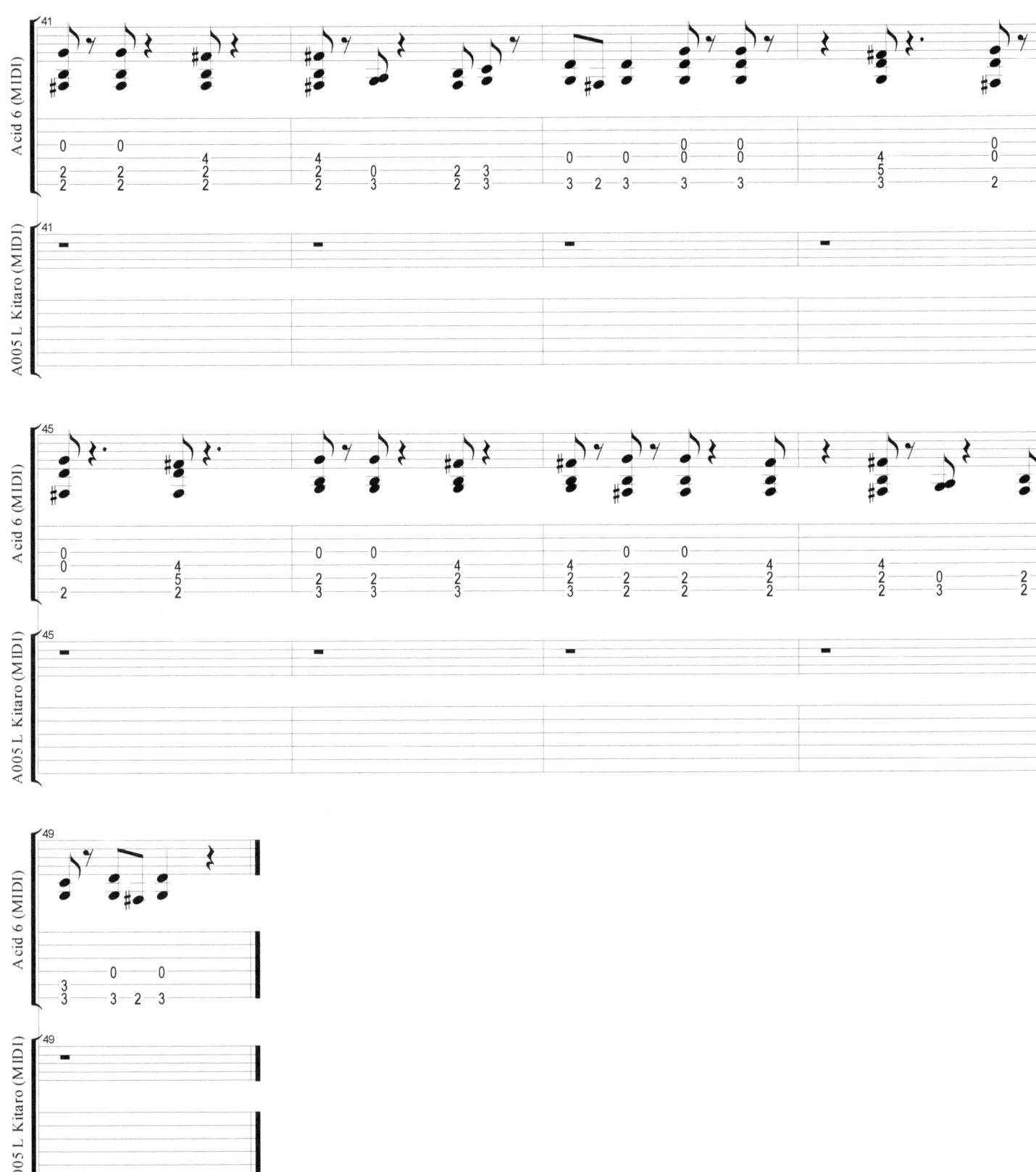

Fight!

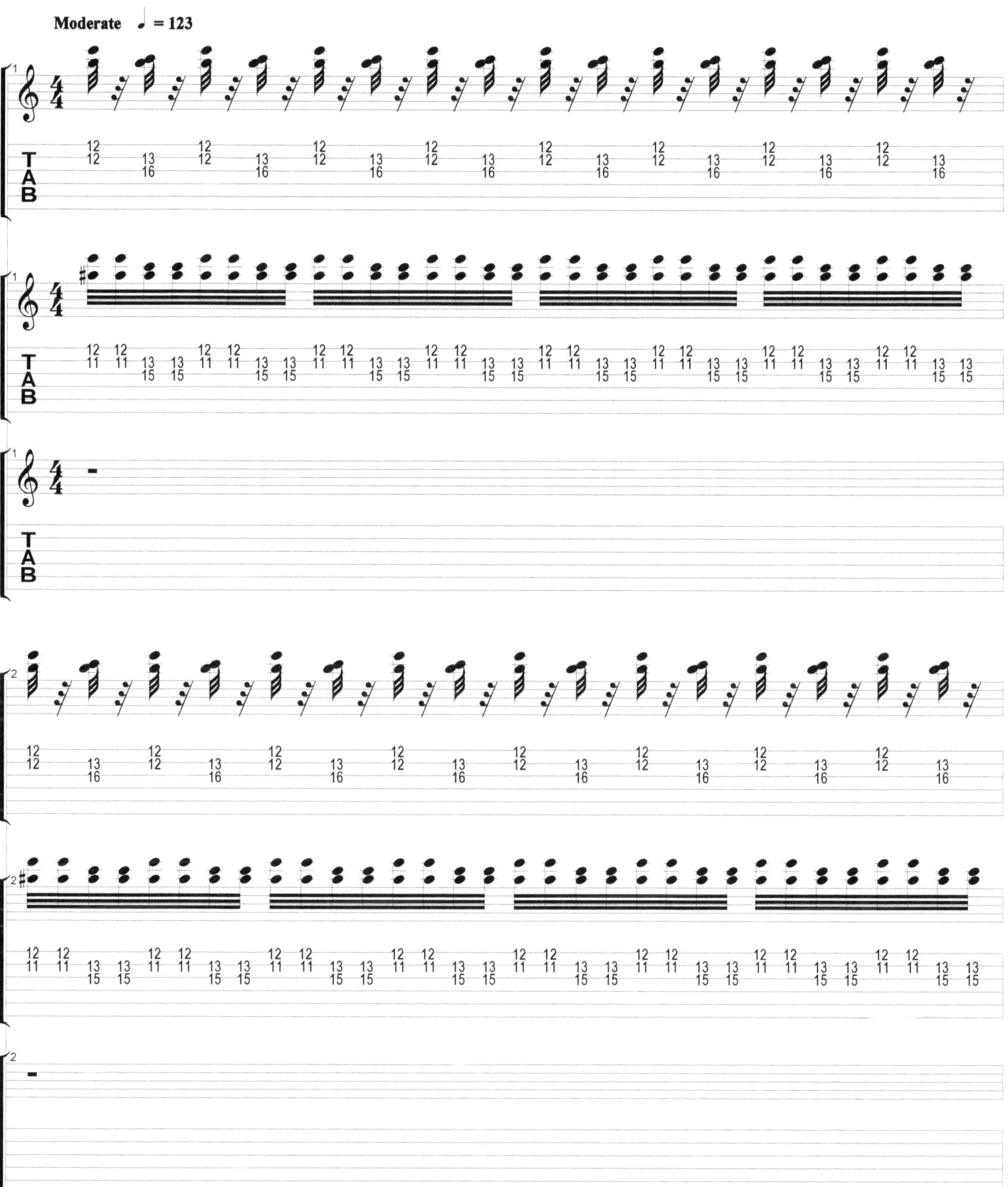

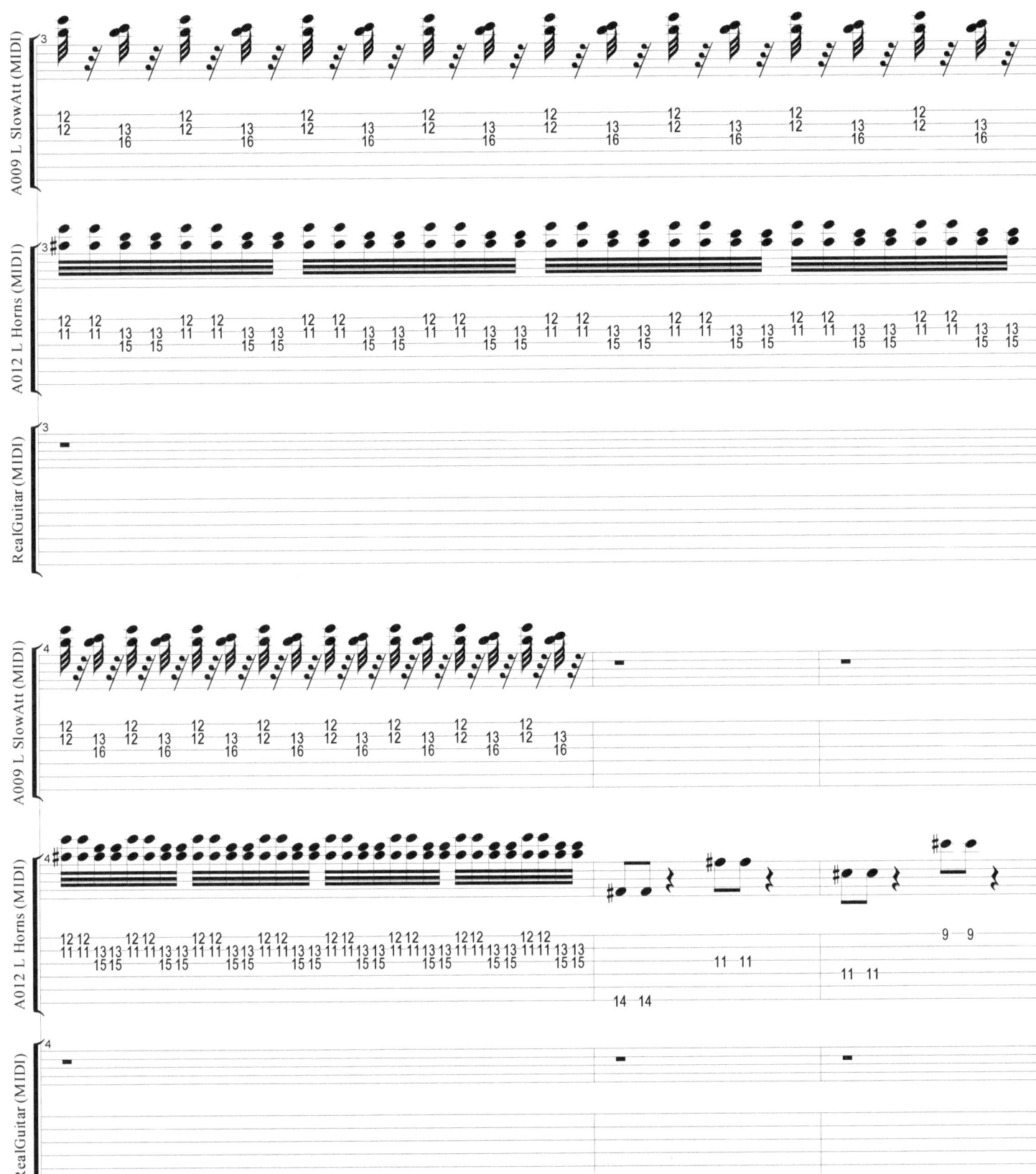

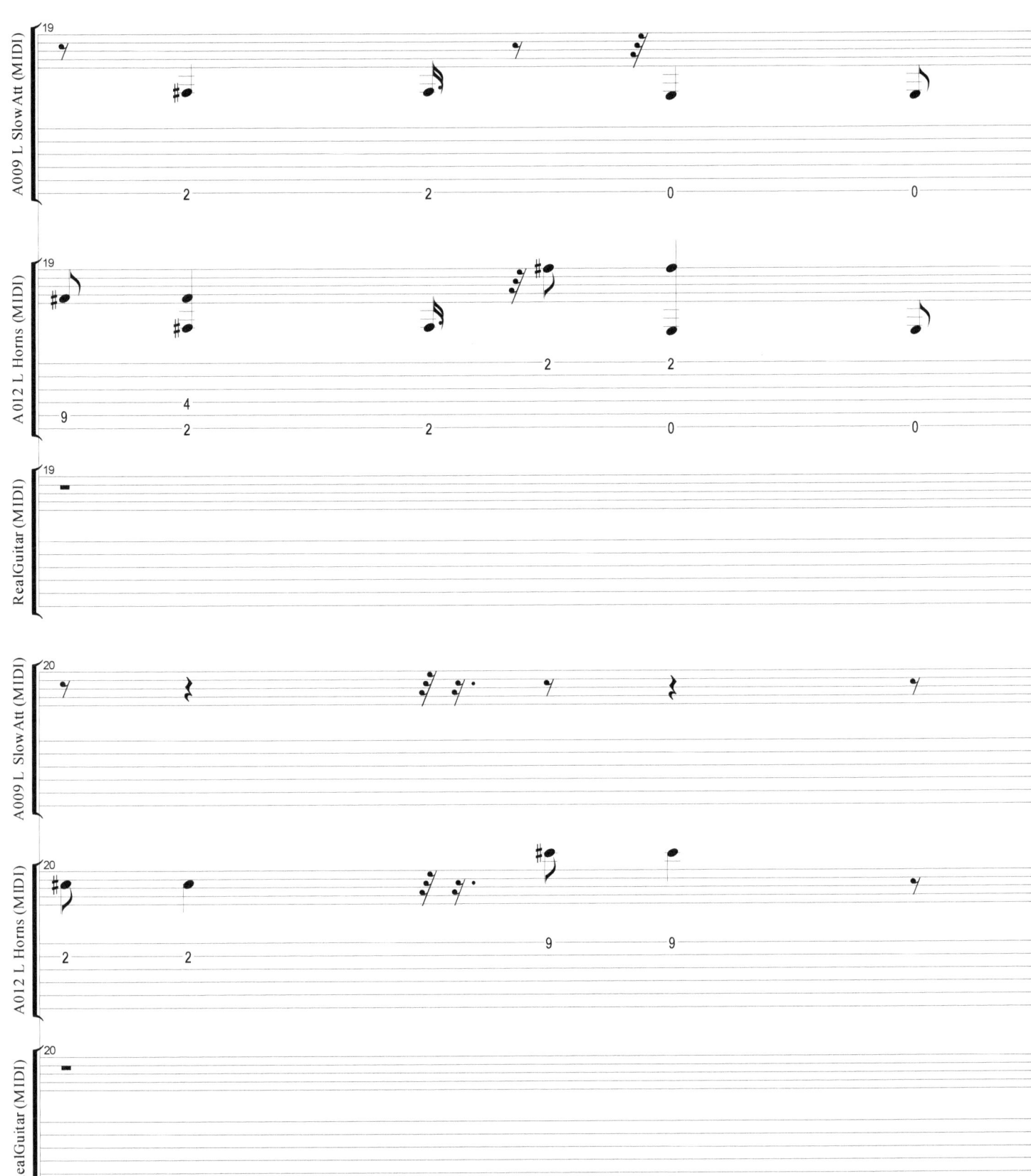

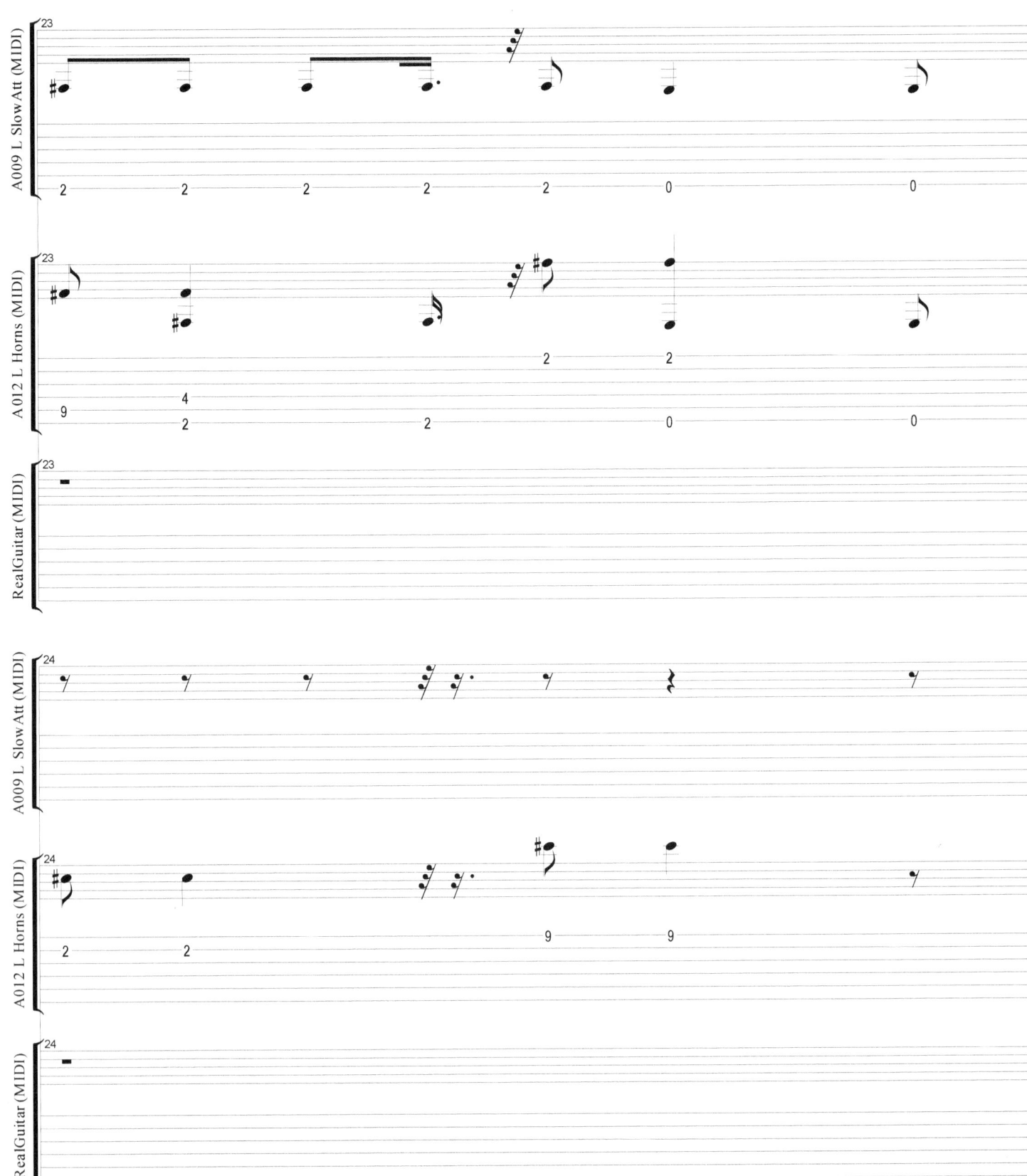

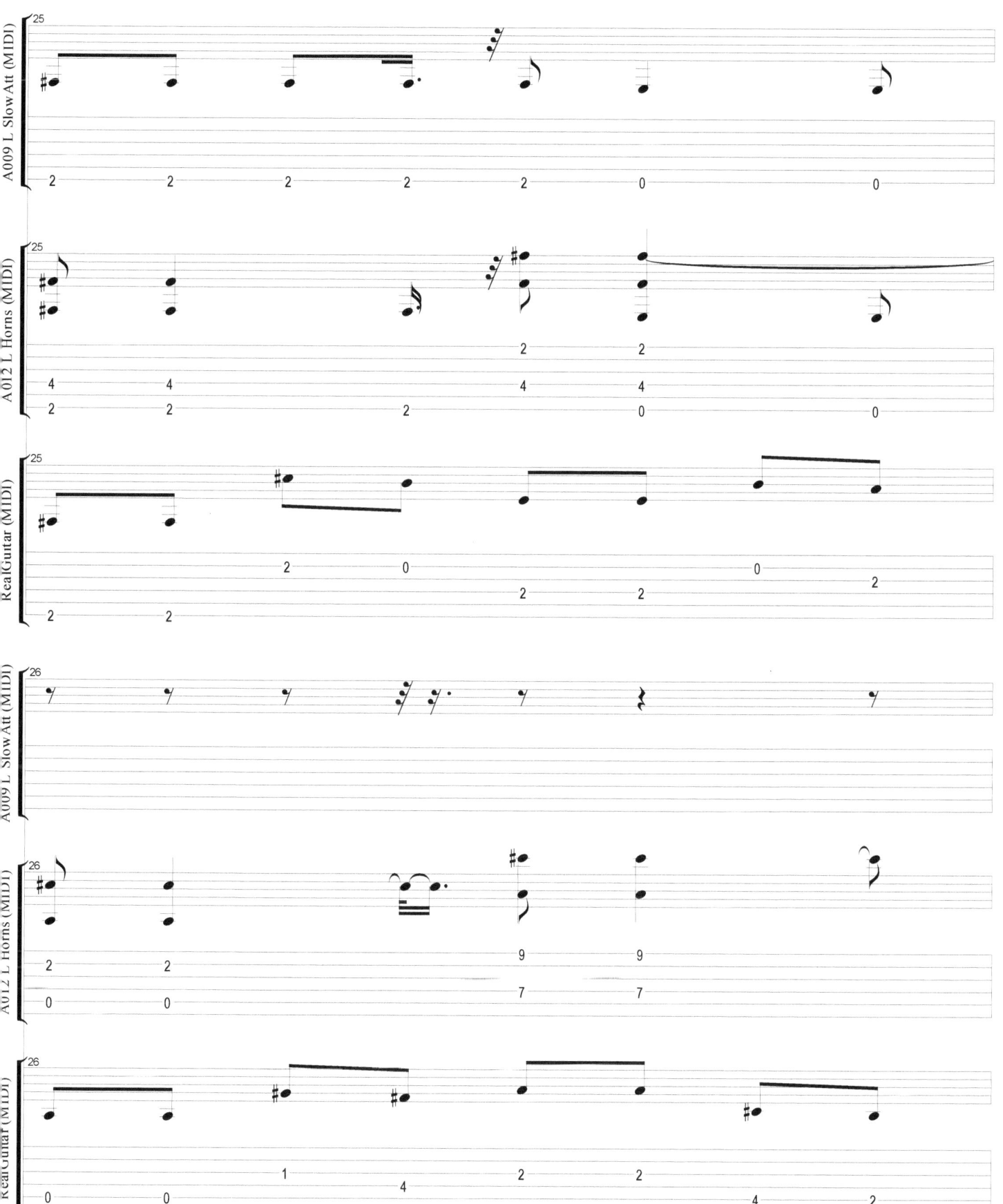

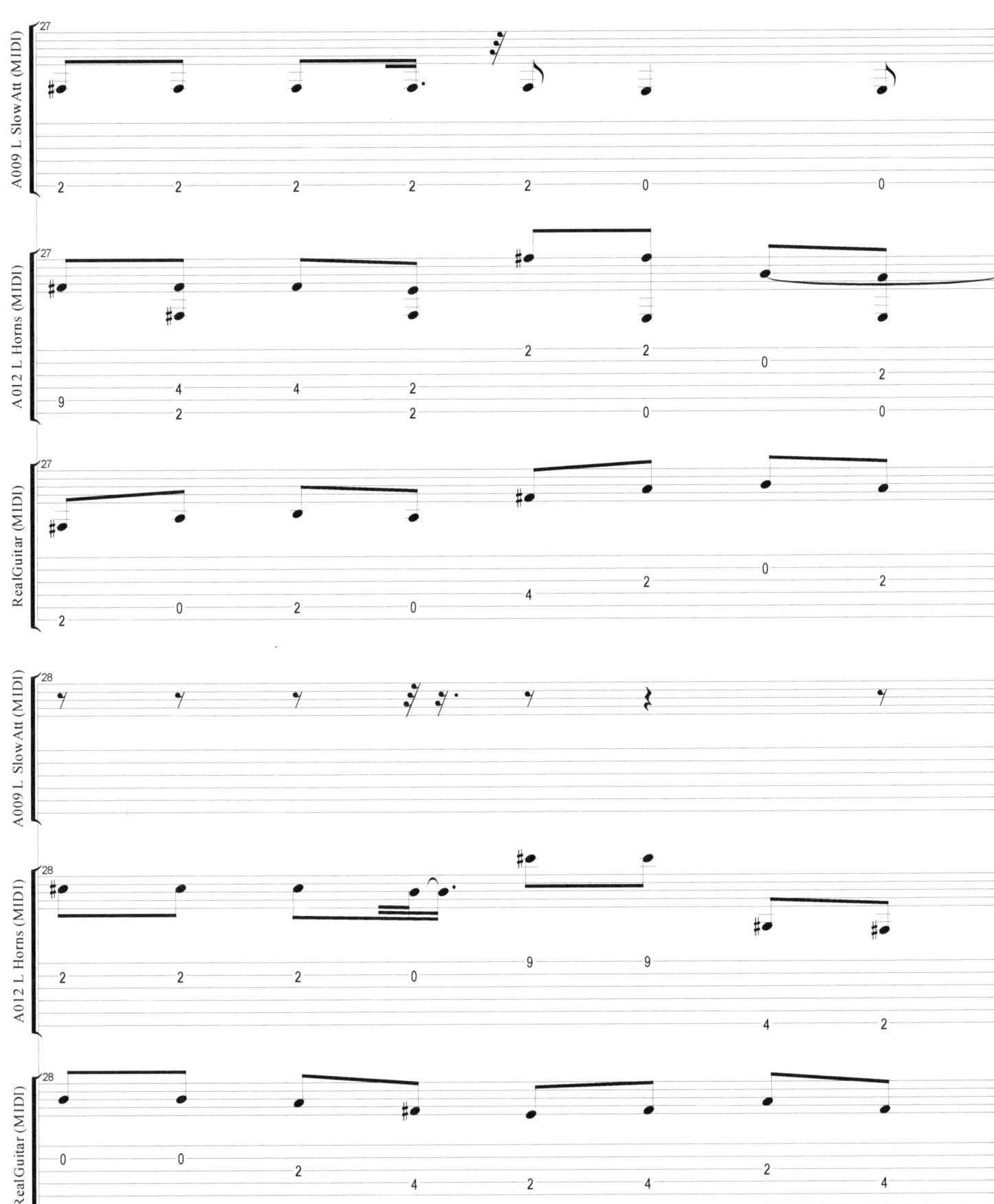

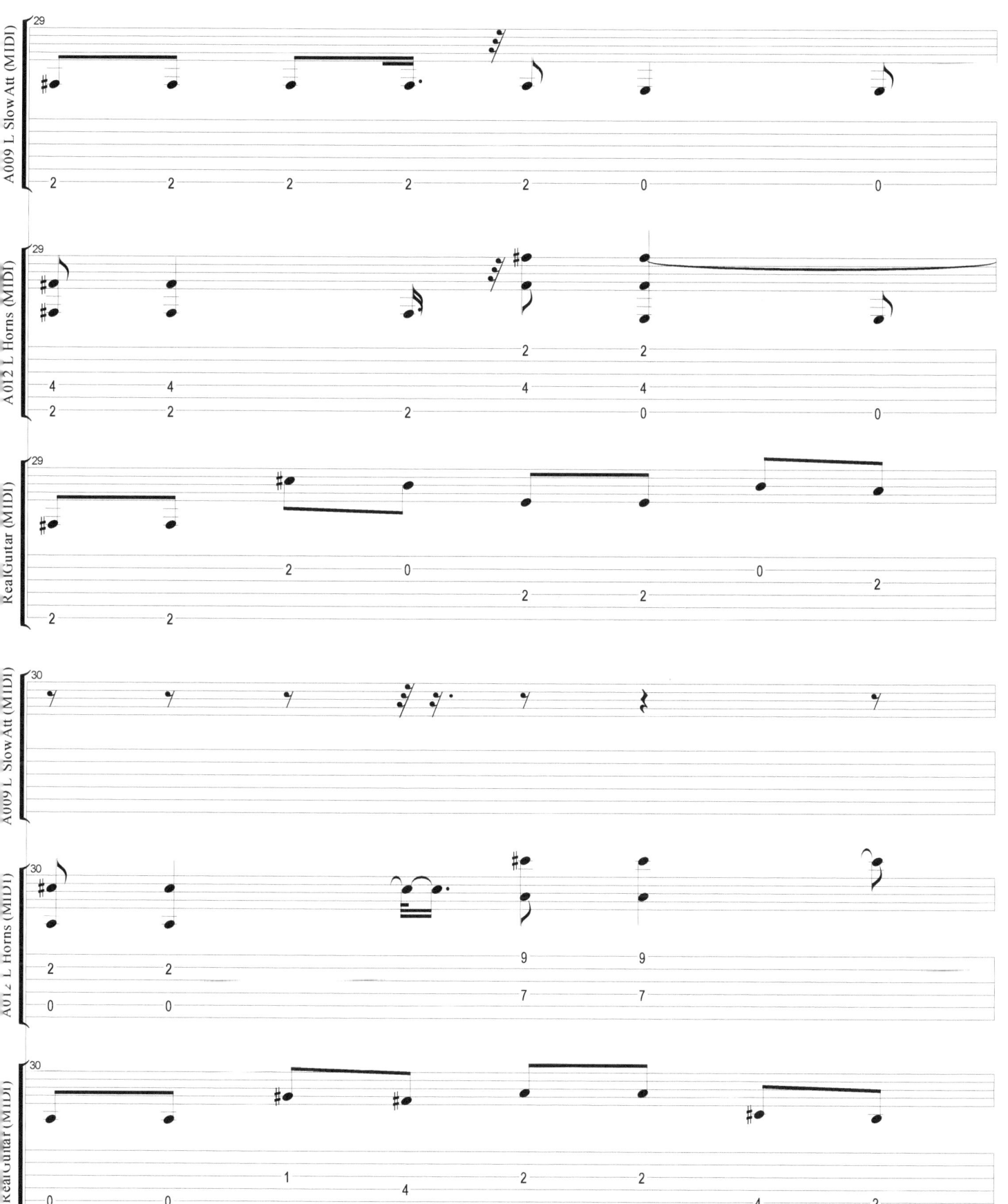

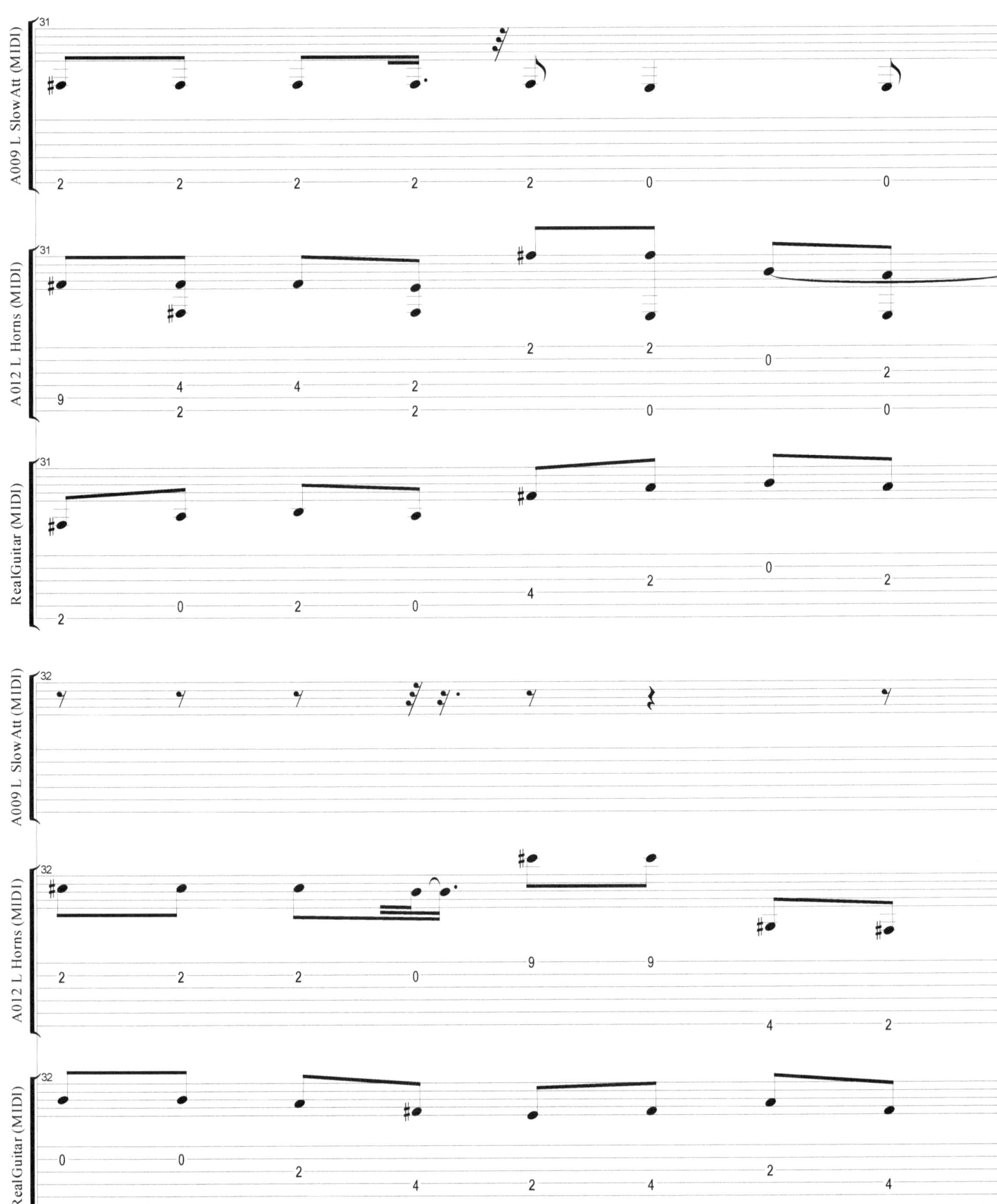

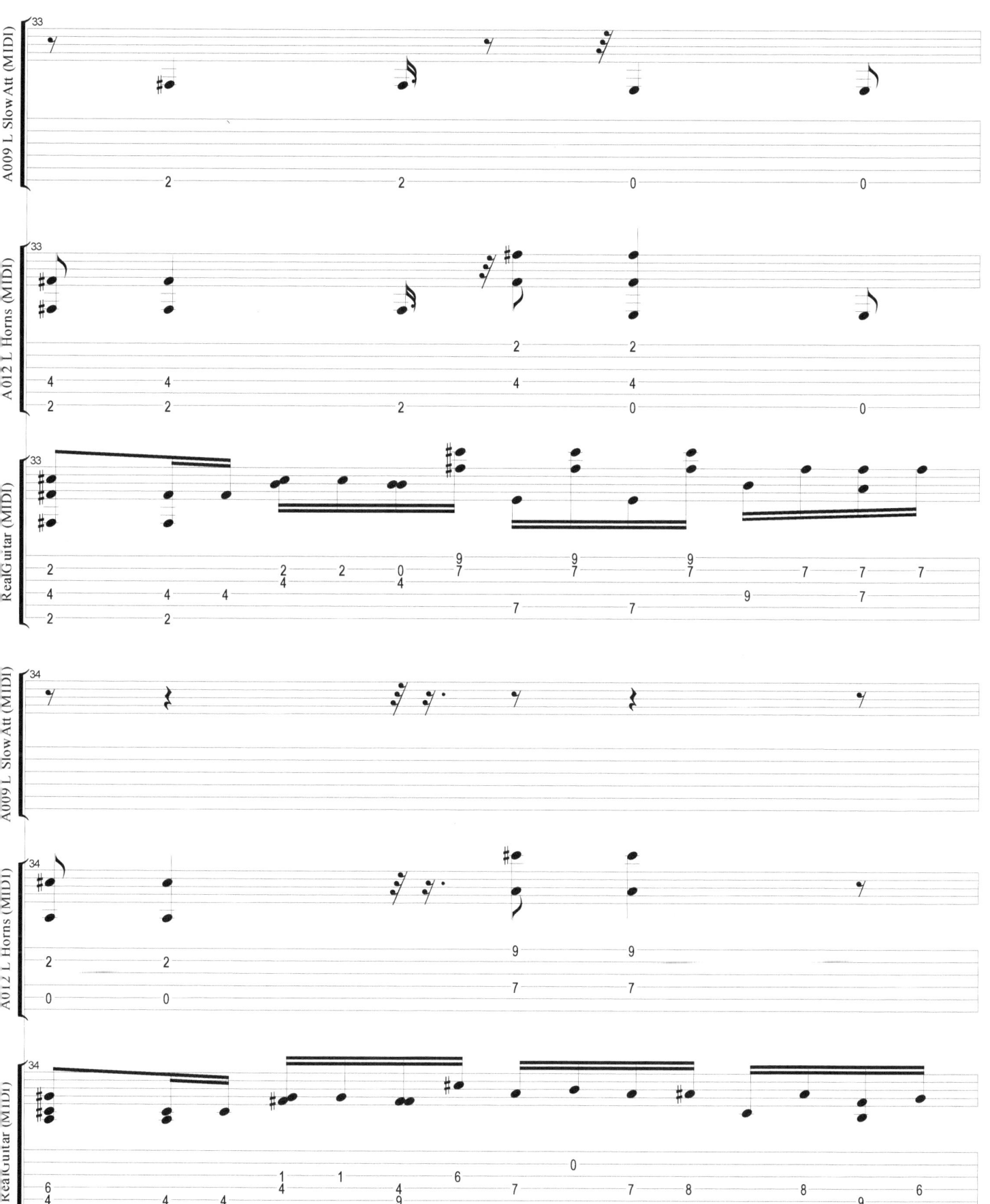

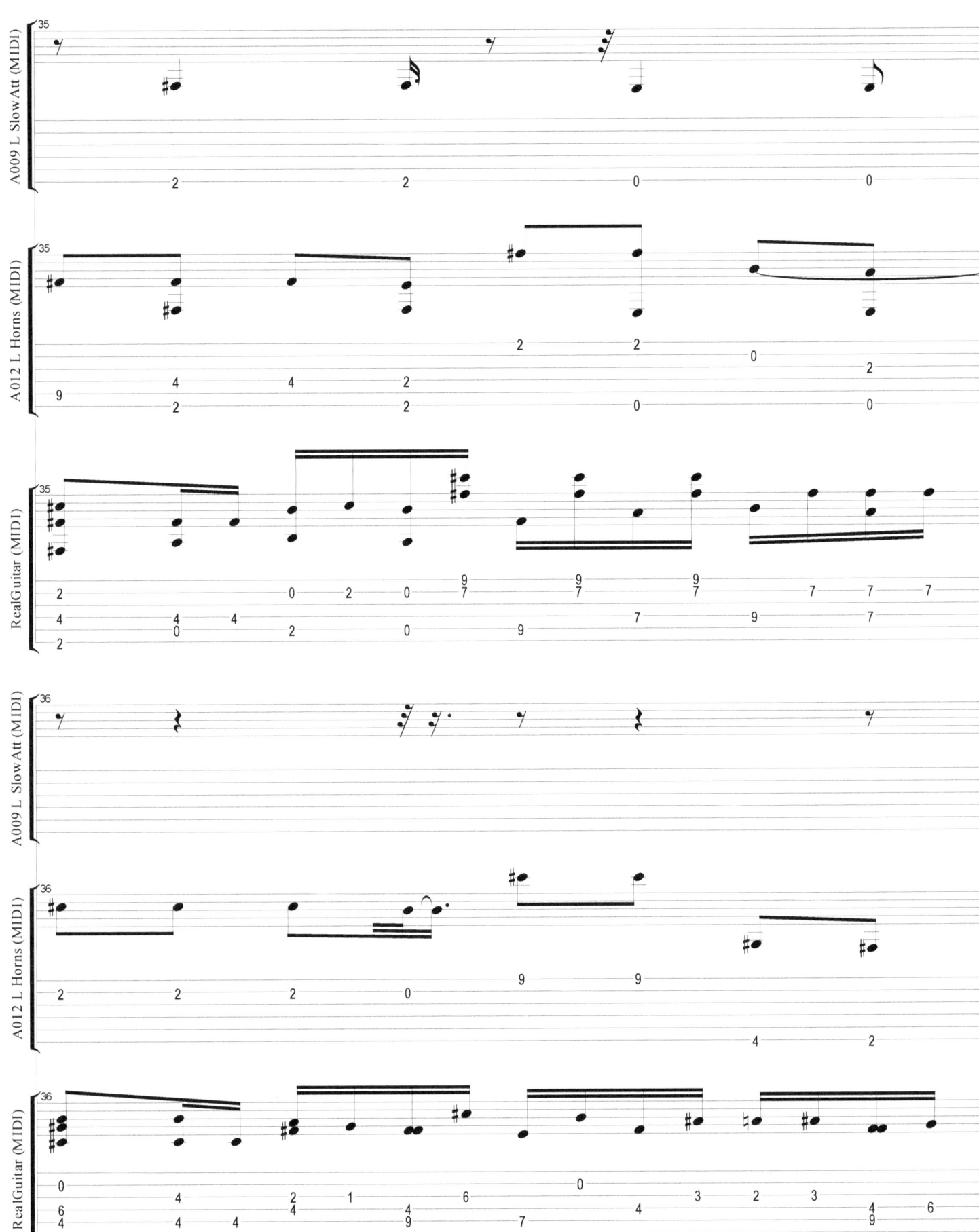

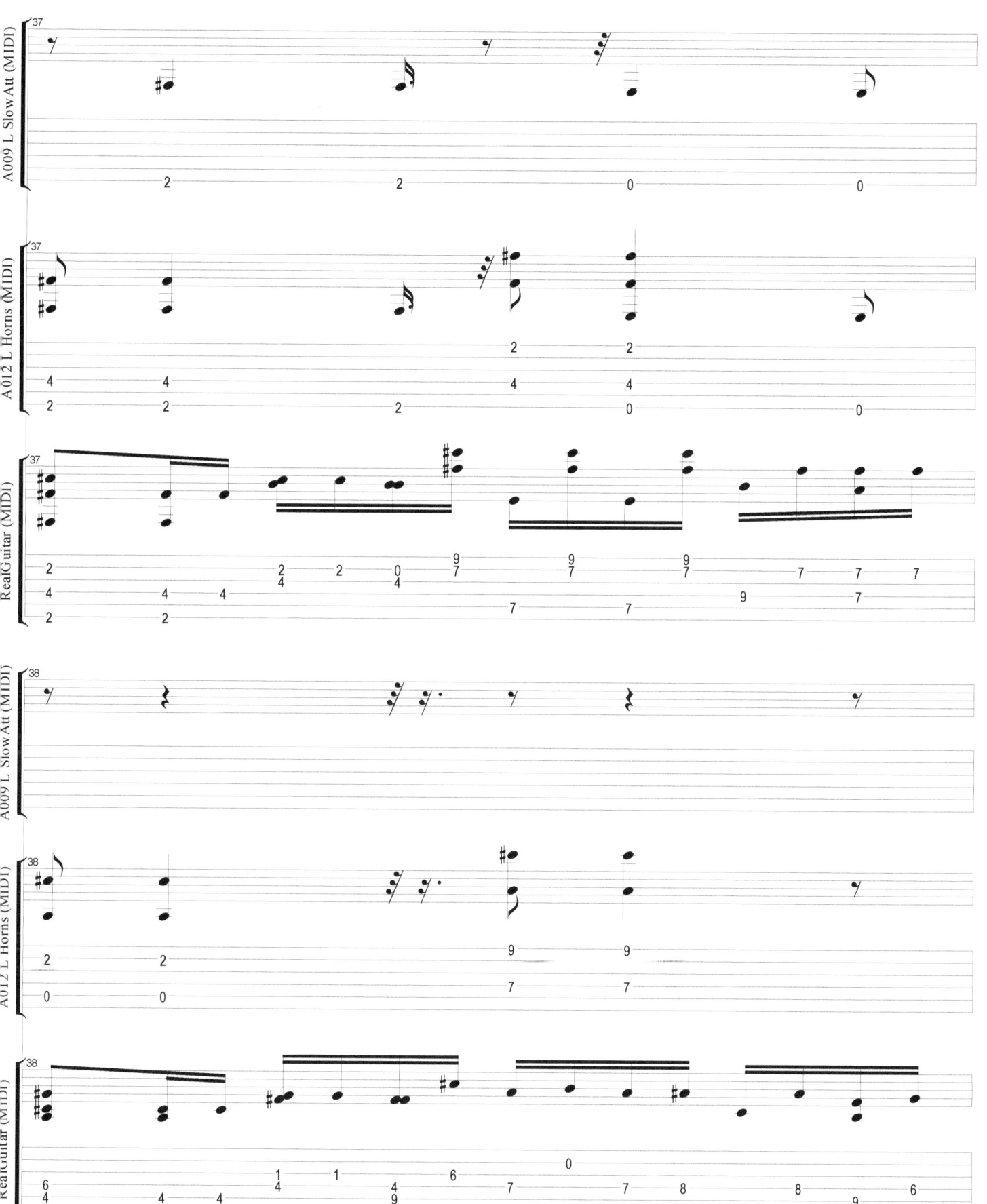

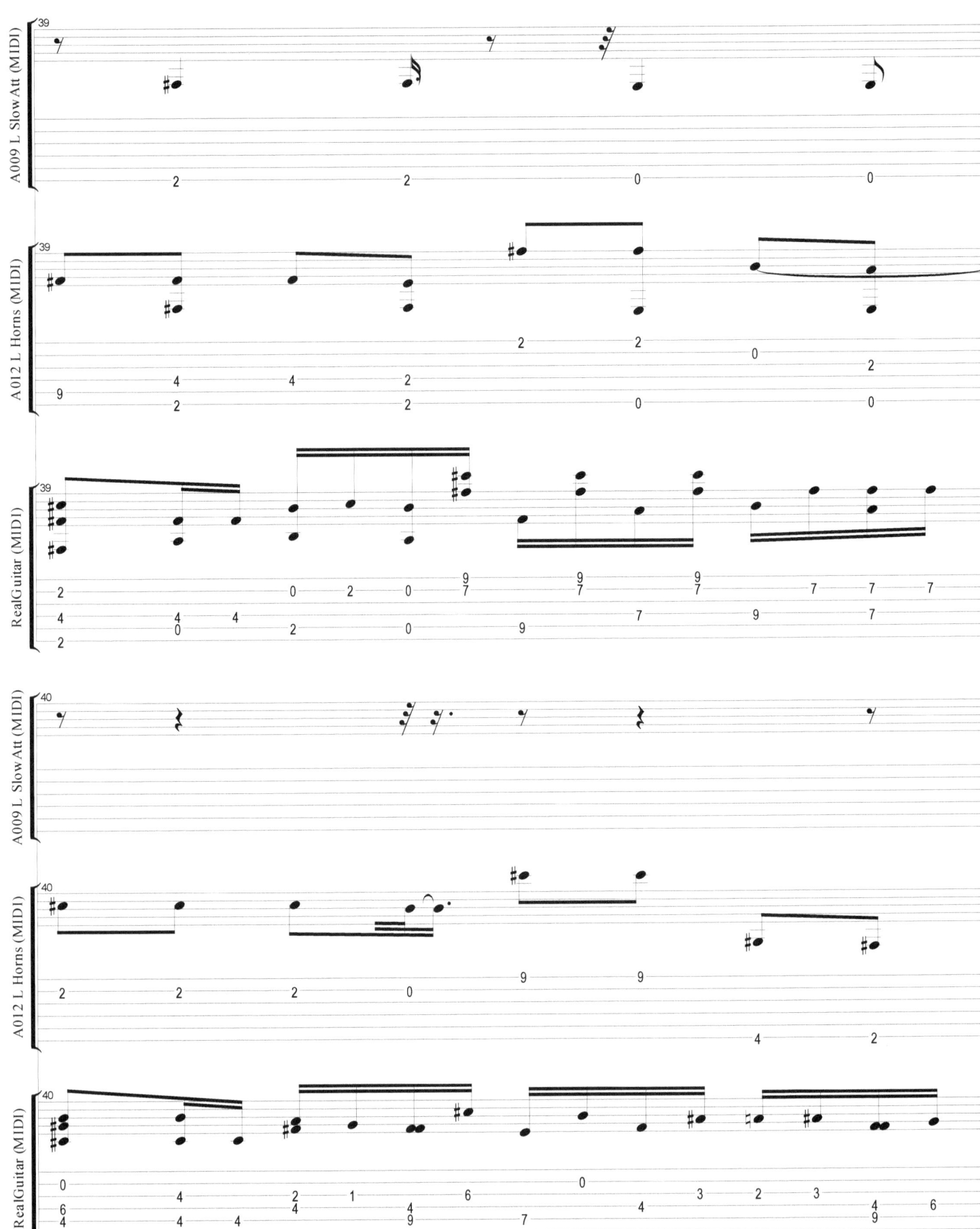

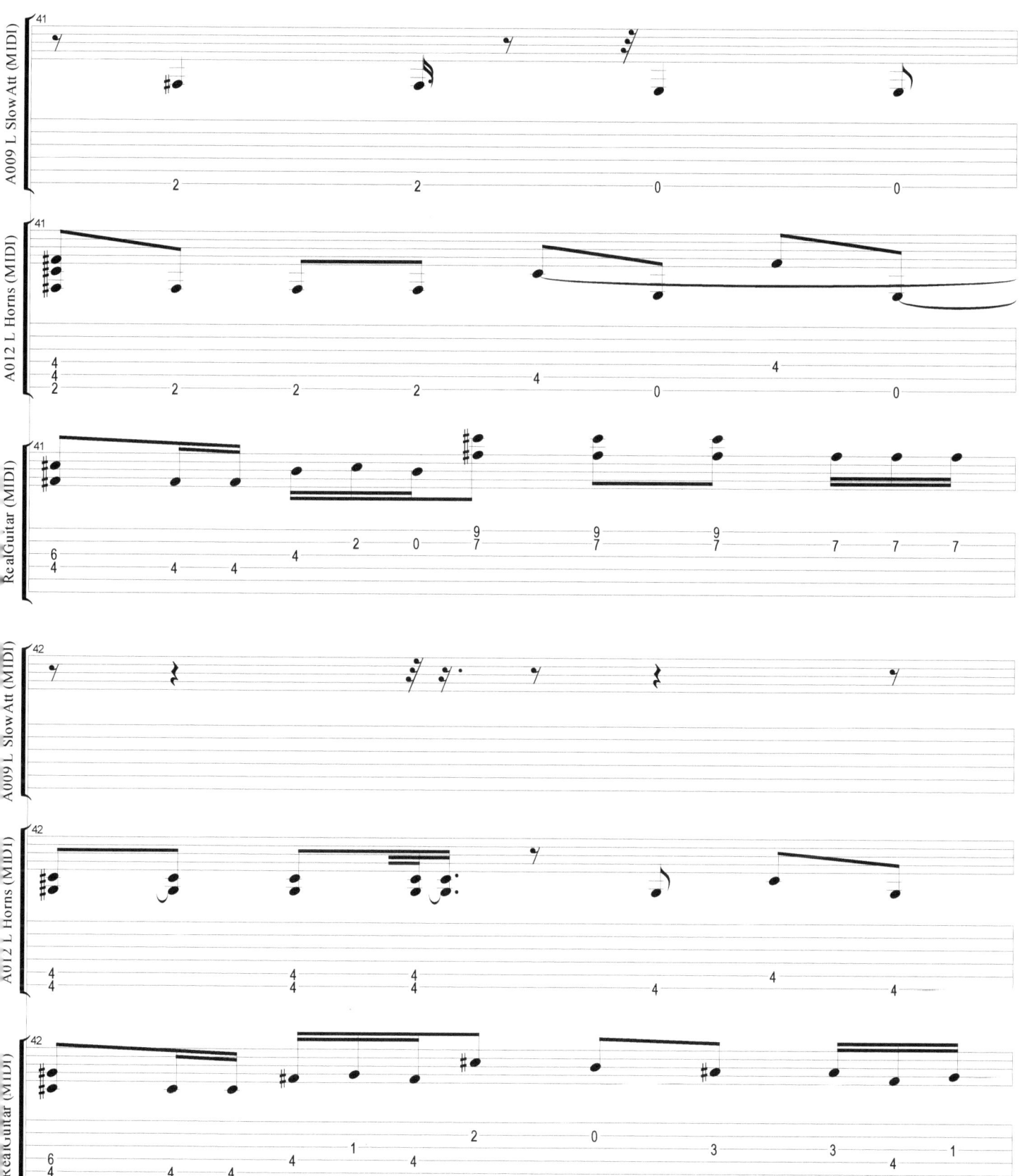

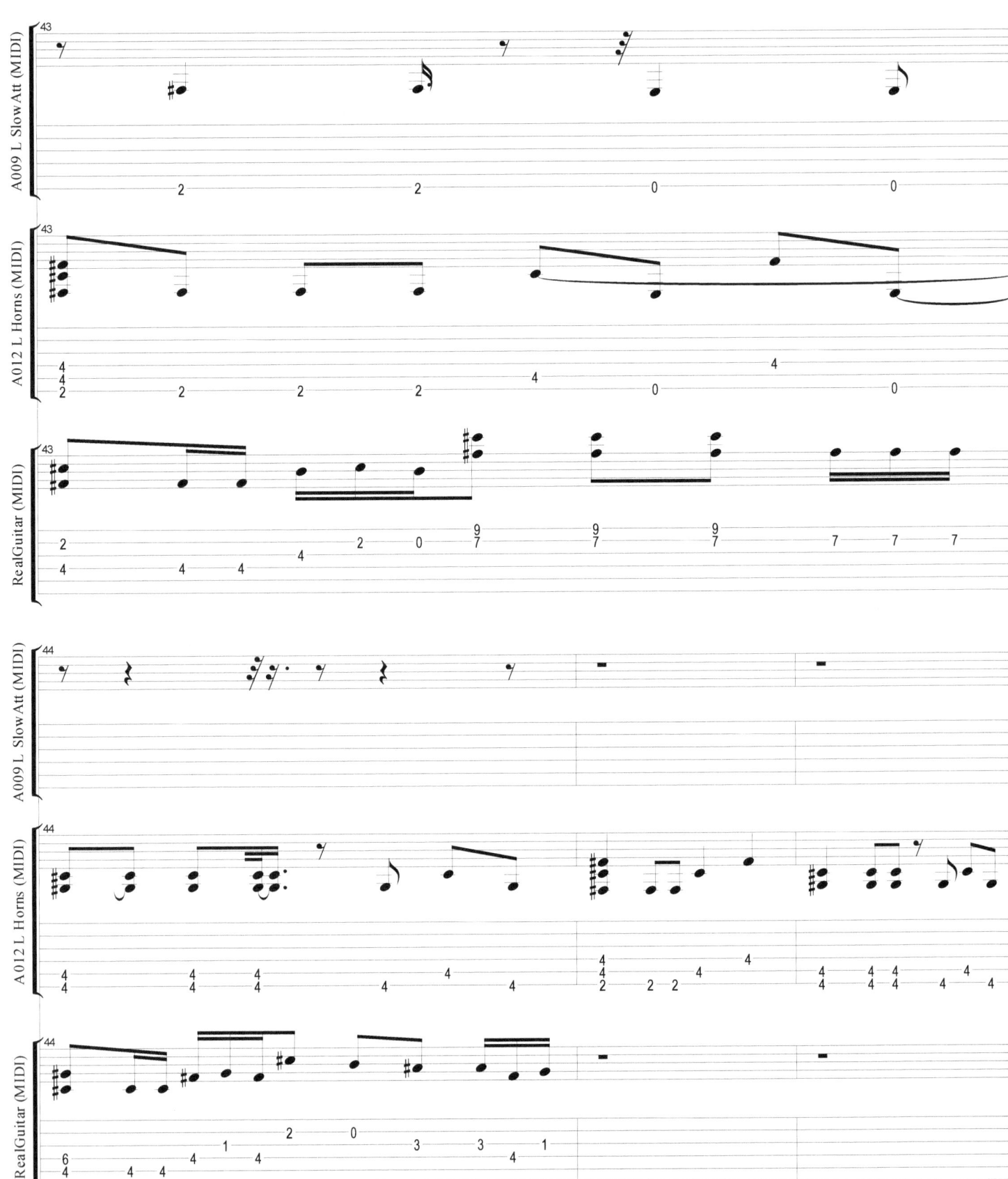

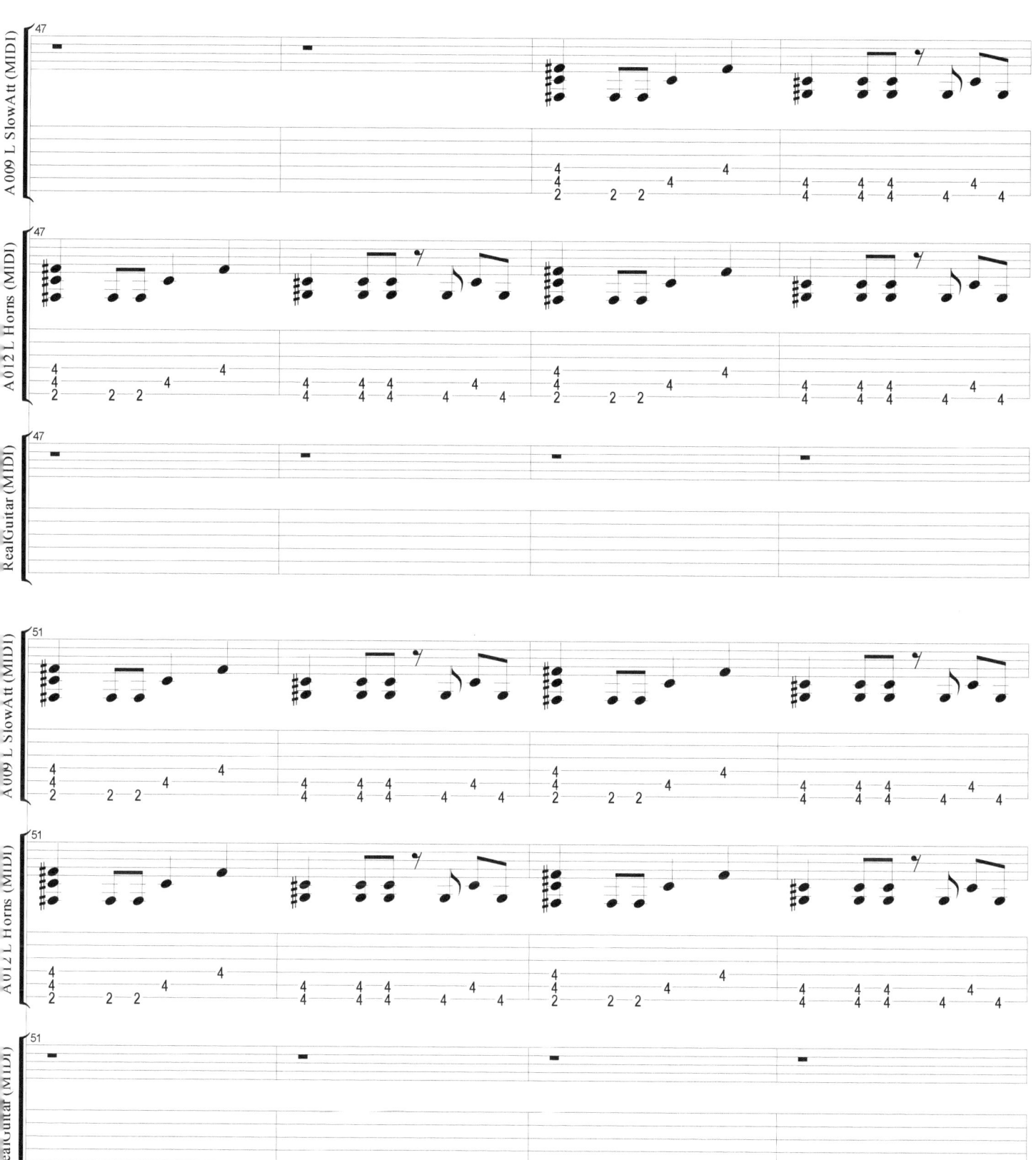

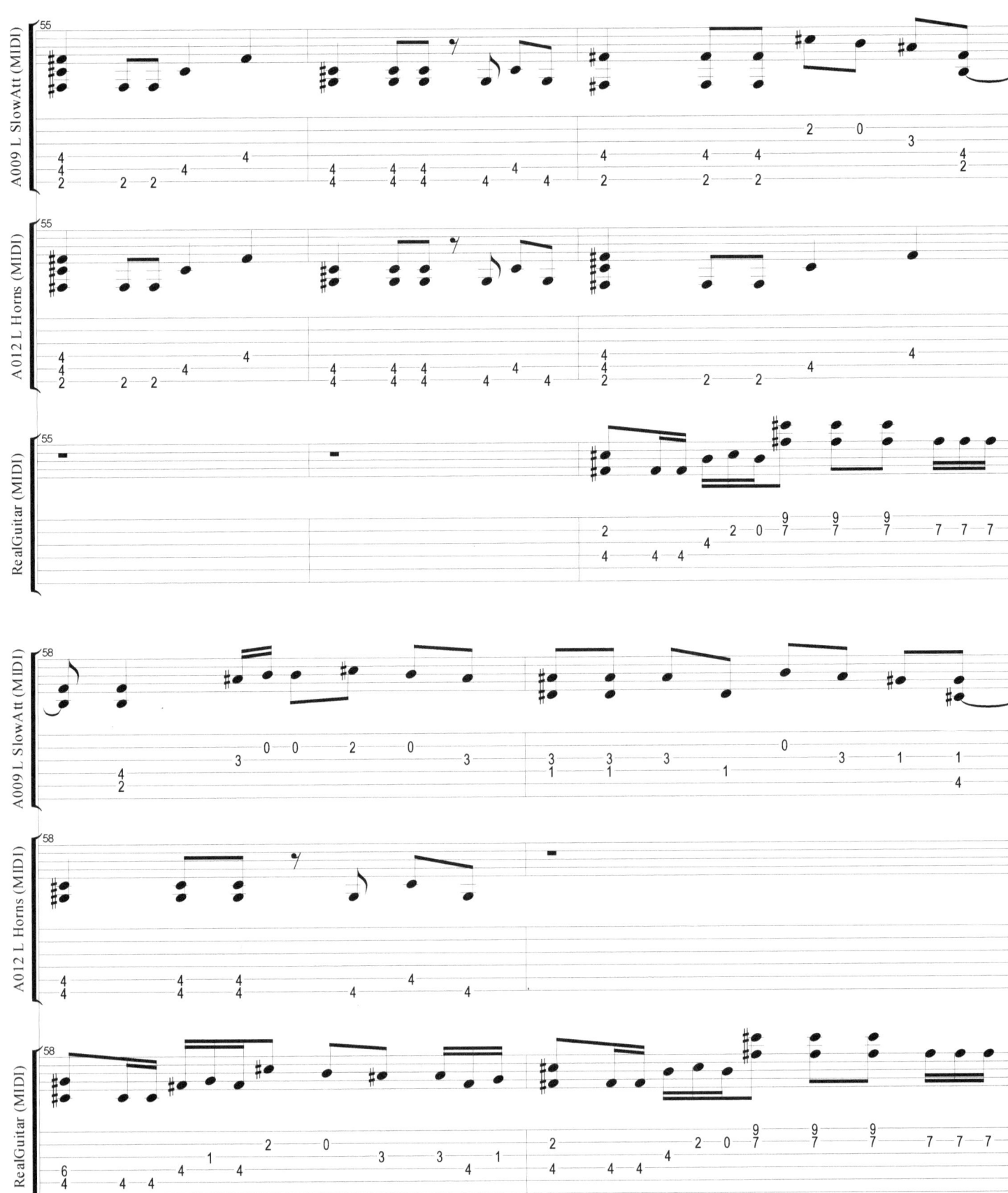

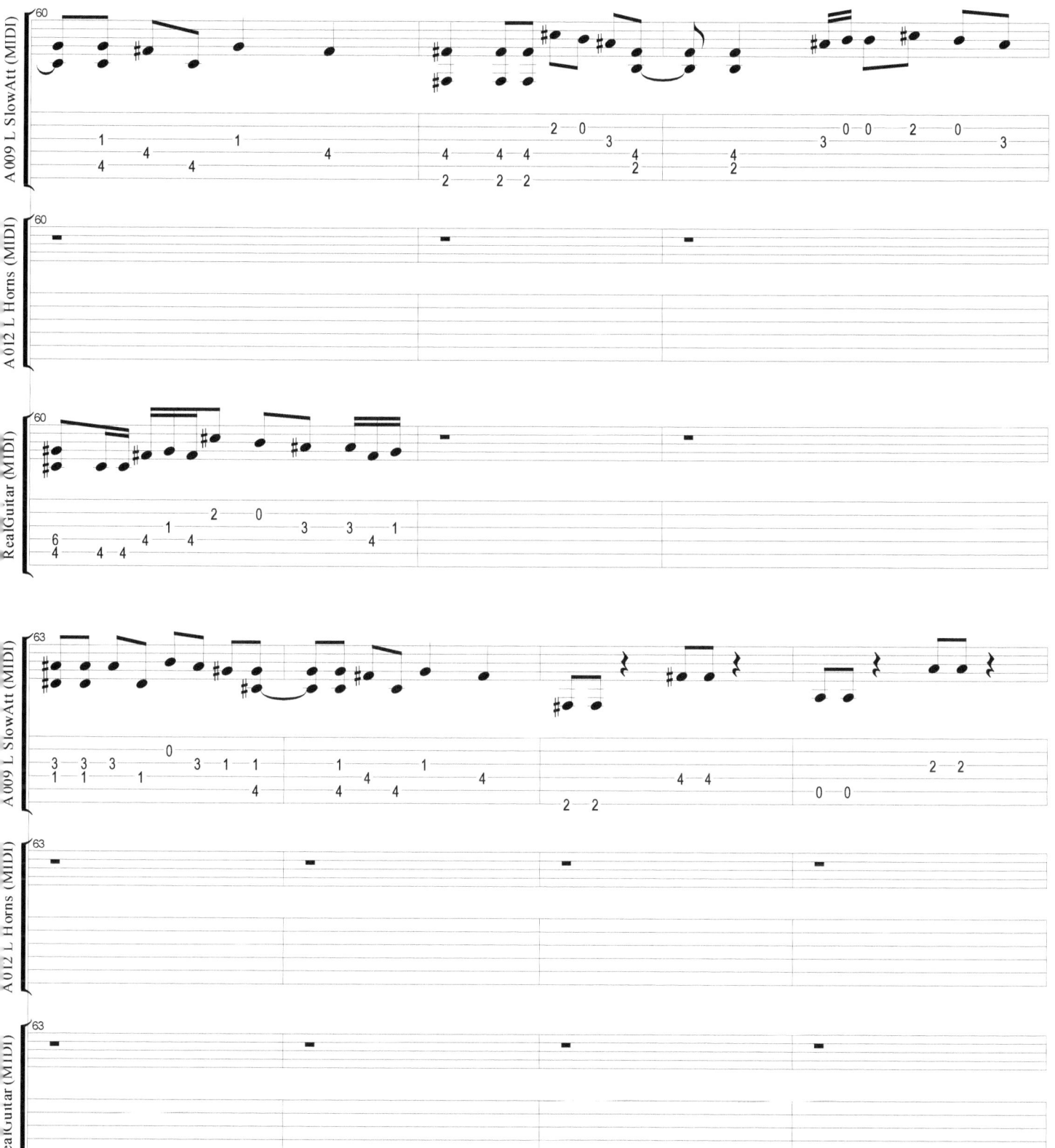

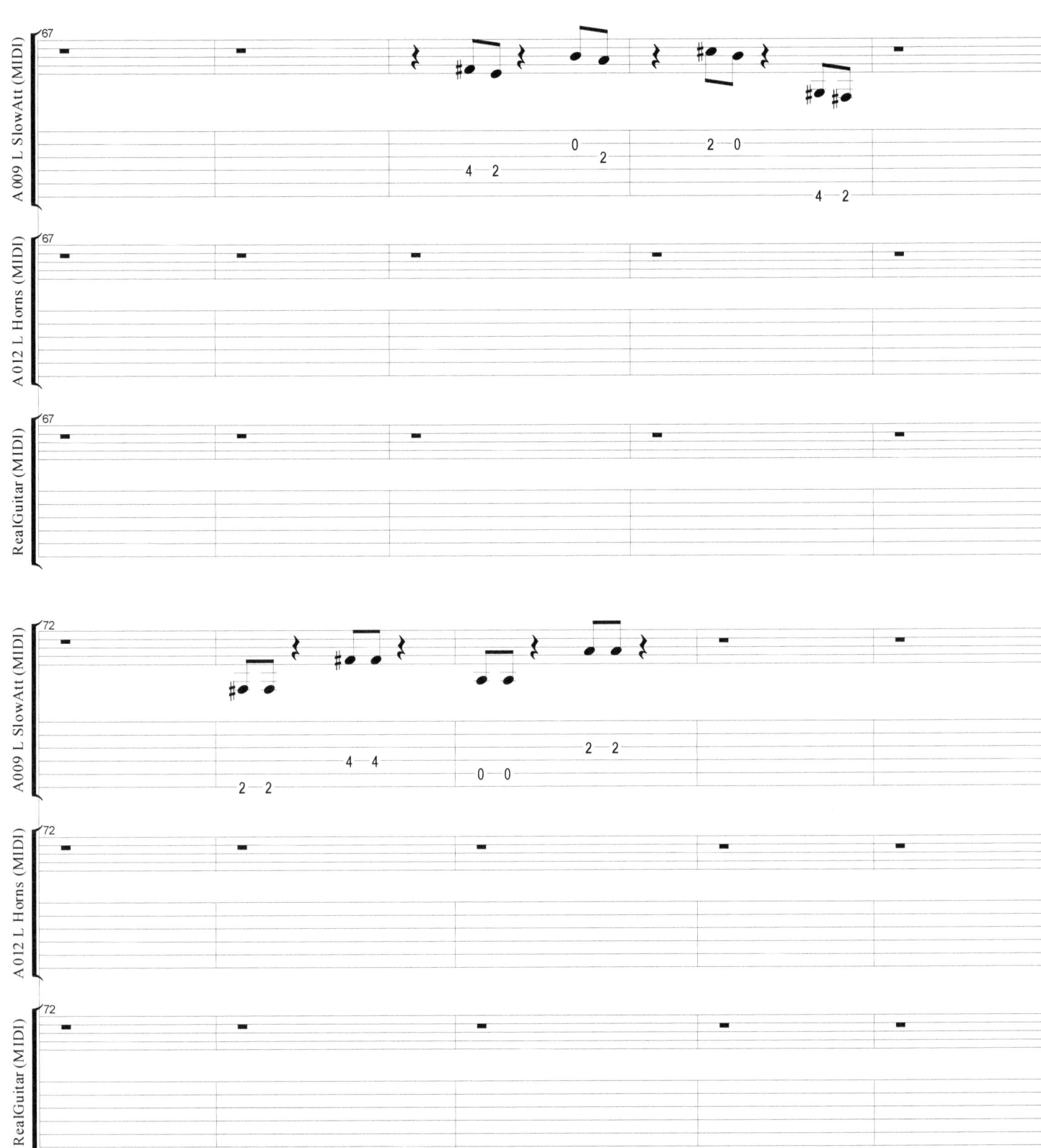

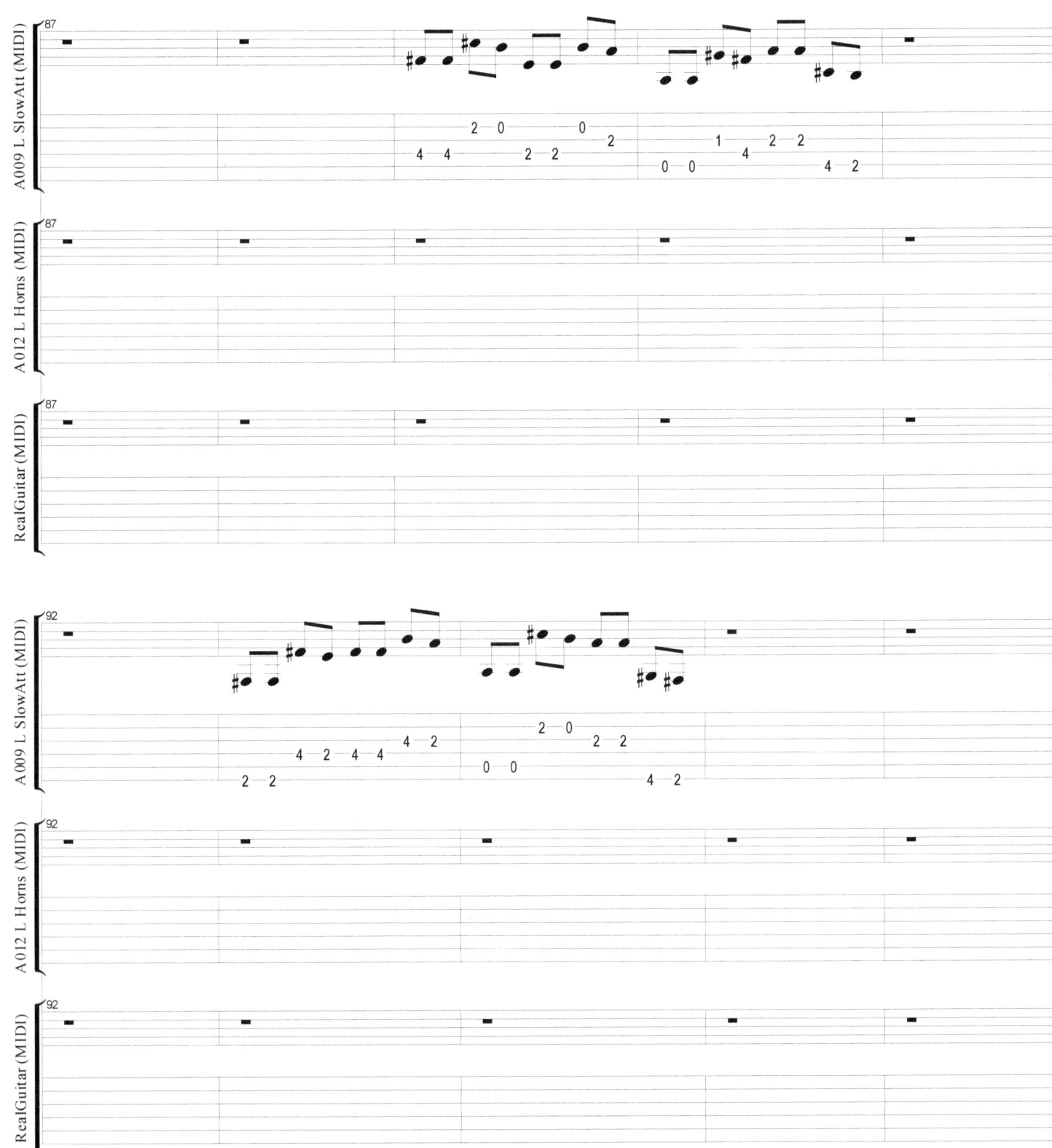

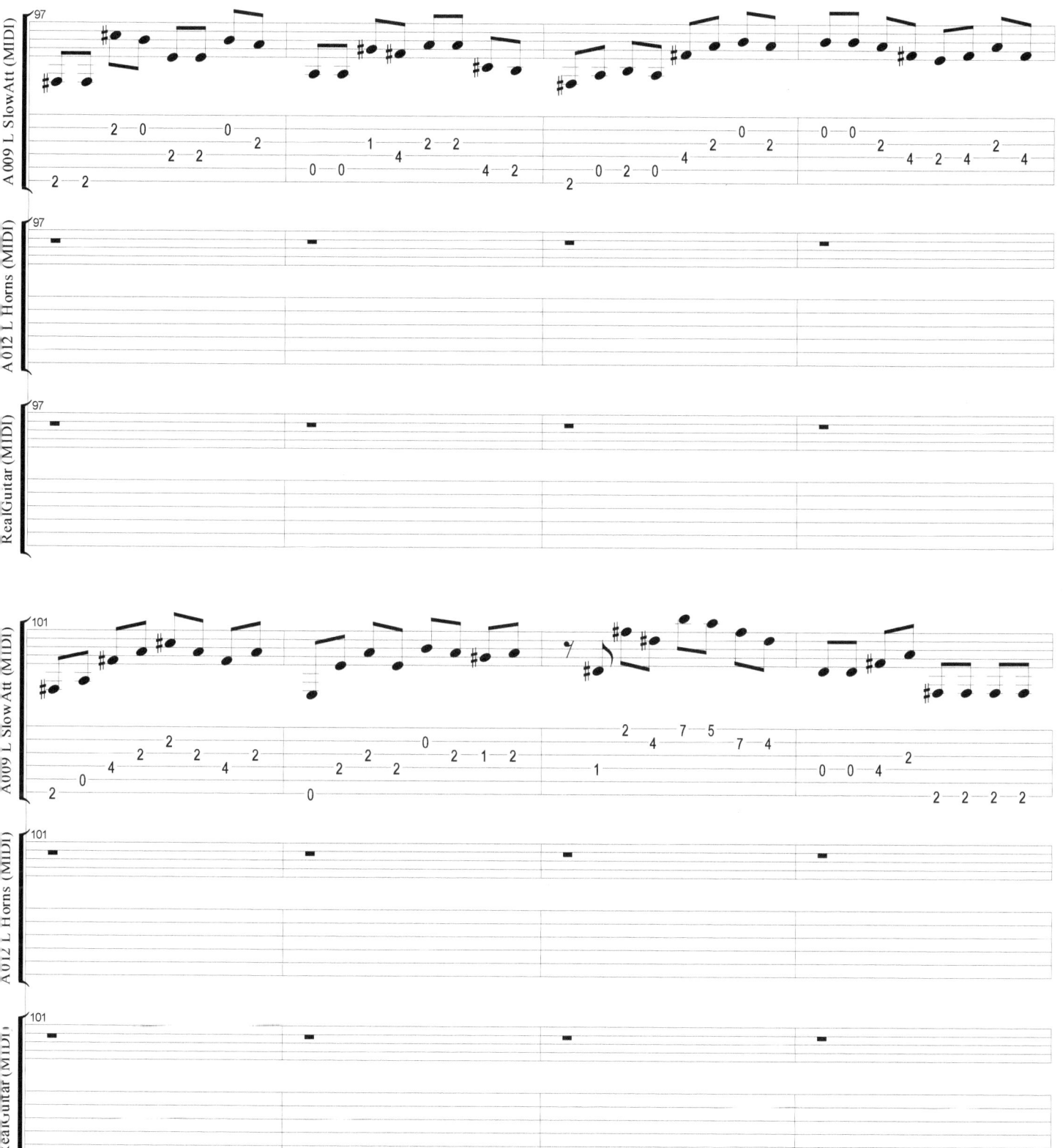

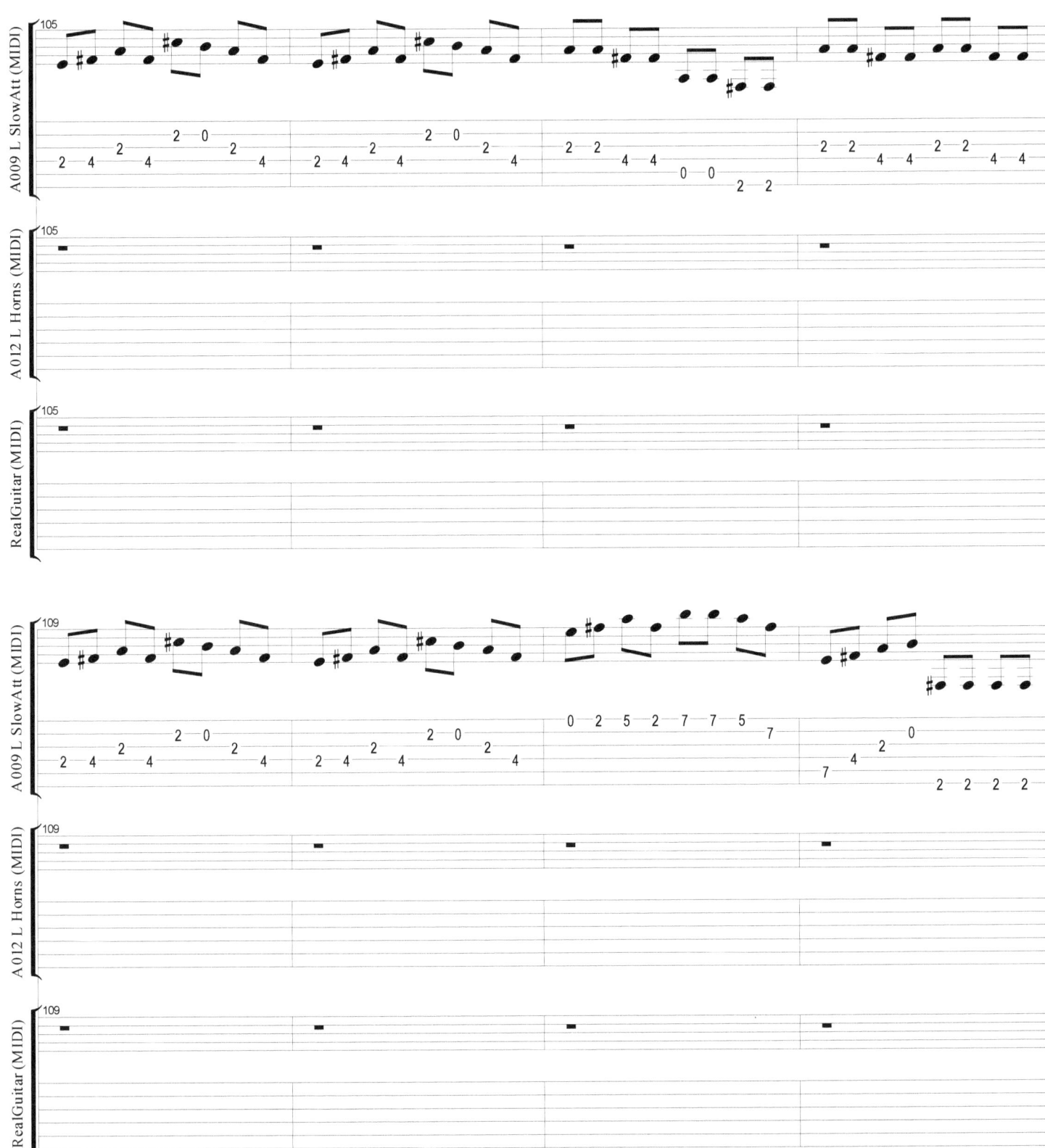

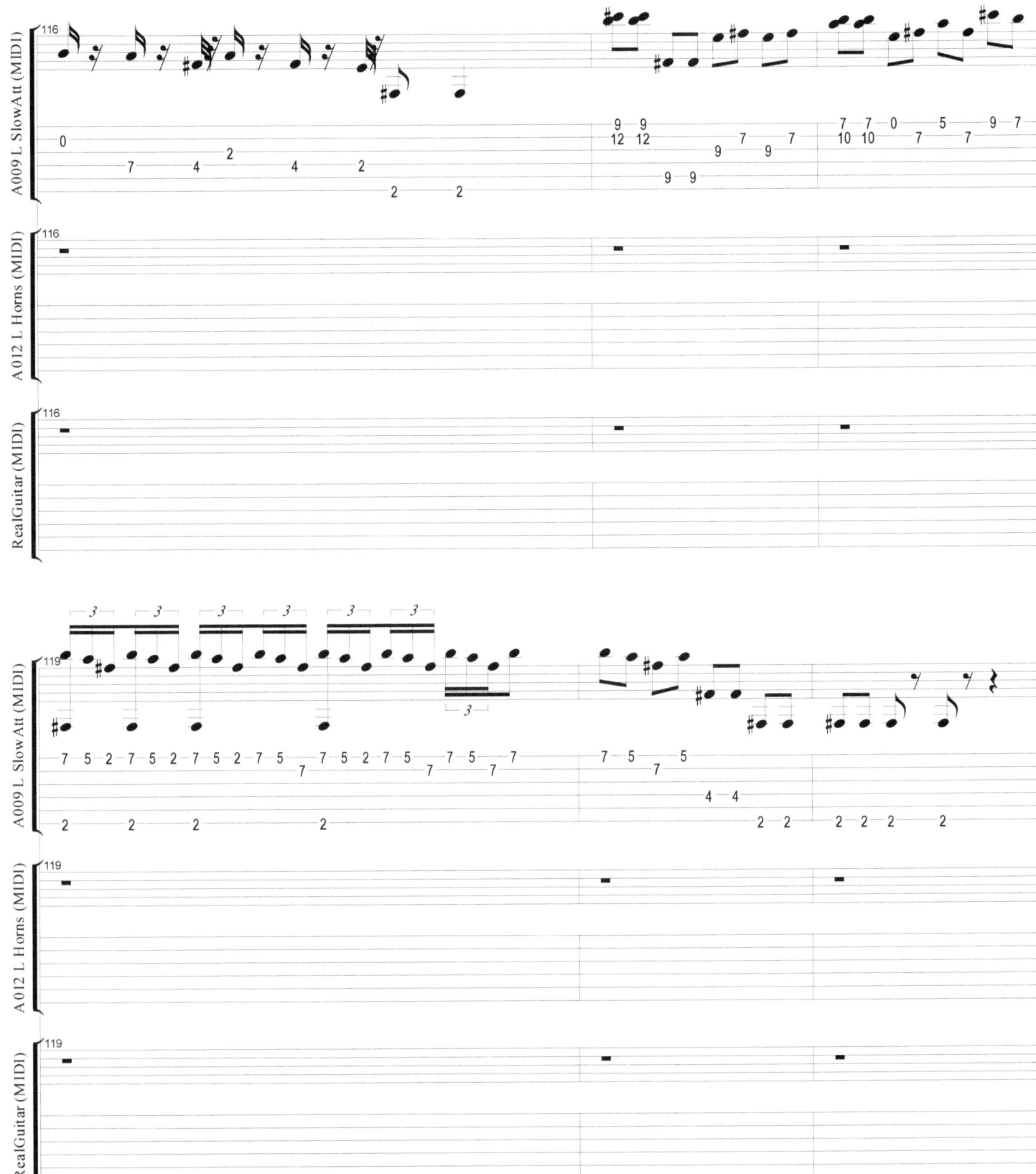

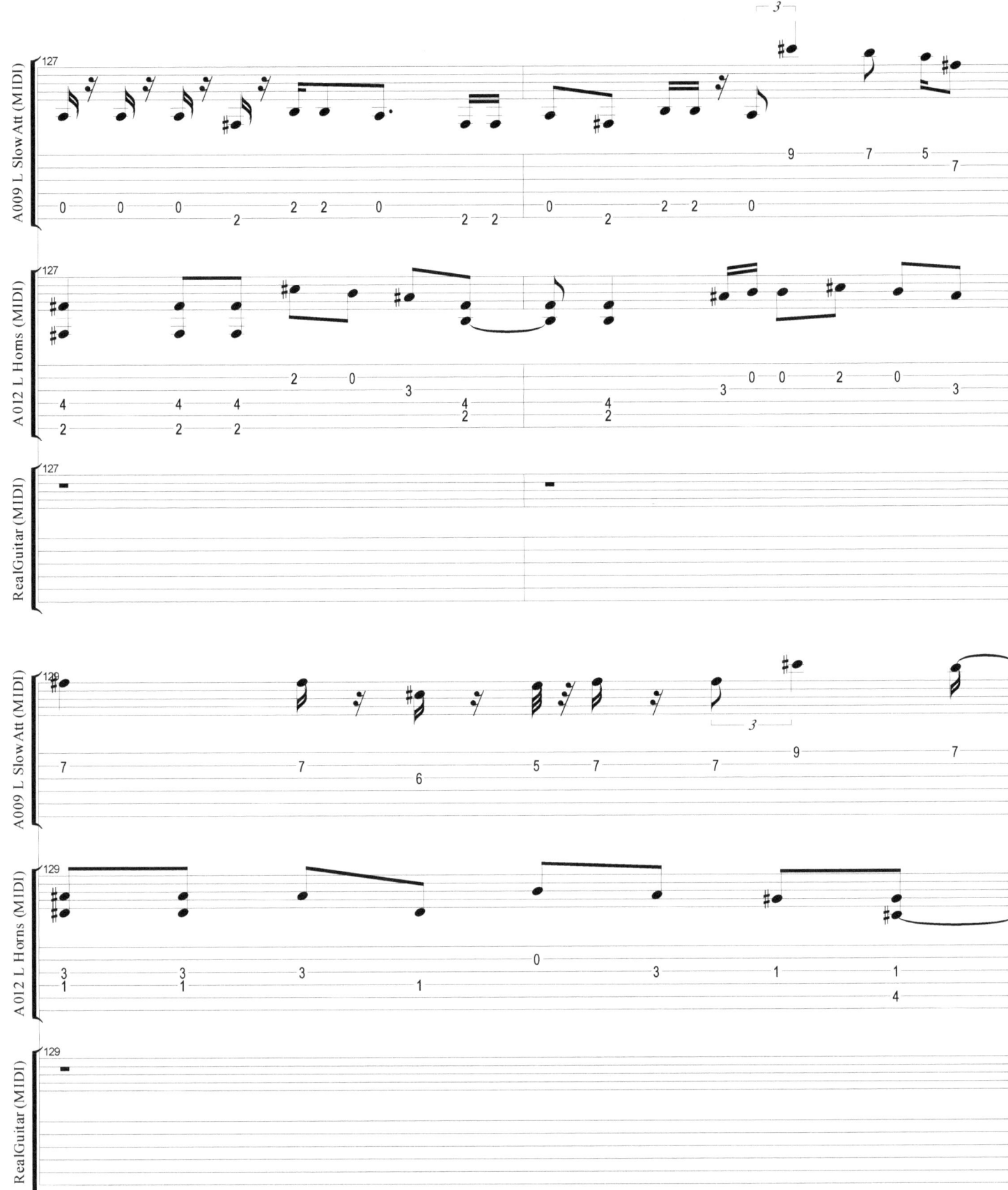

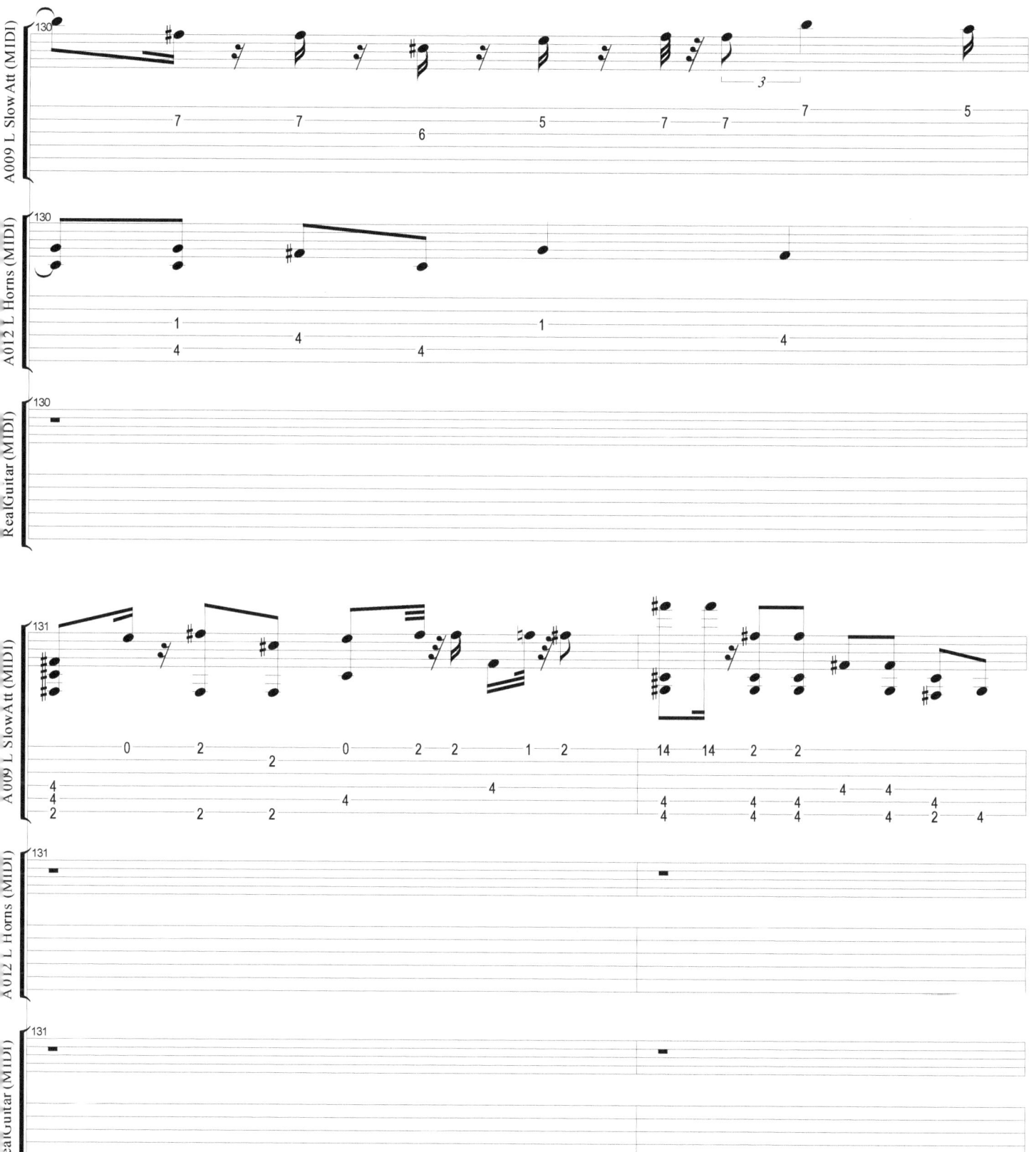

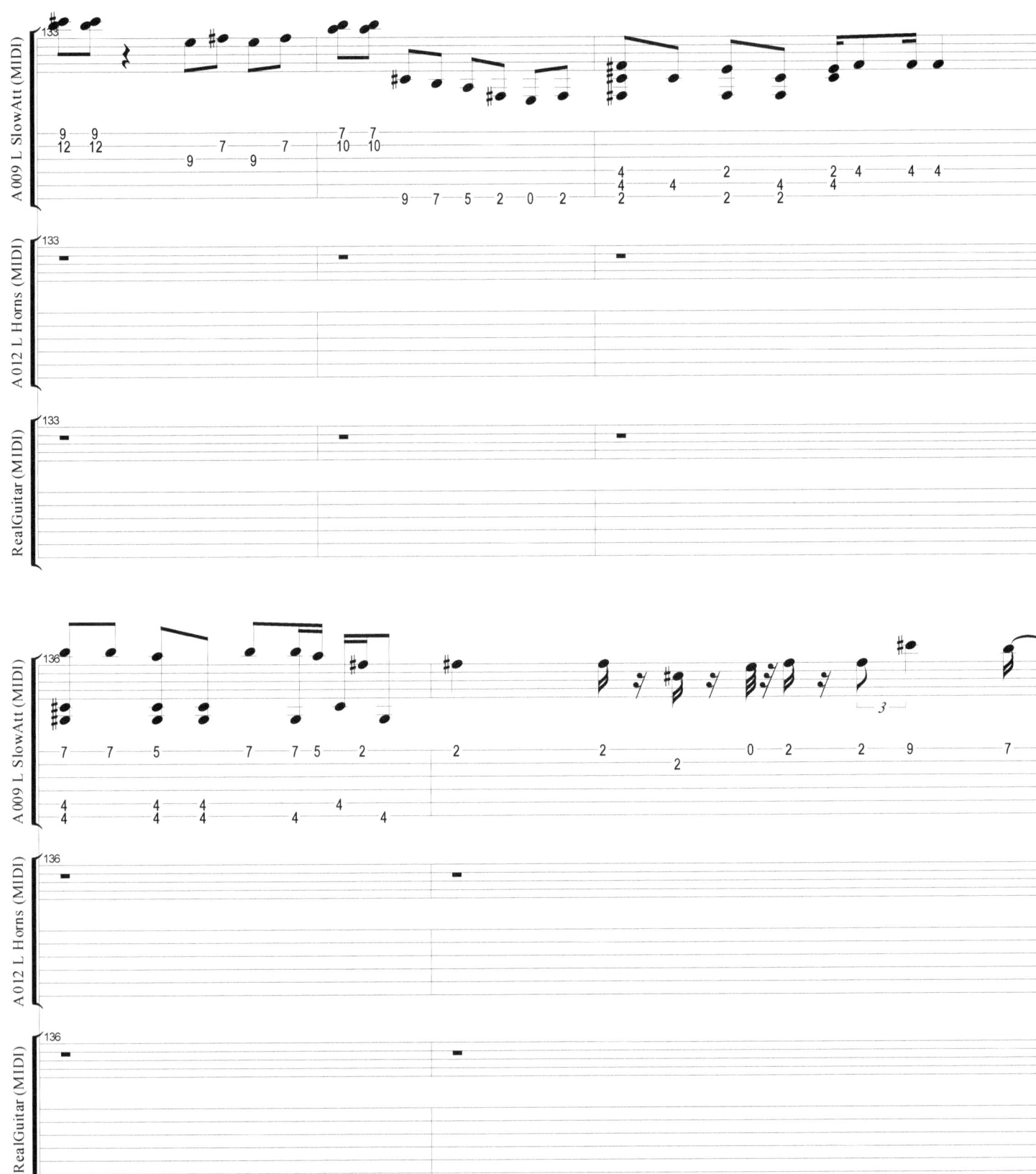

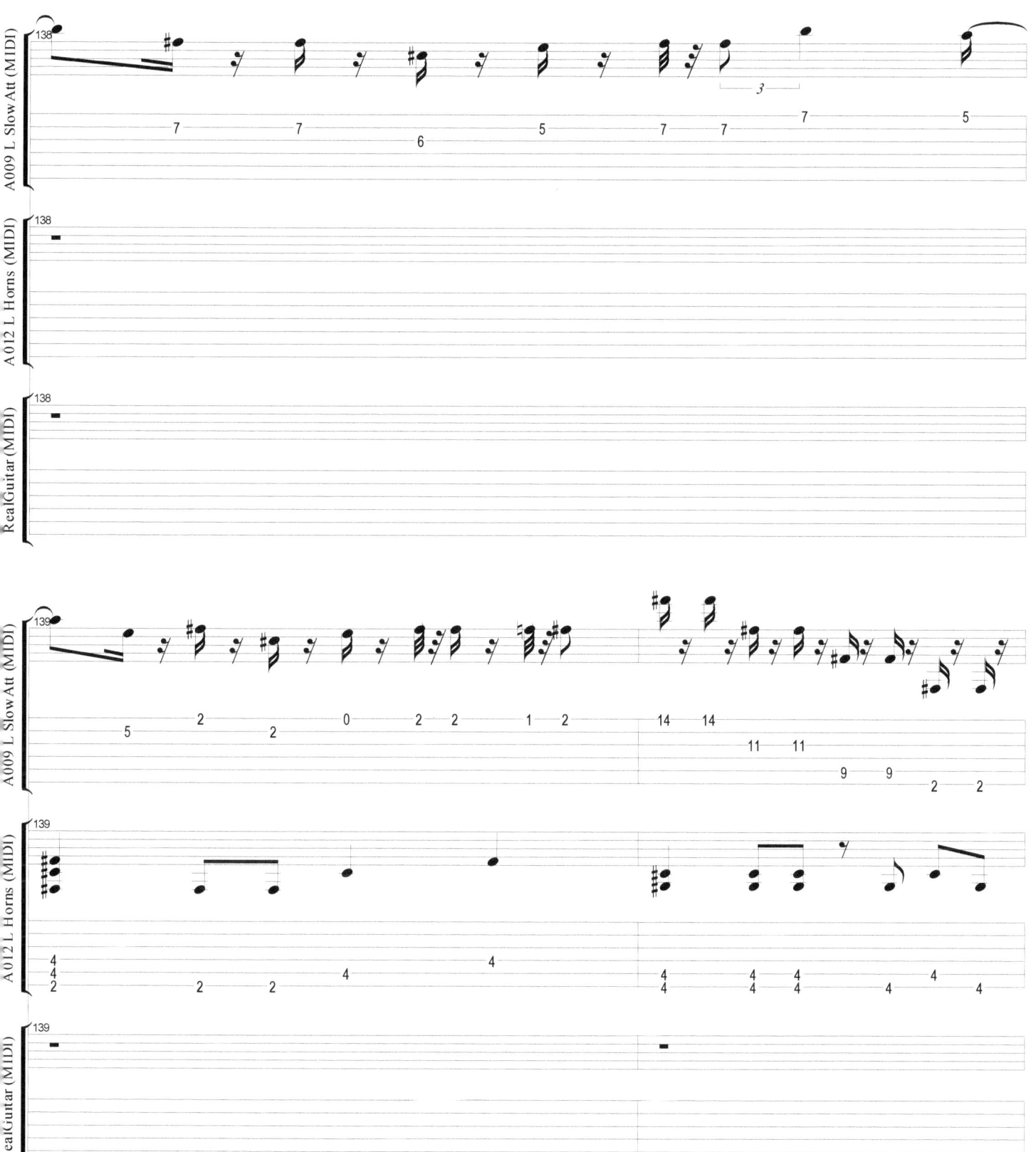

Forget Her

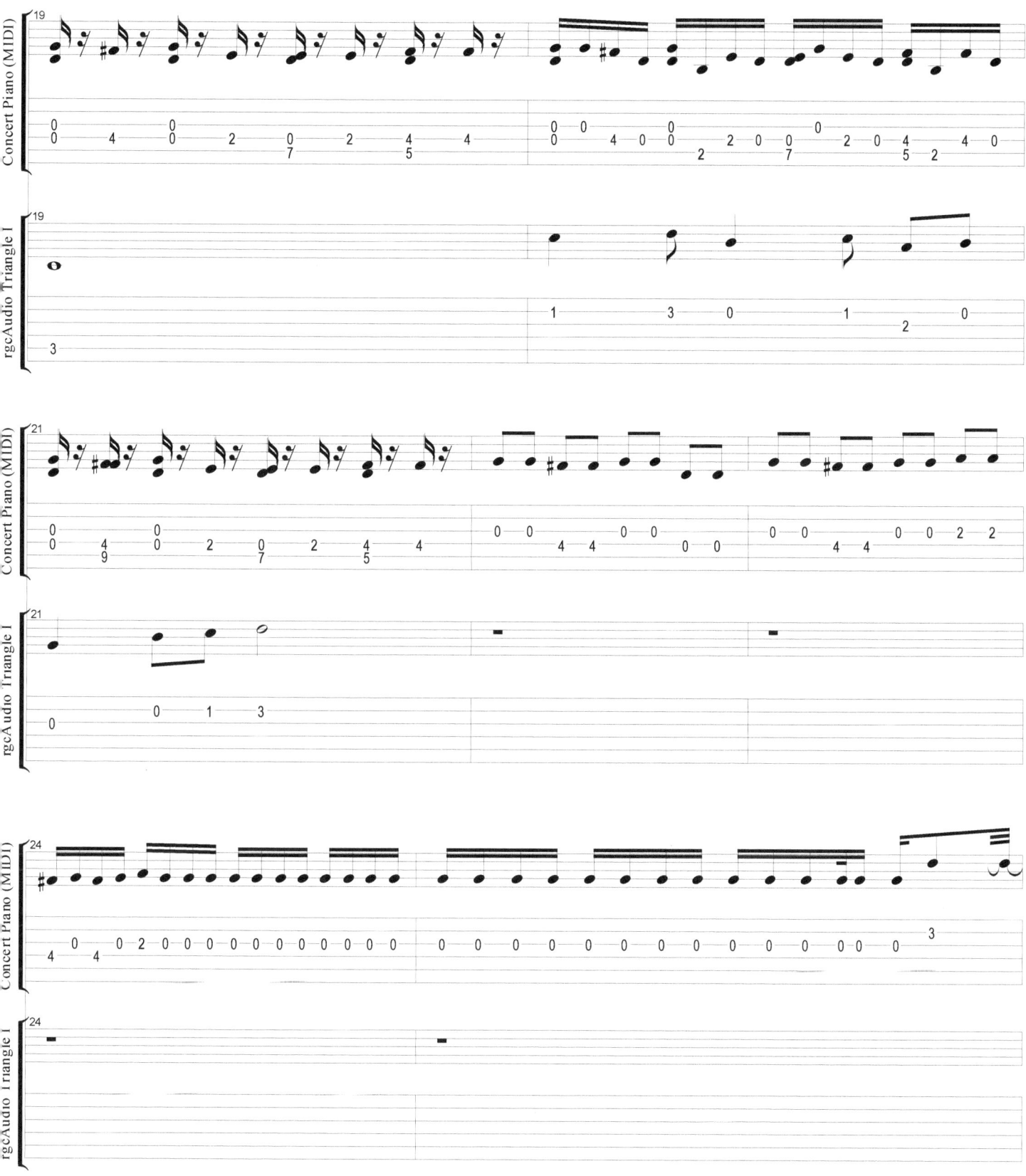

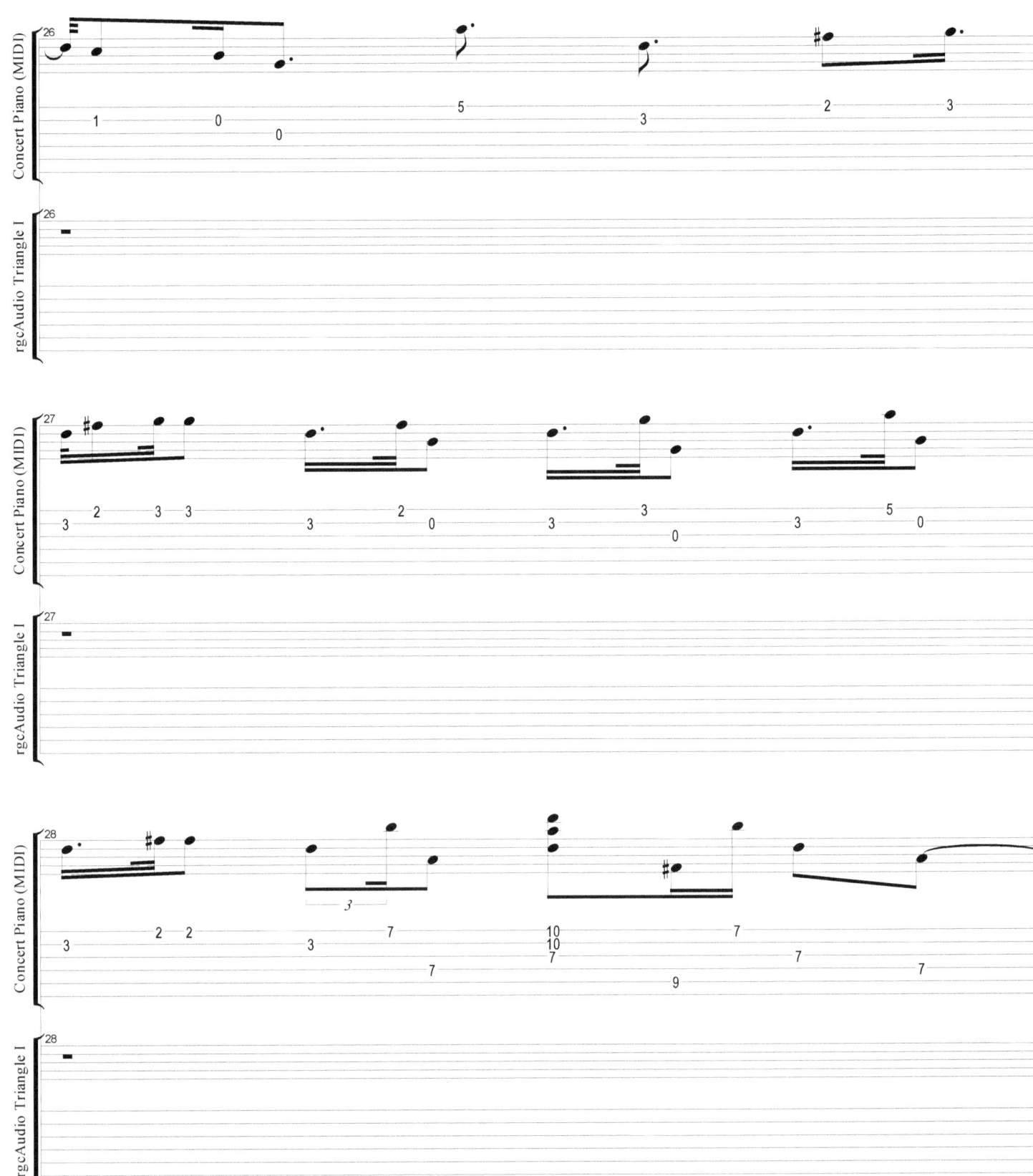

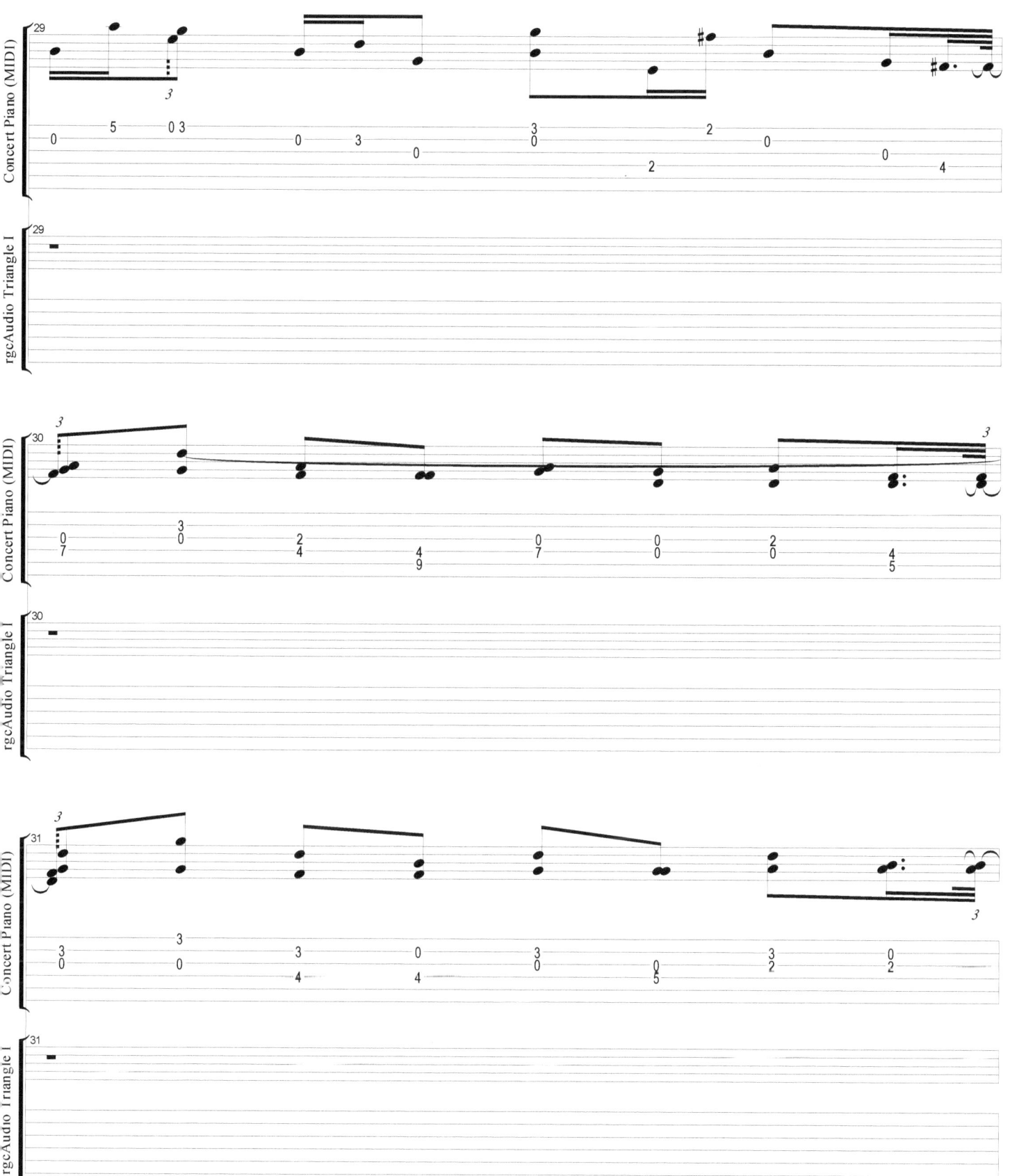

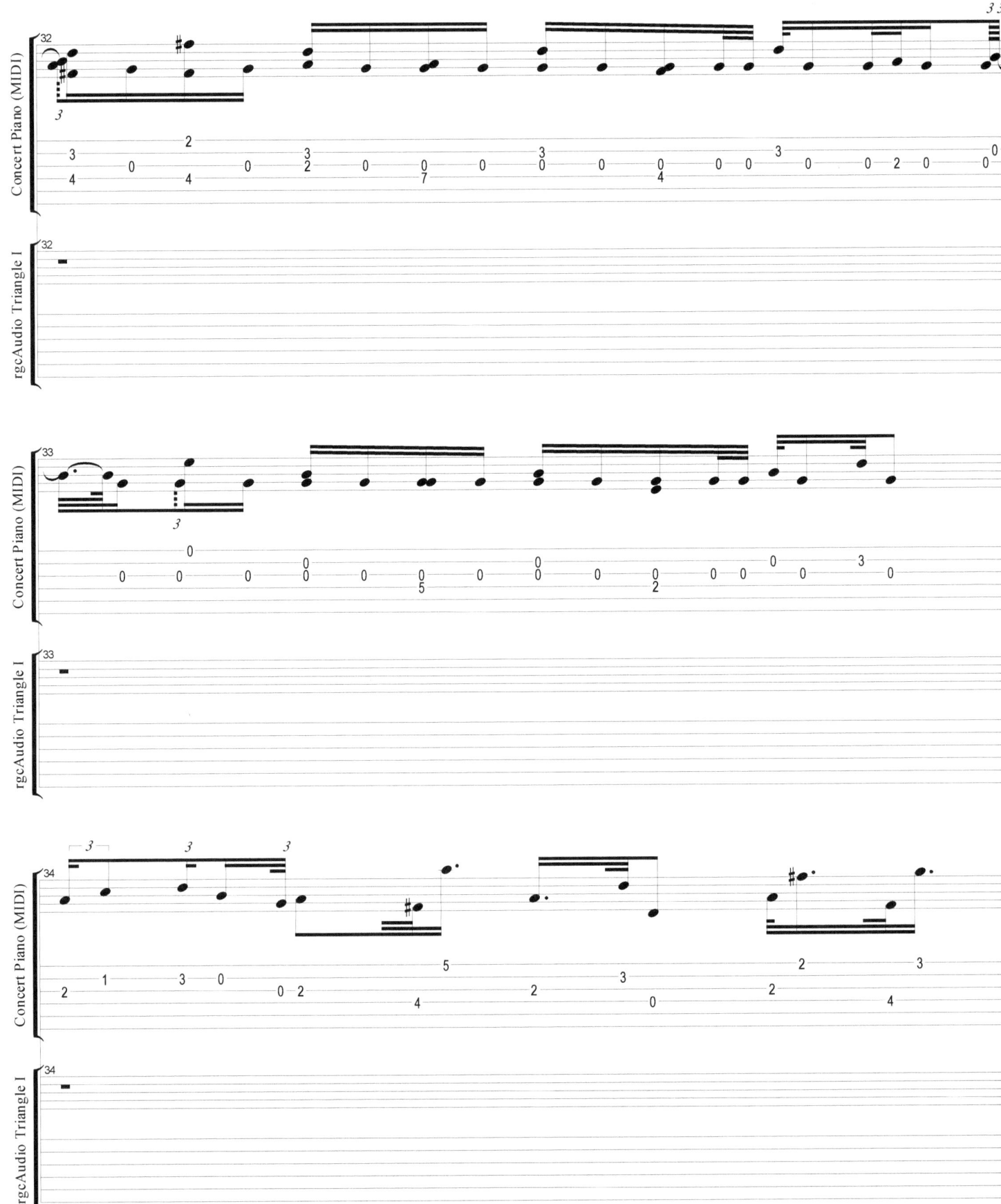

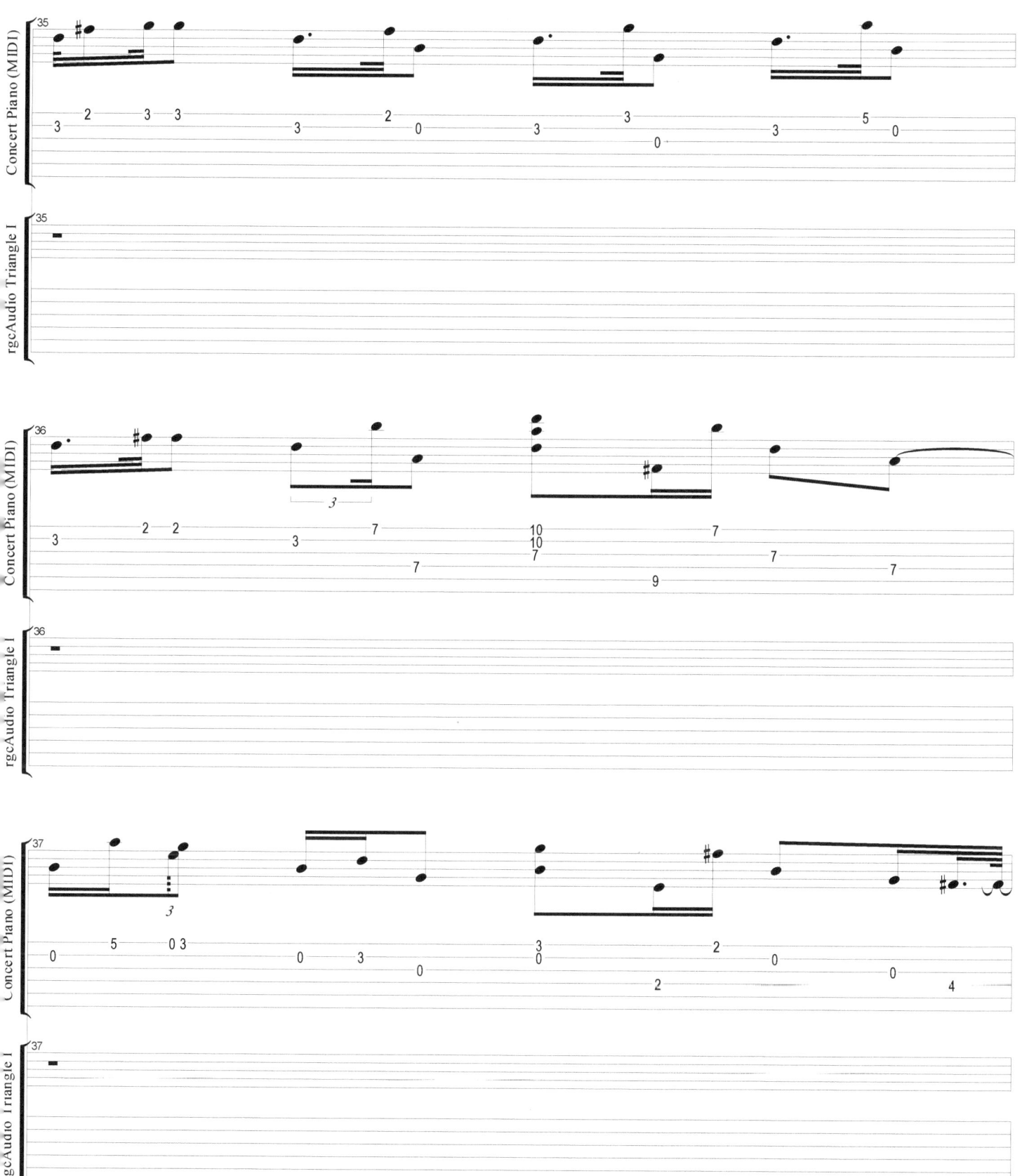

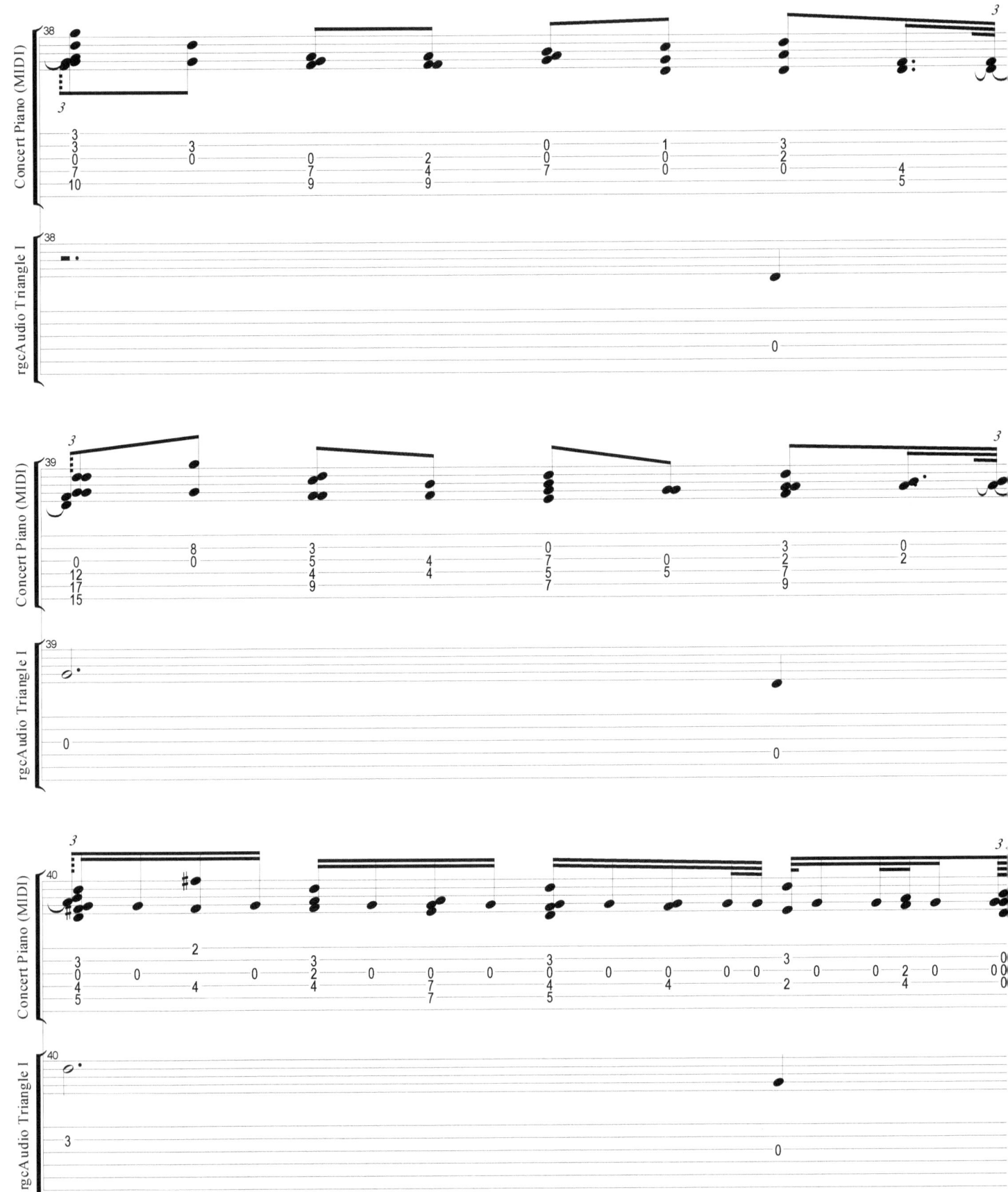

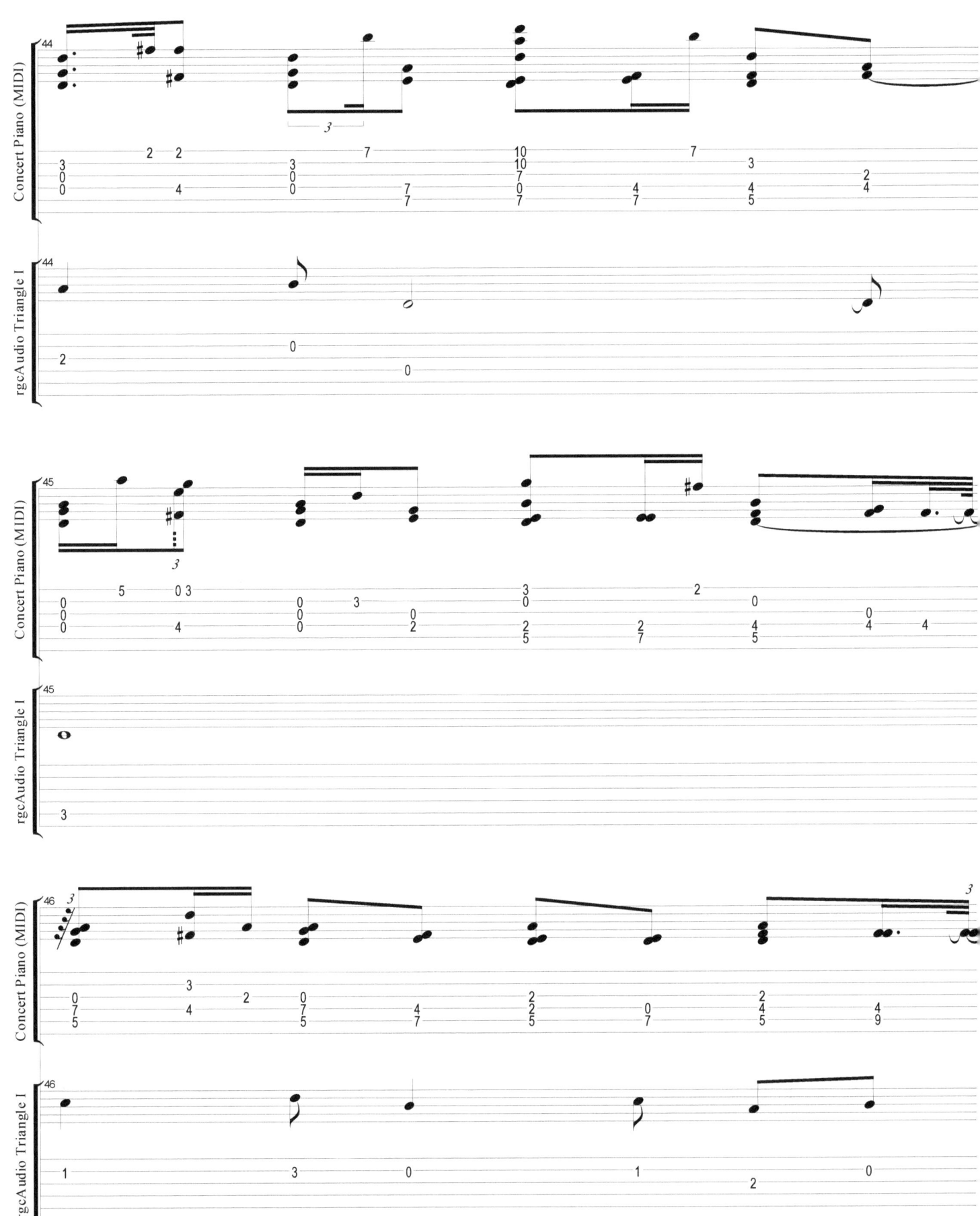

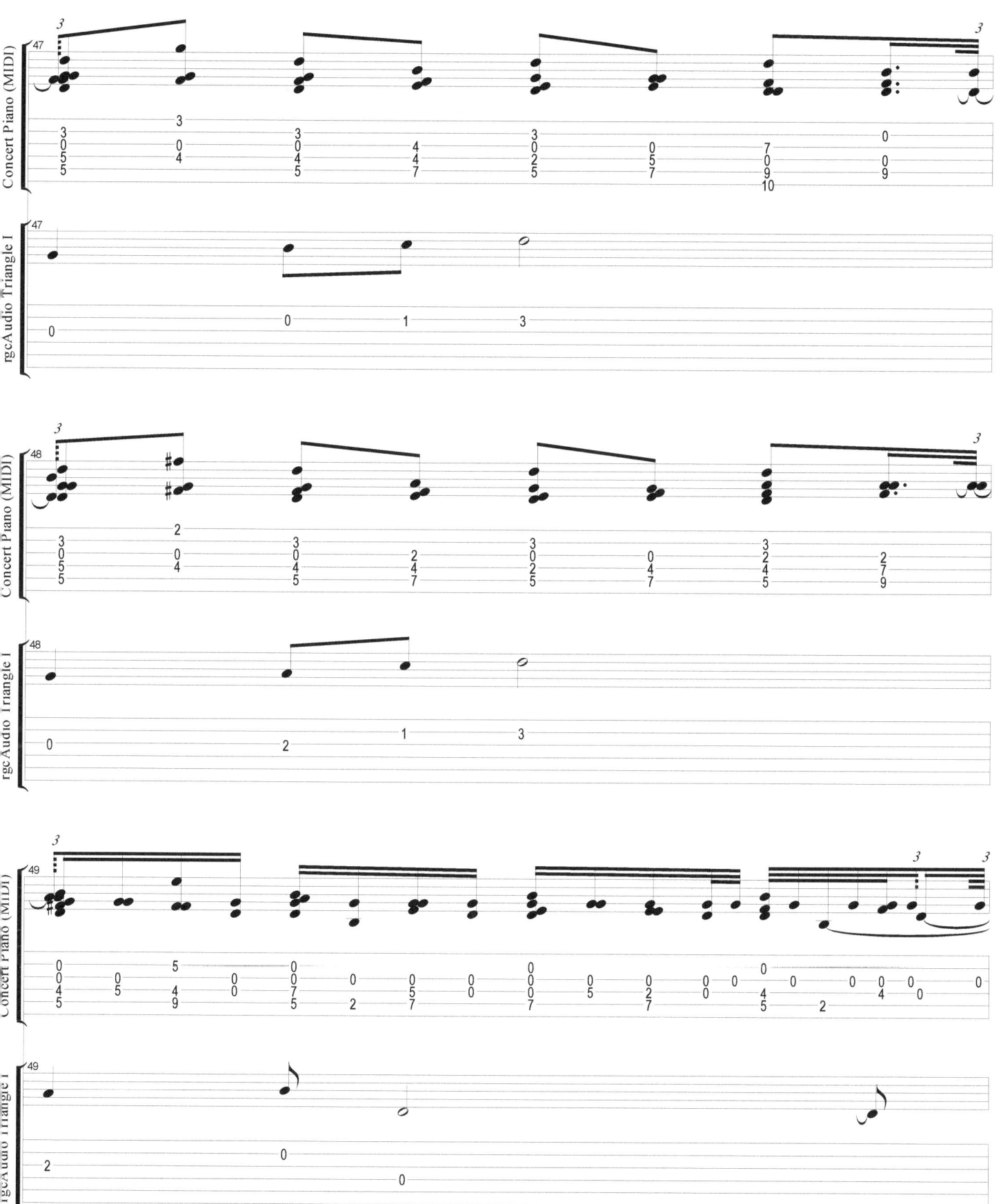

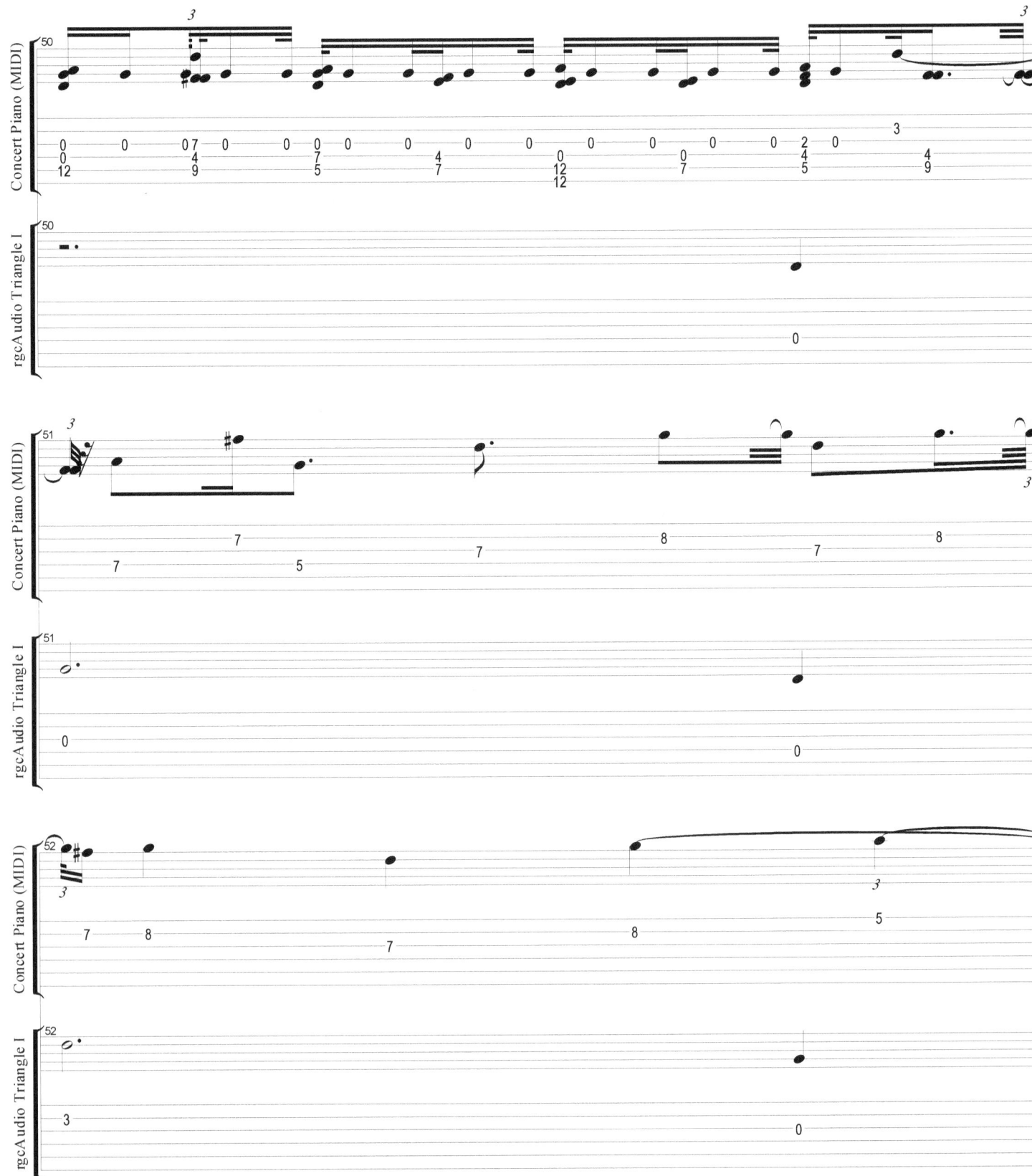

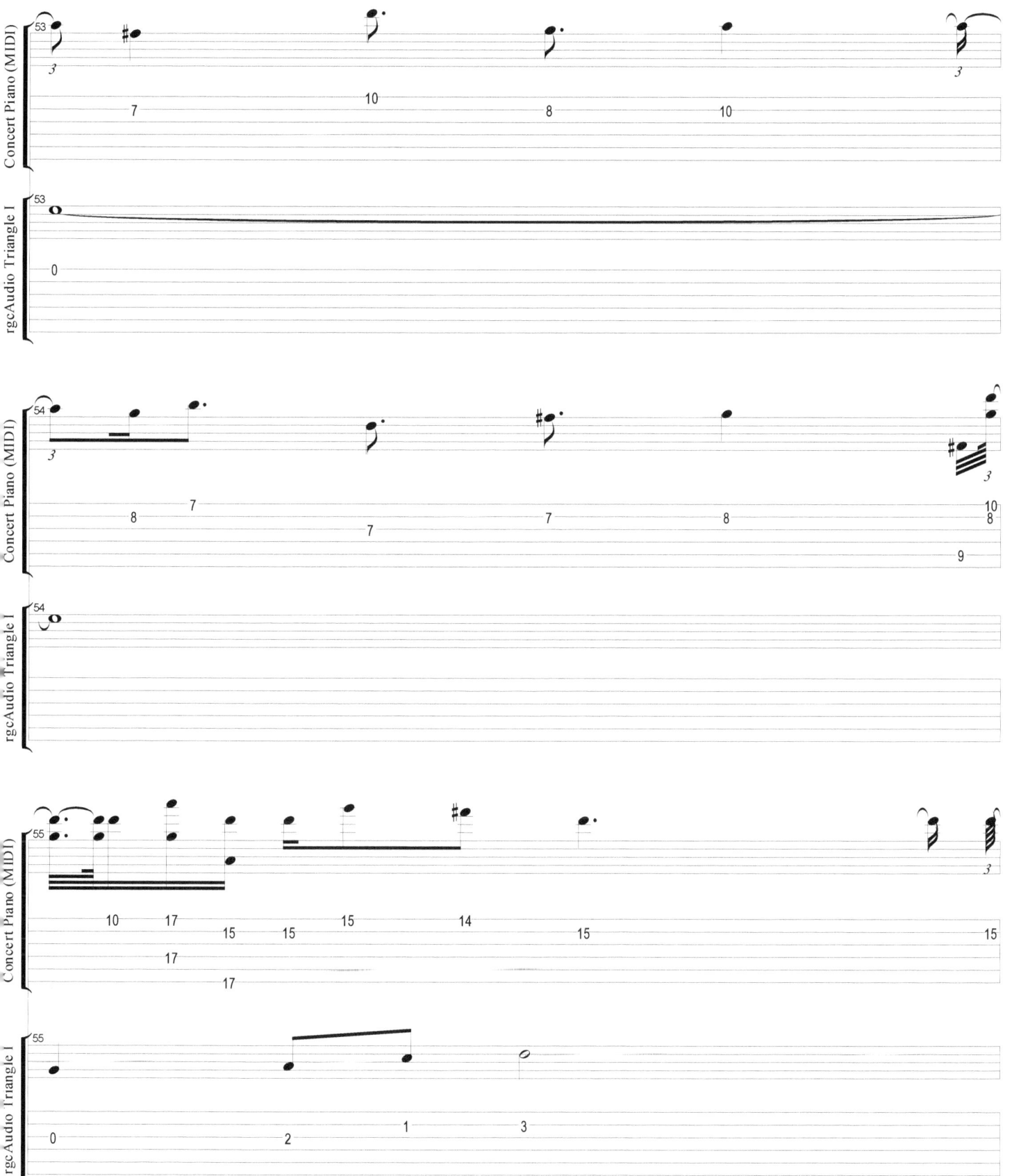

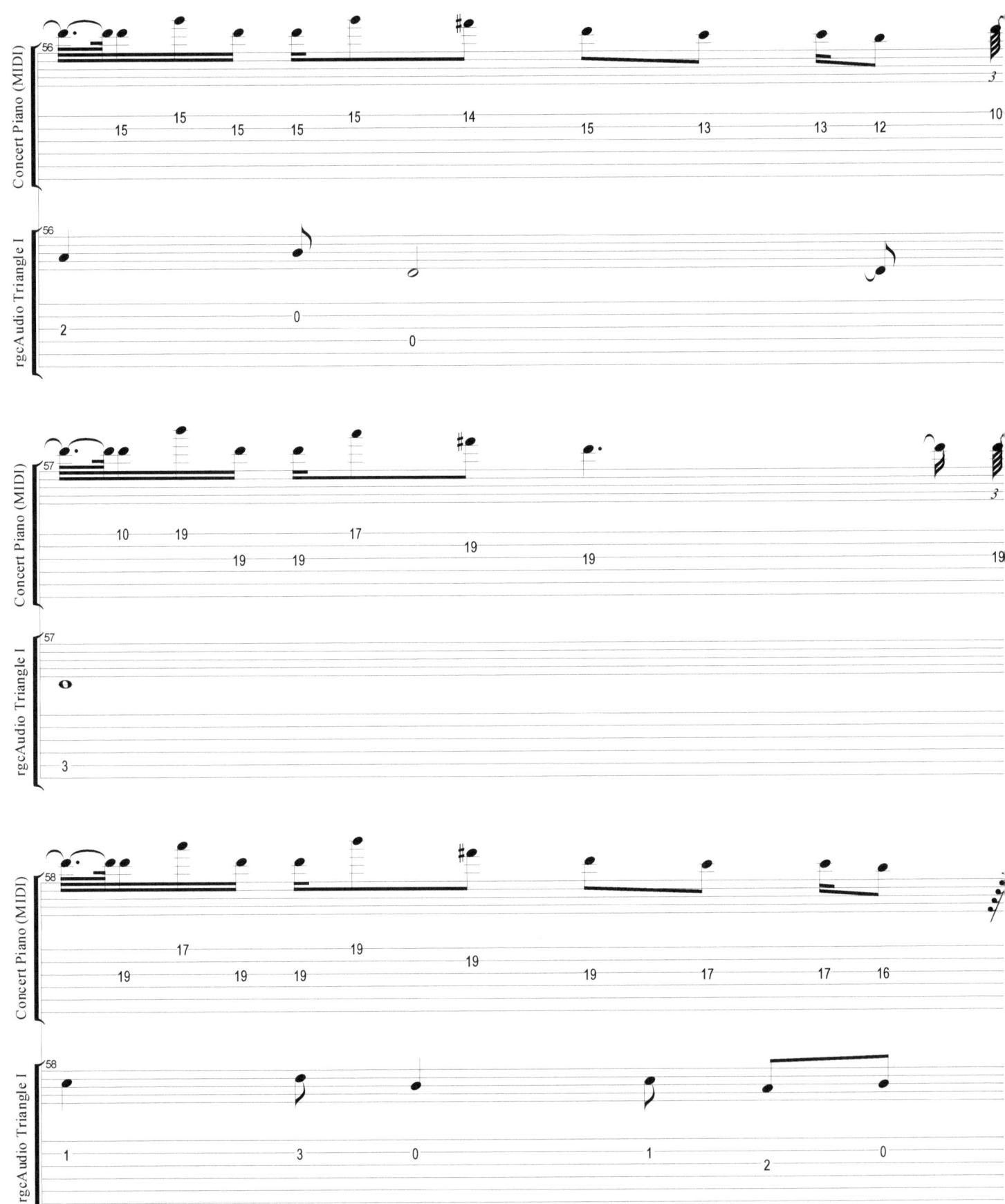

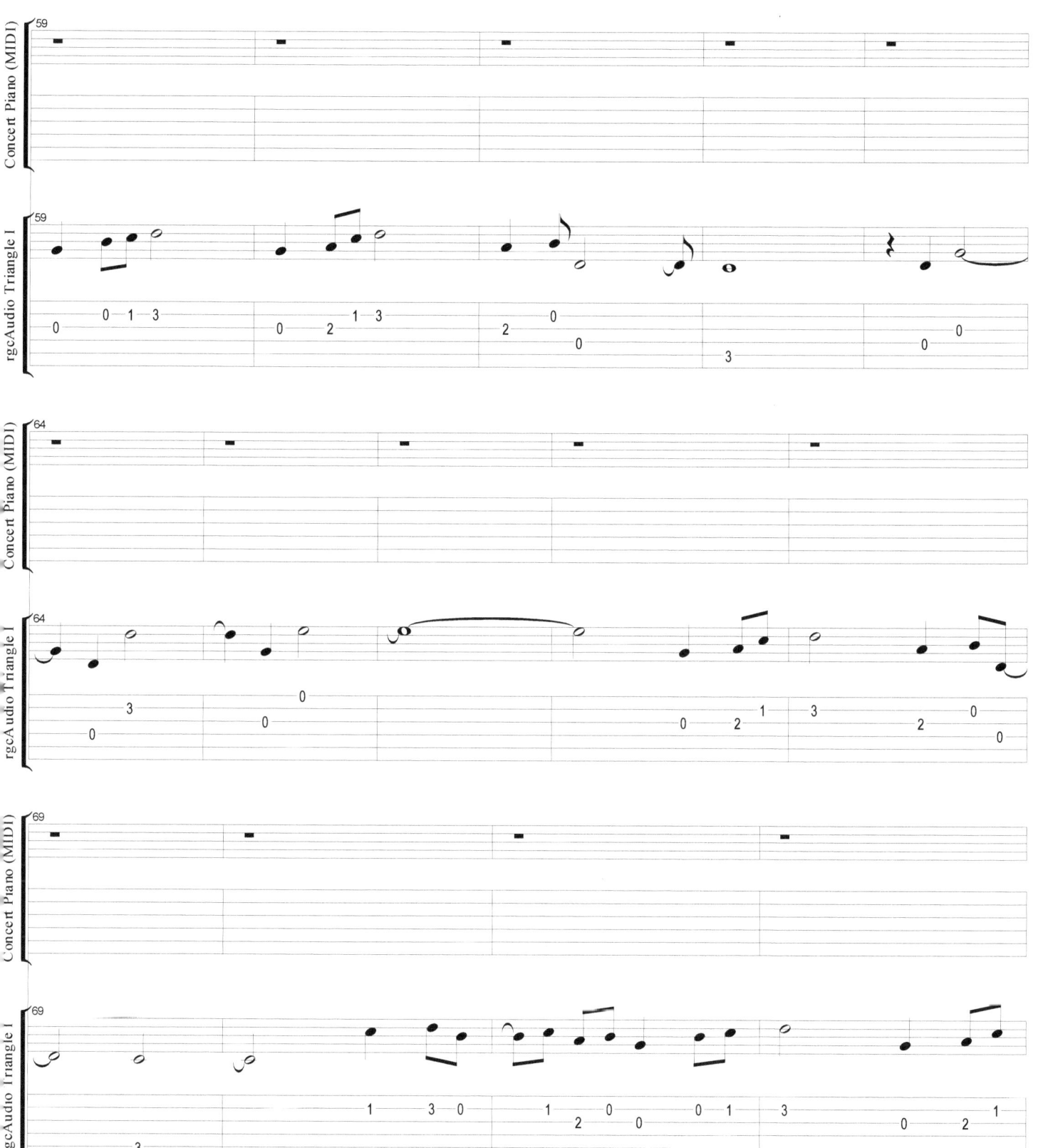

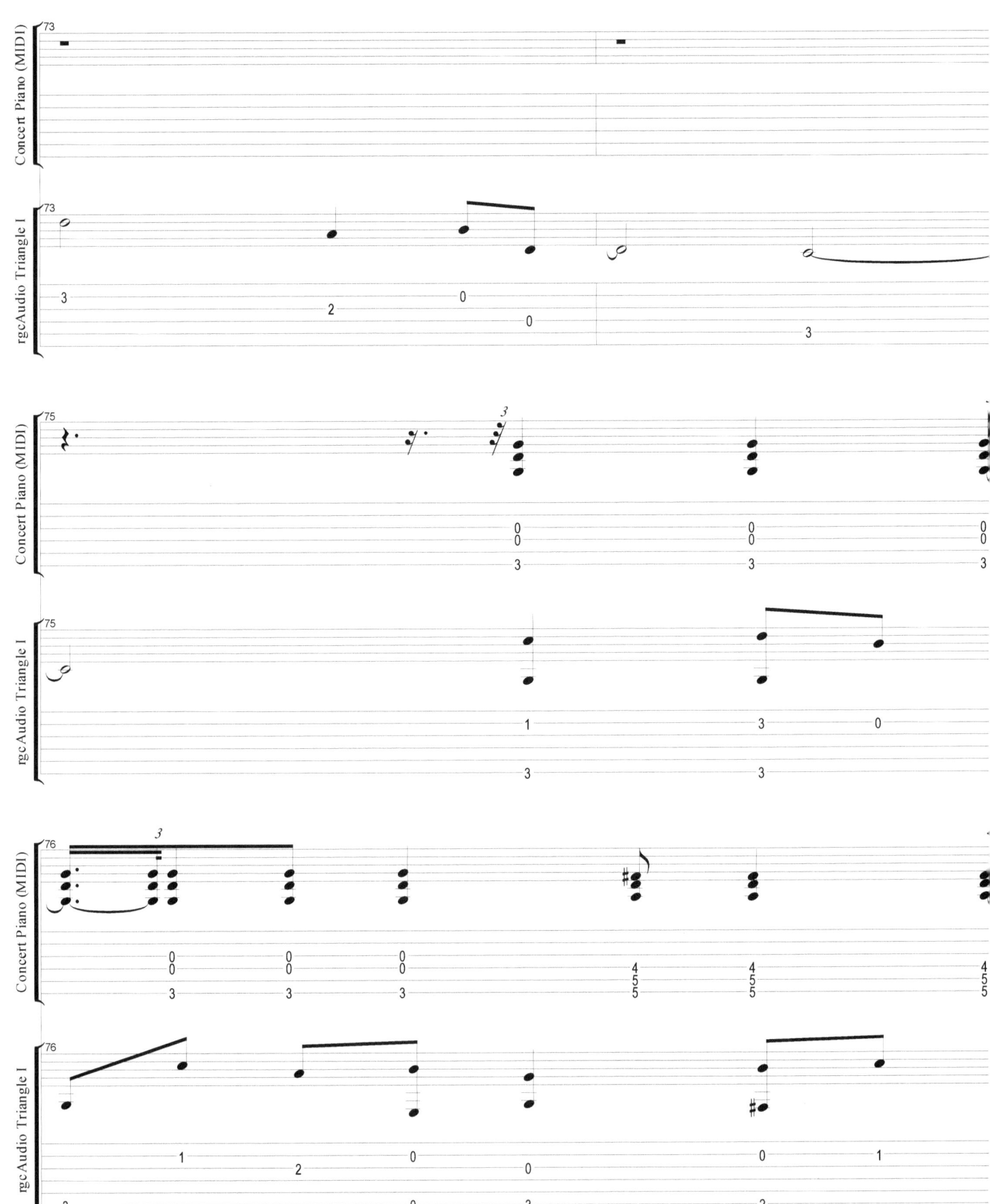

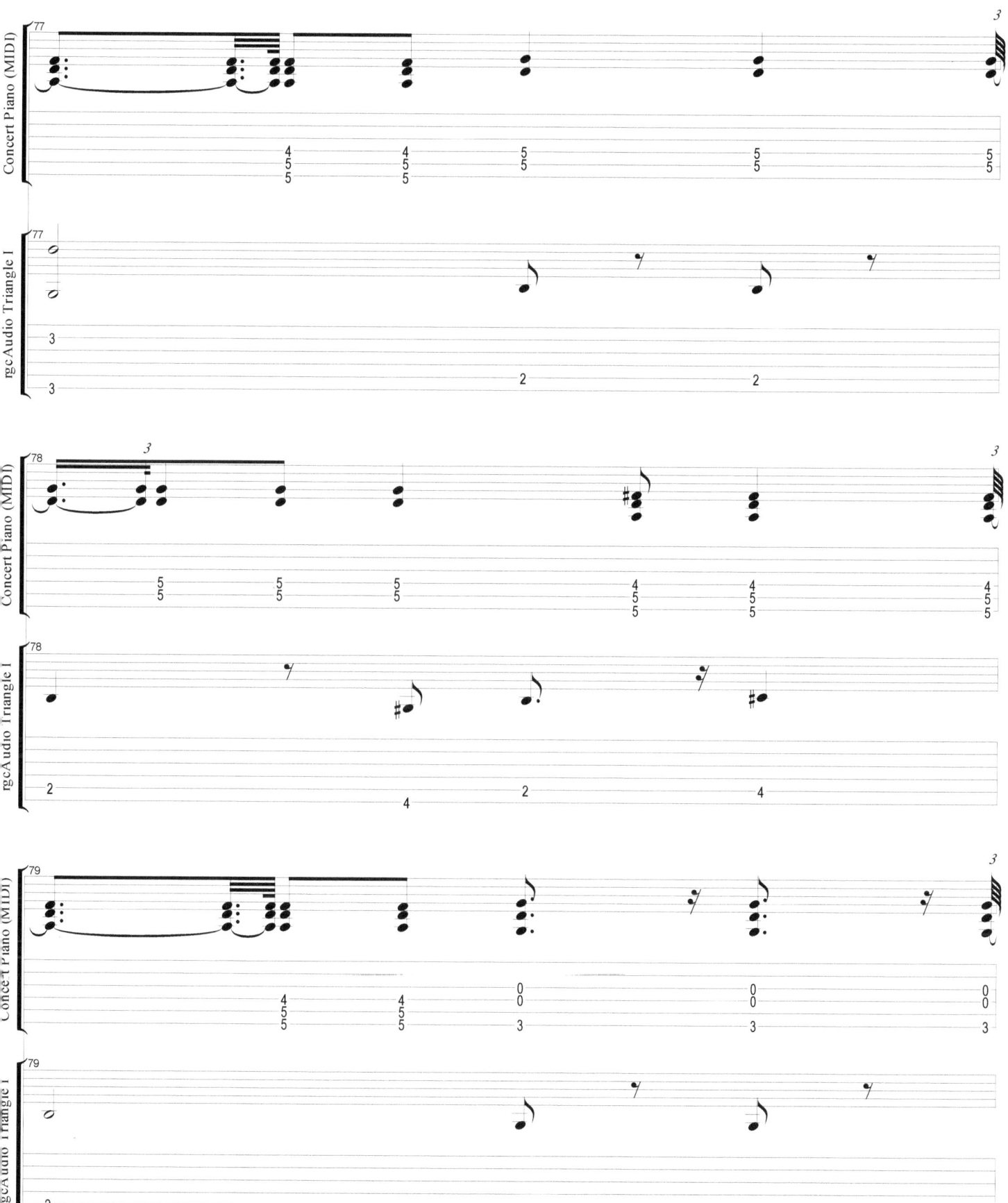

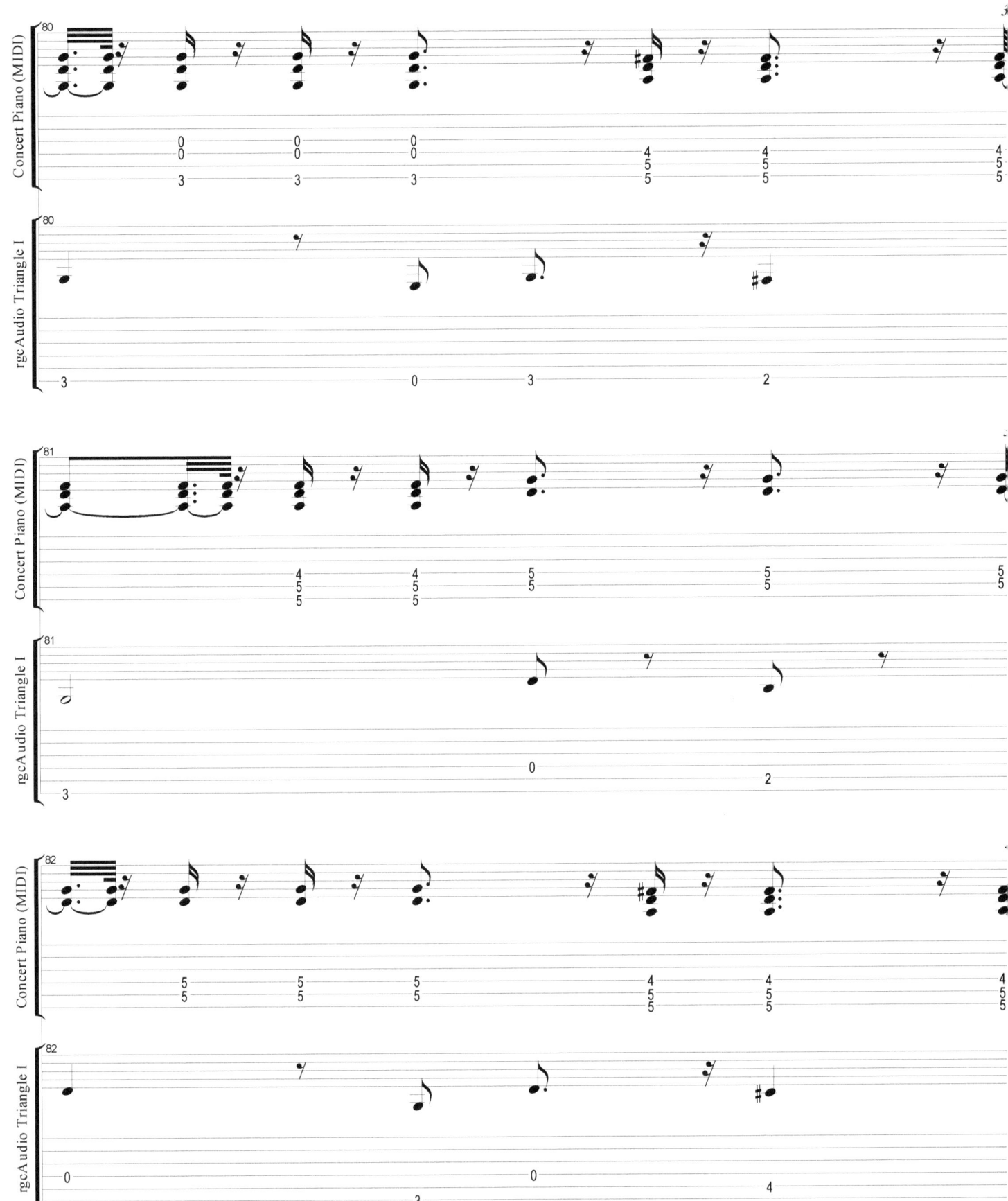

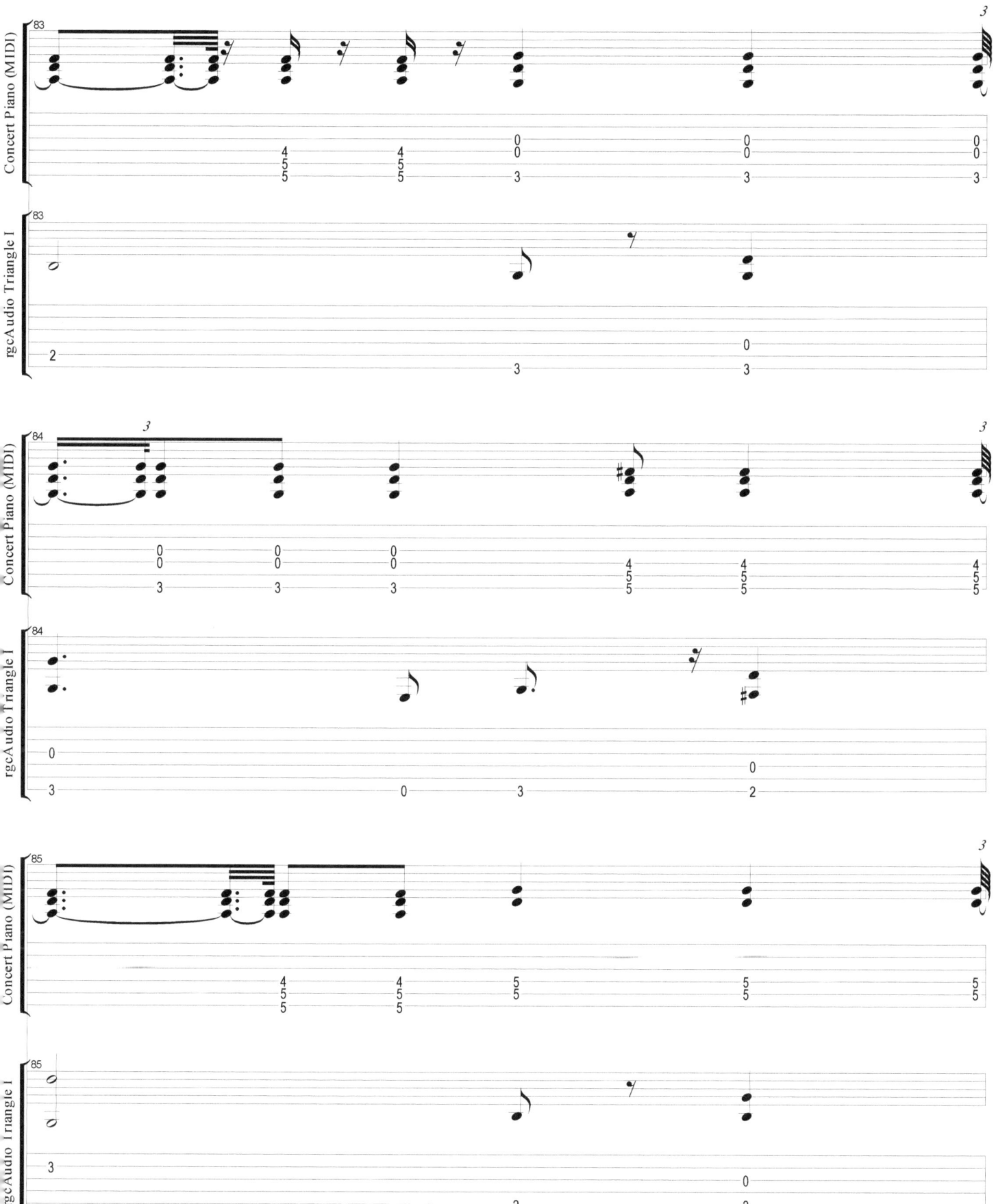

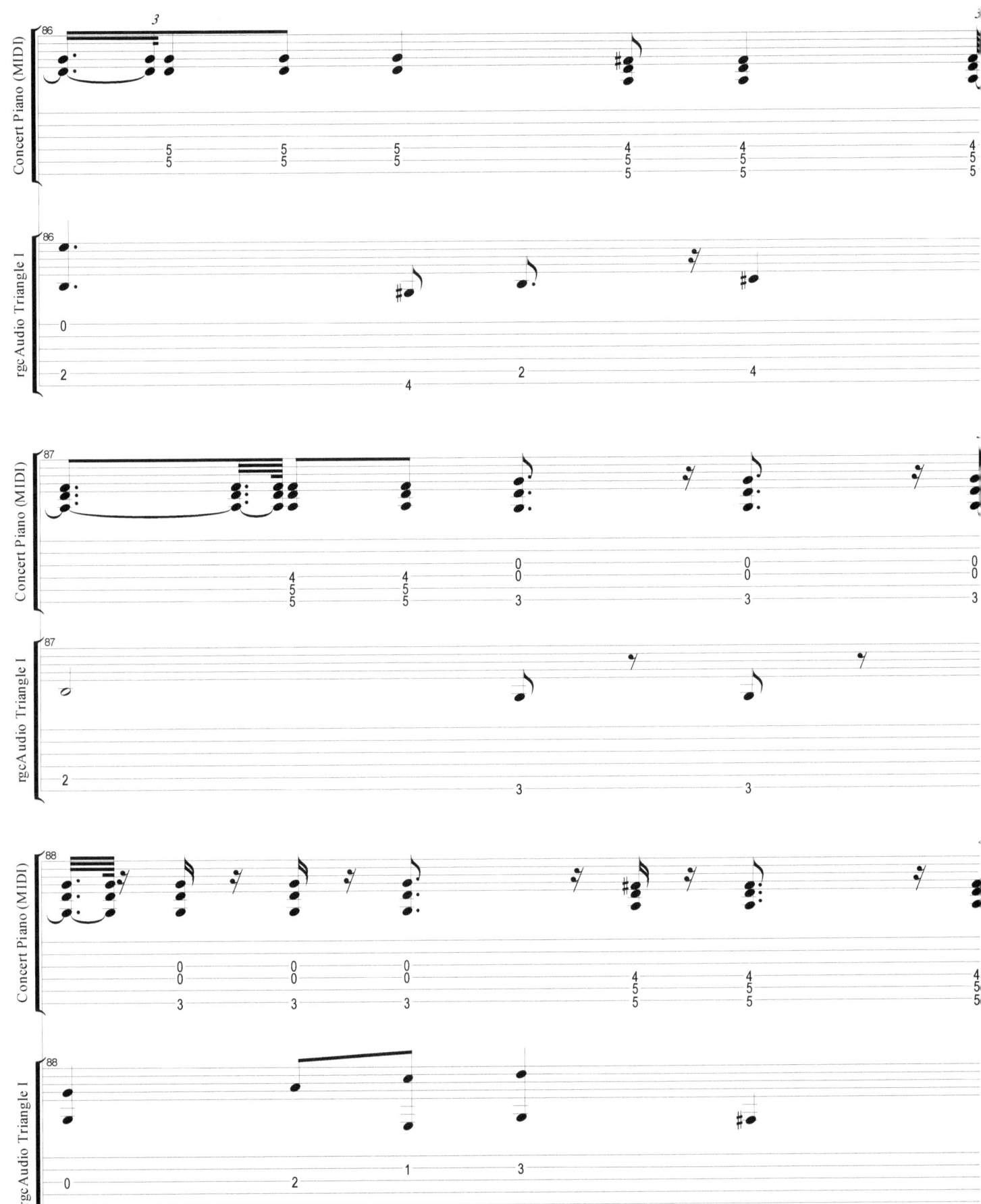

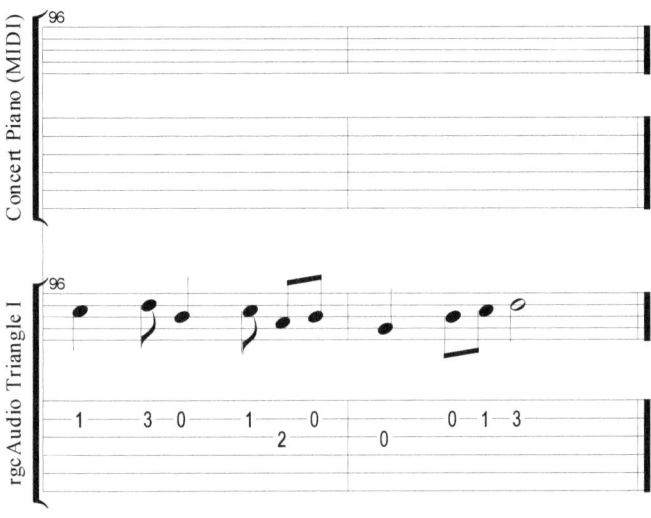

Hello My Friend, Hello

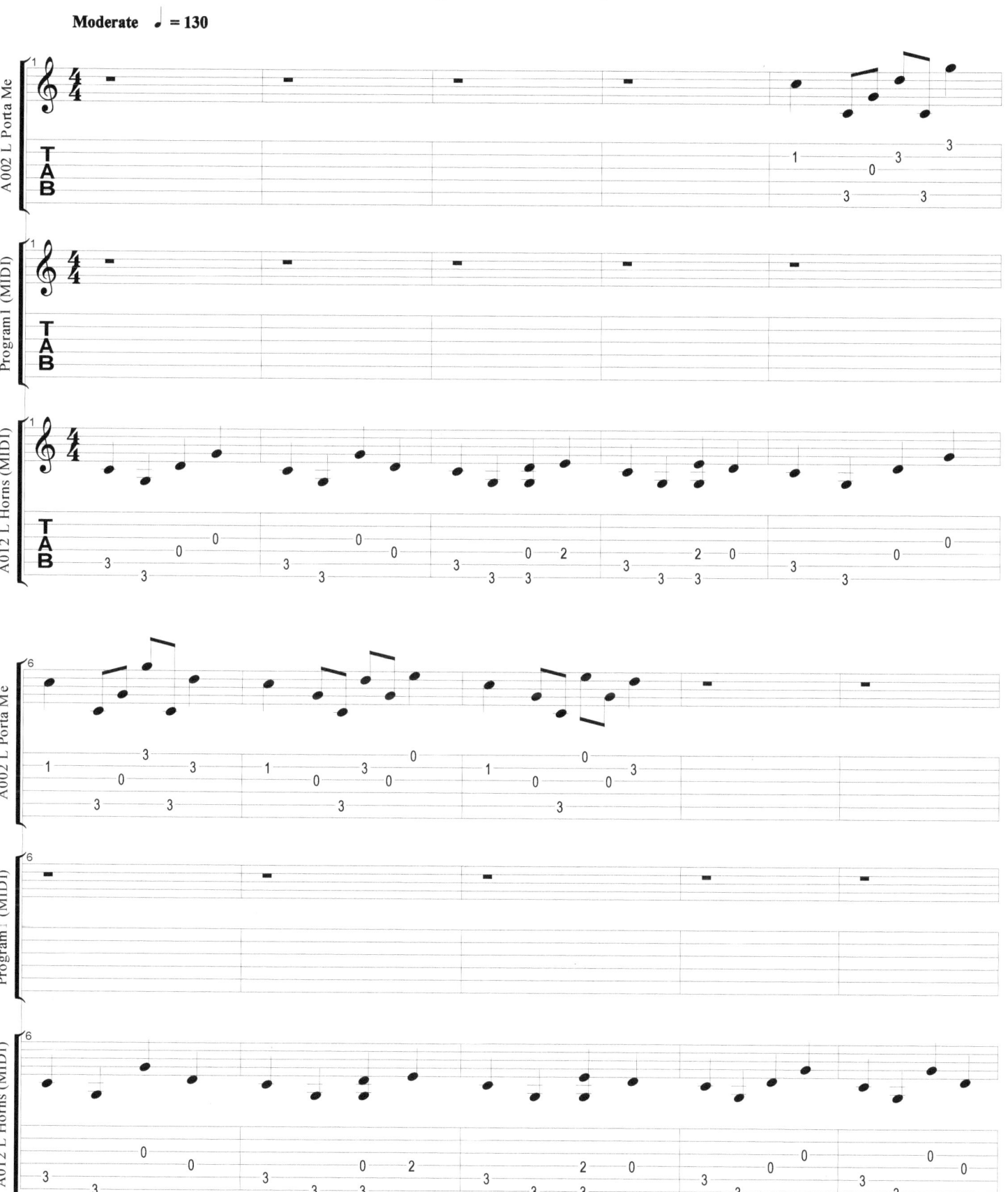

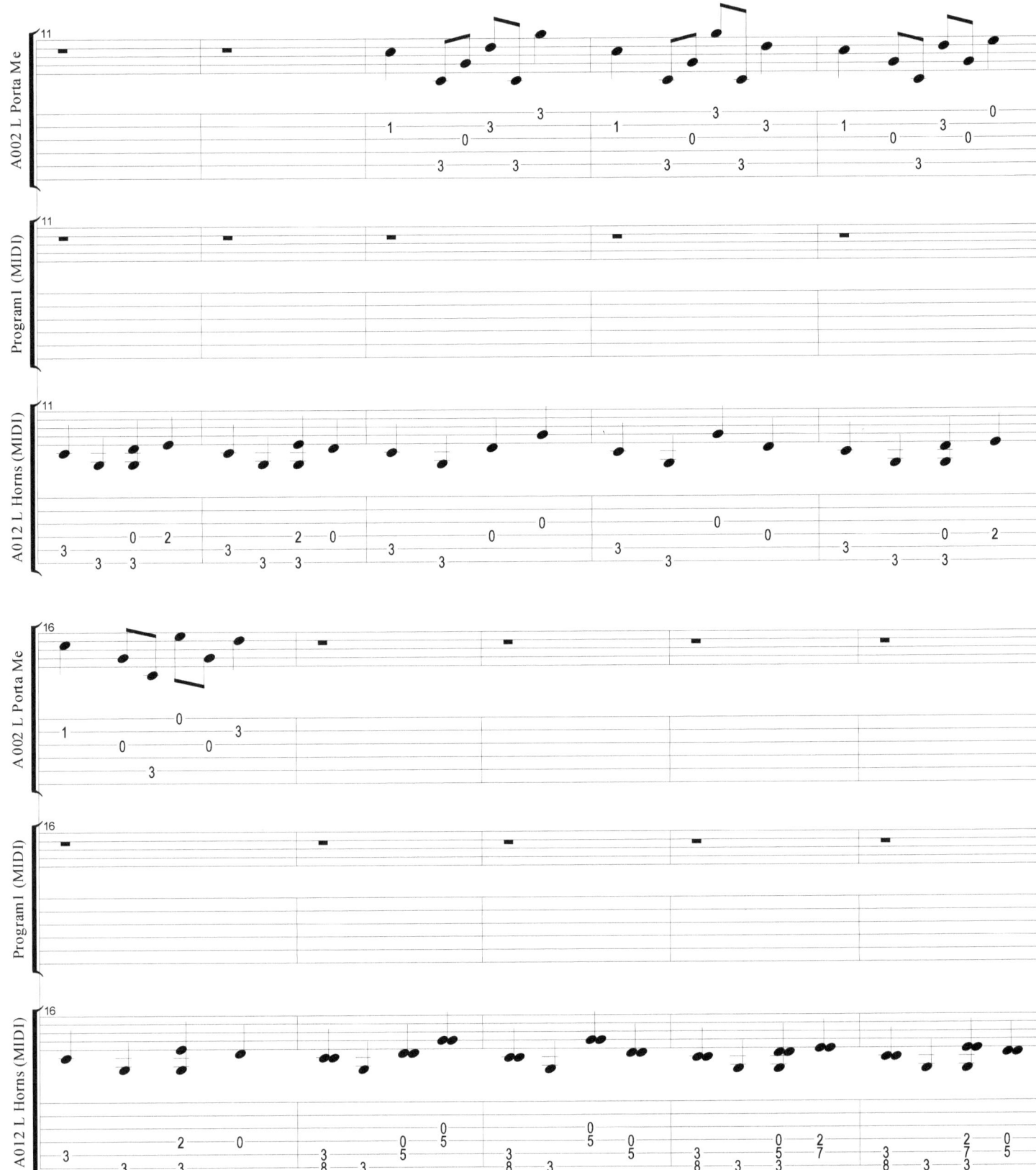

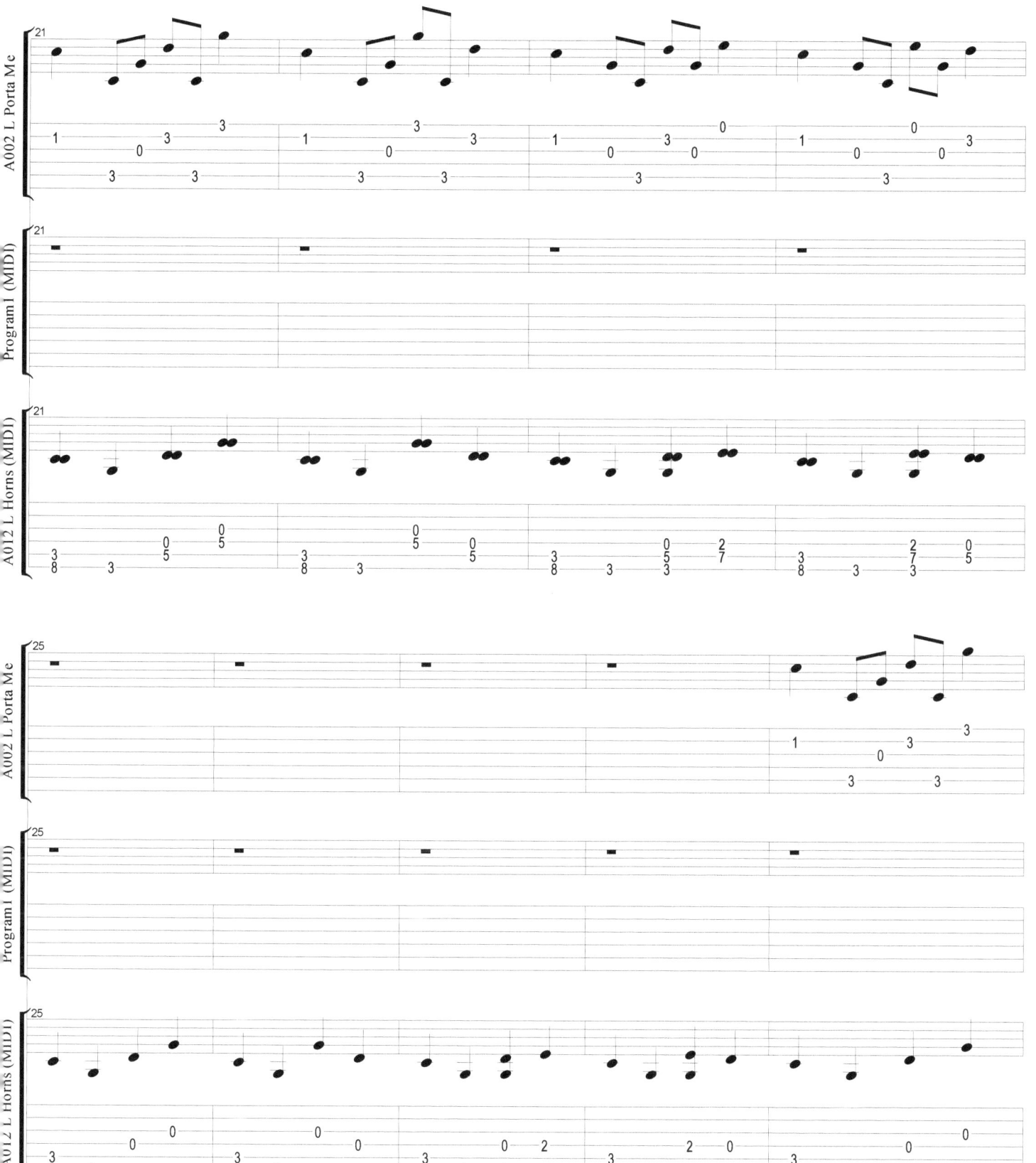

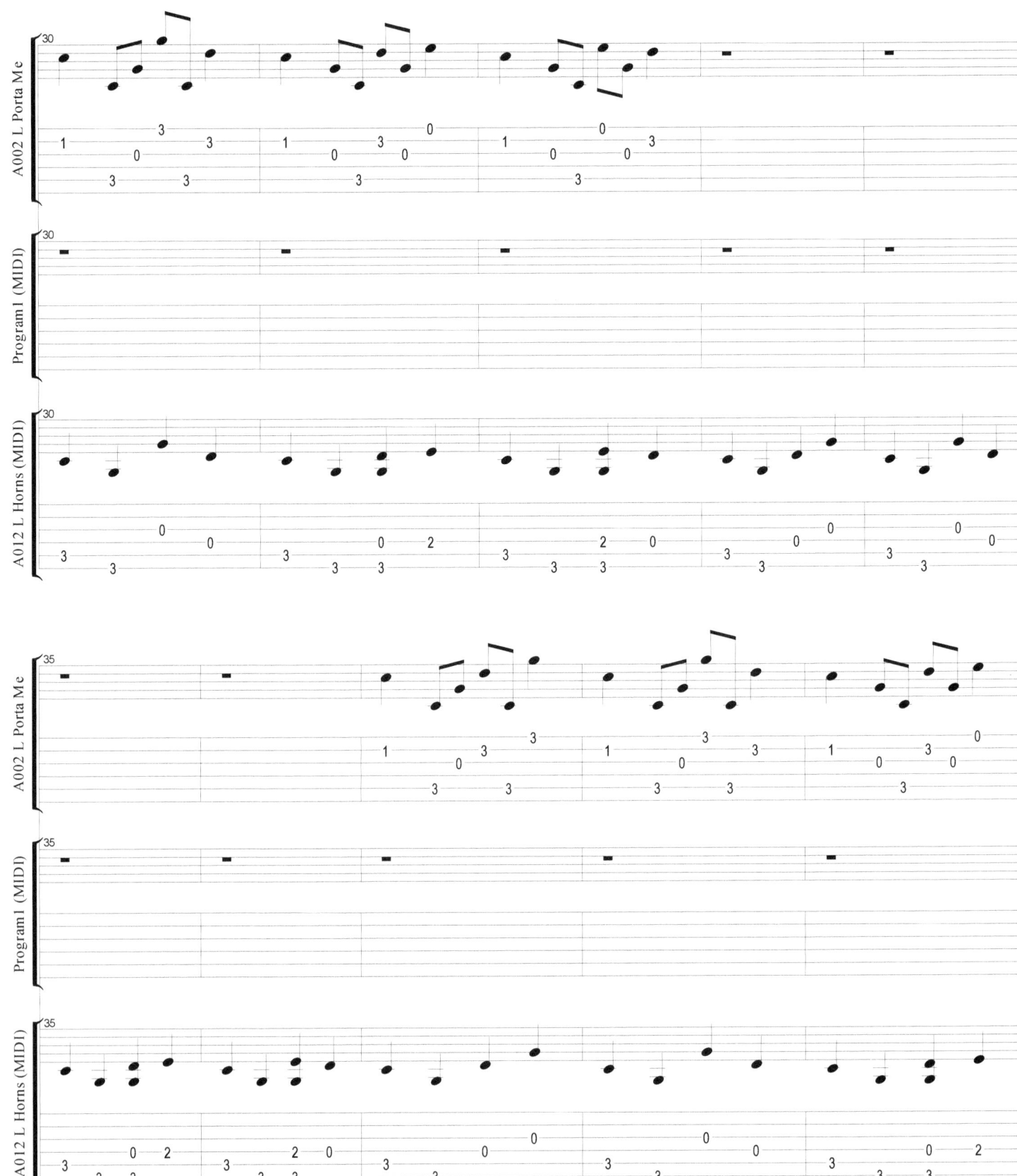

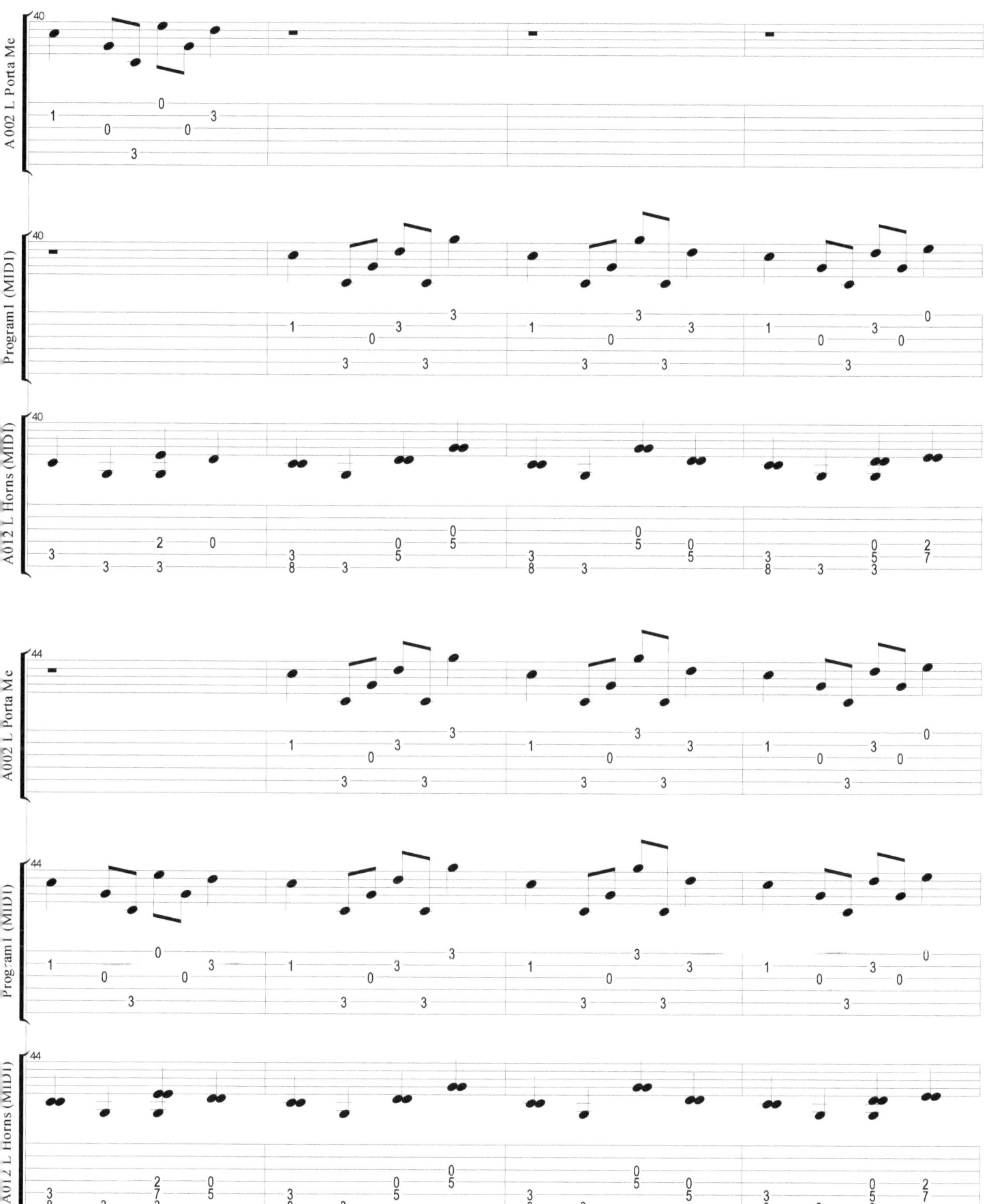

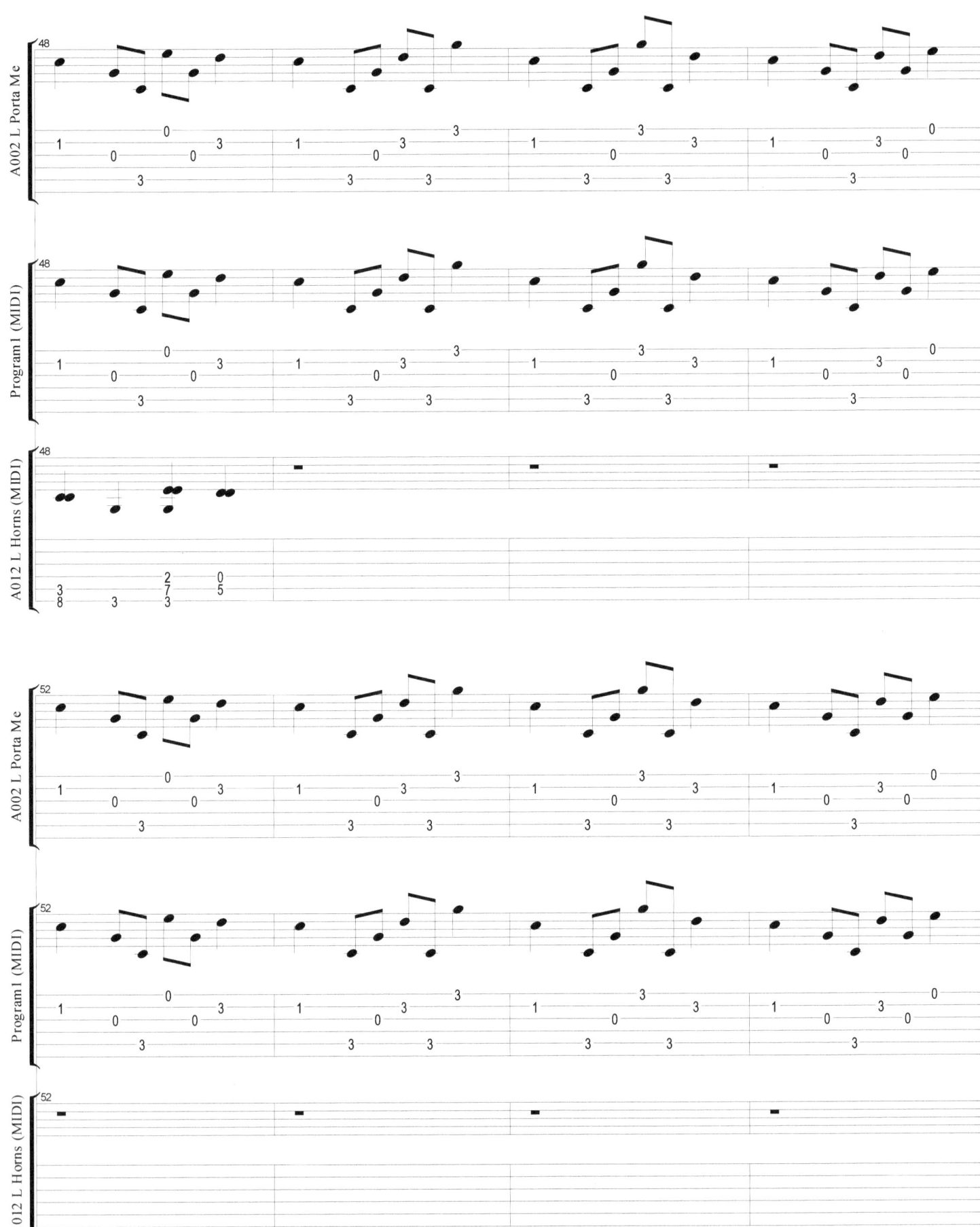

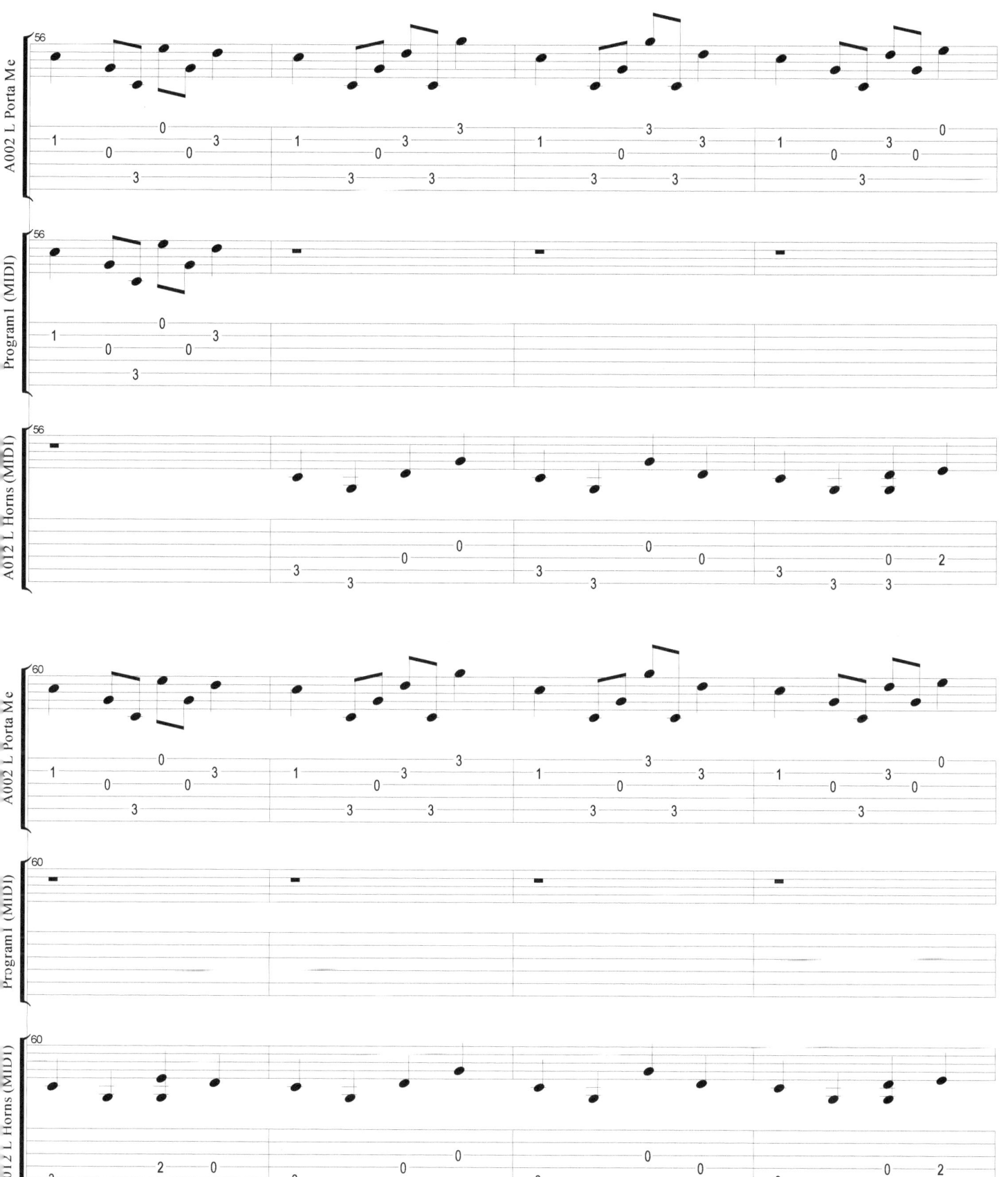

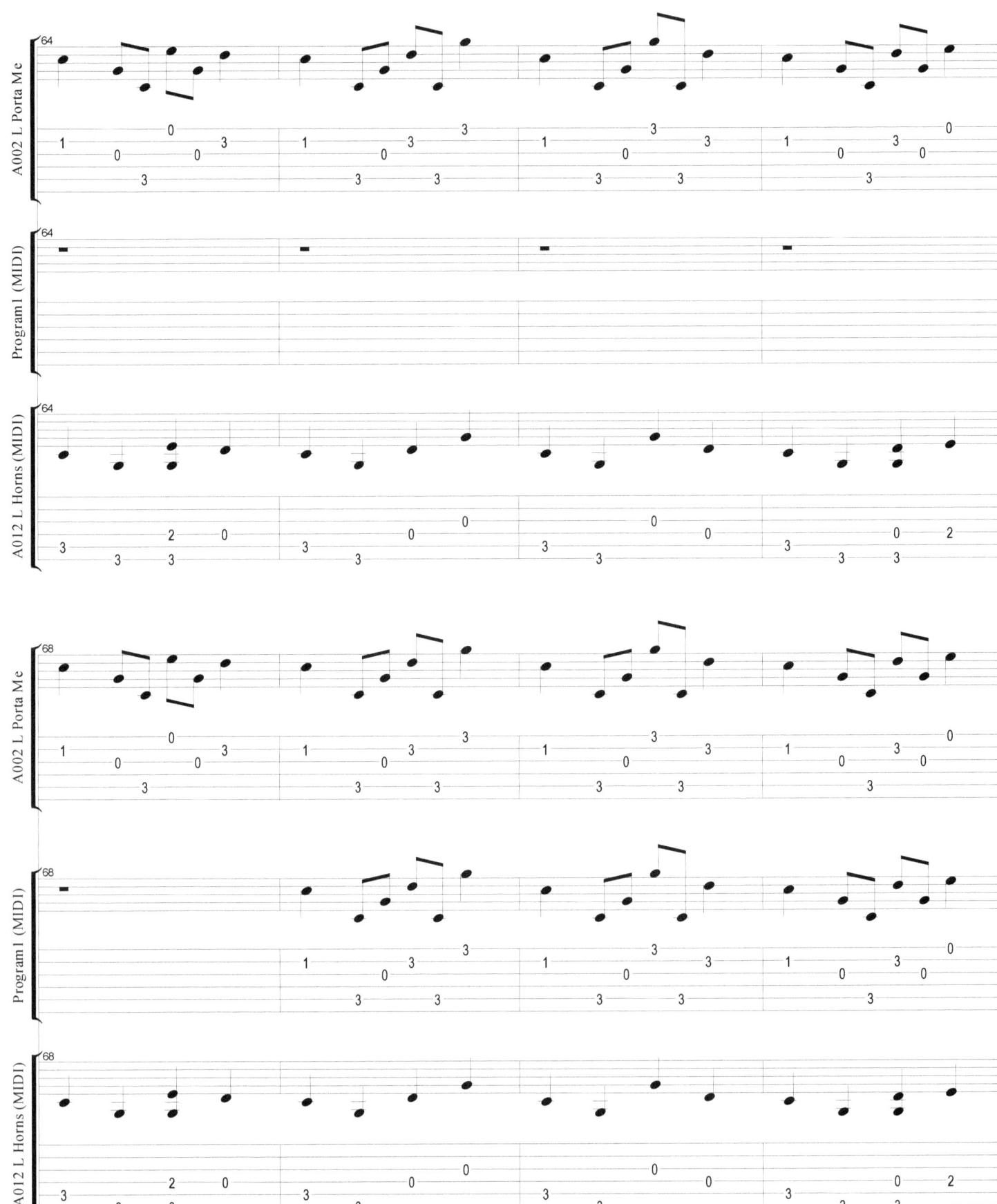

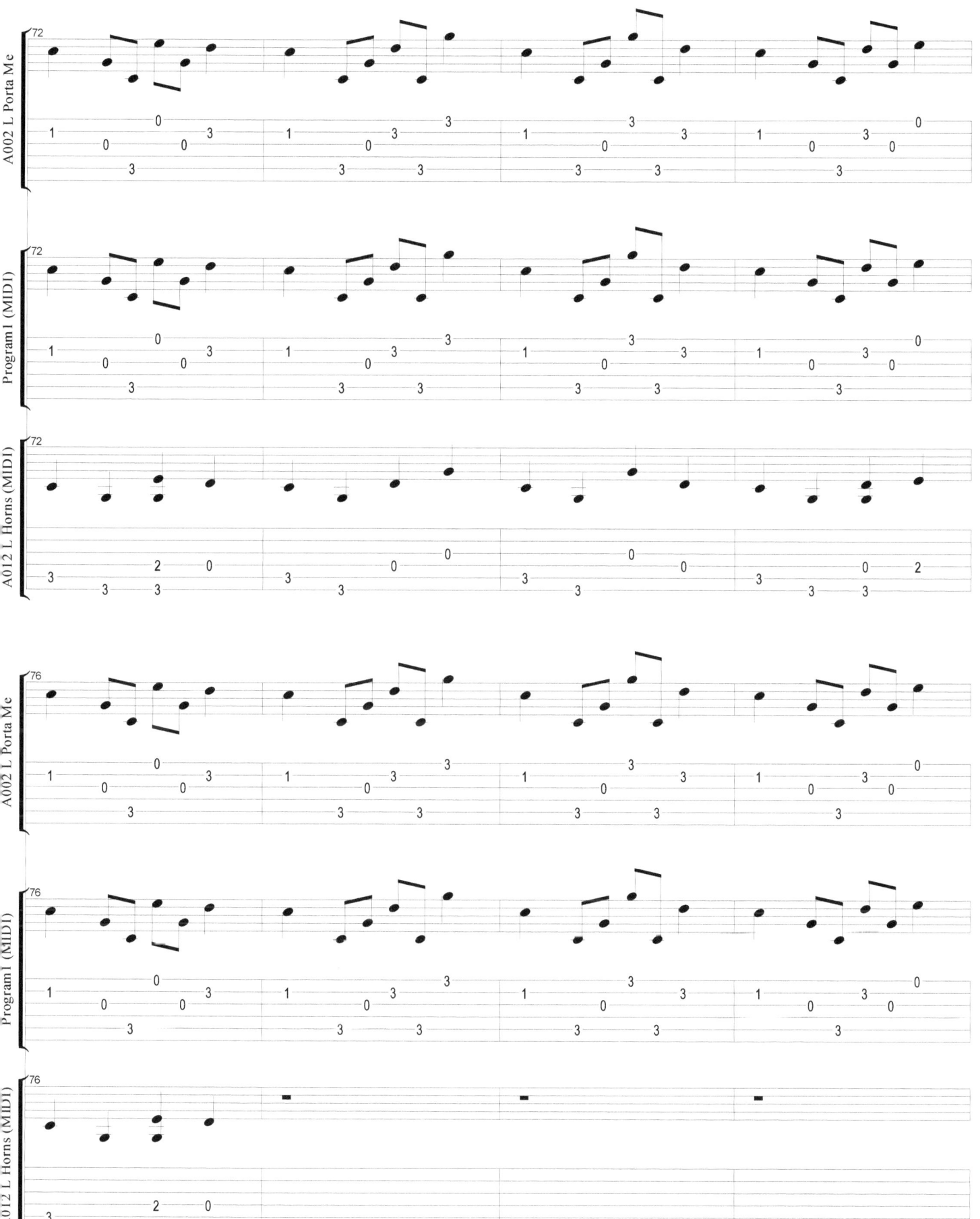

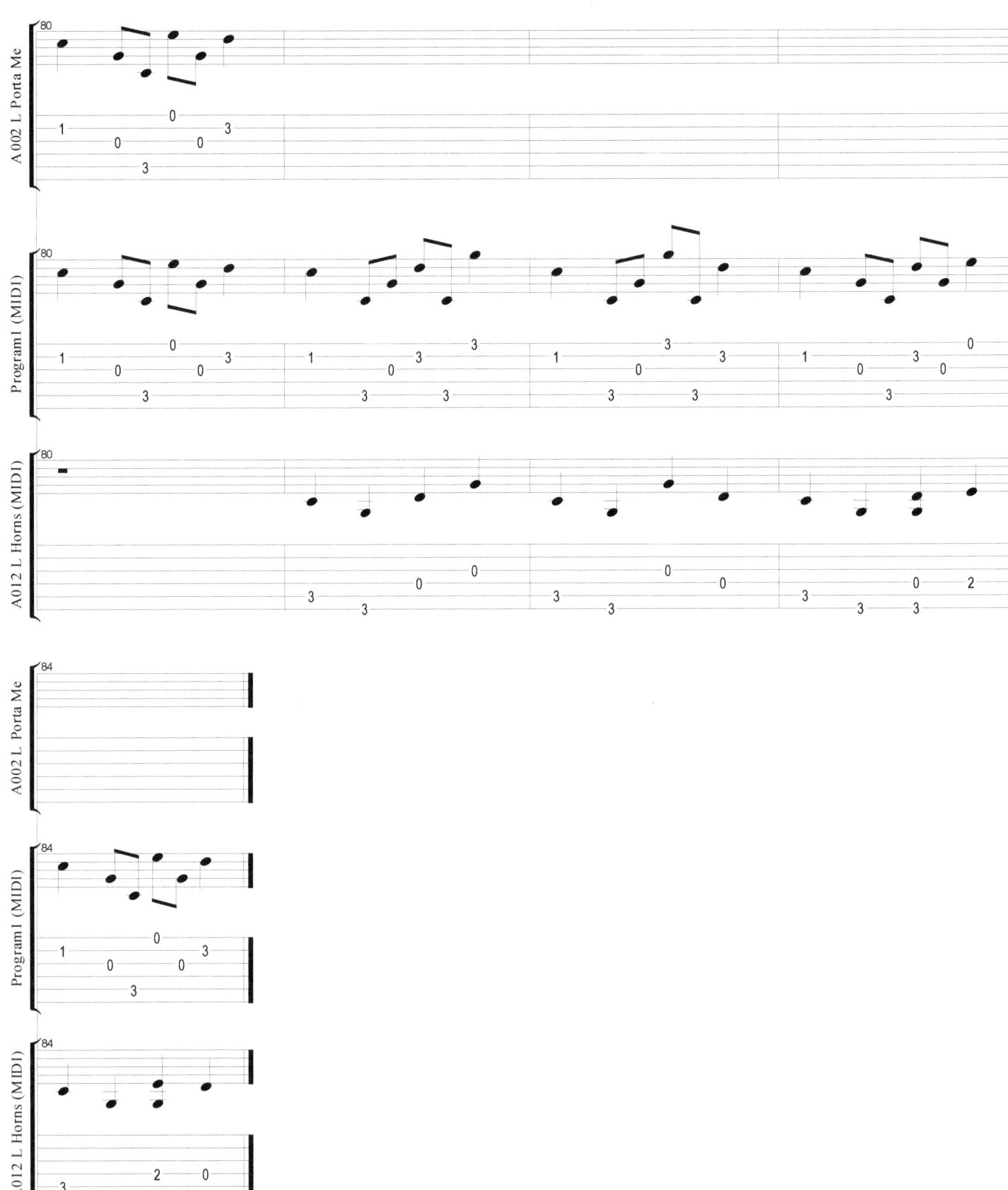

I Never Thought

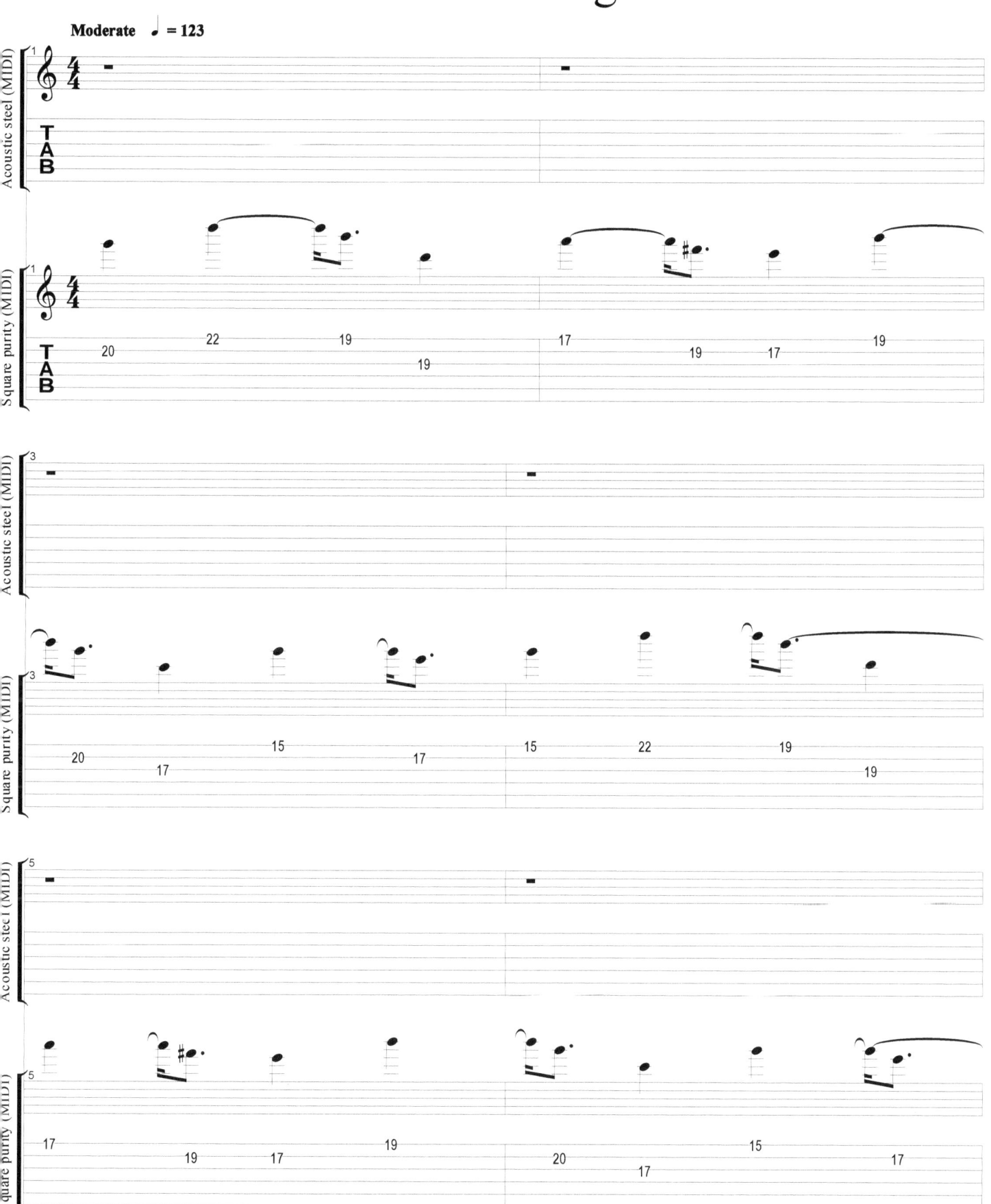

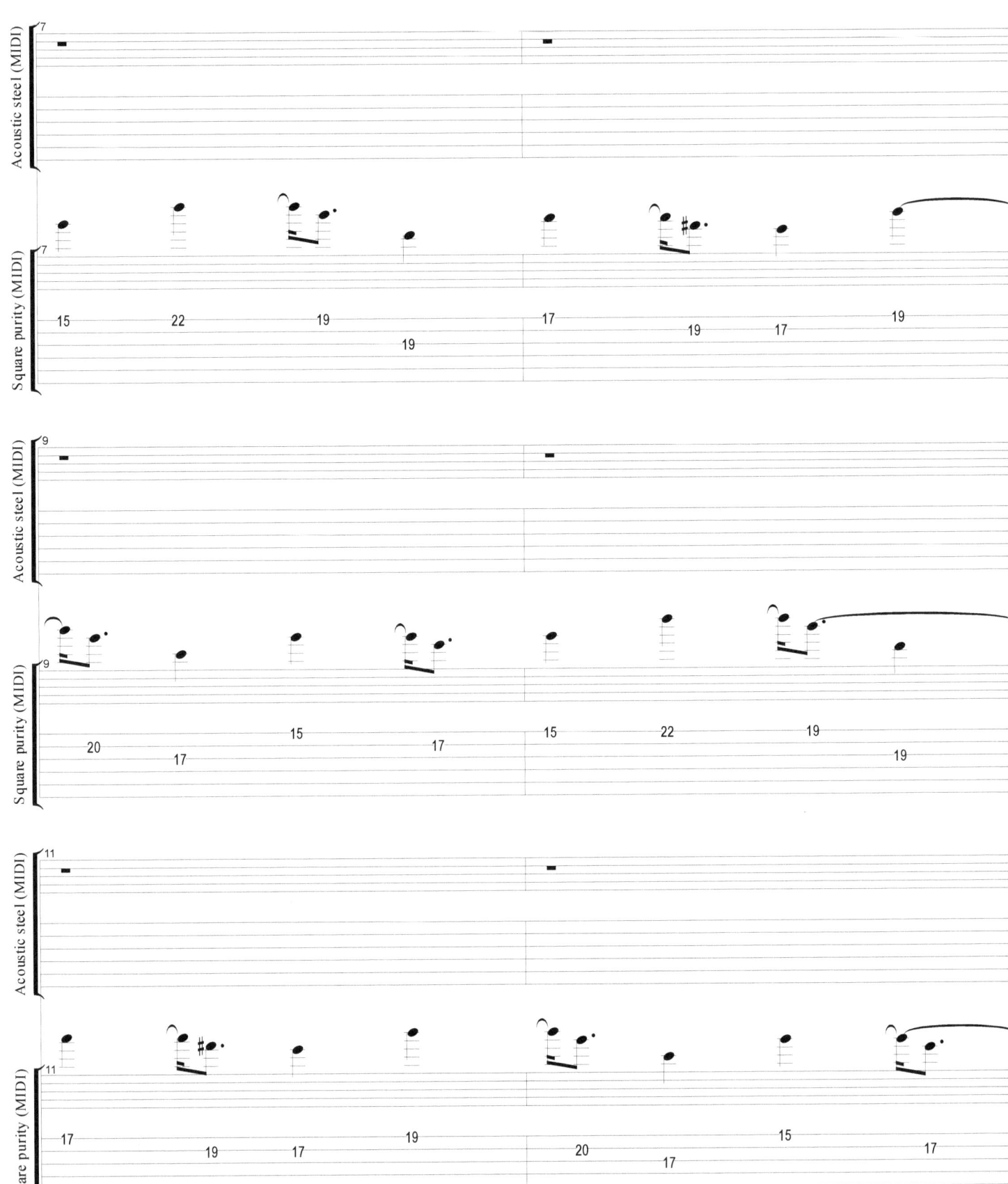

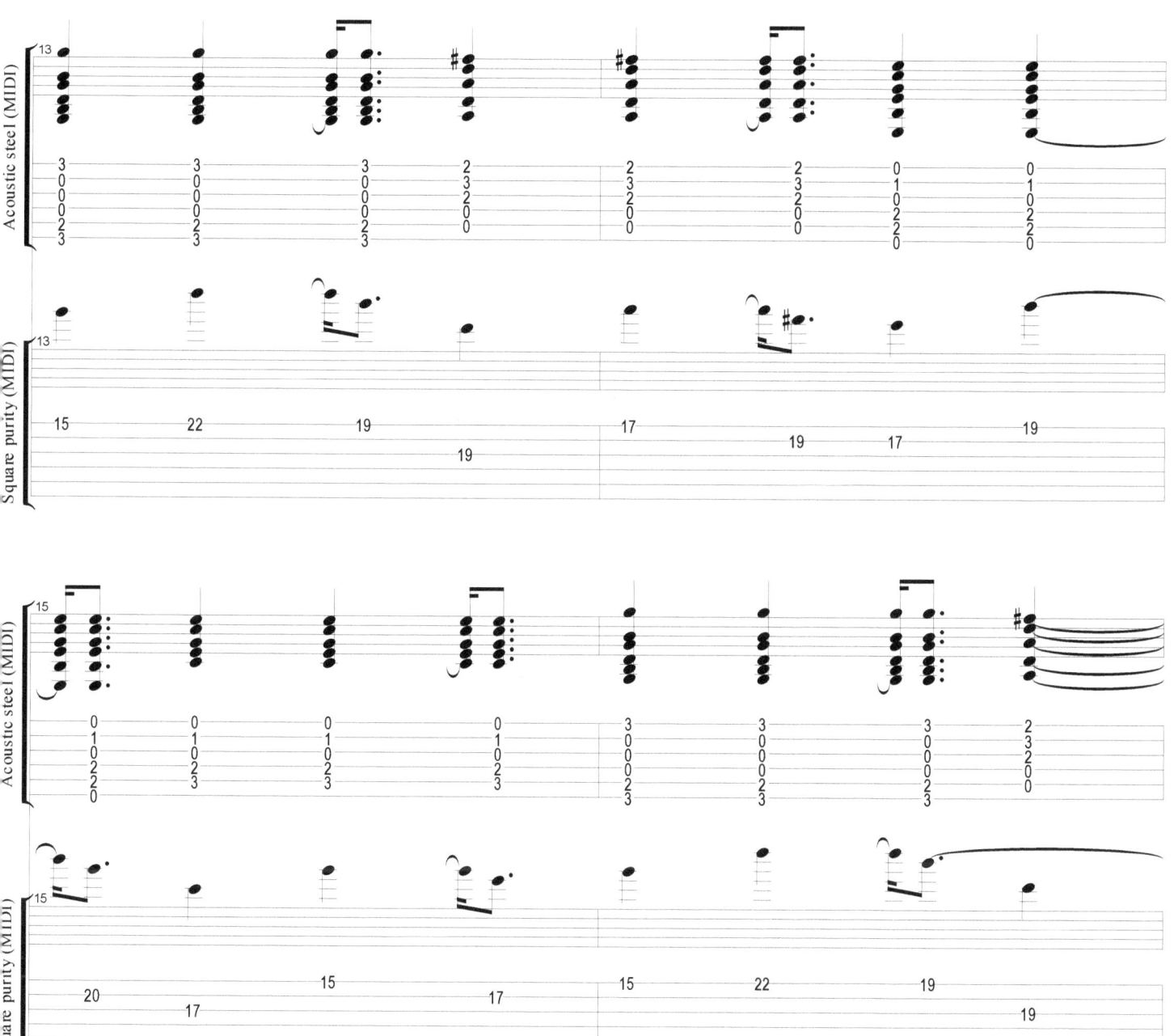

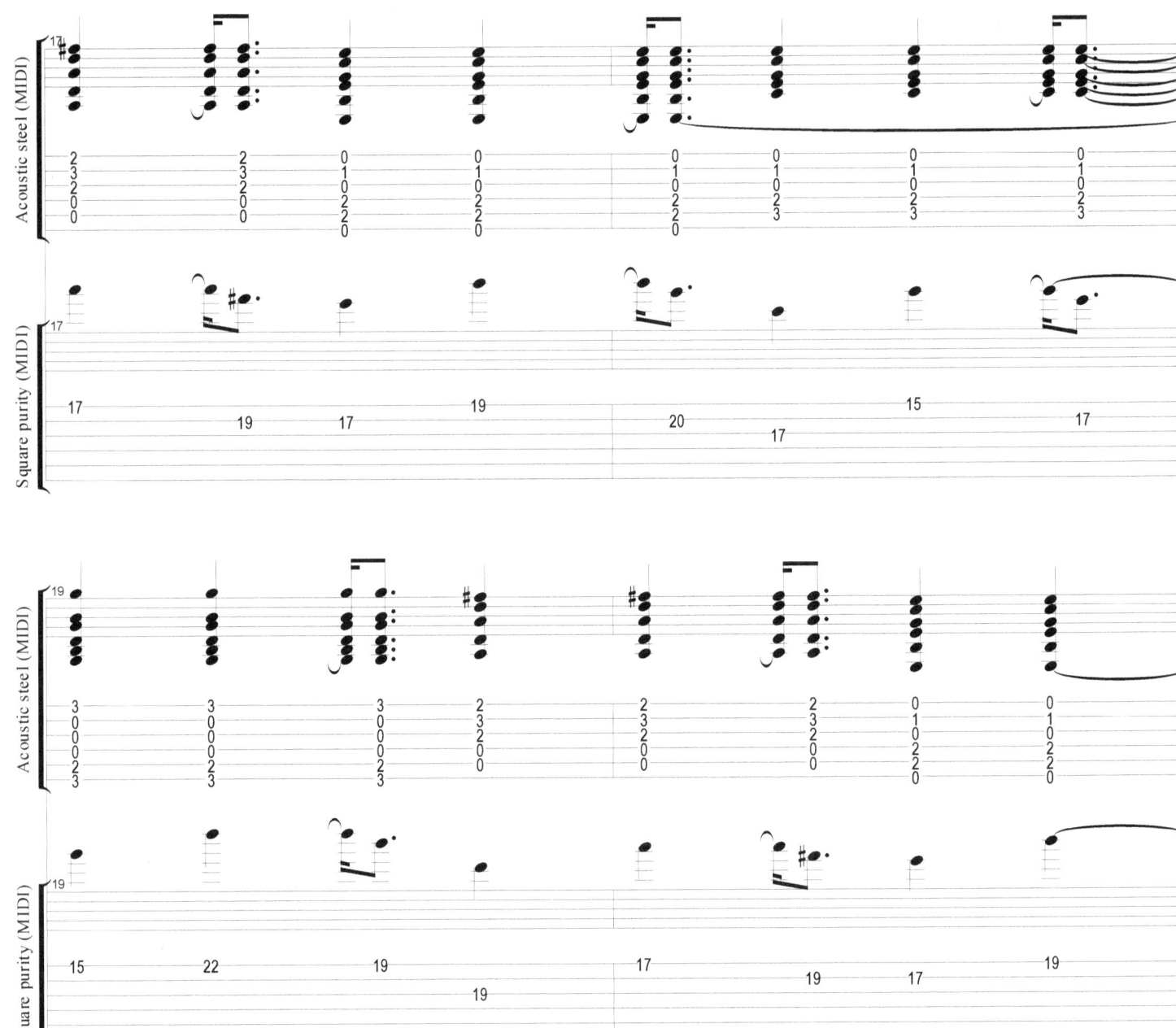

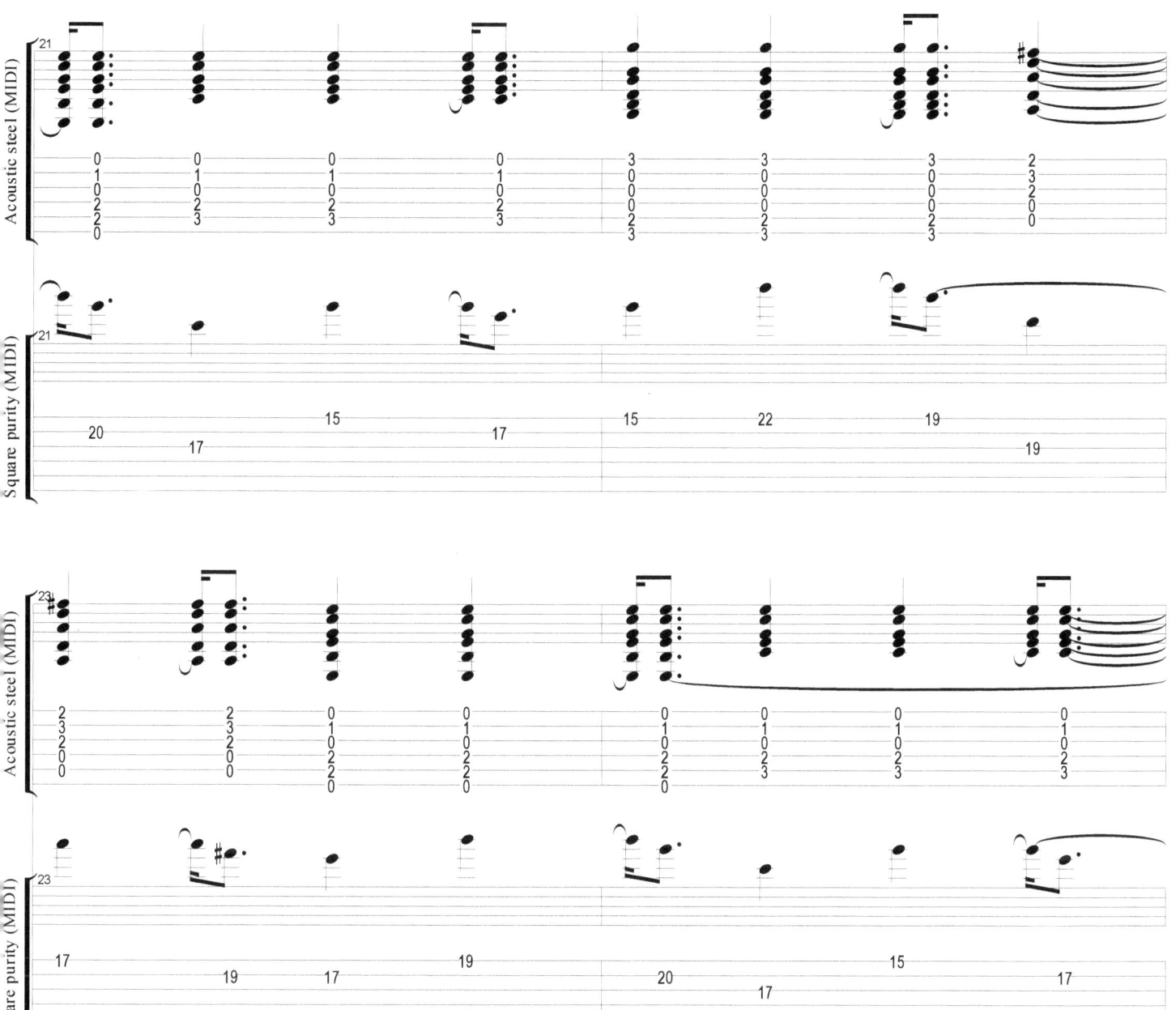

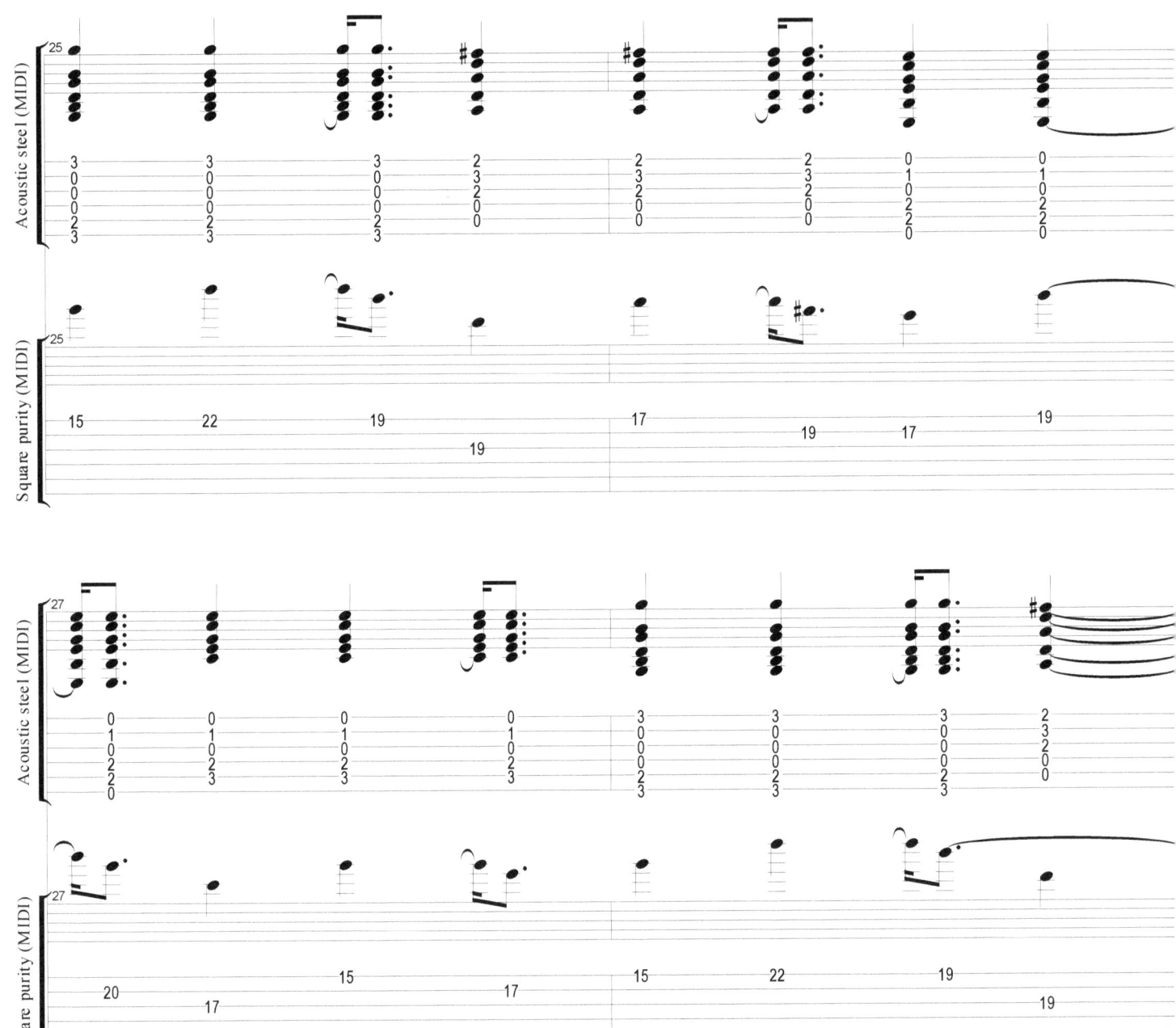

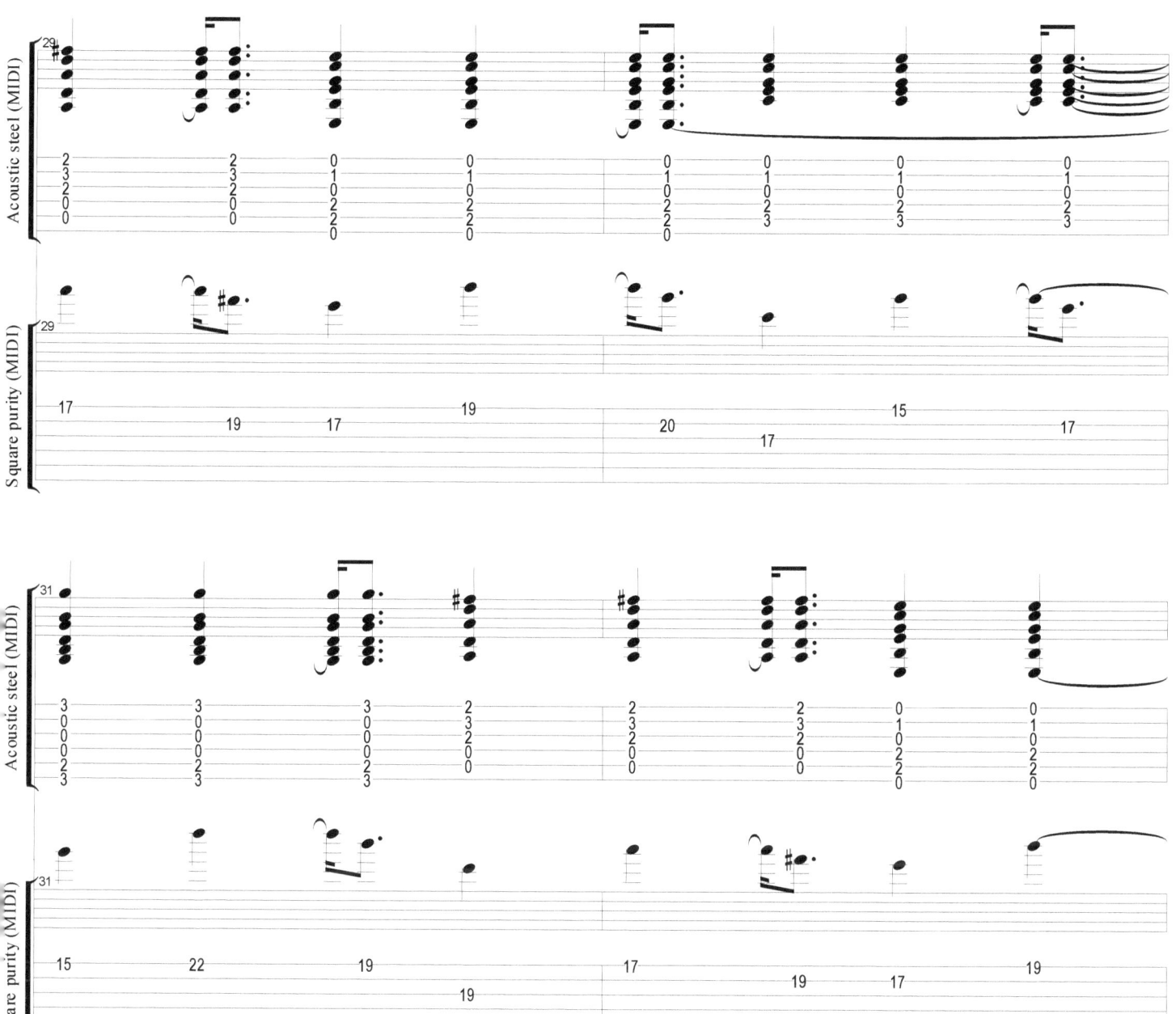

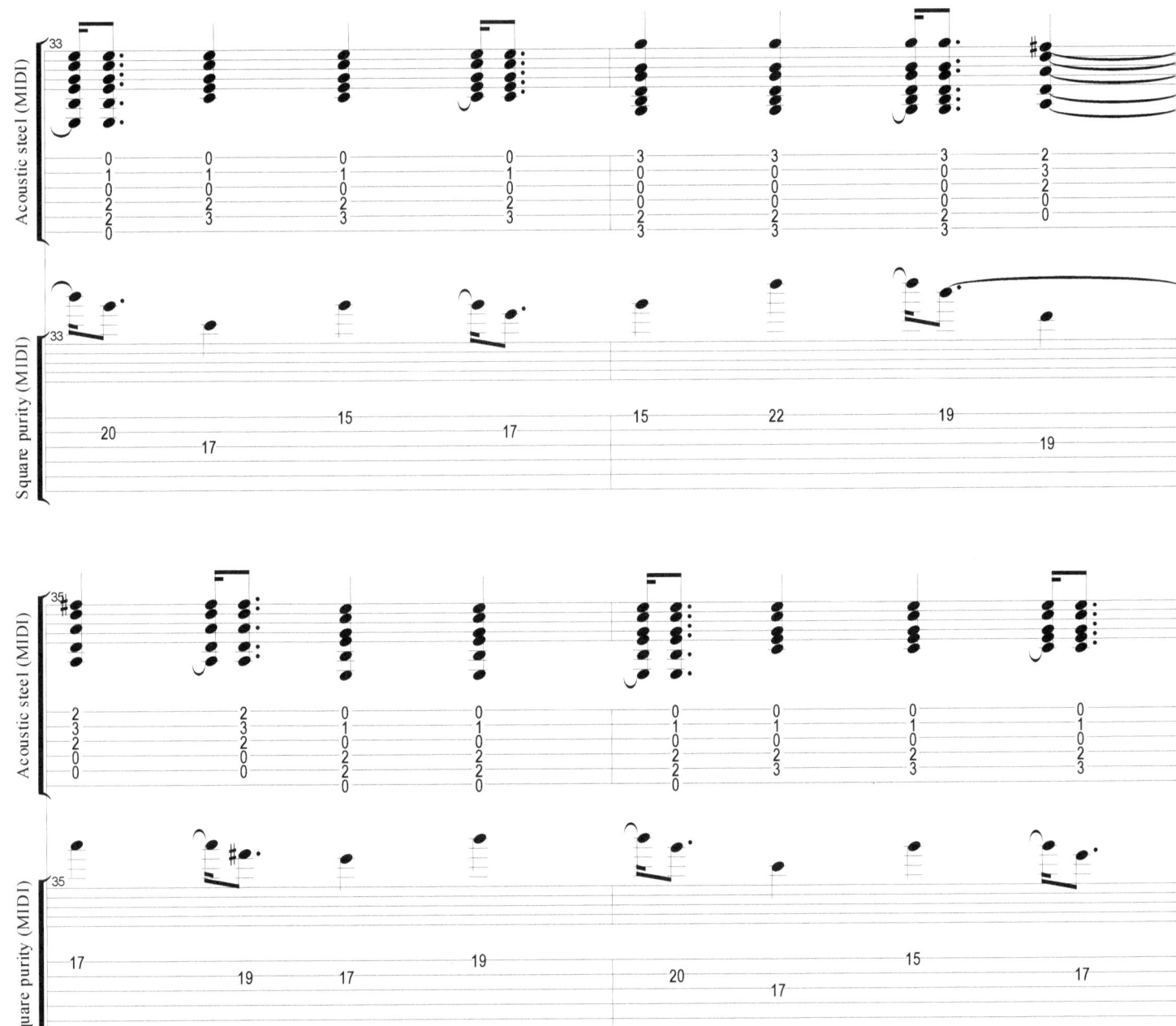

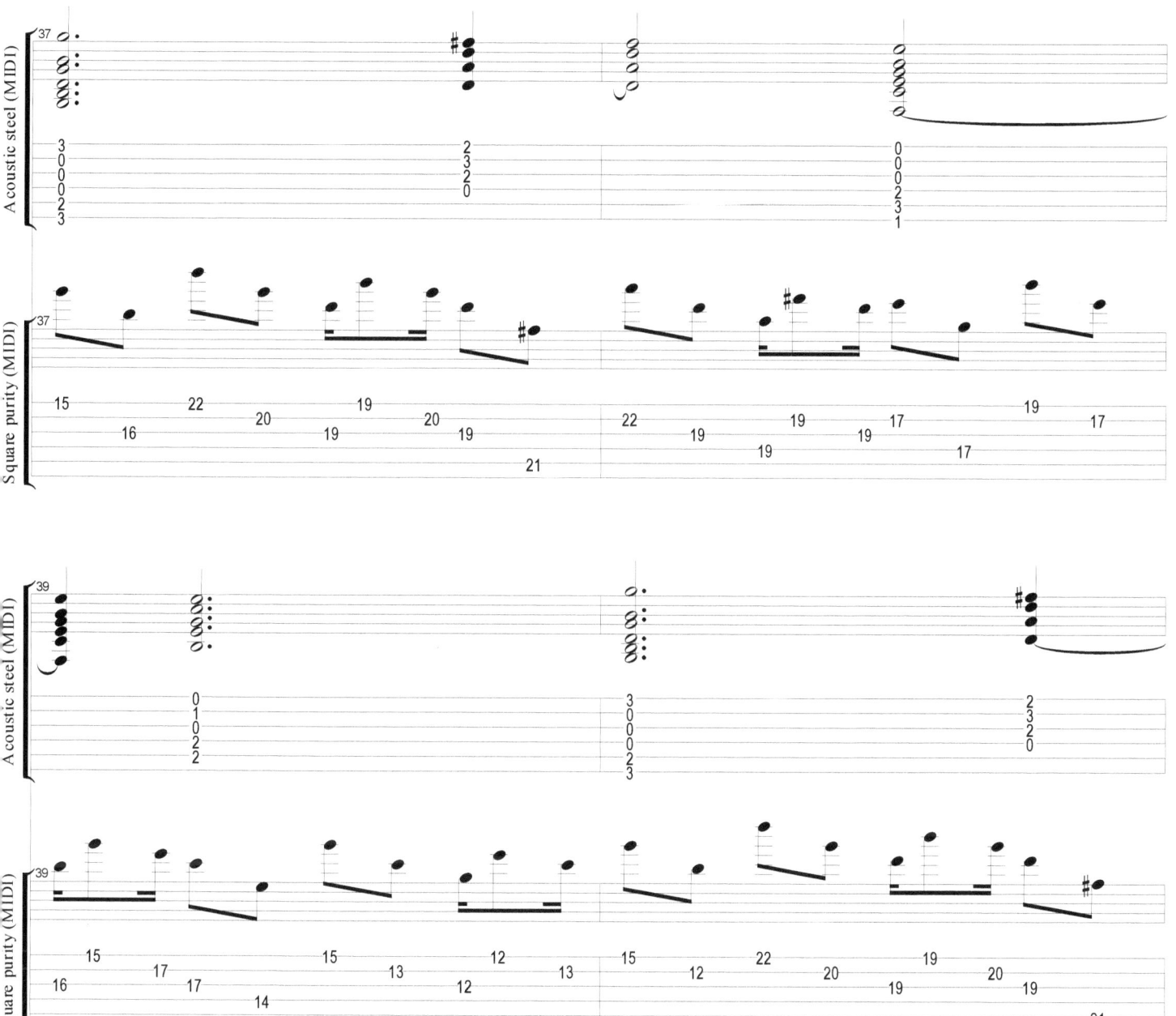

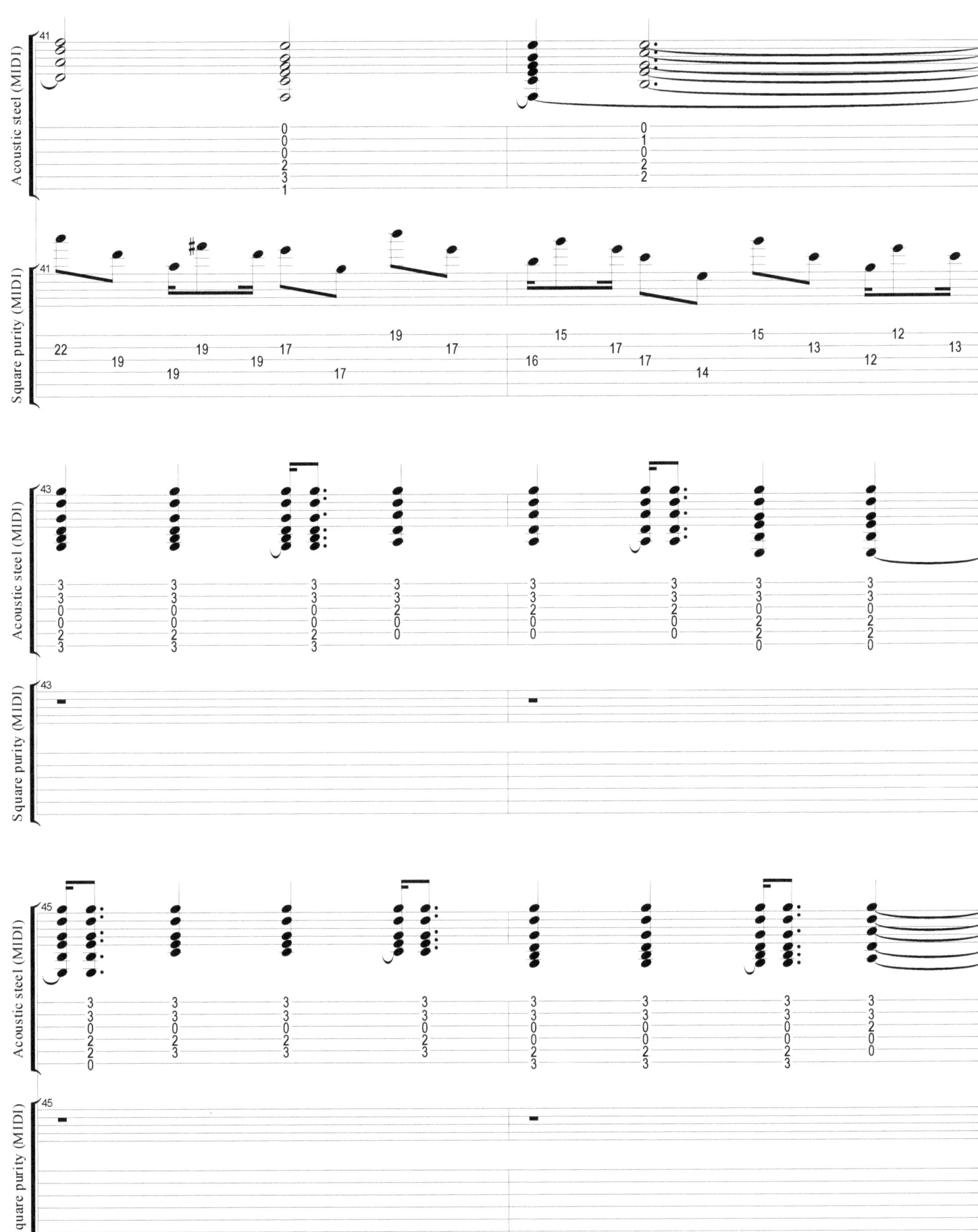

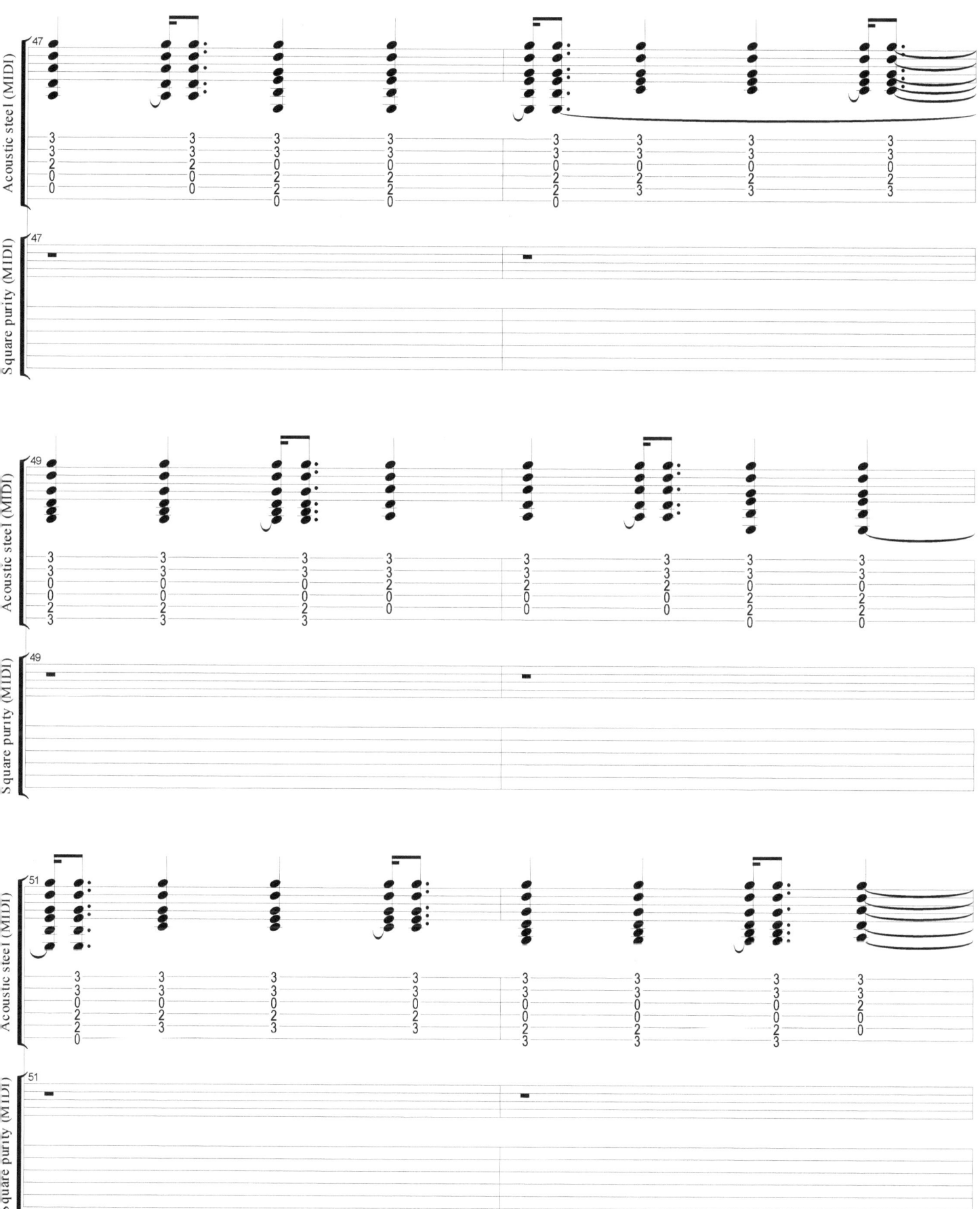

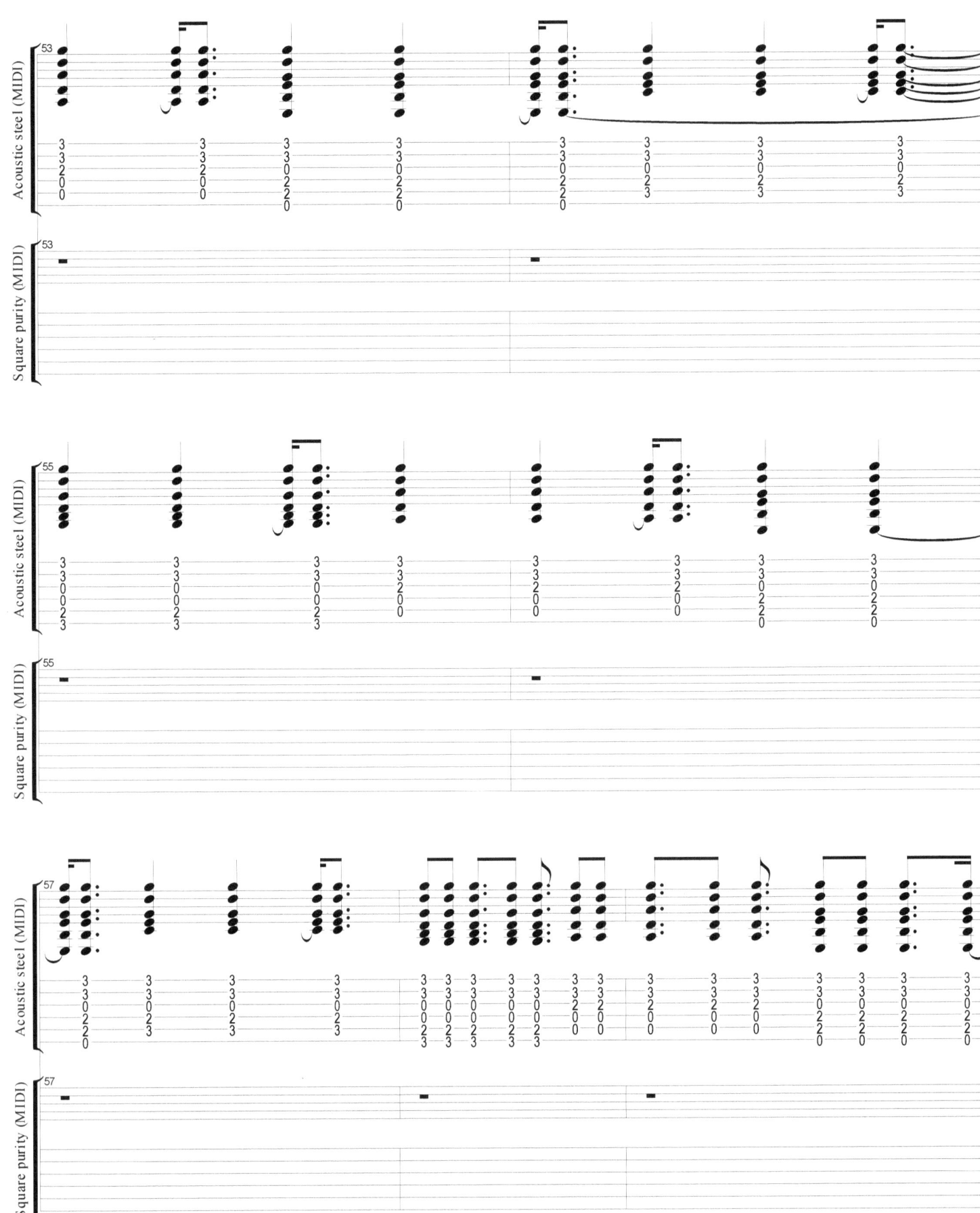

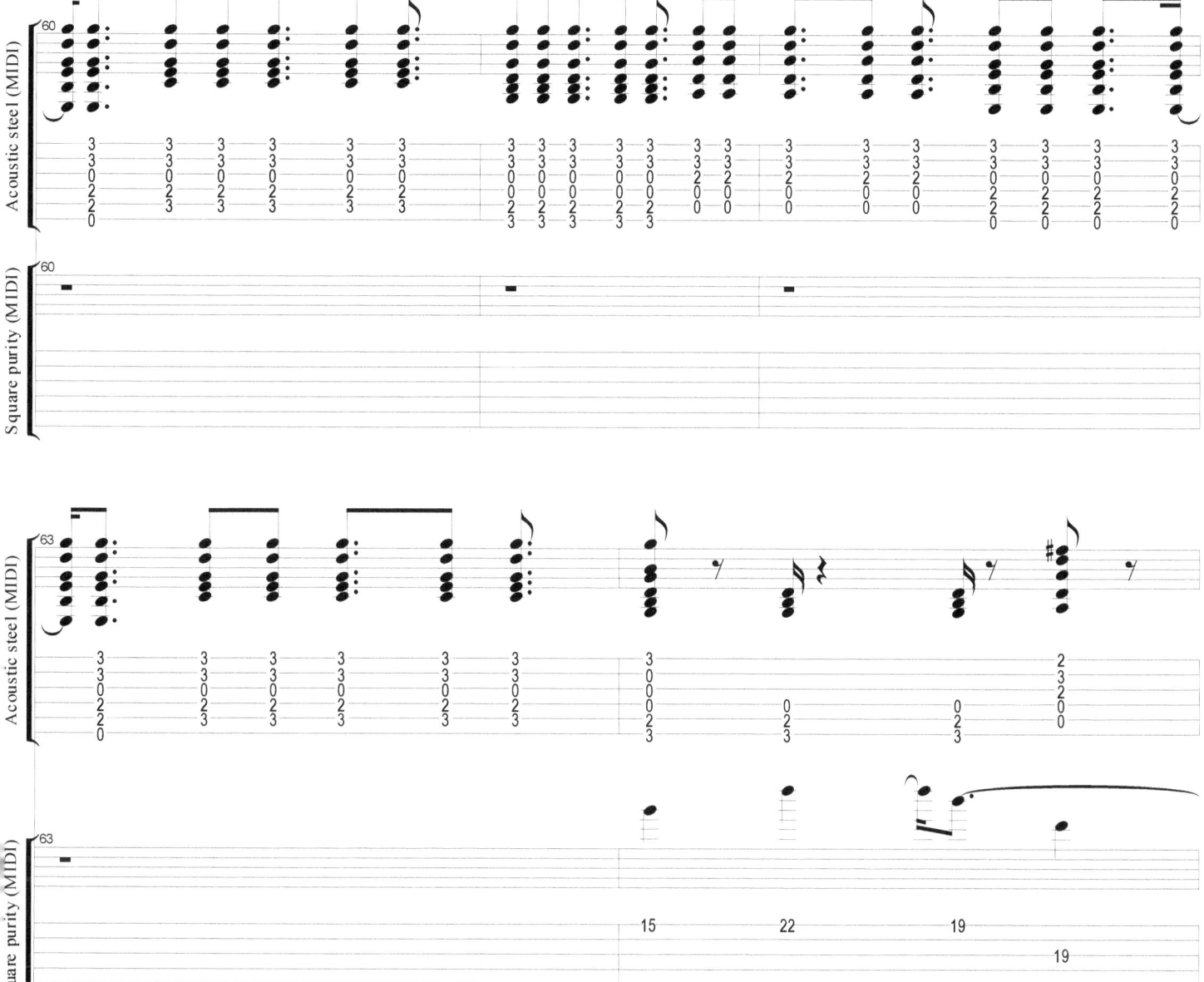

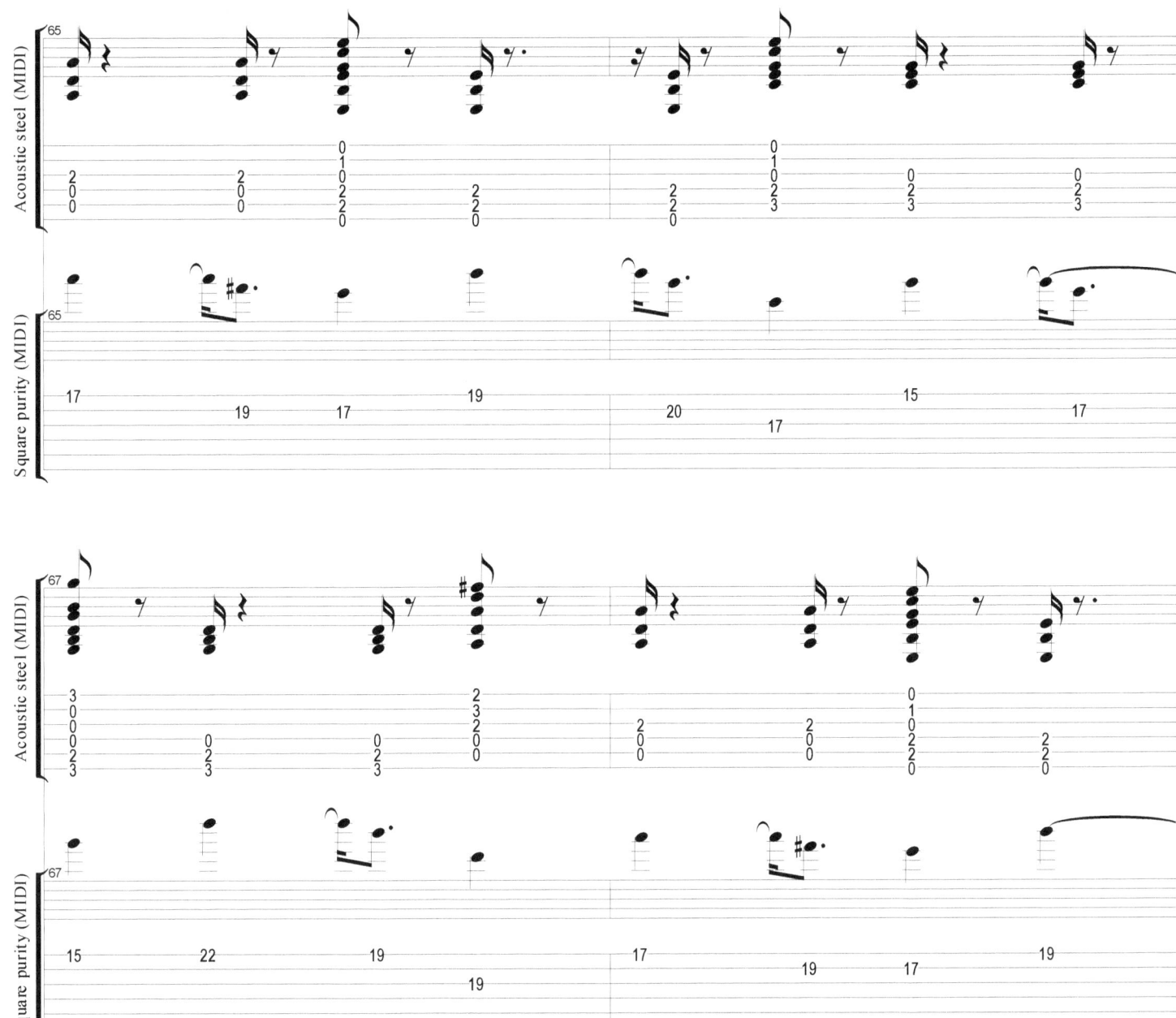

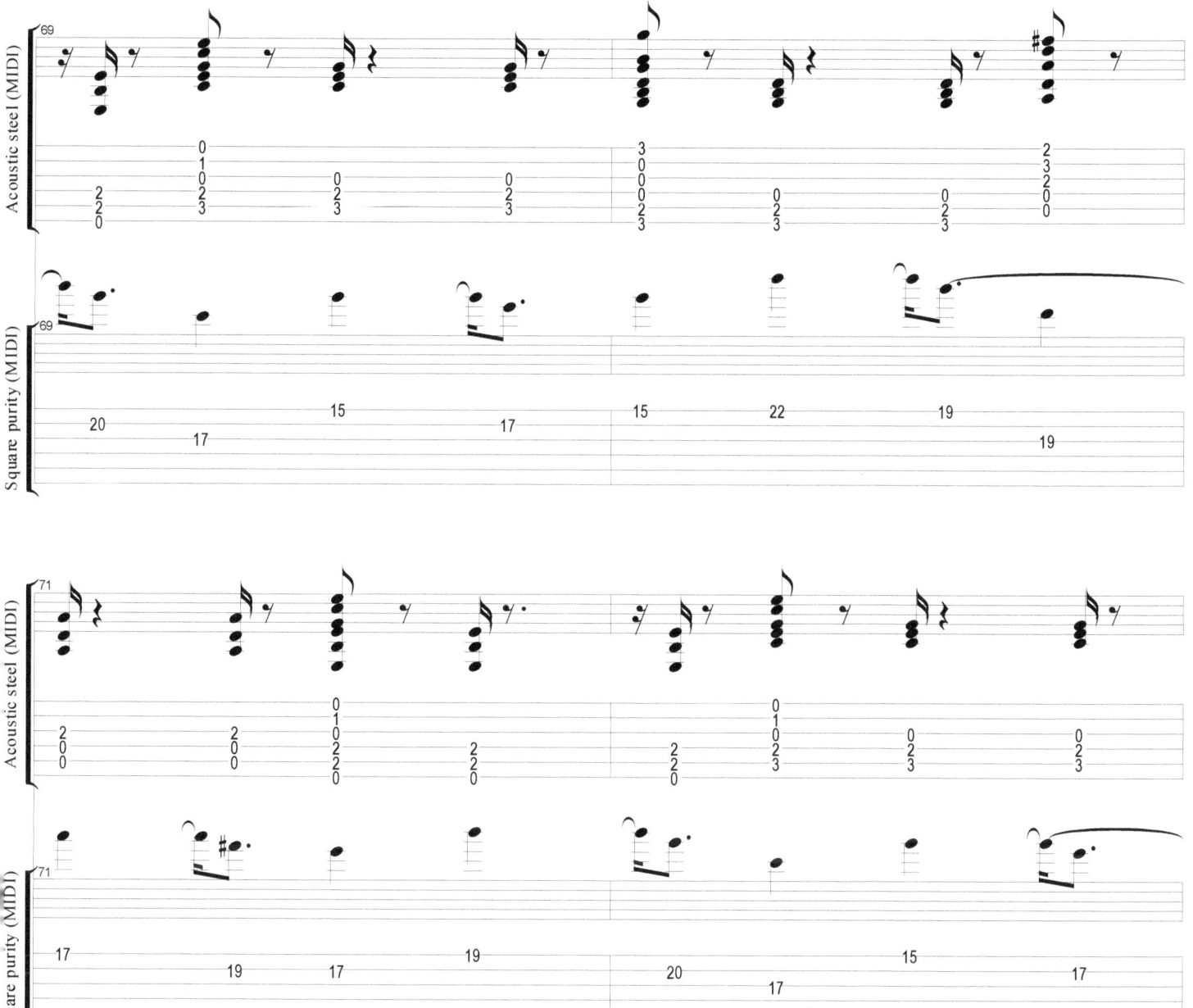

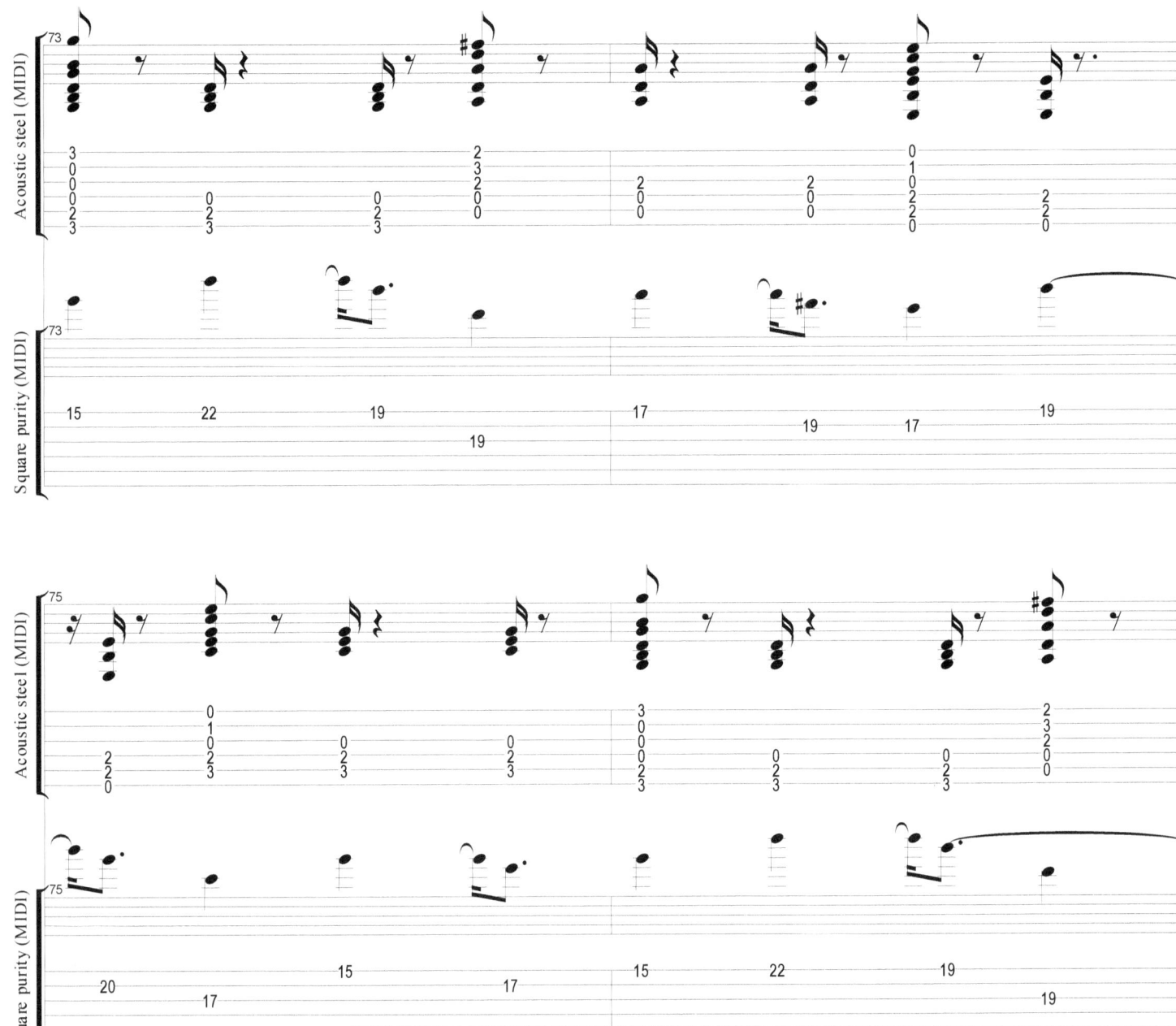

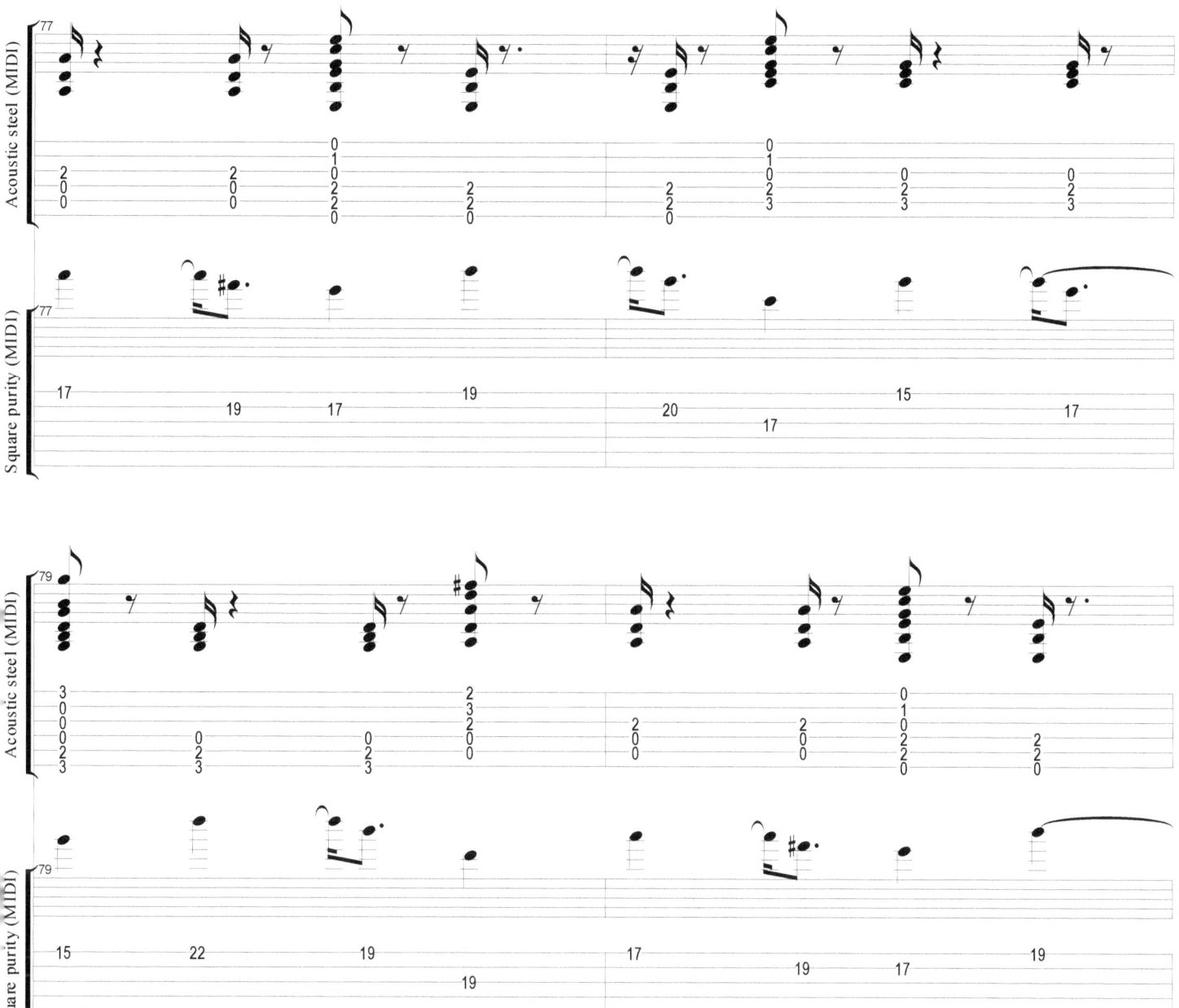

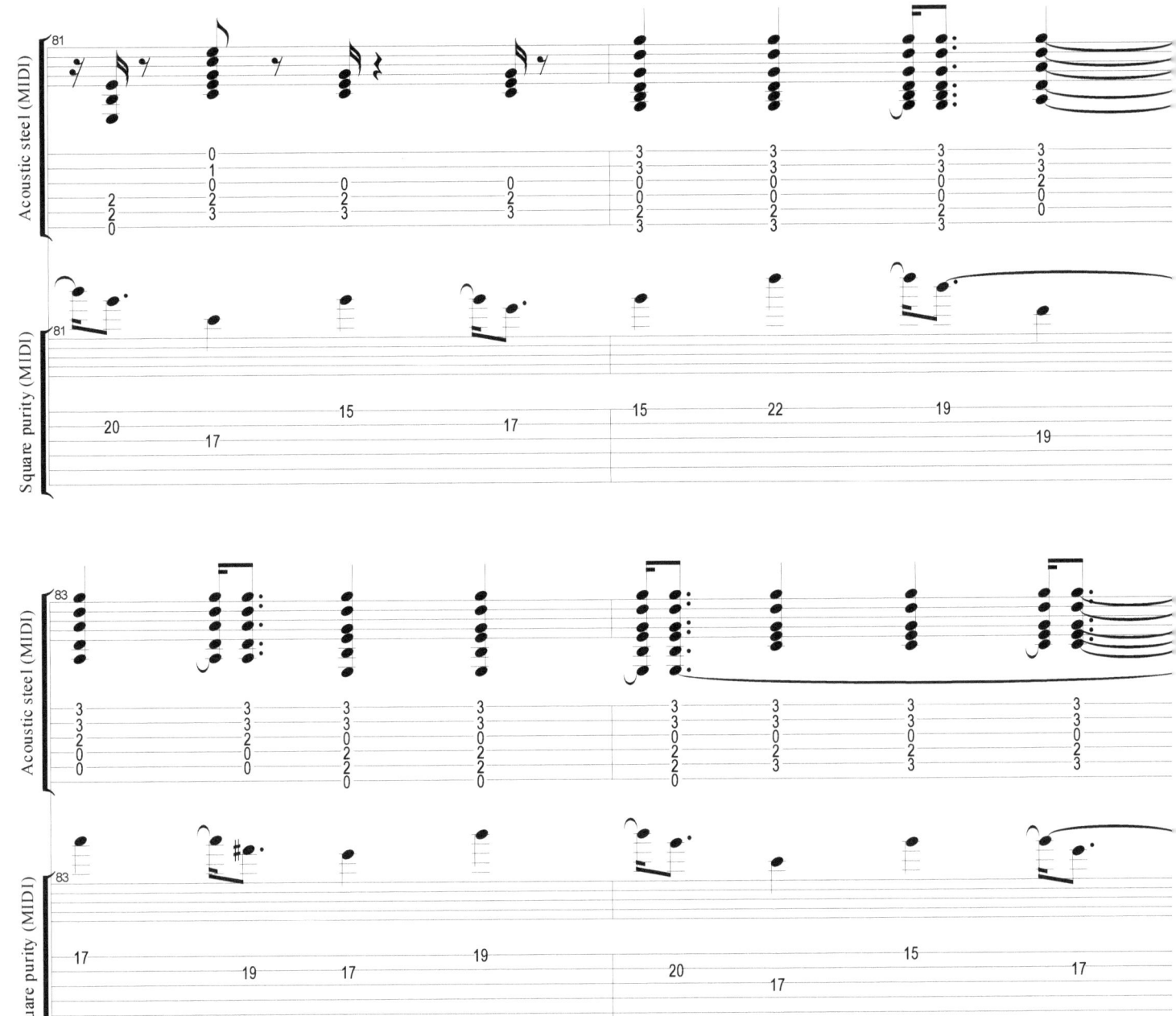

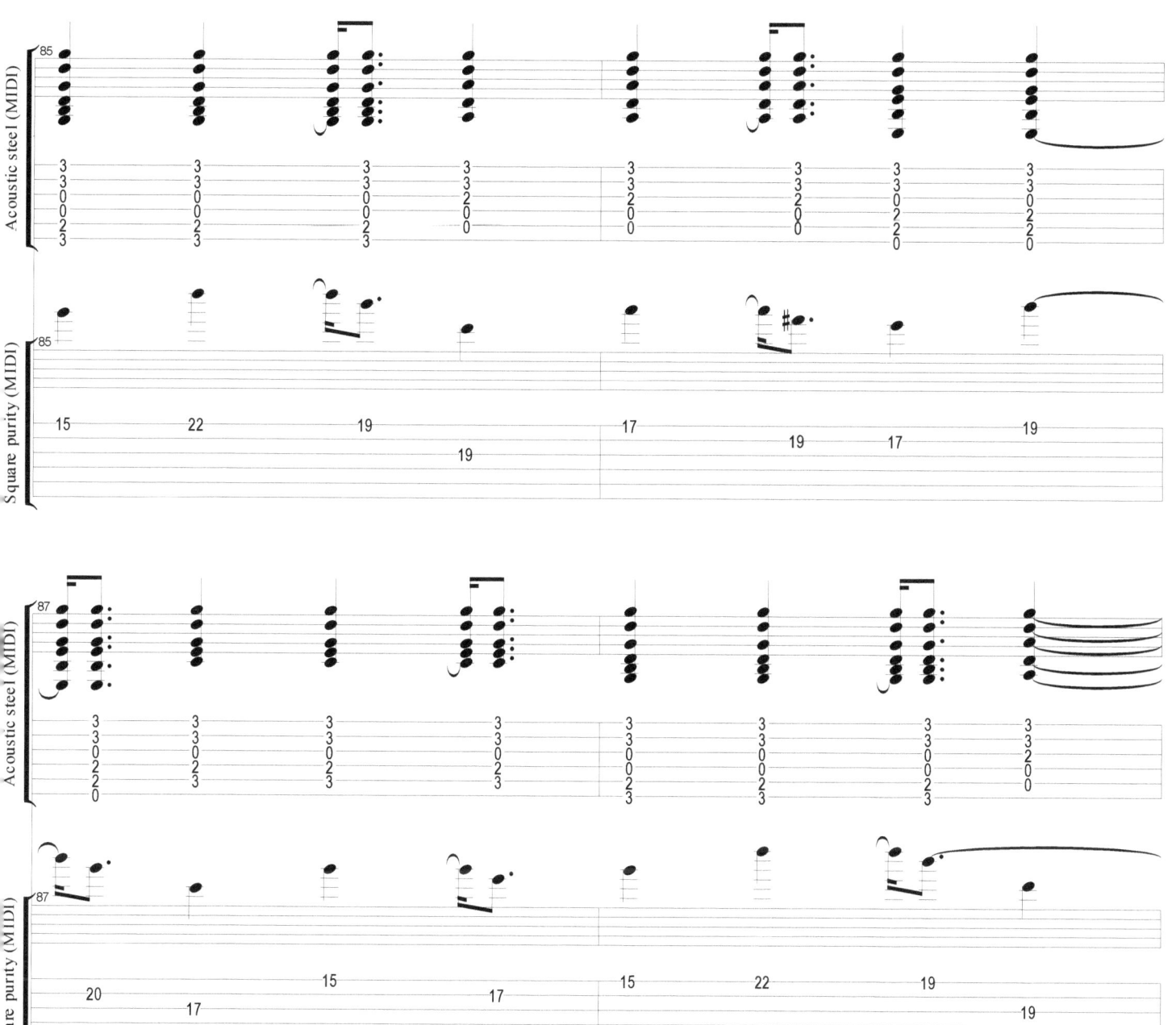

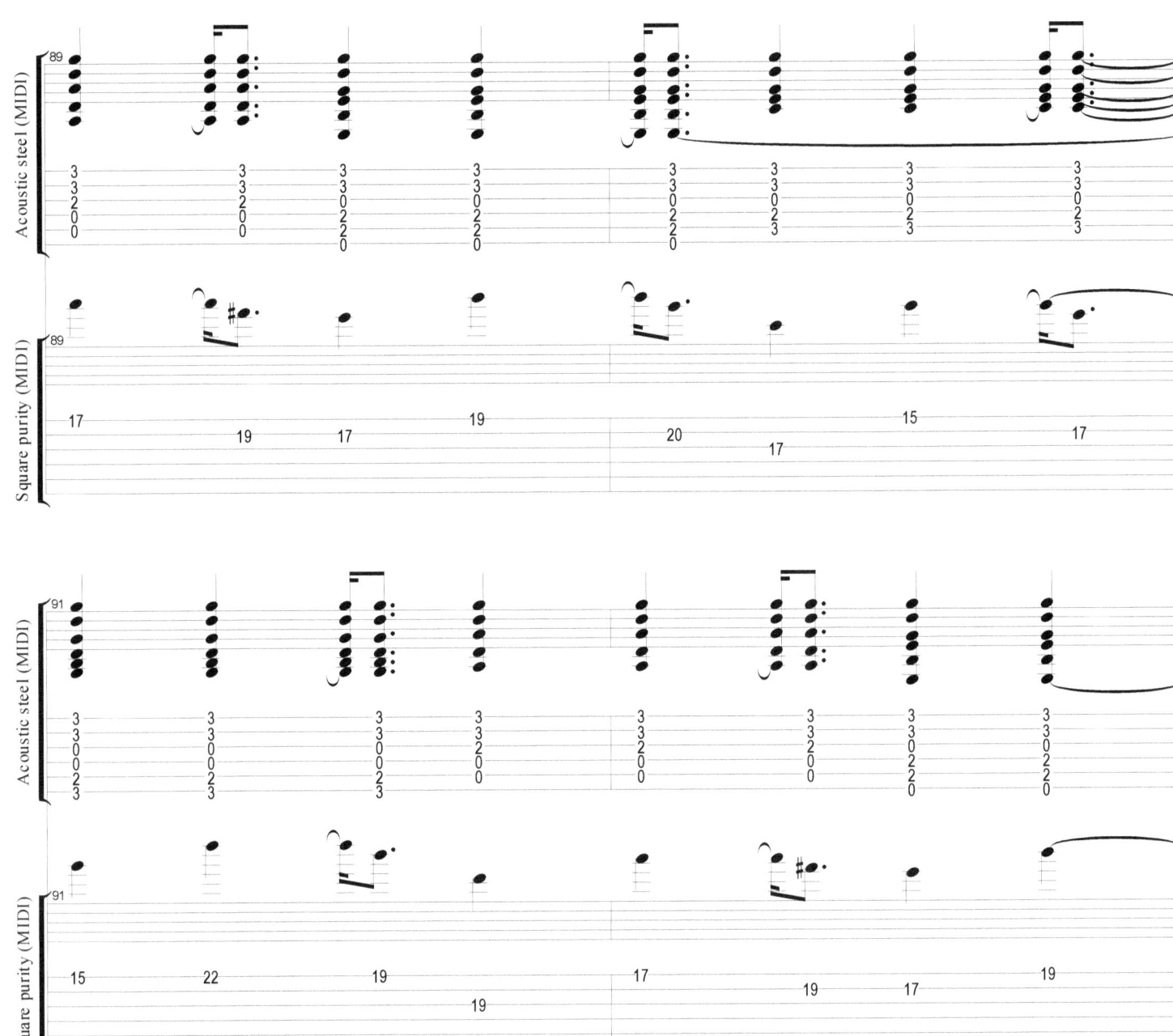

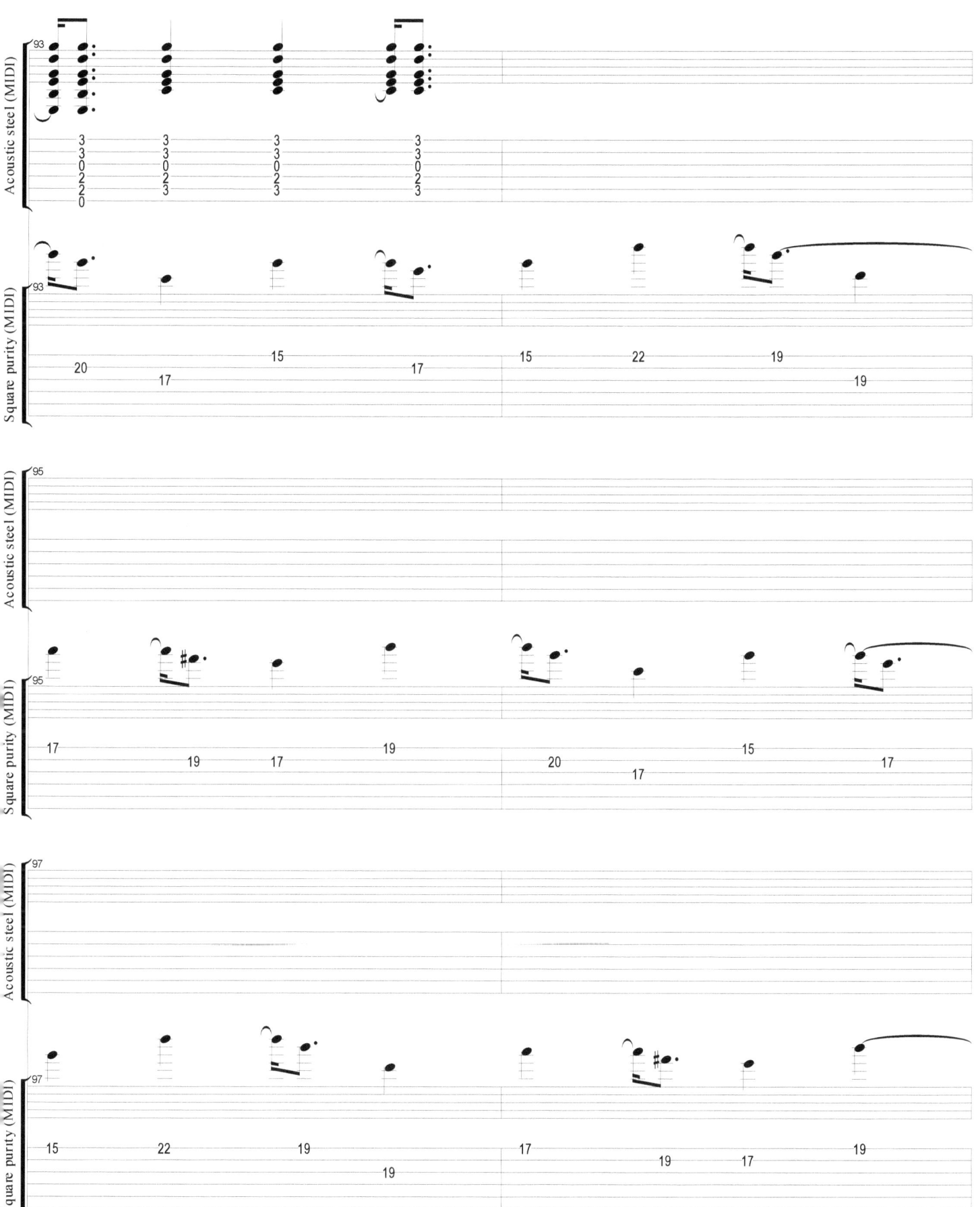

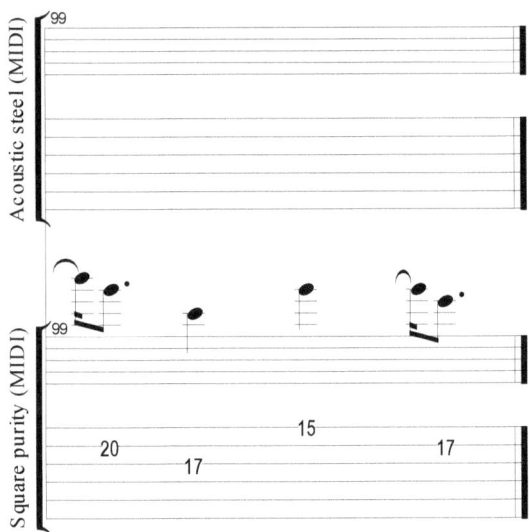

Last Night

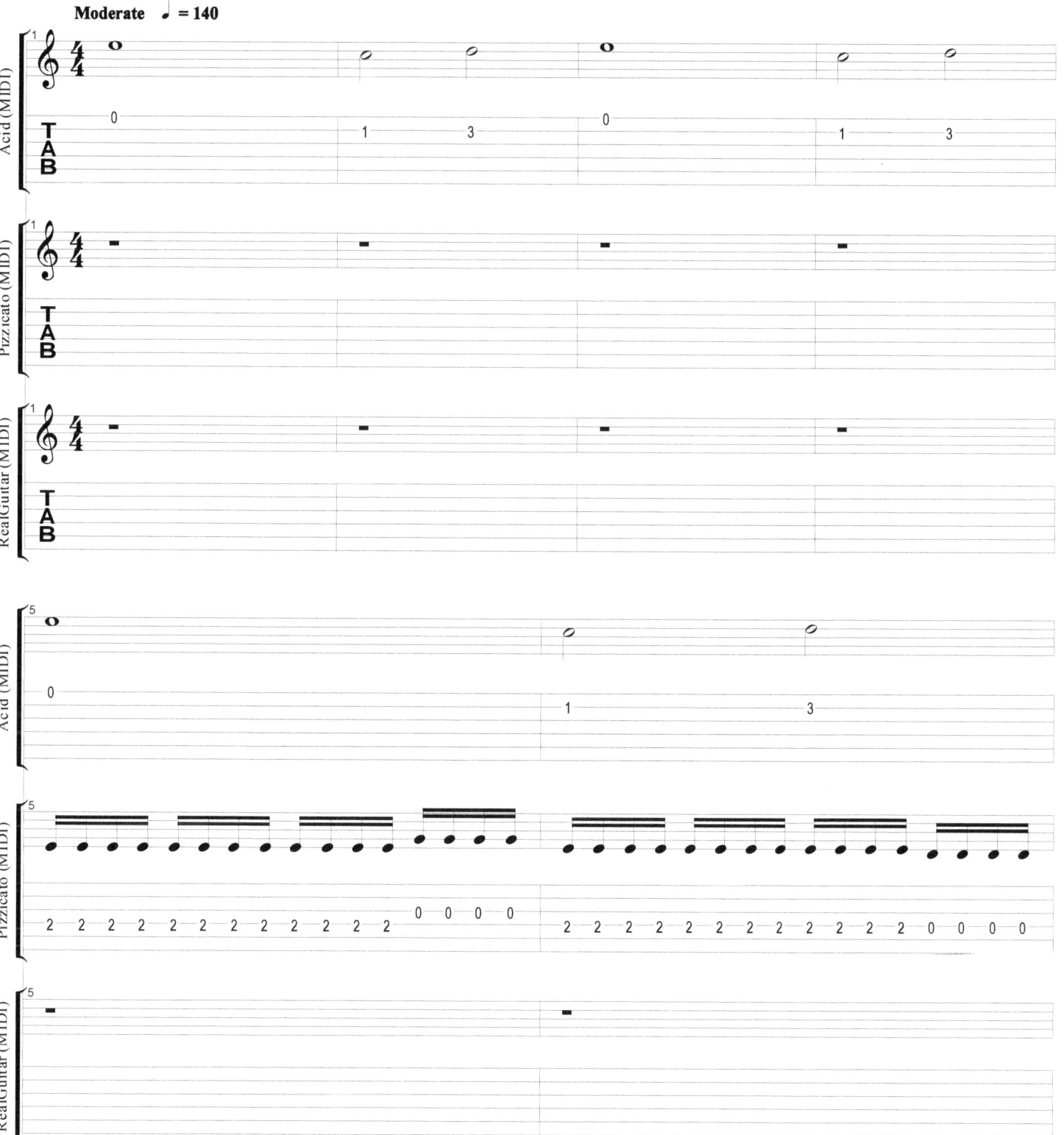

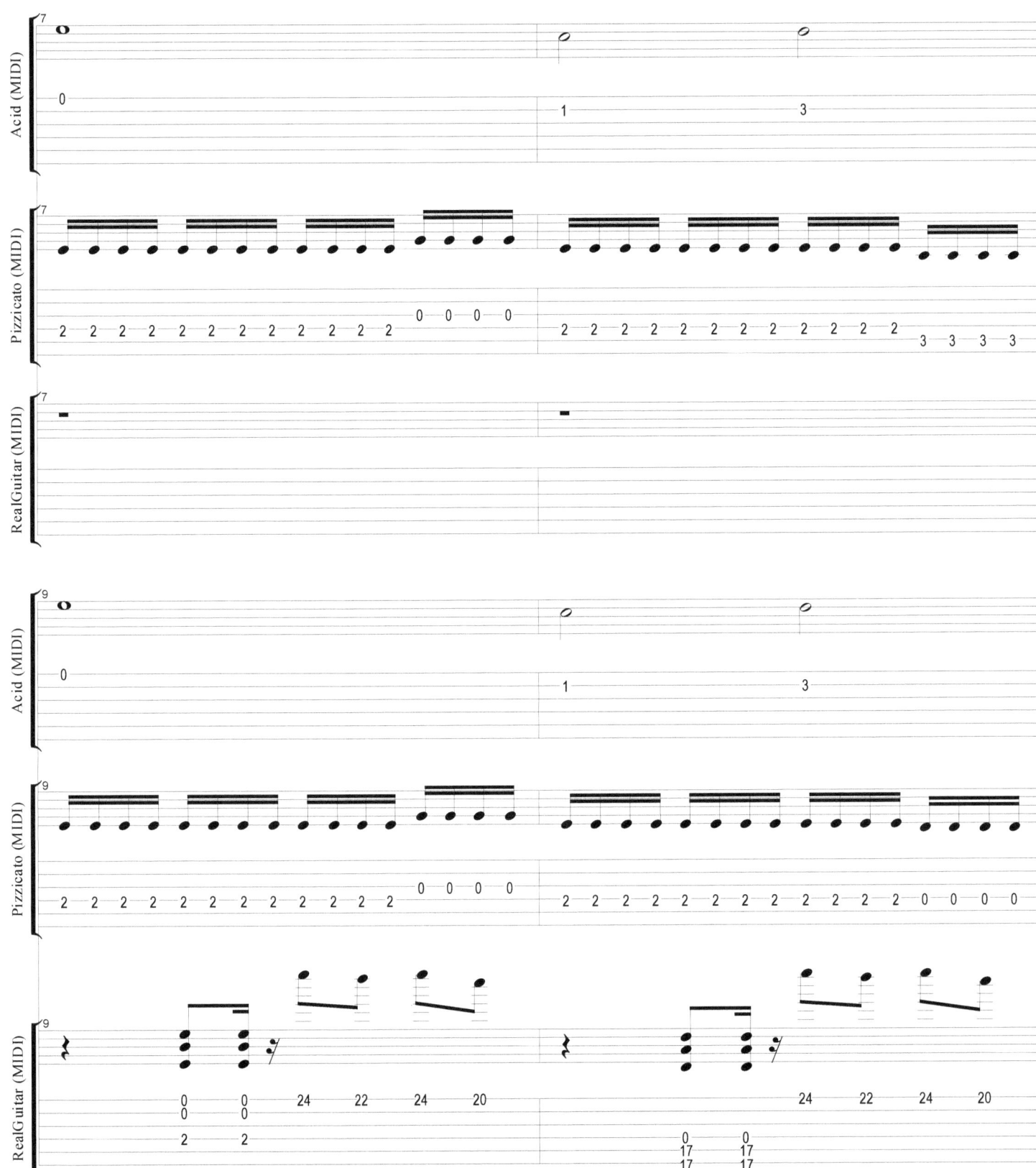

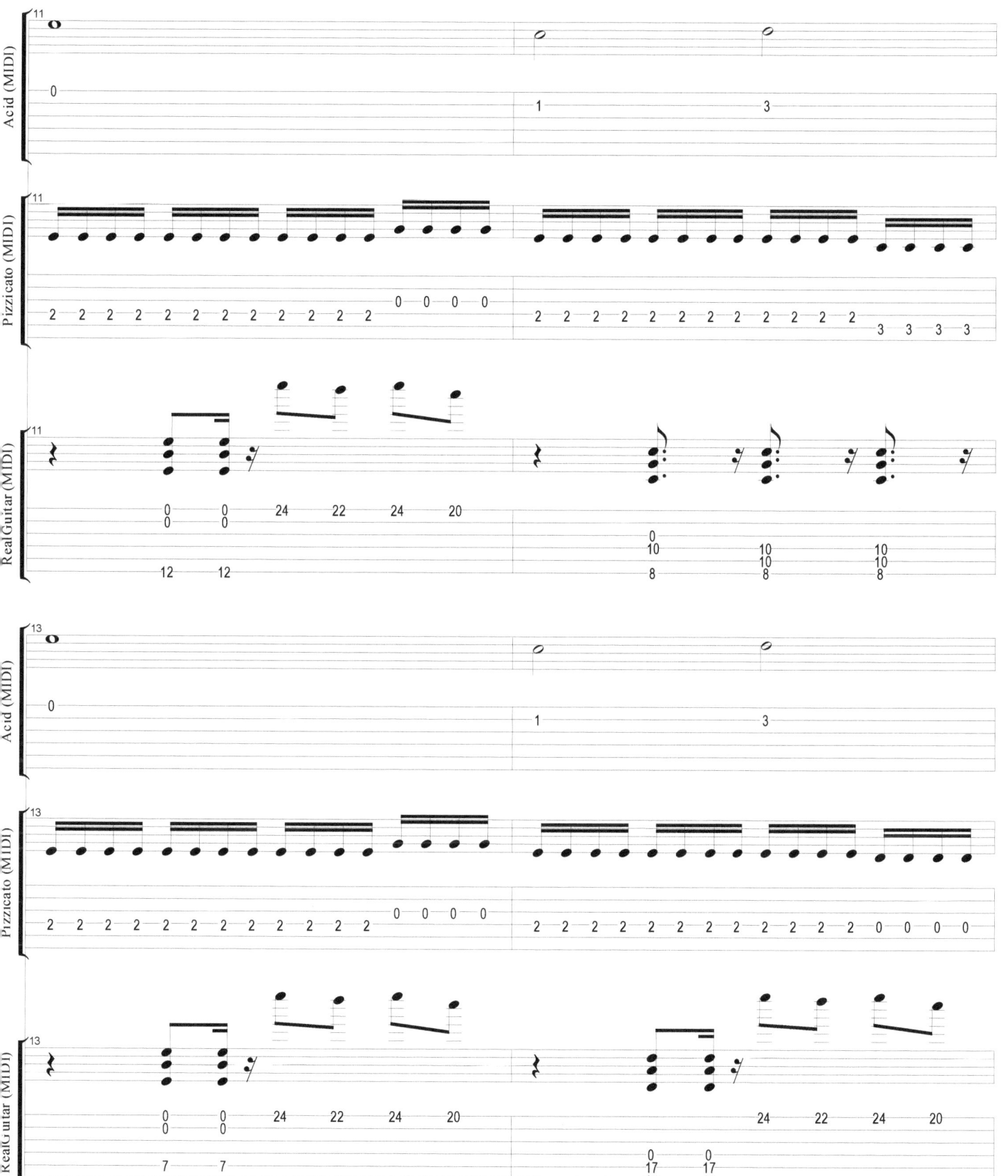

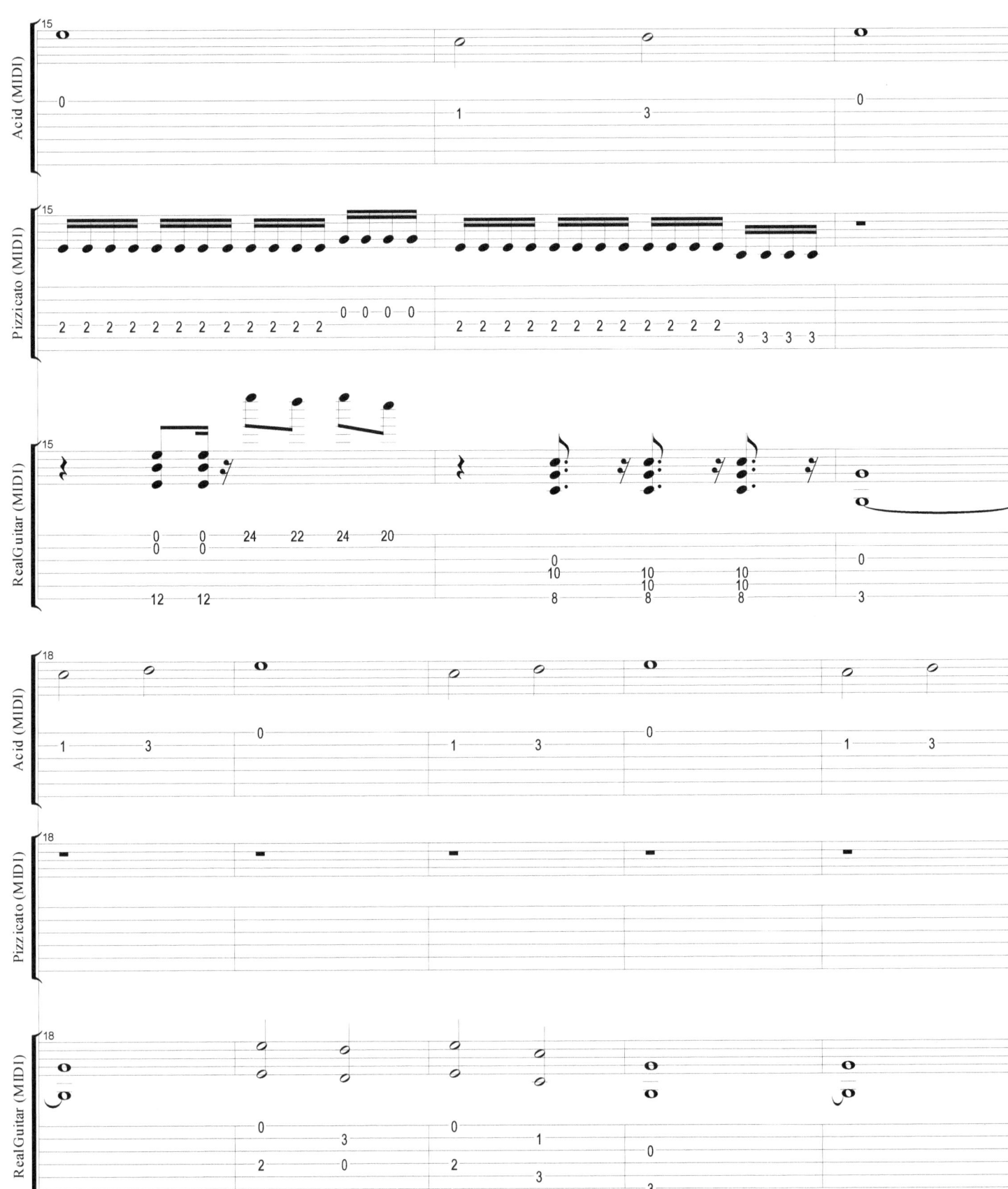

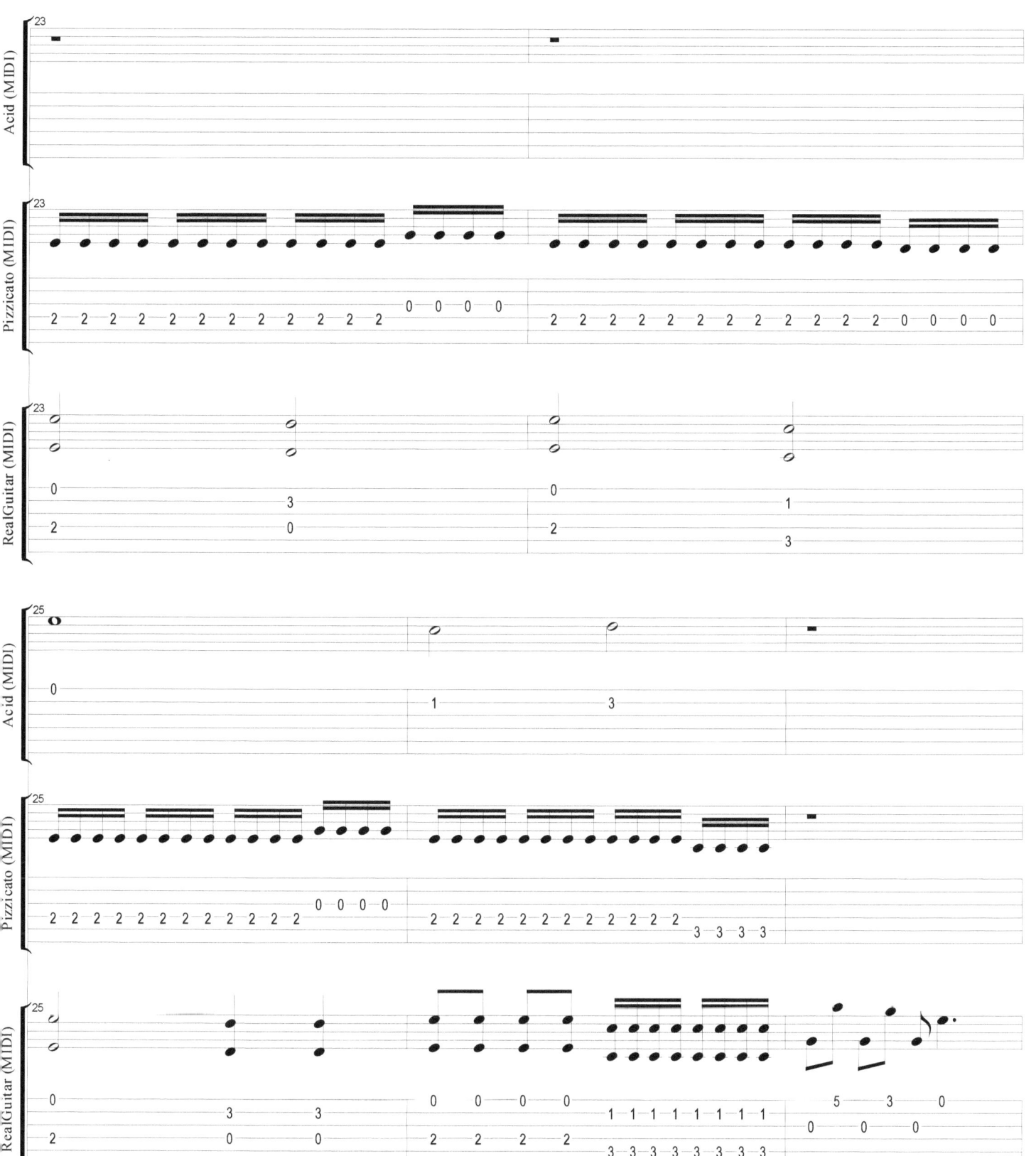

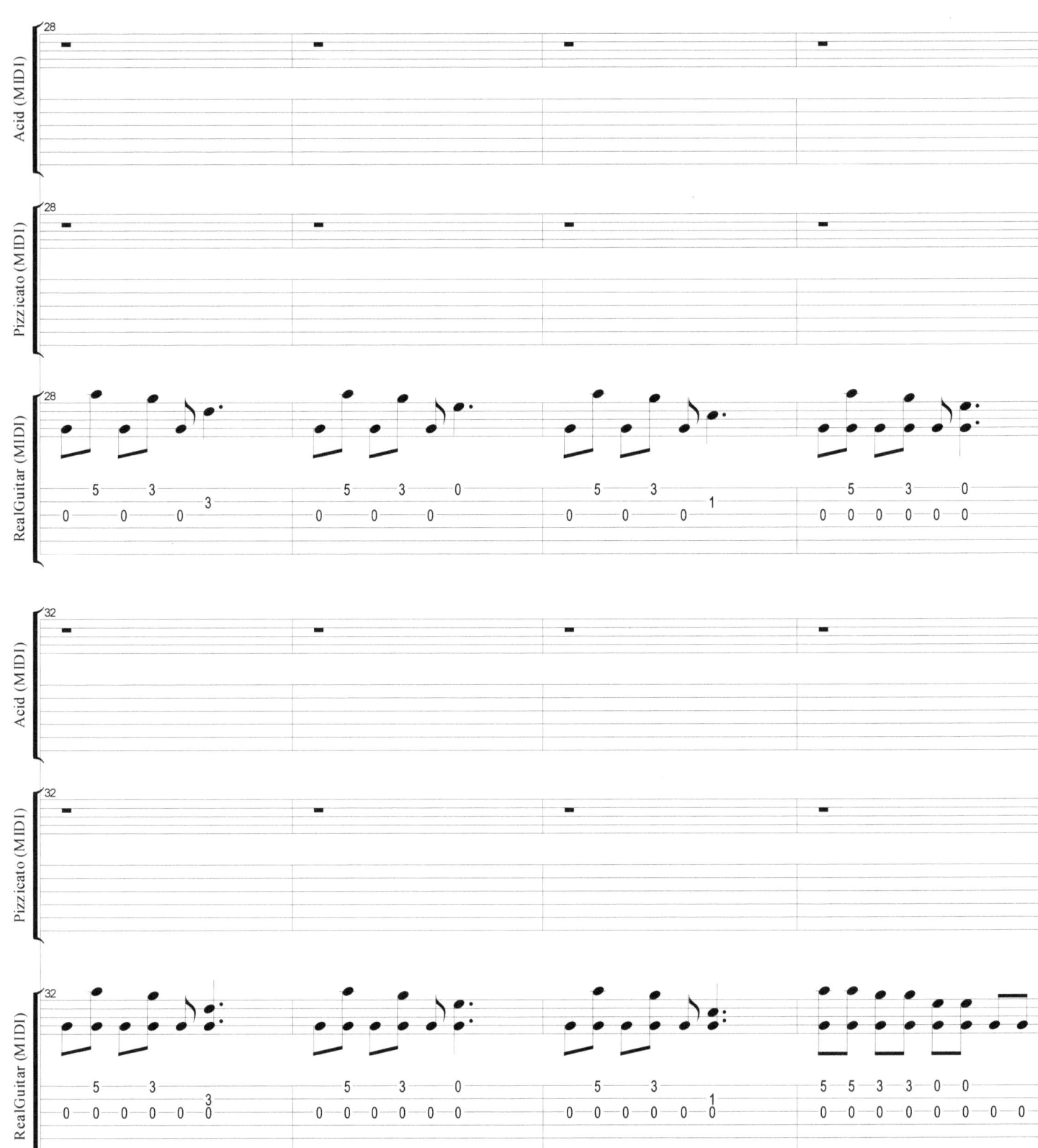

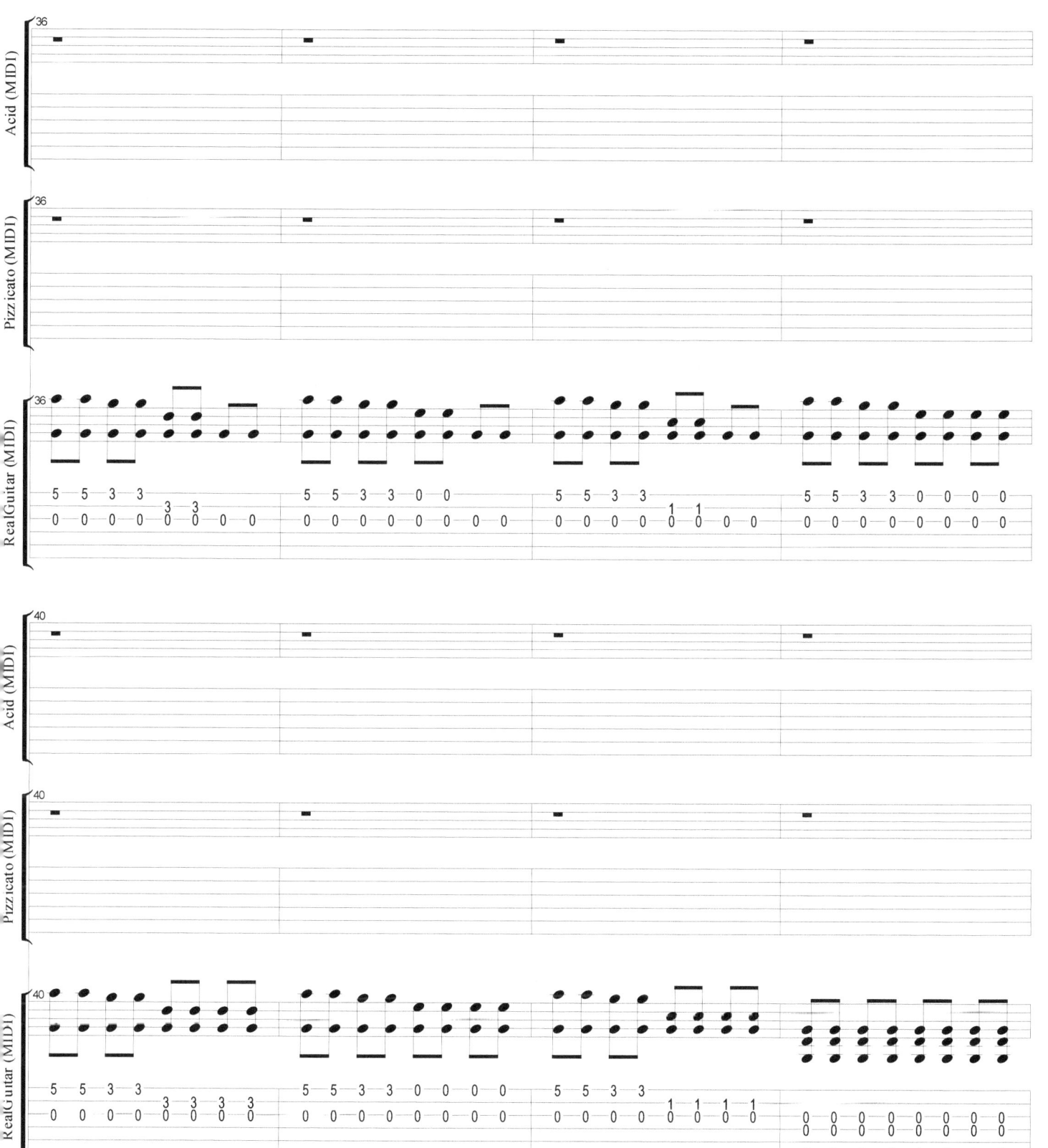

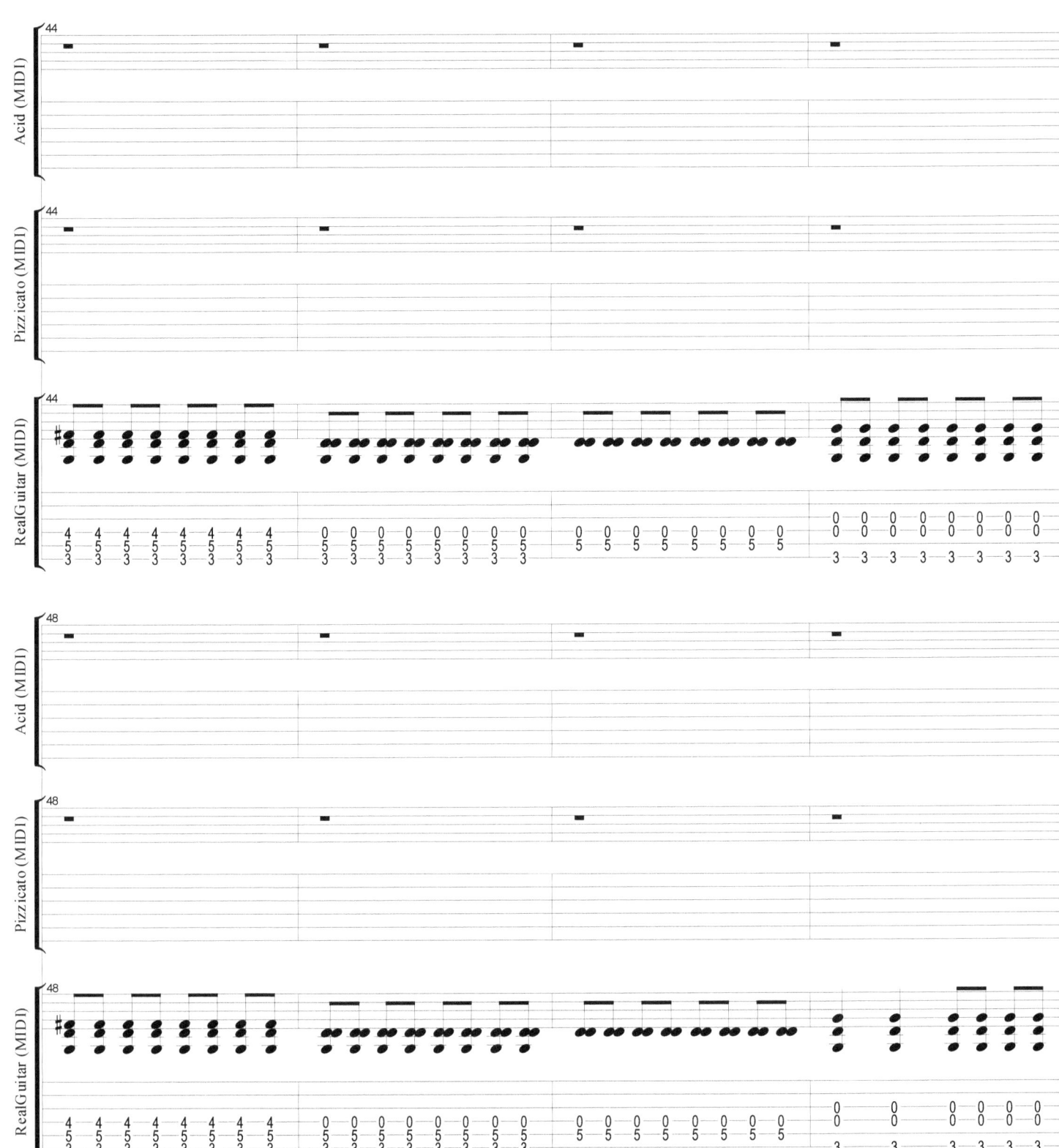

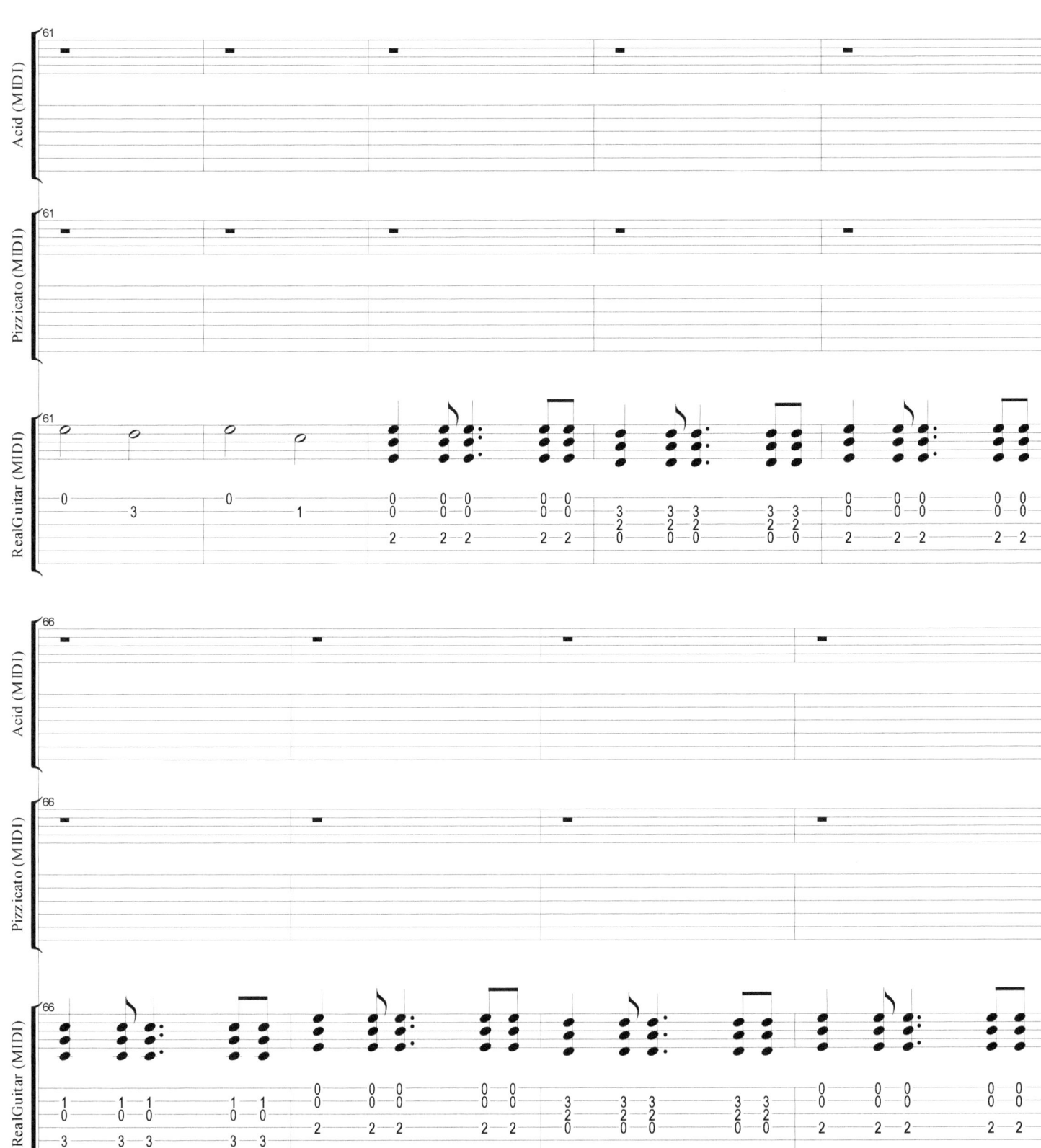

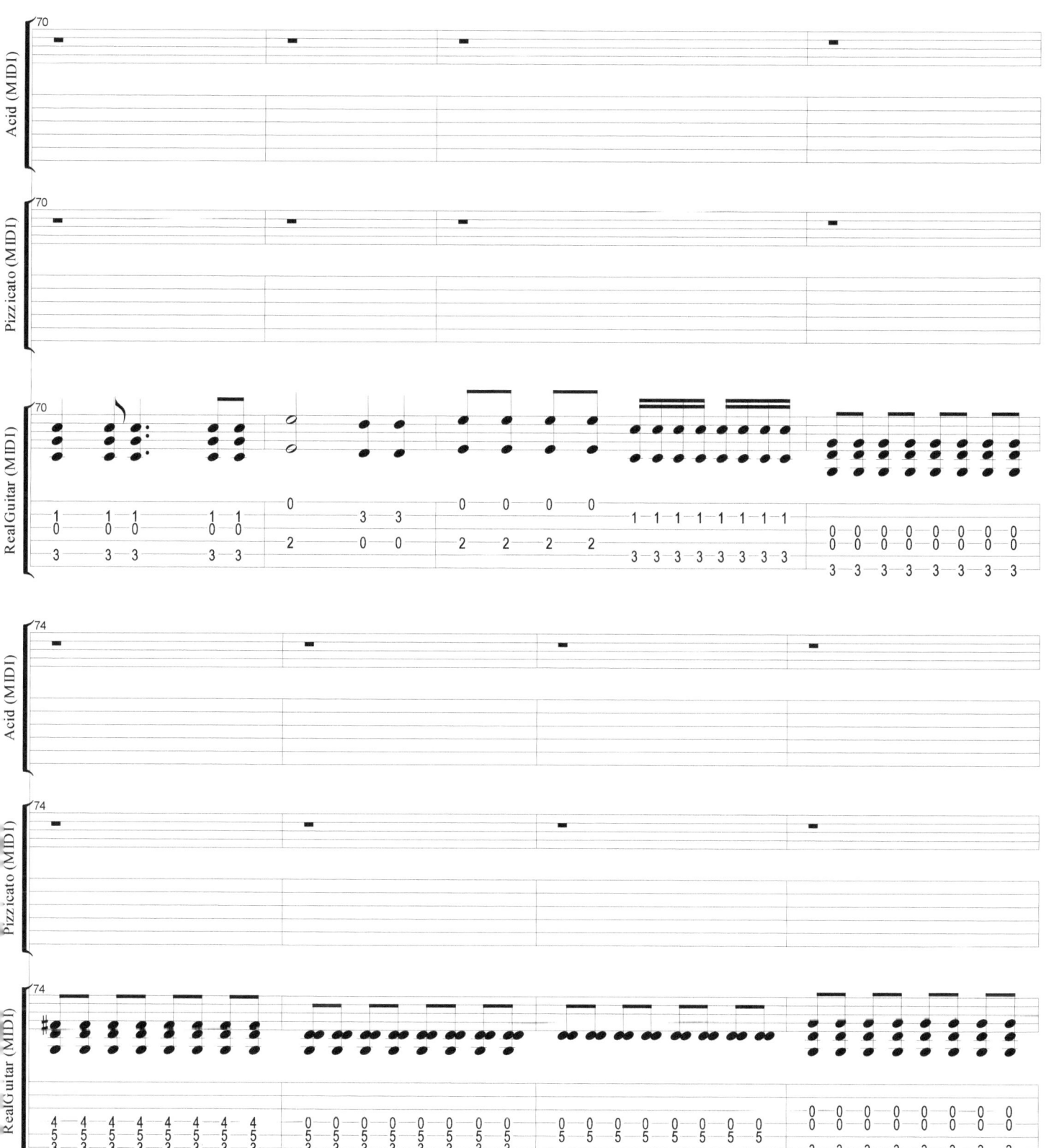

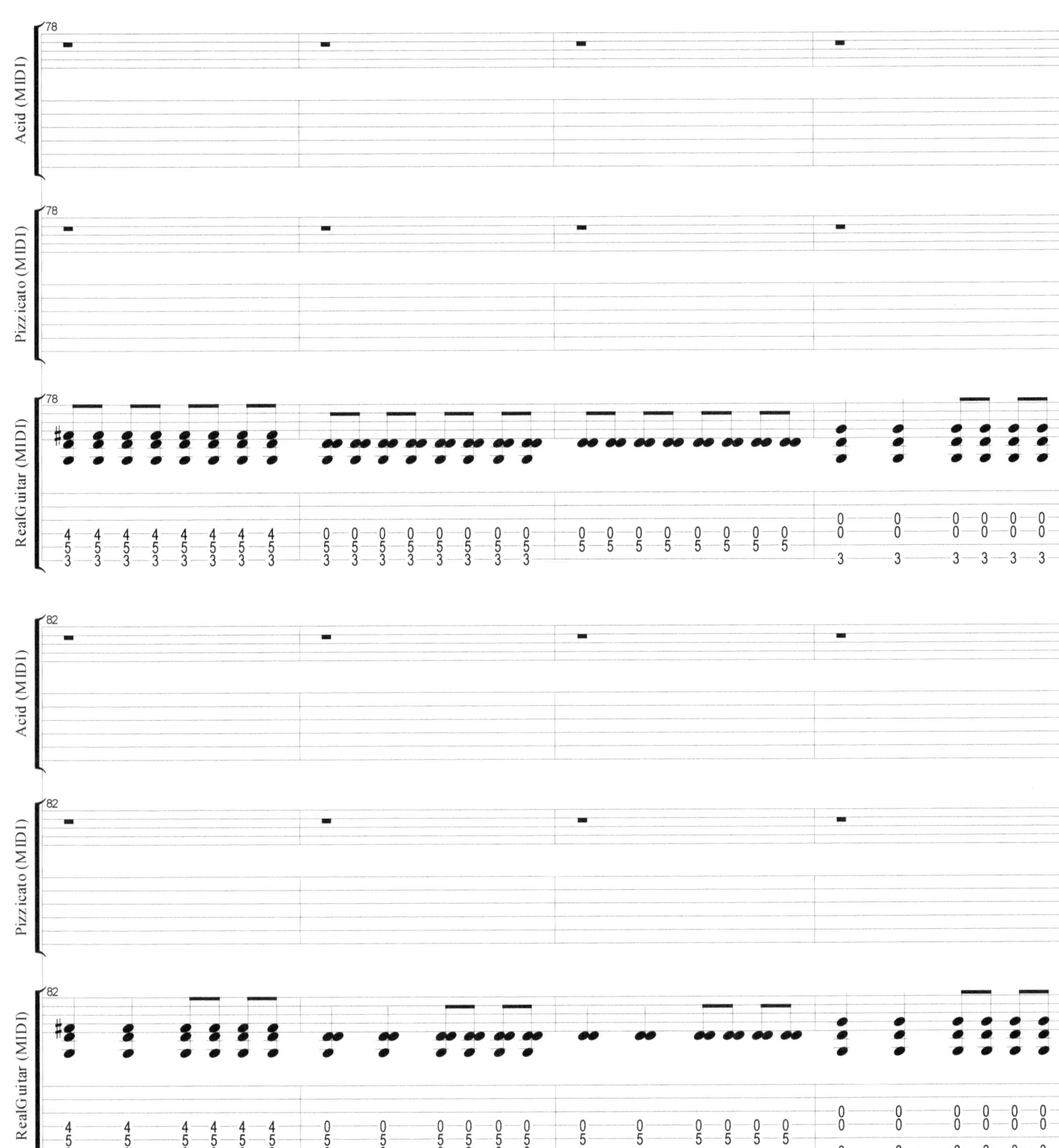

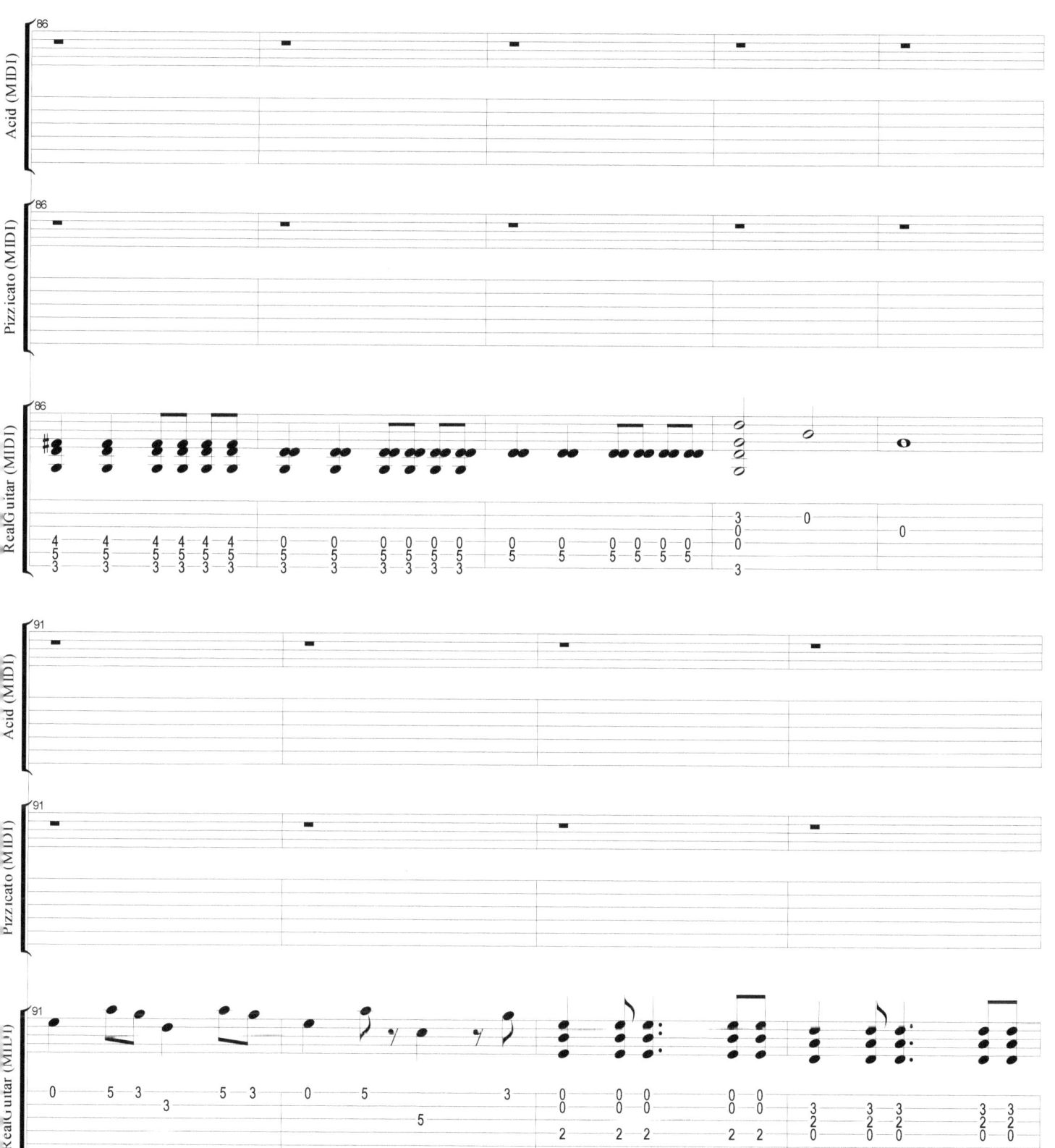

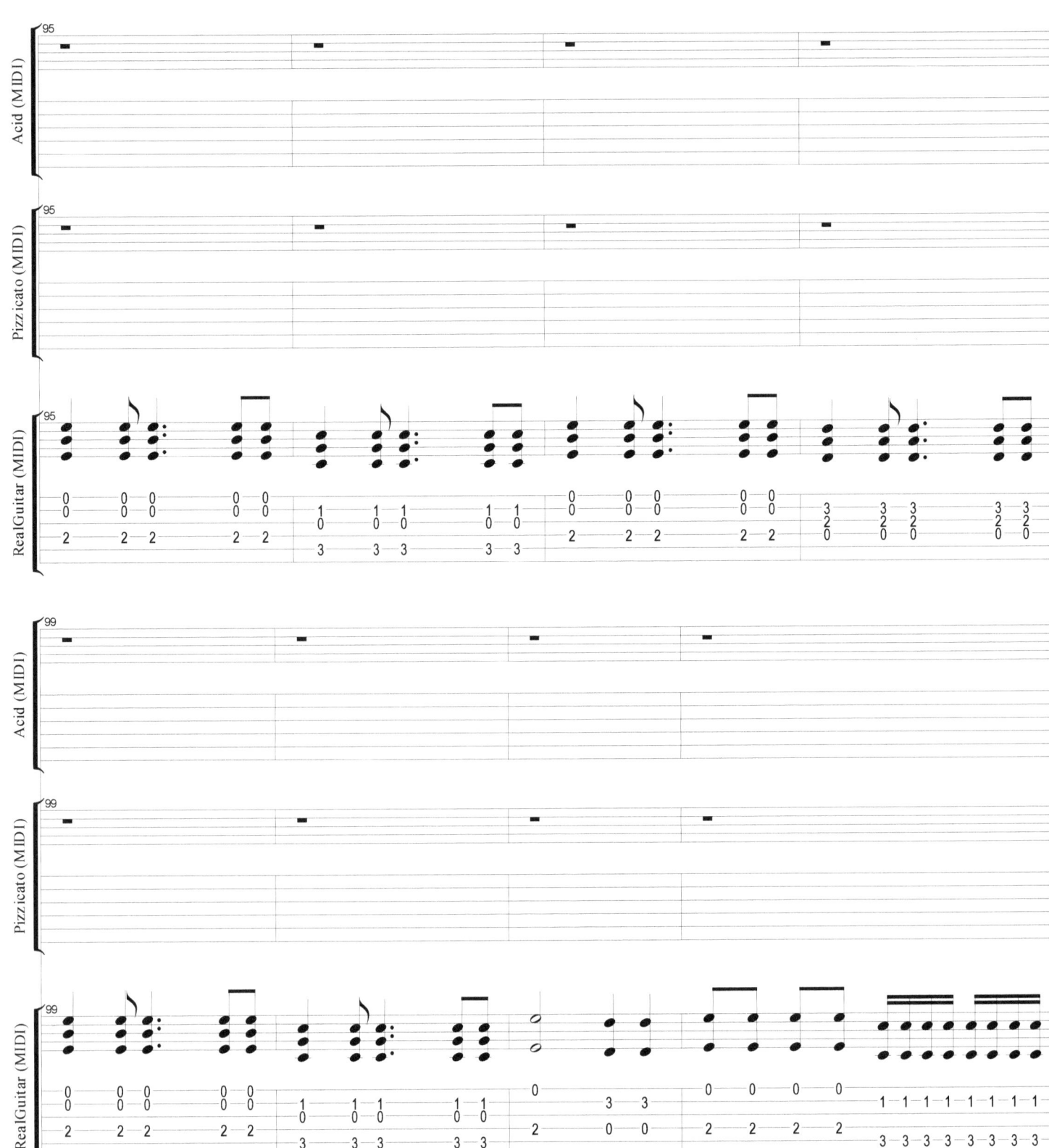

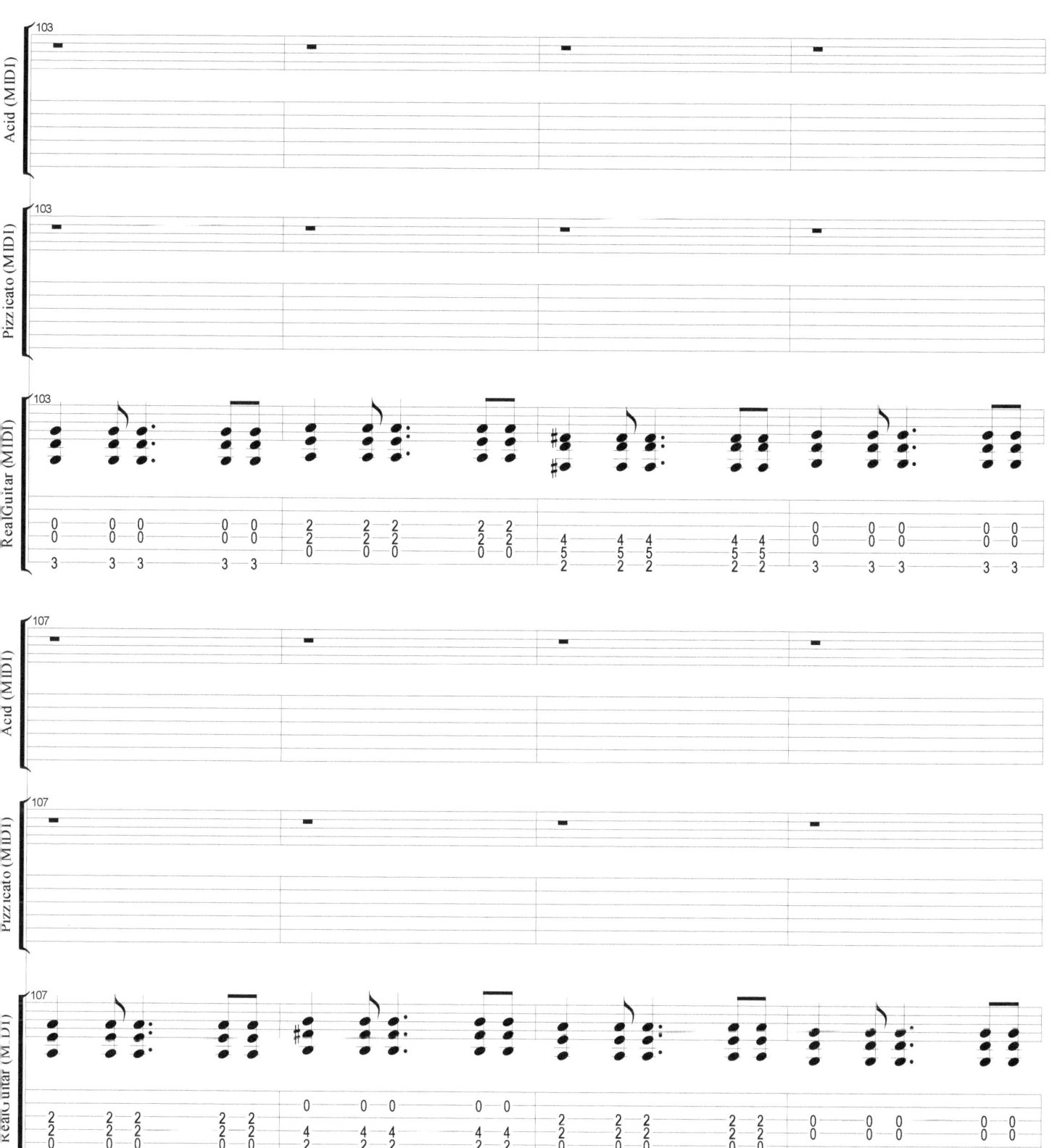

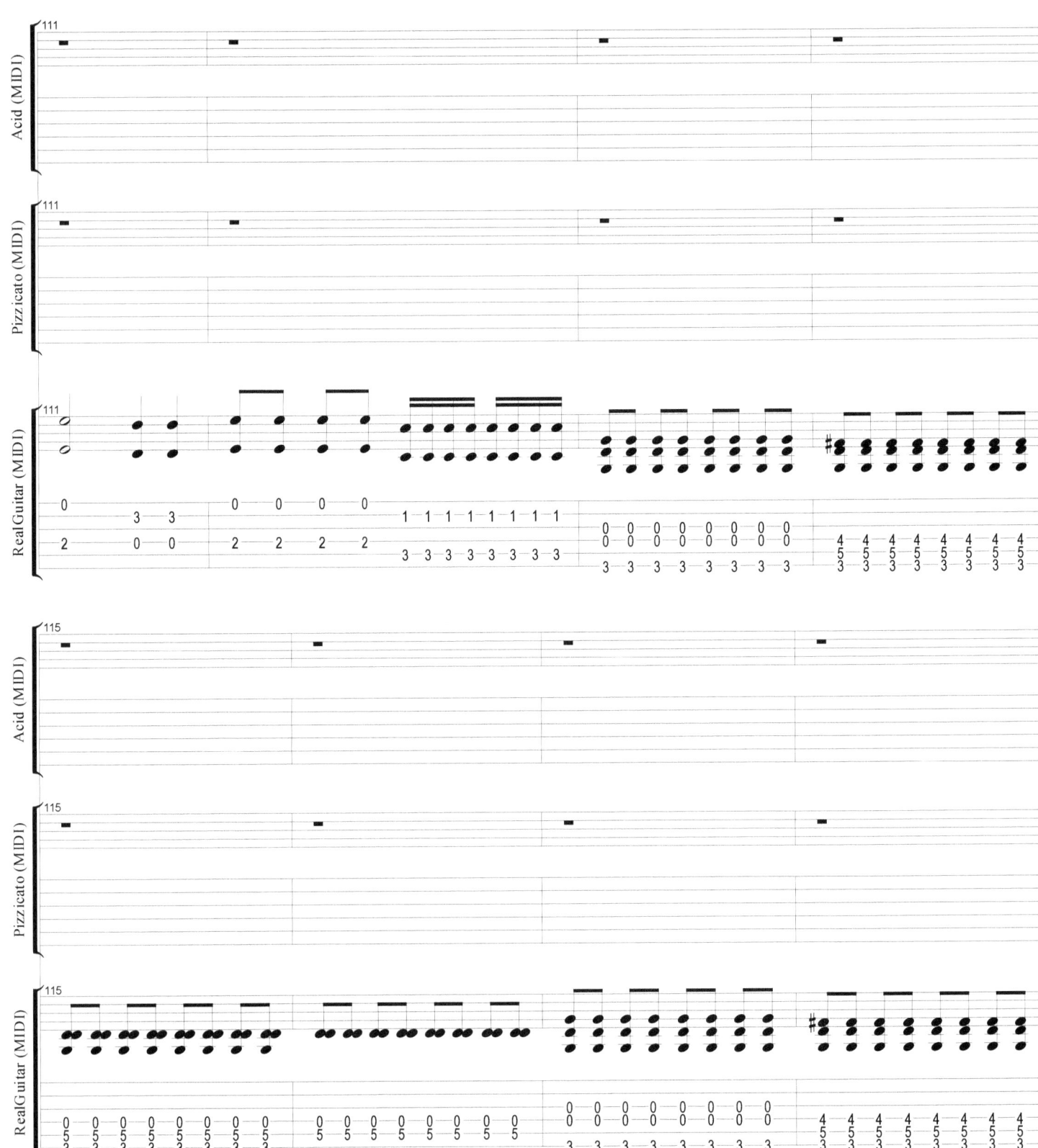

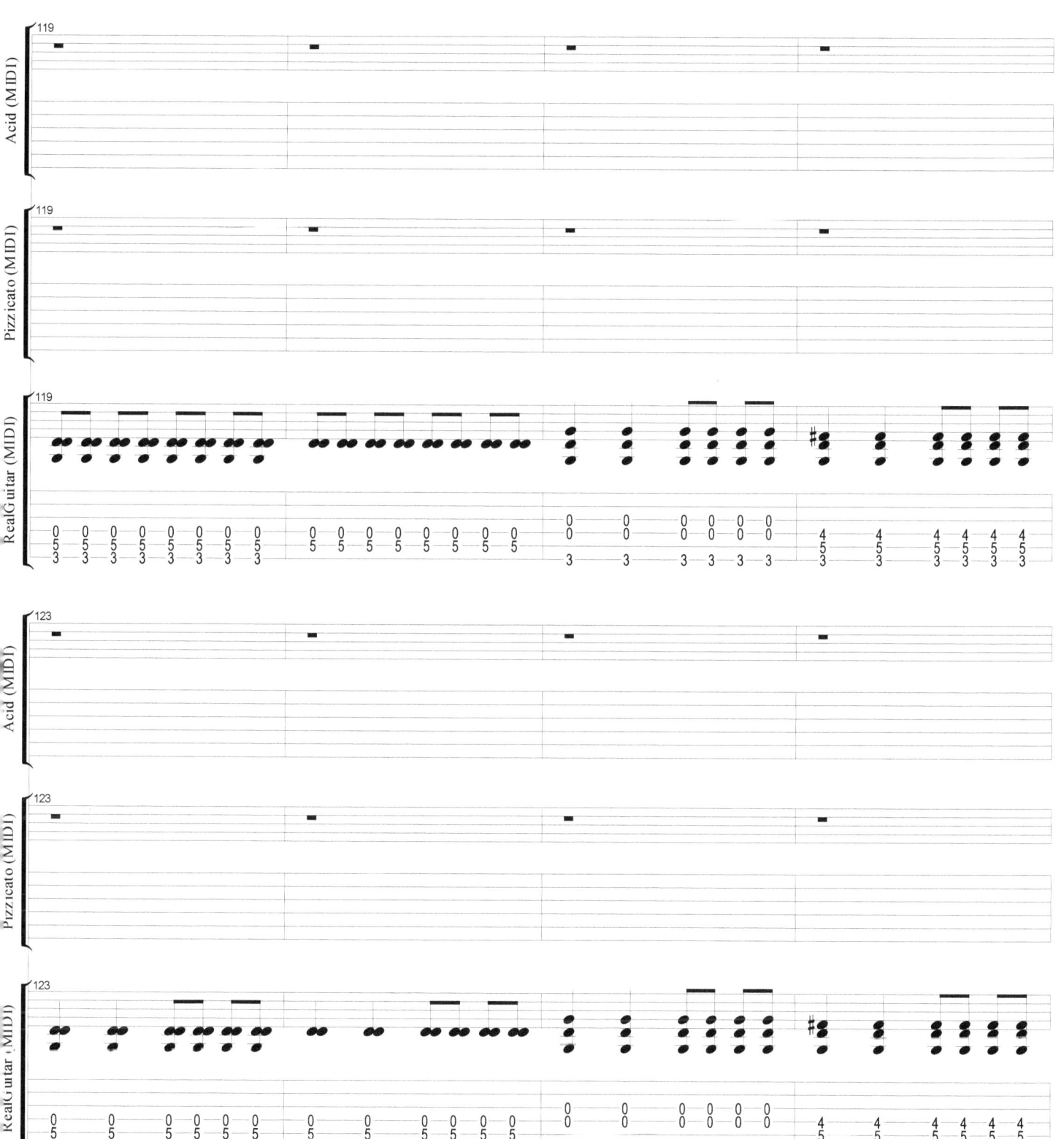

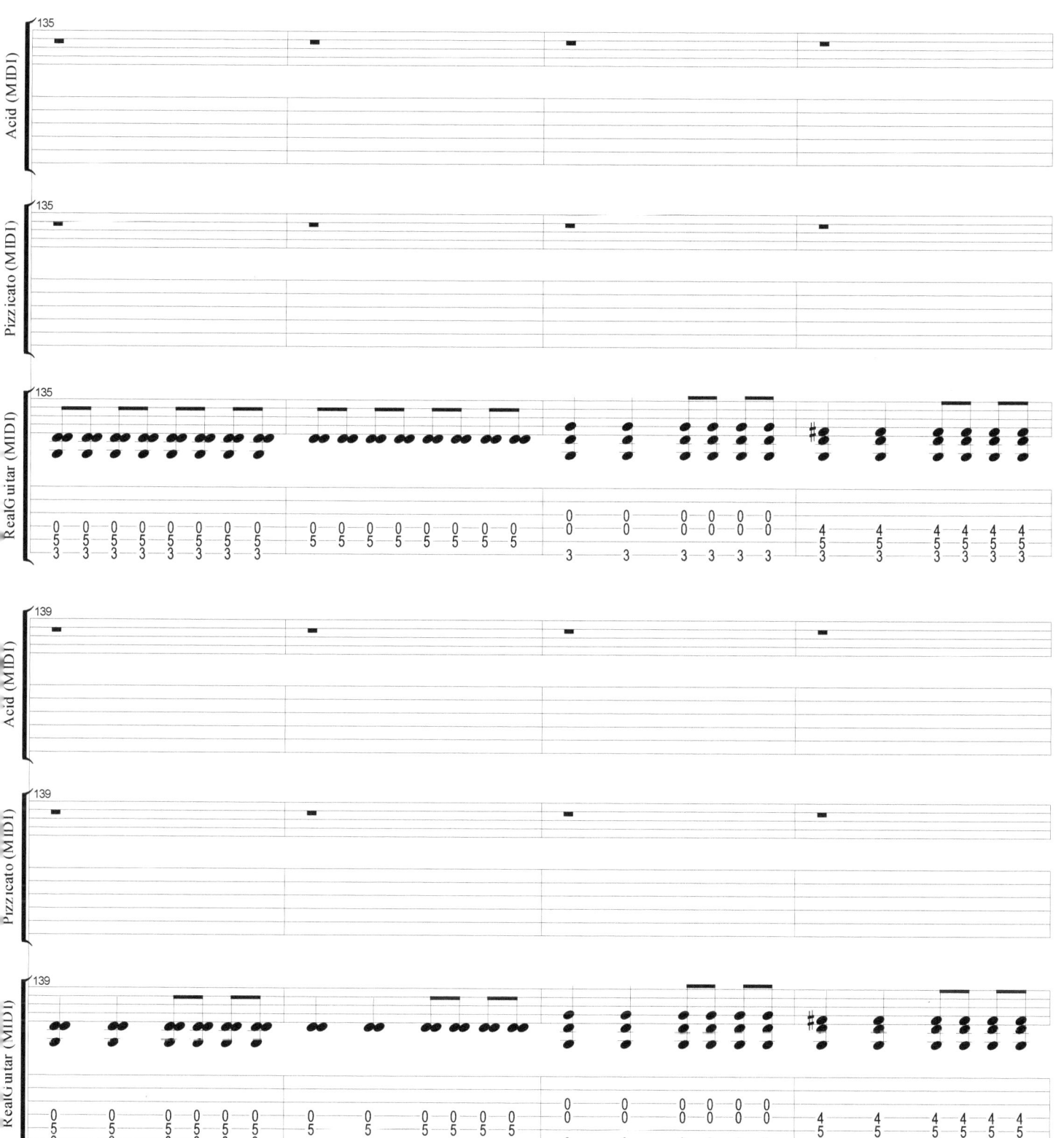

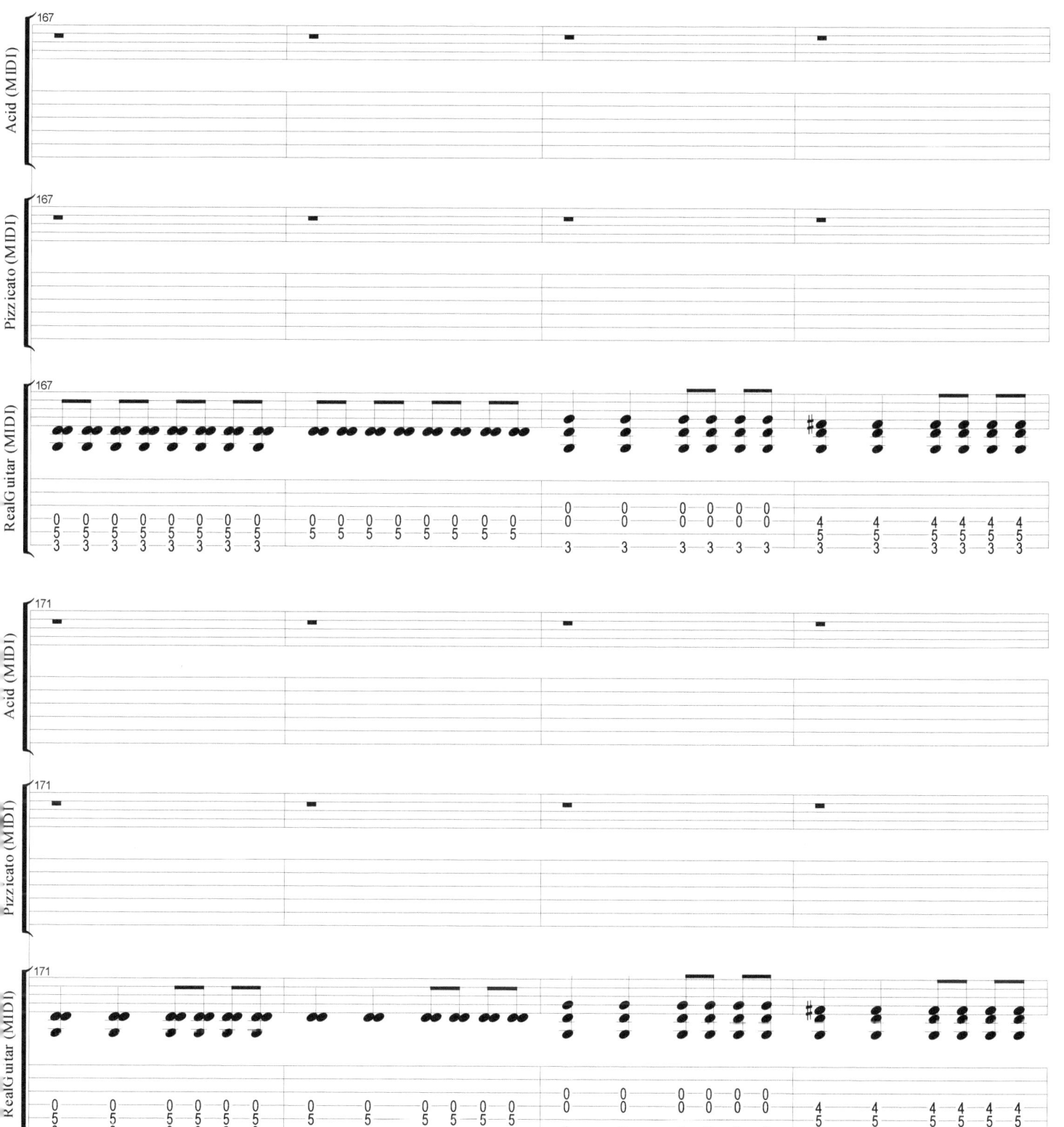

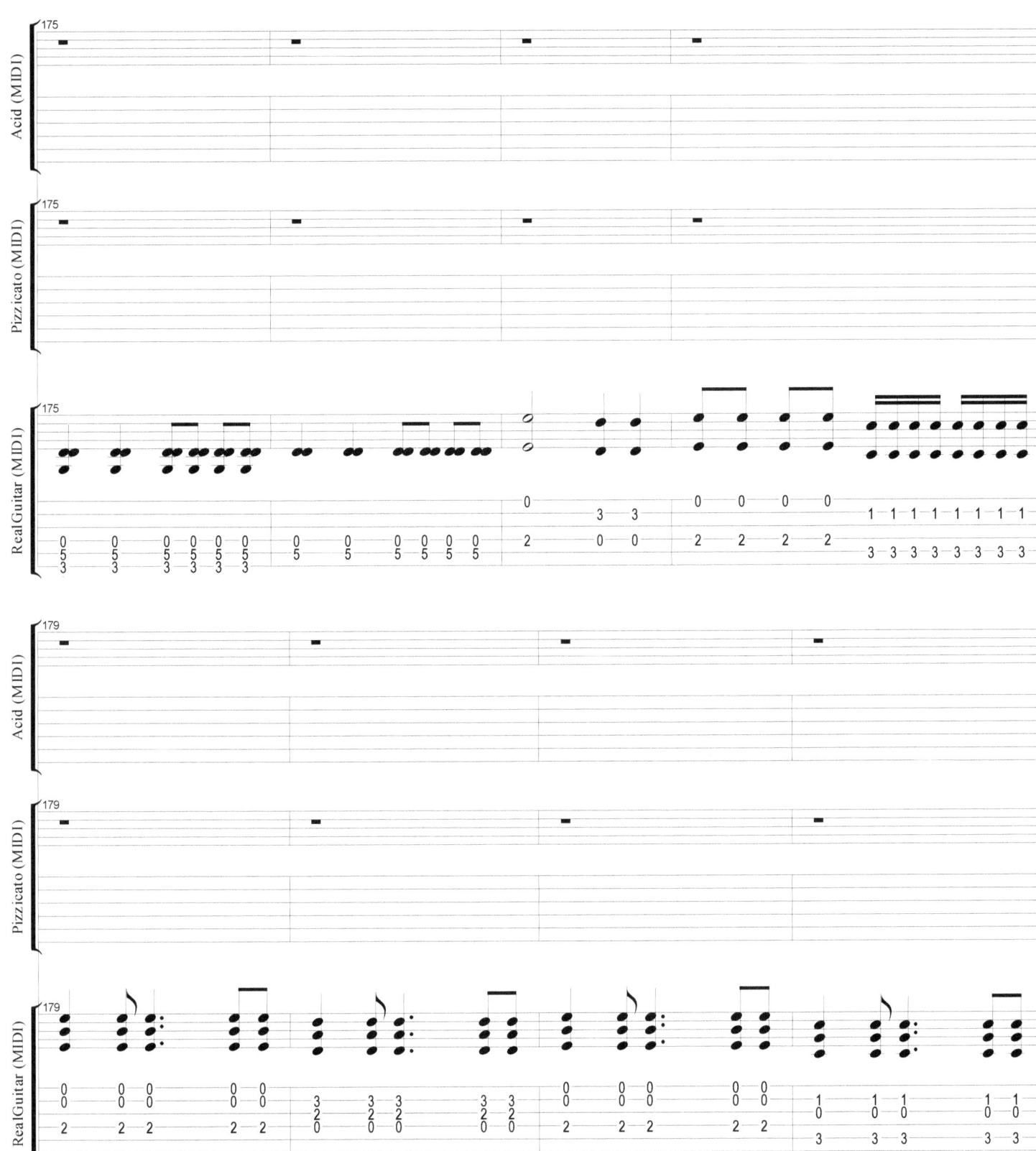

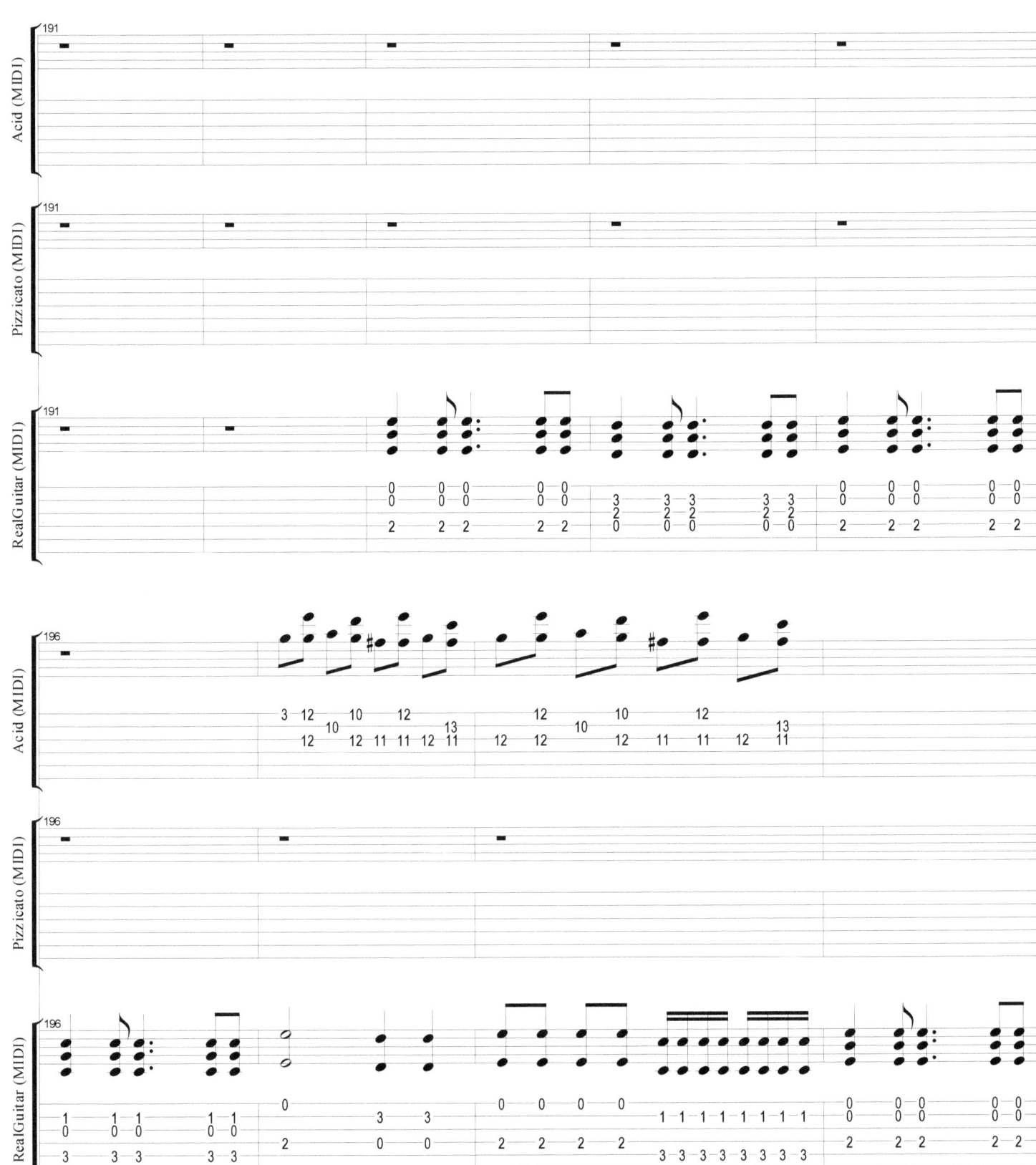

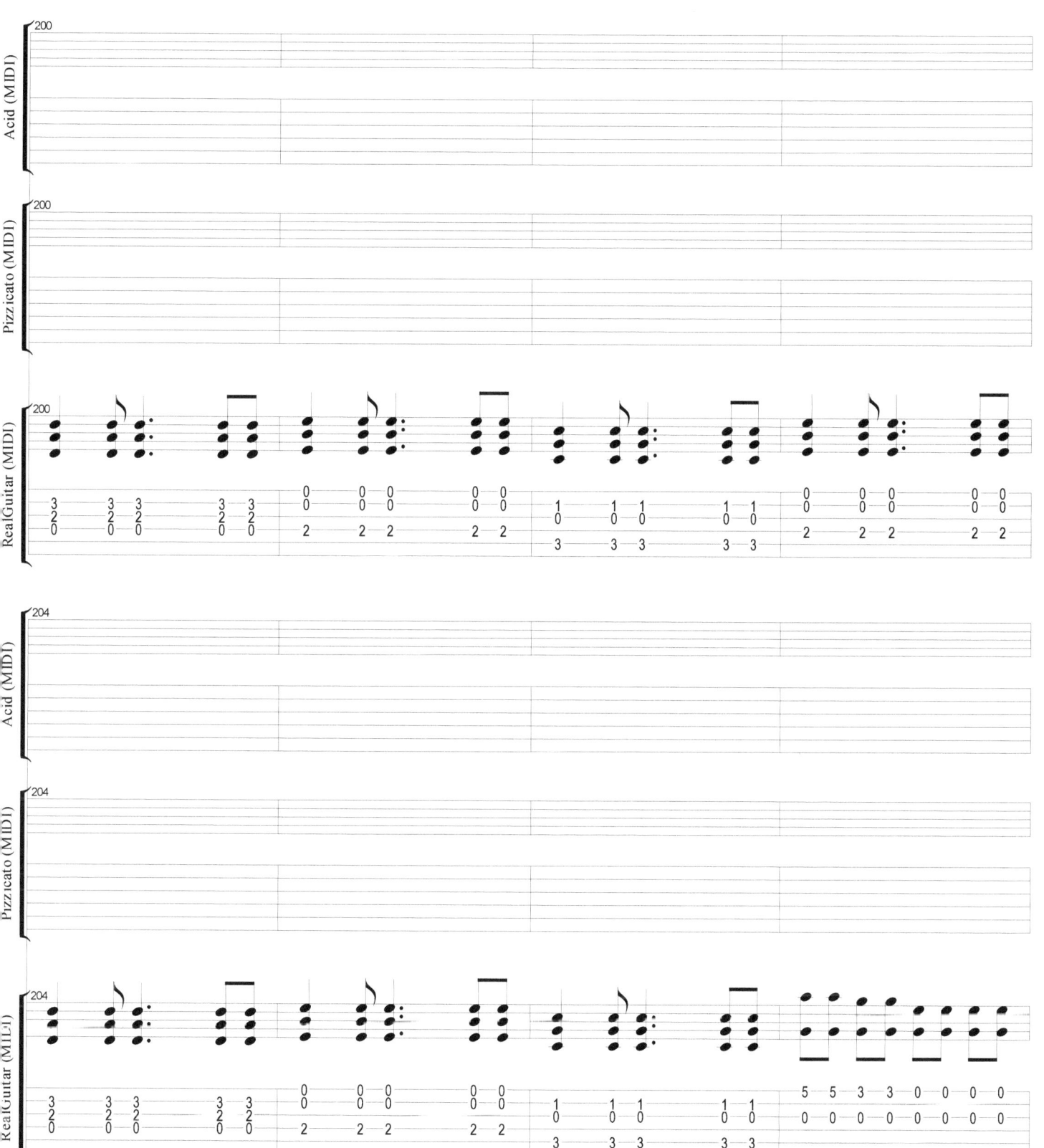

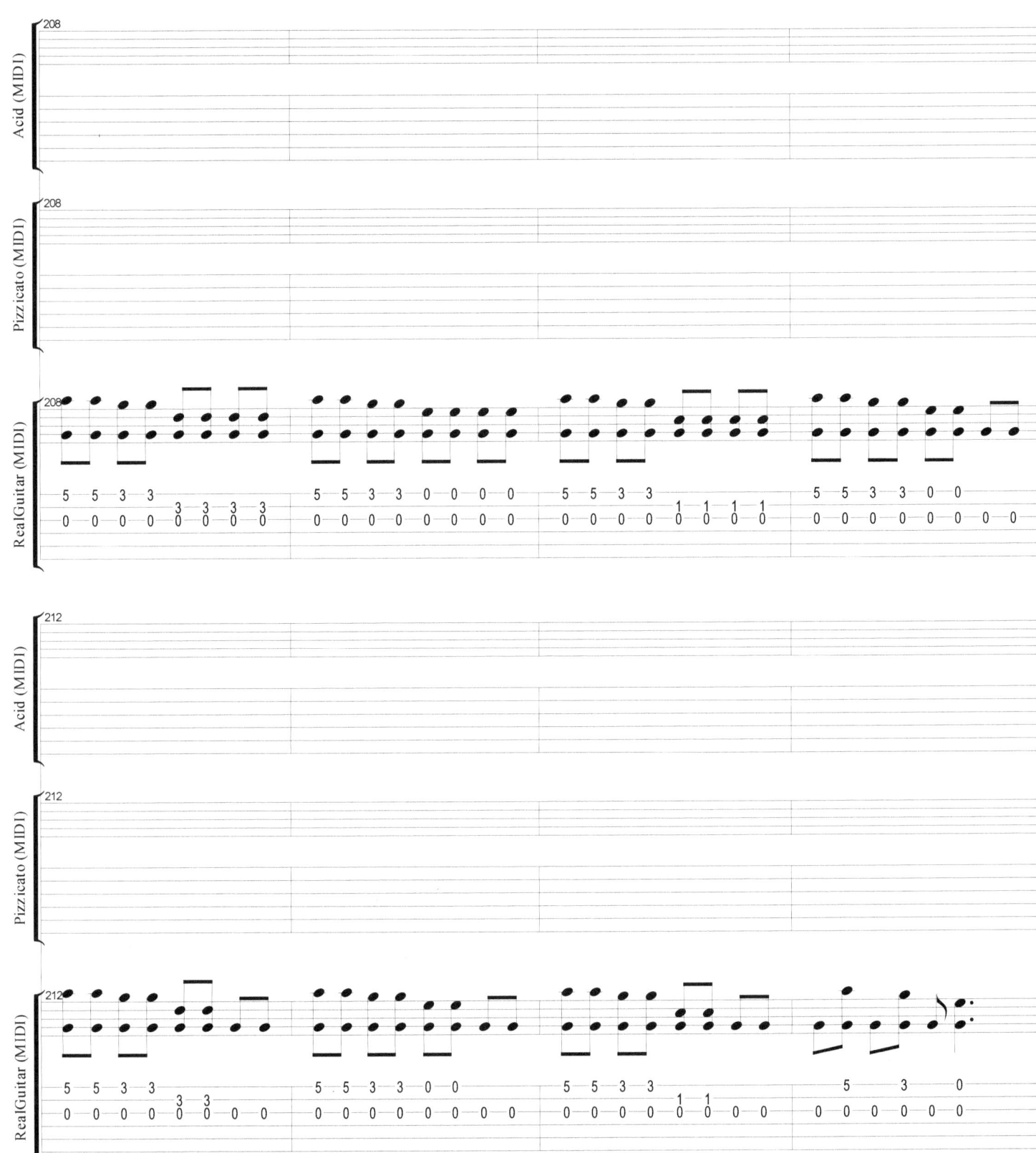

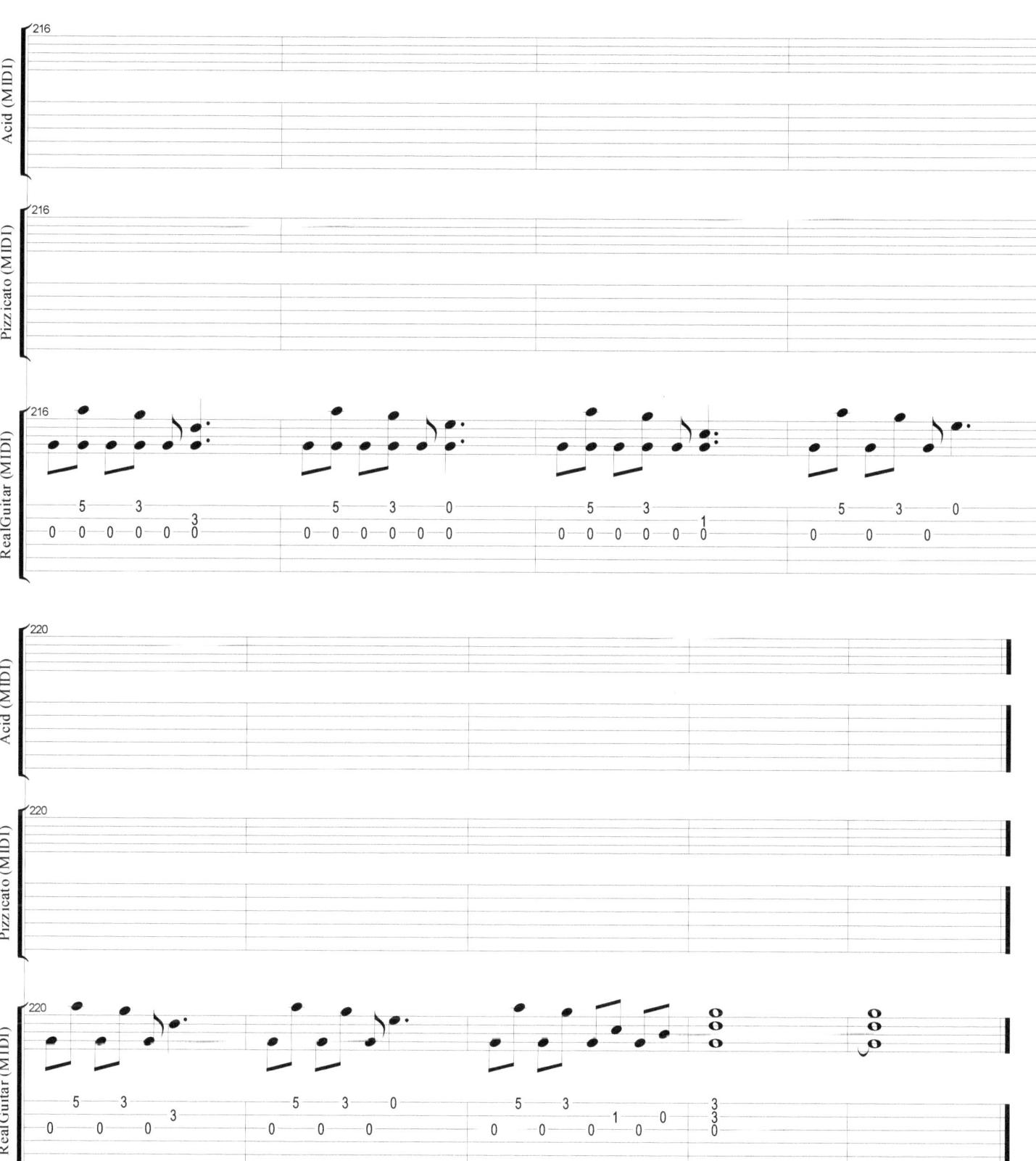

Anti-Christ

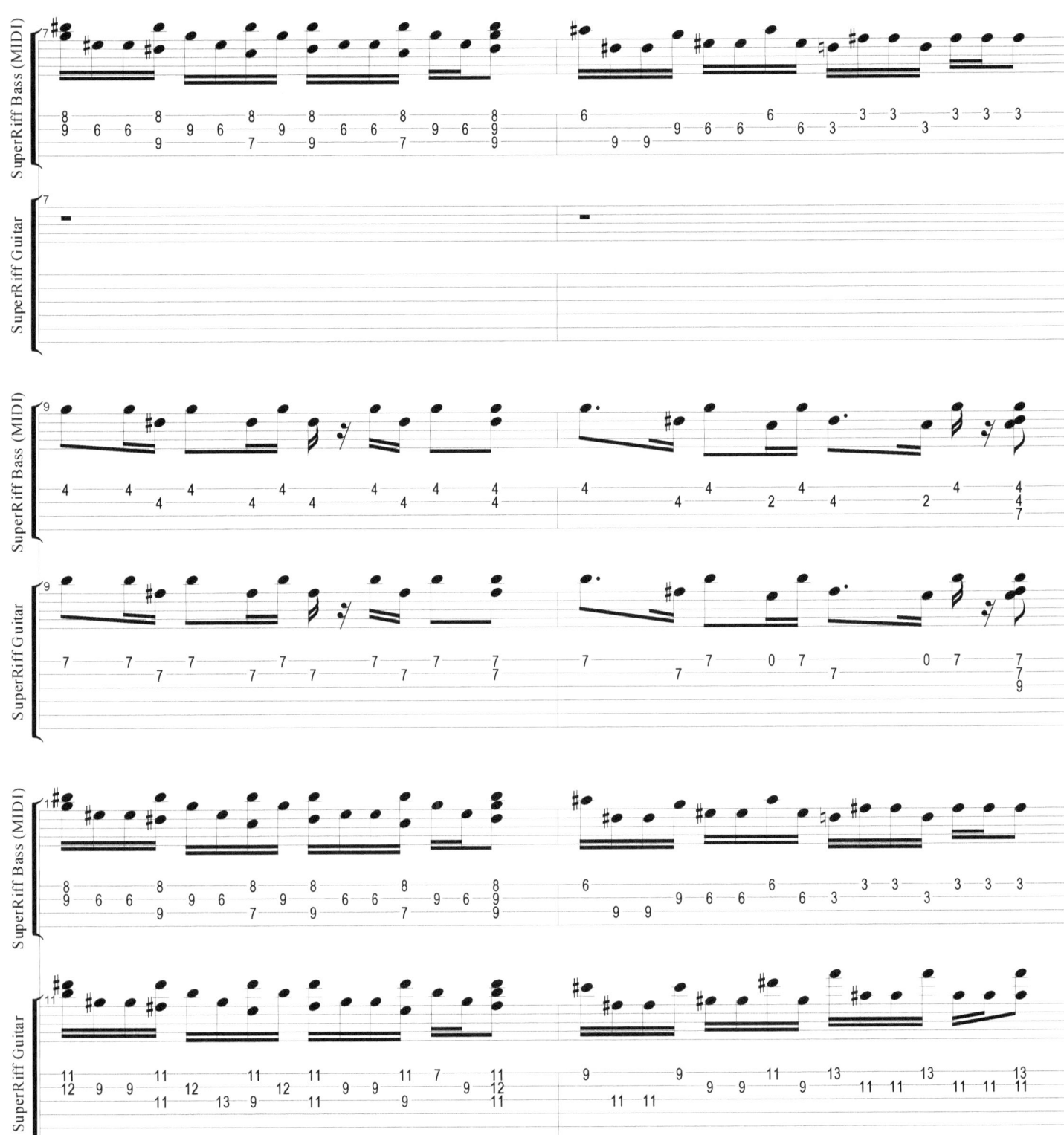

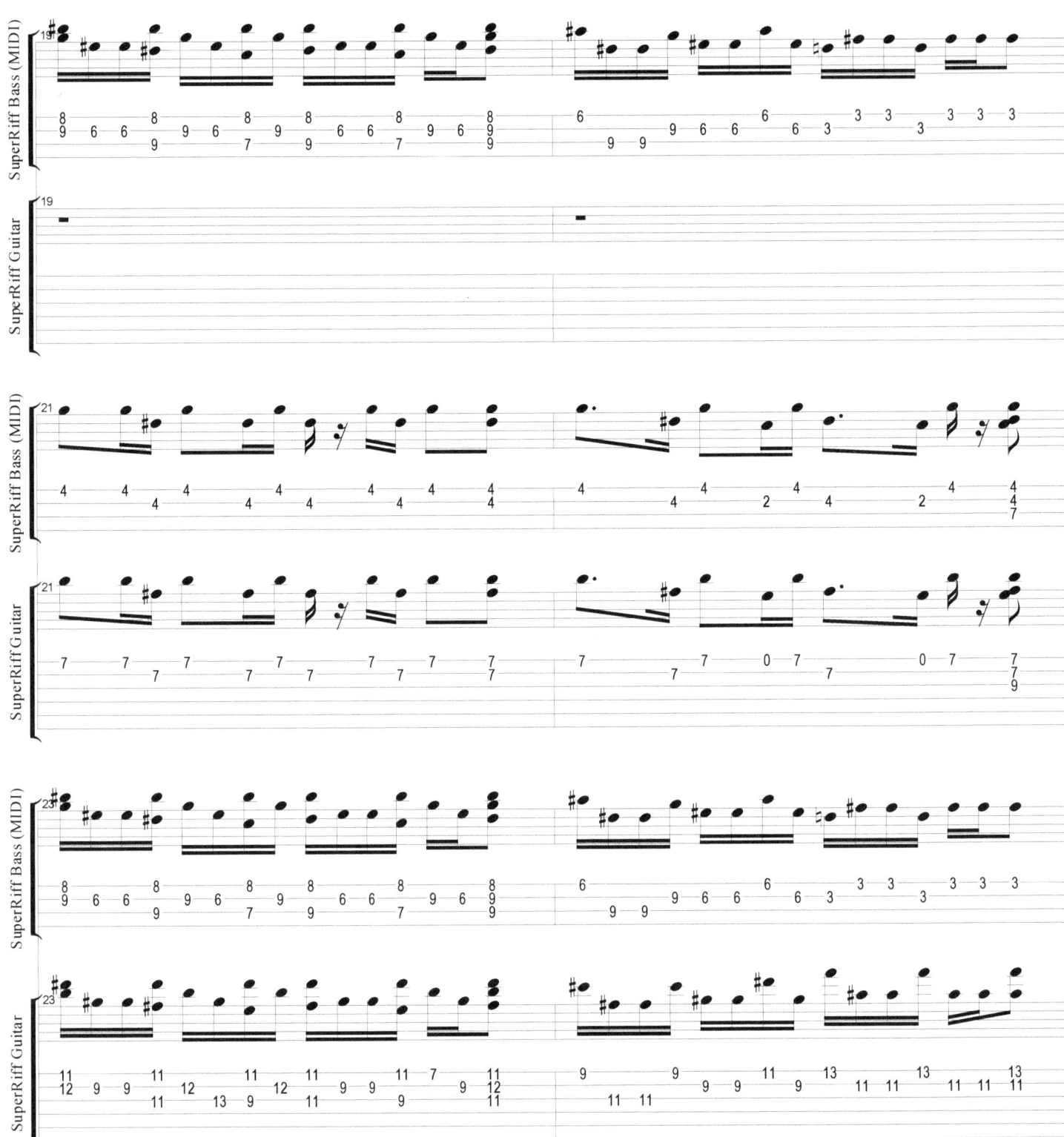

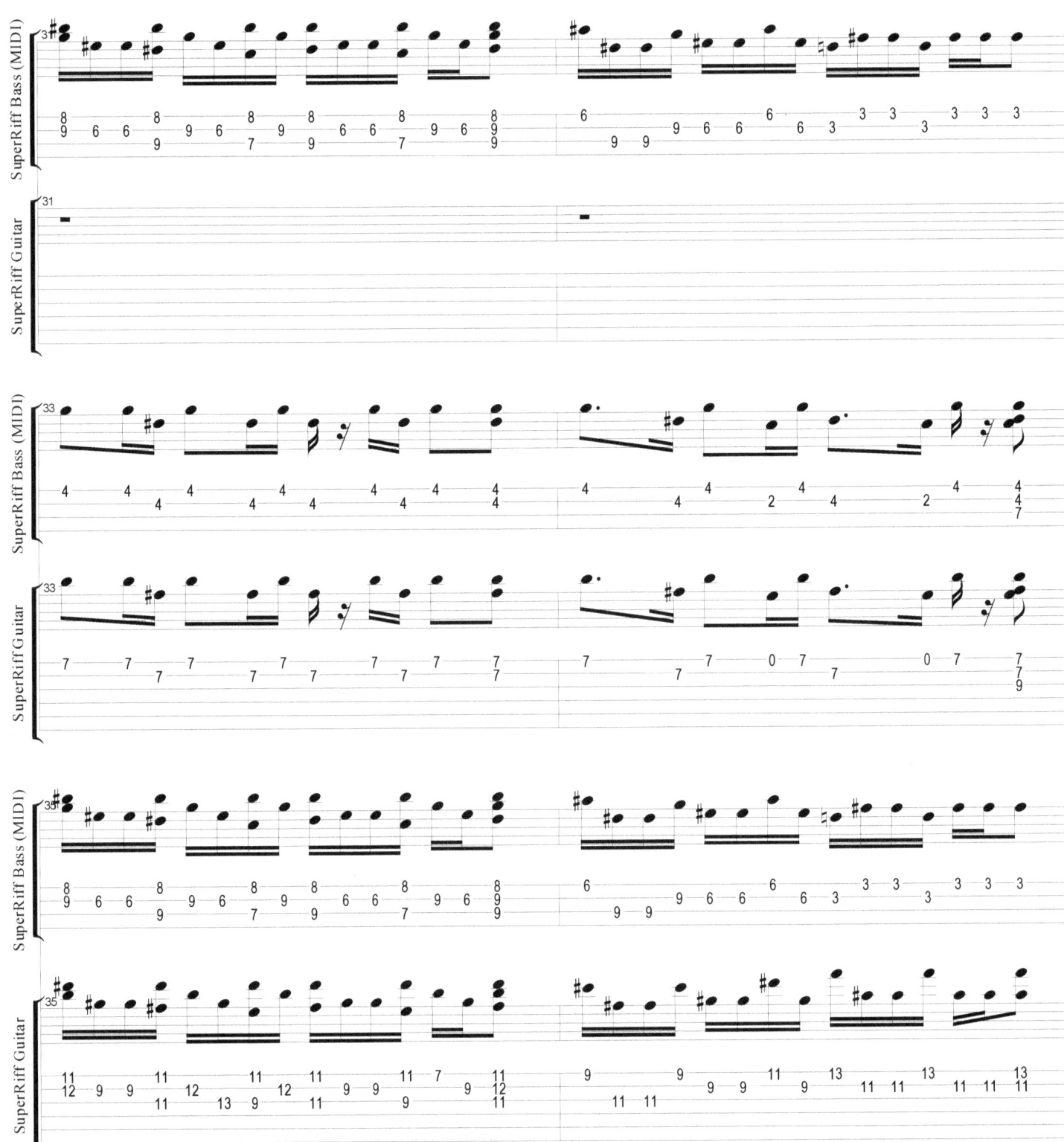

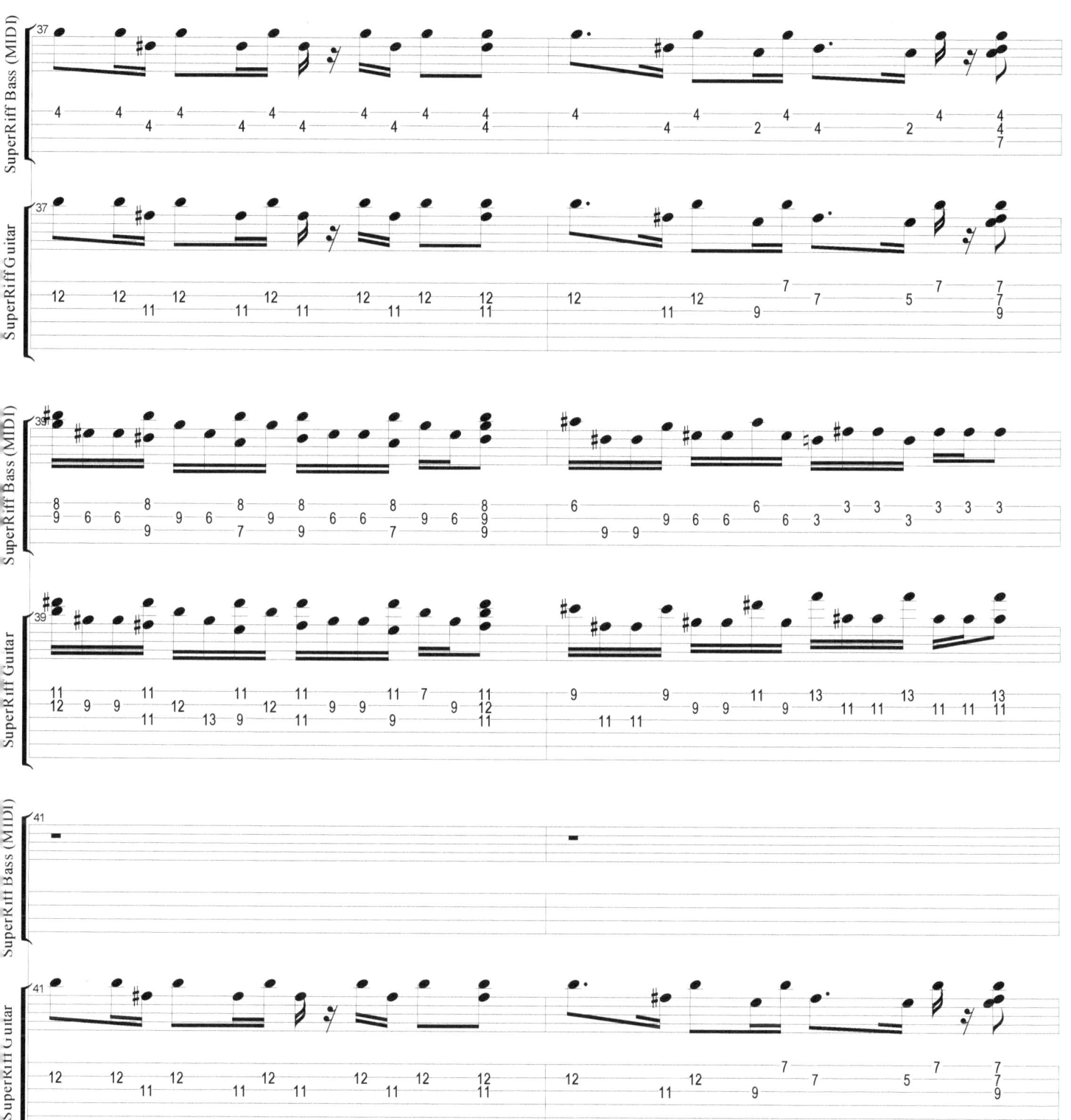

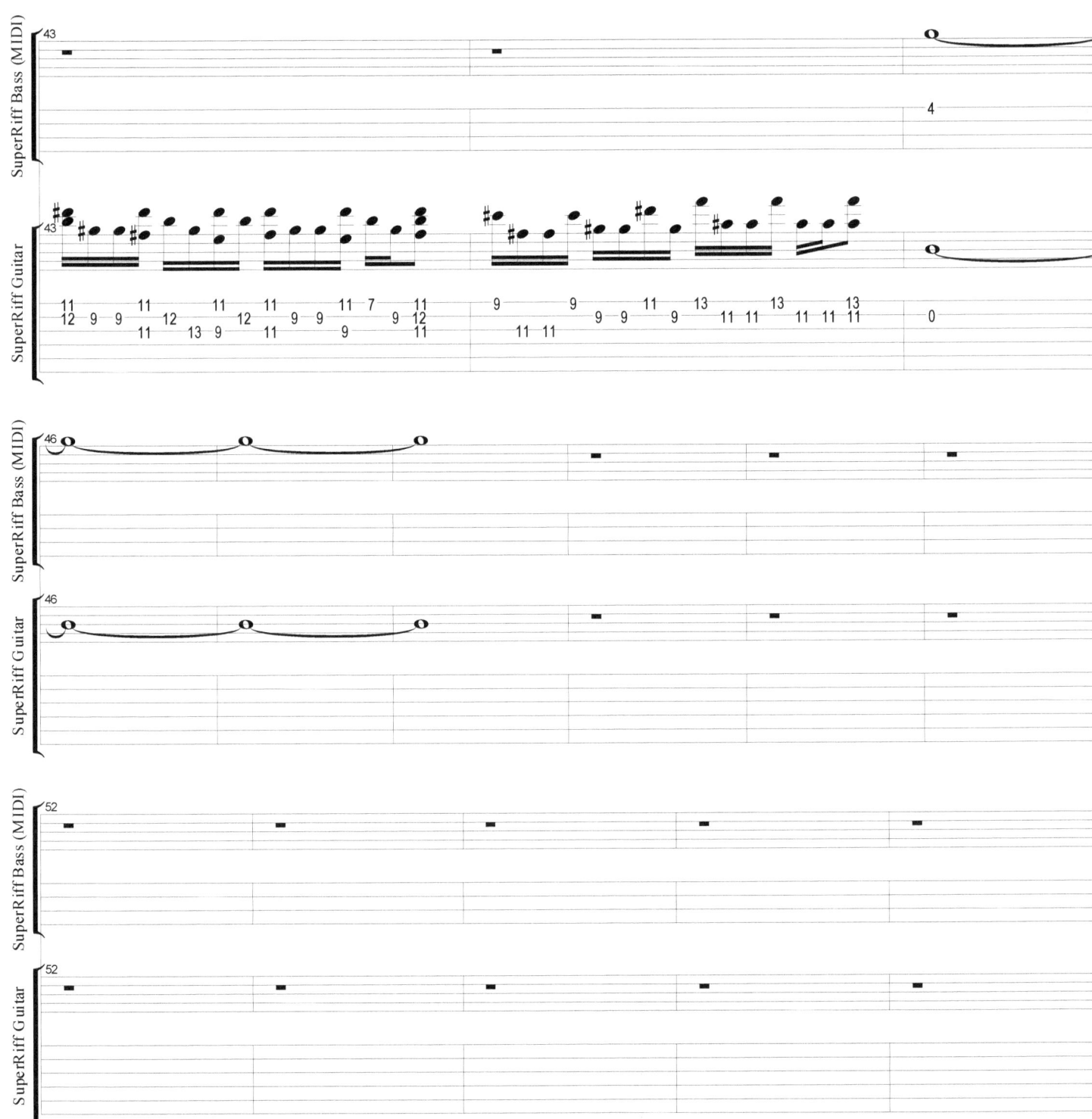

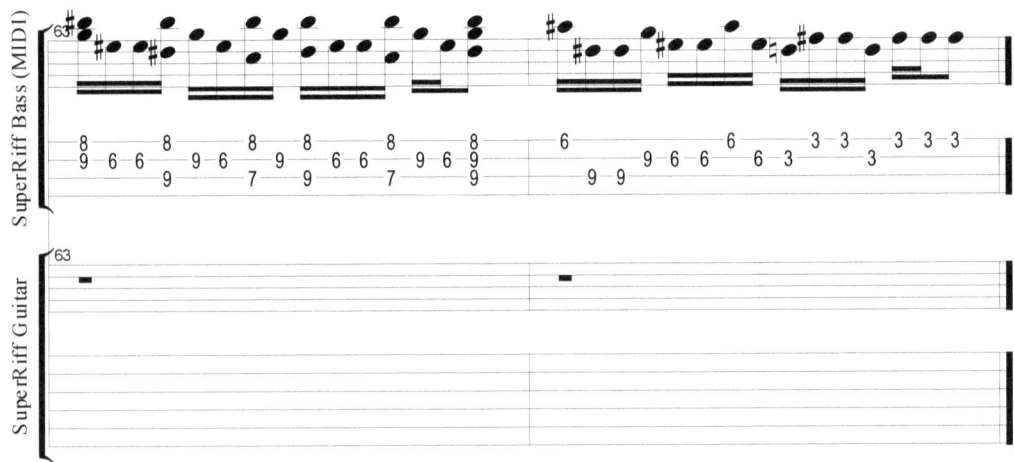

OMG We Like To Party

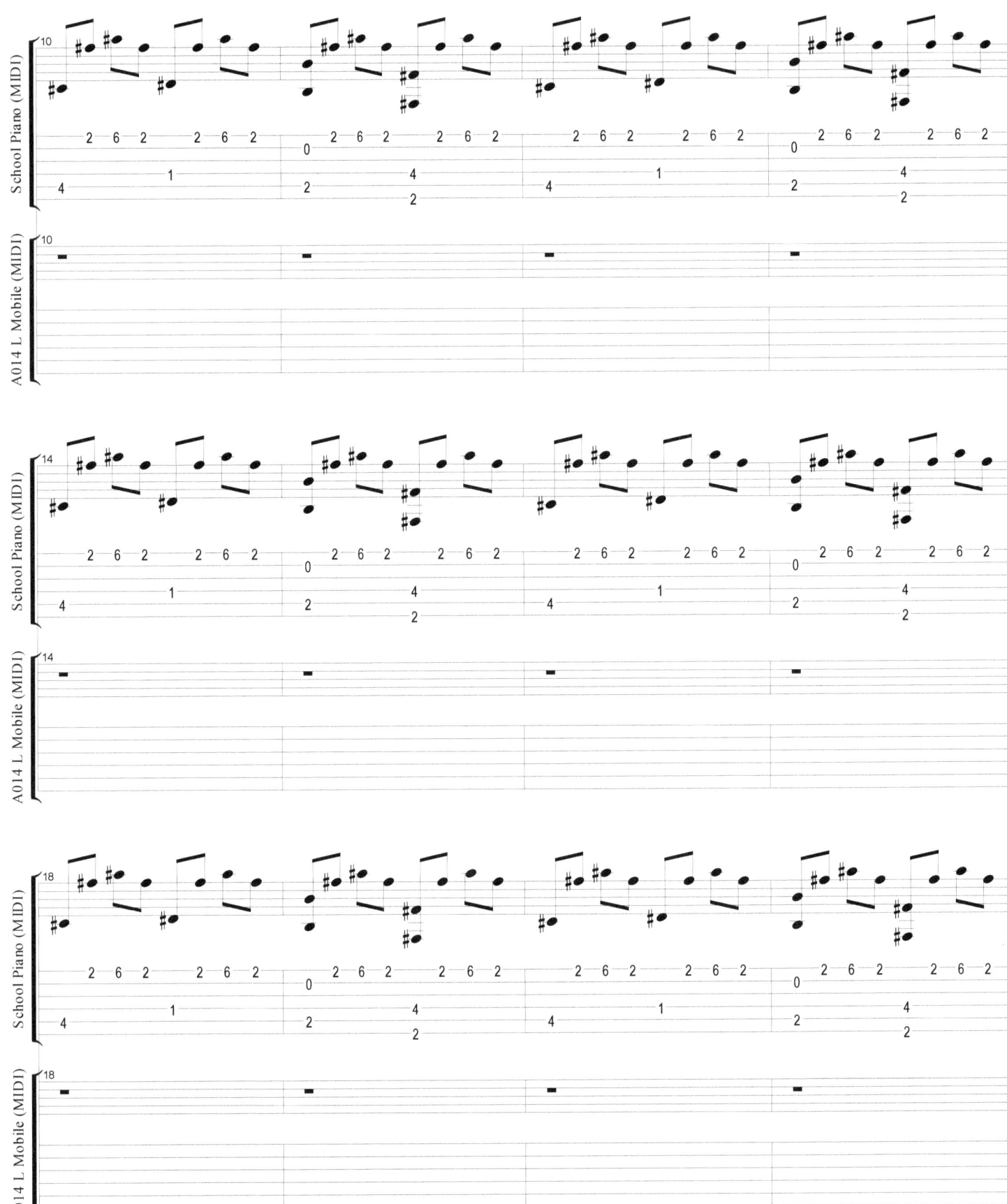

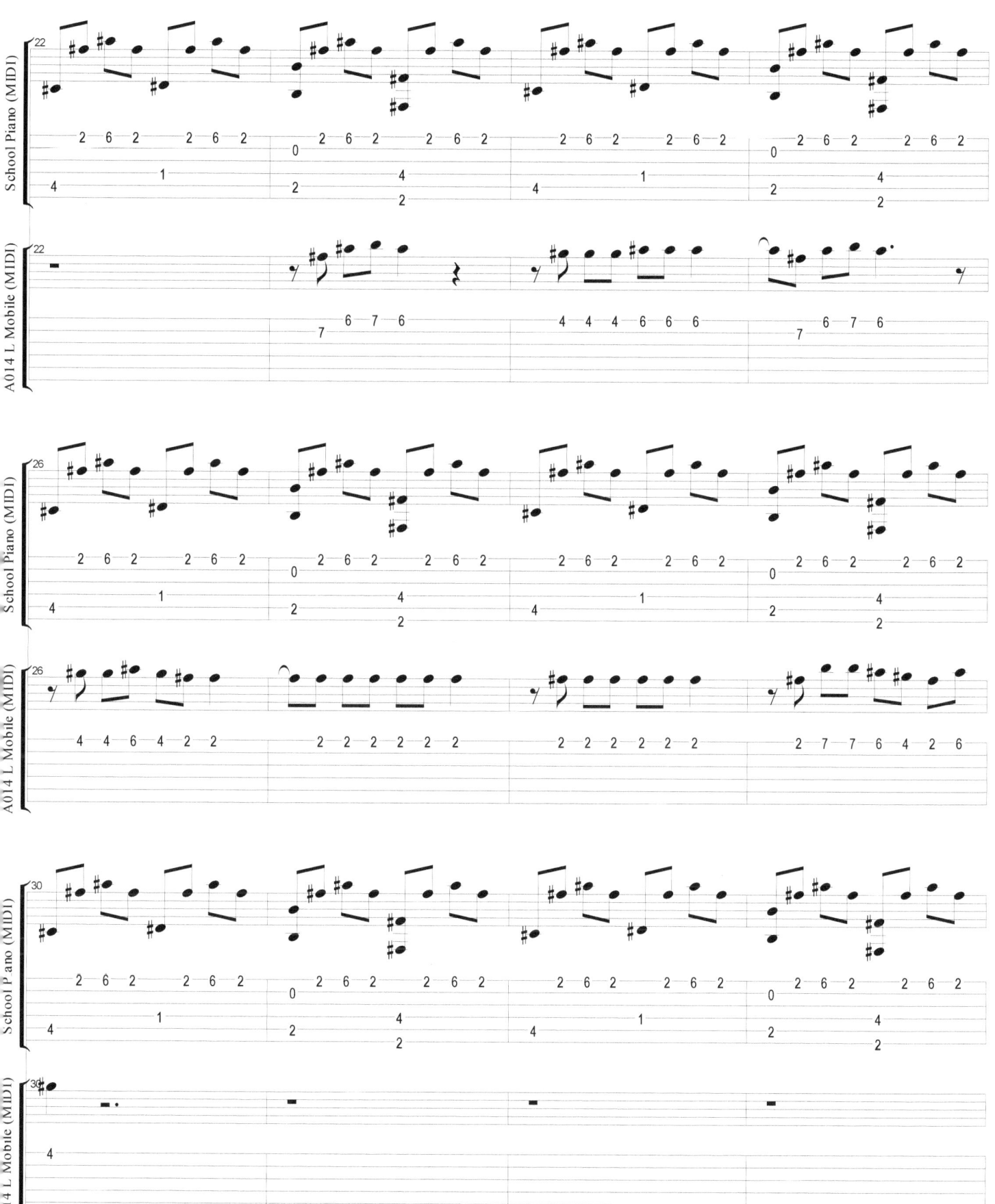

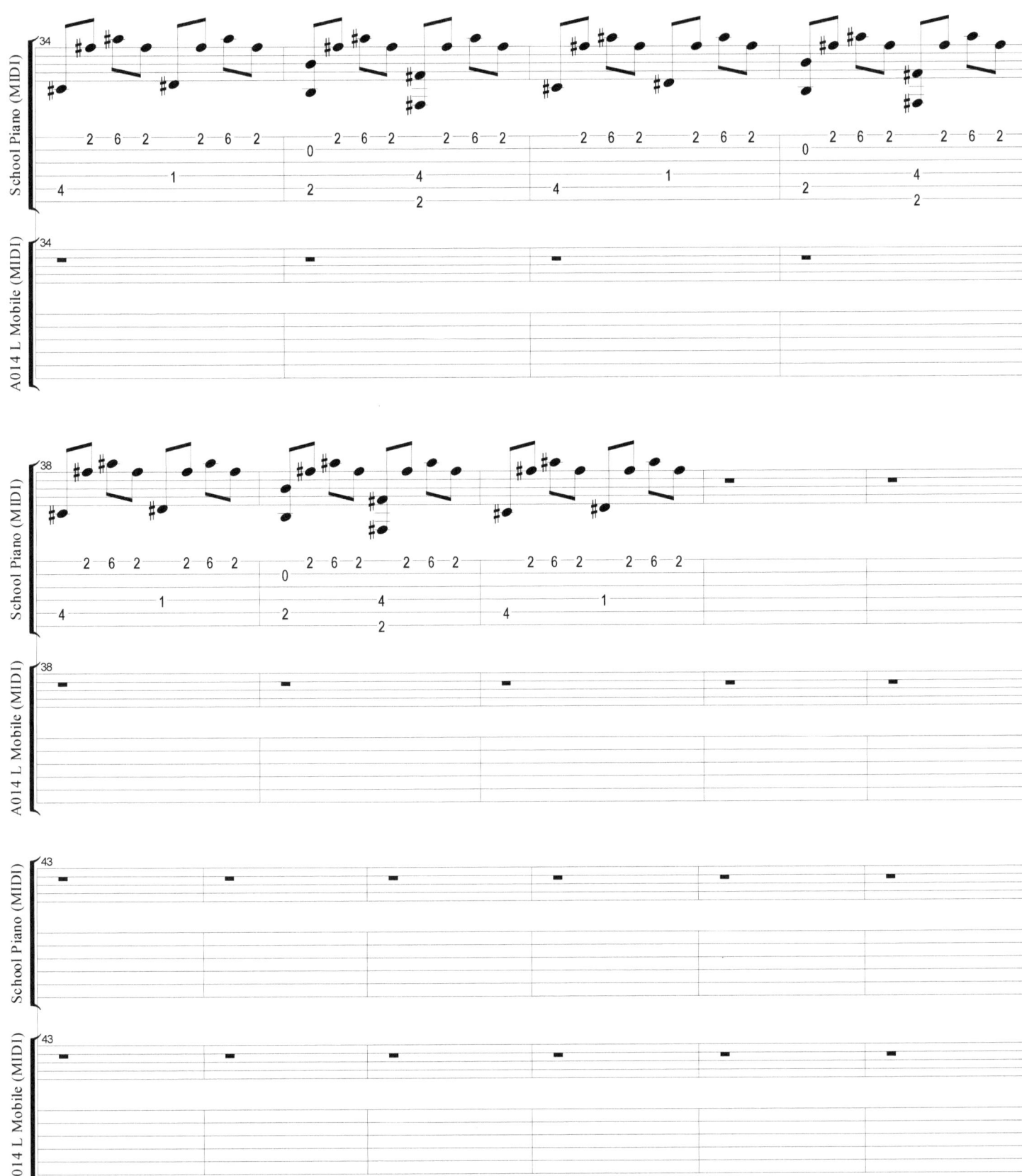

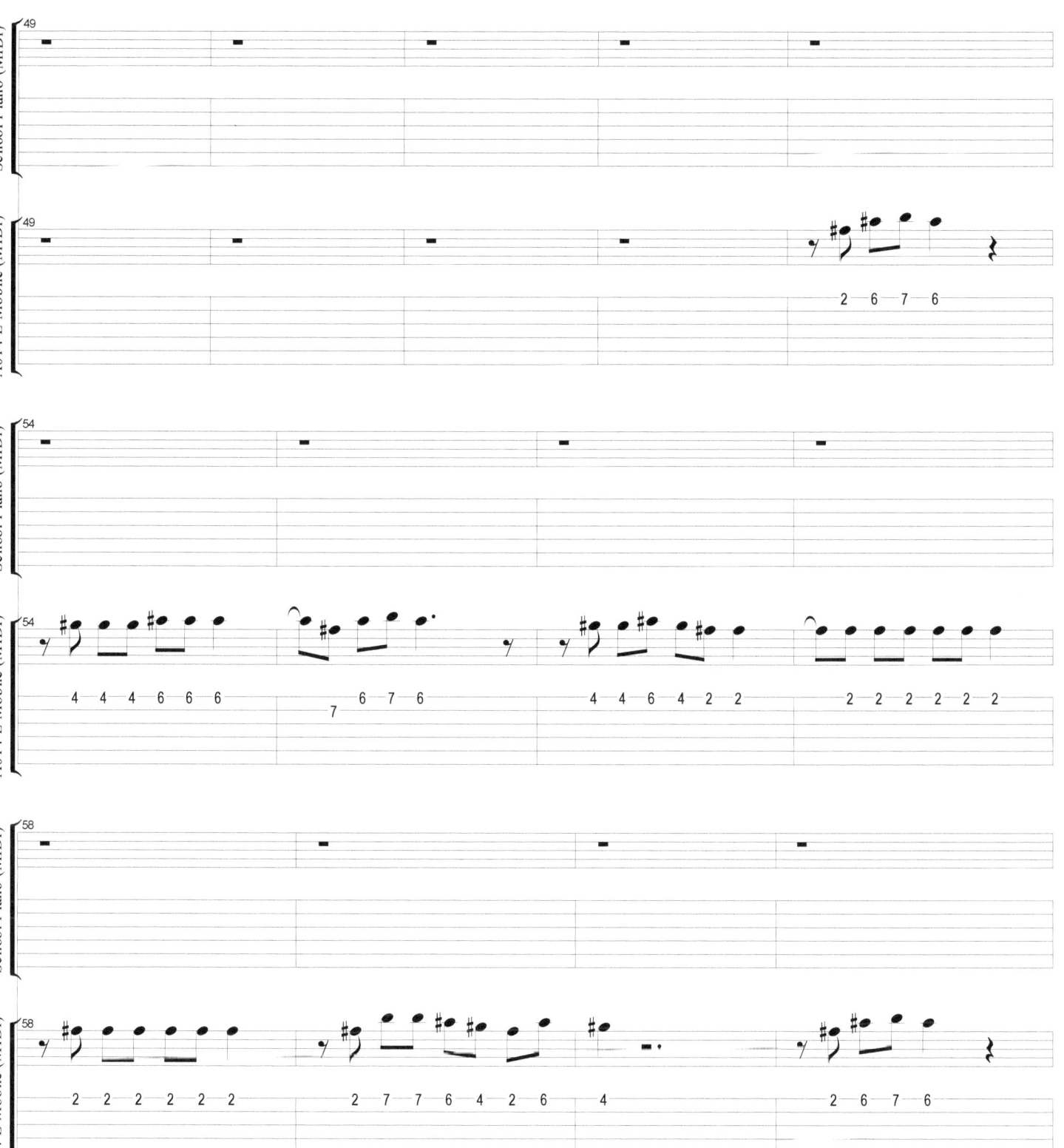

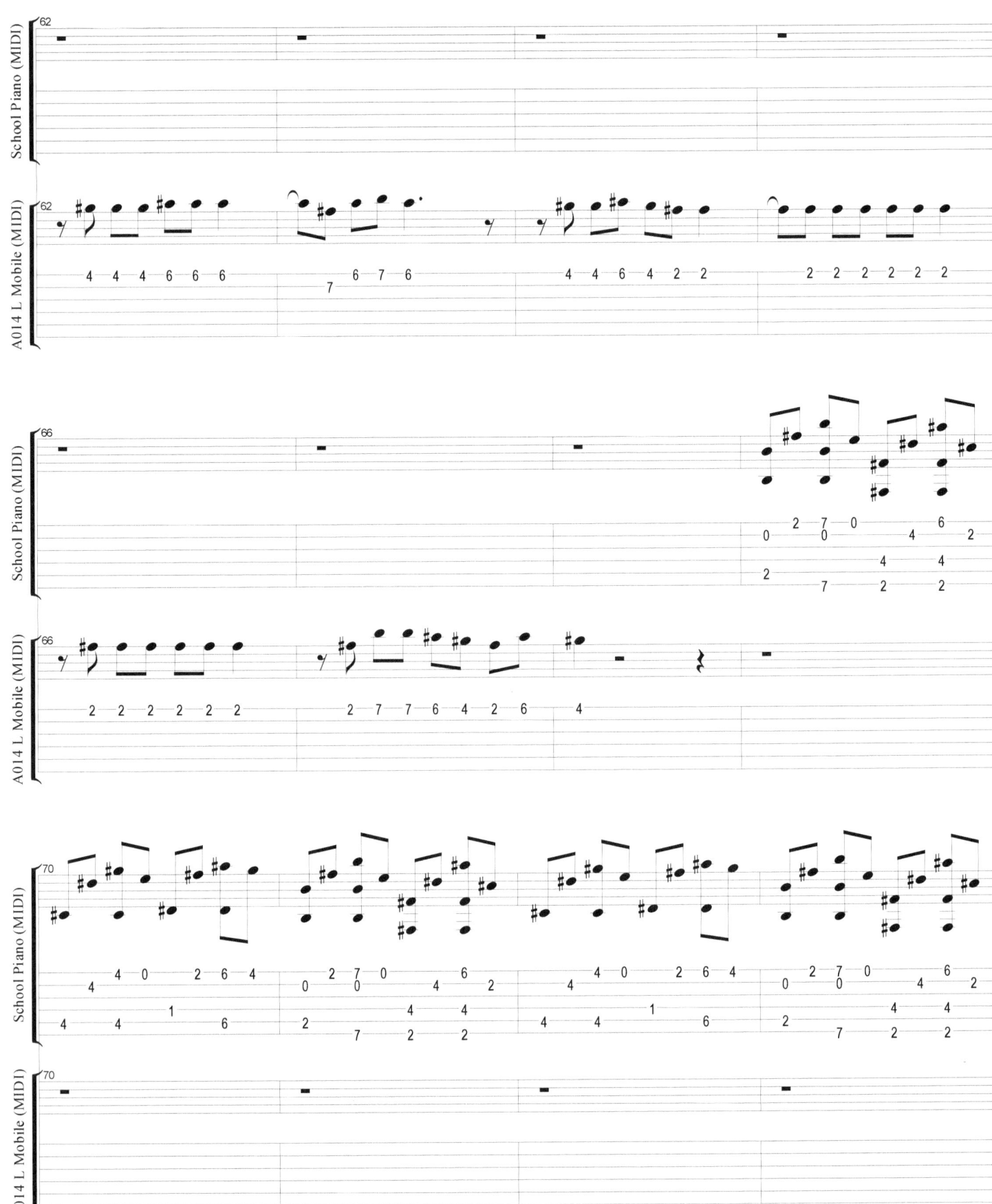

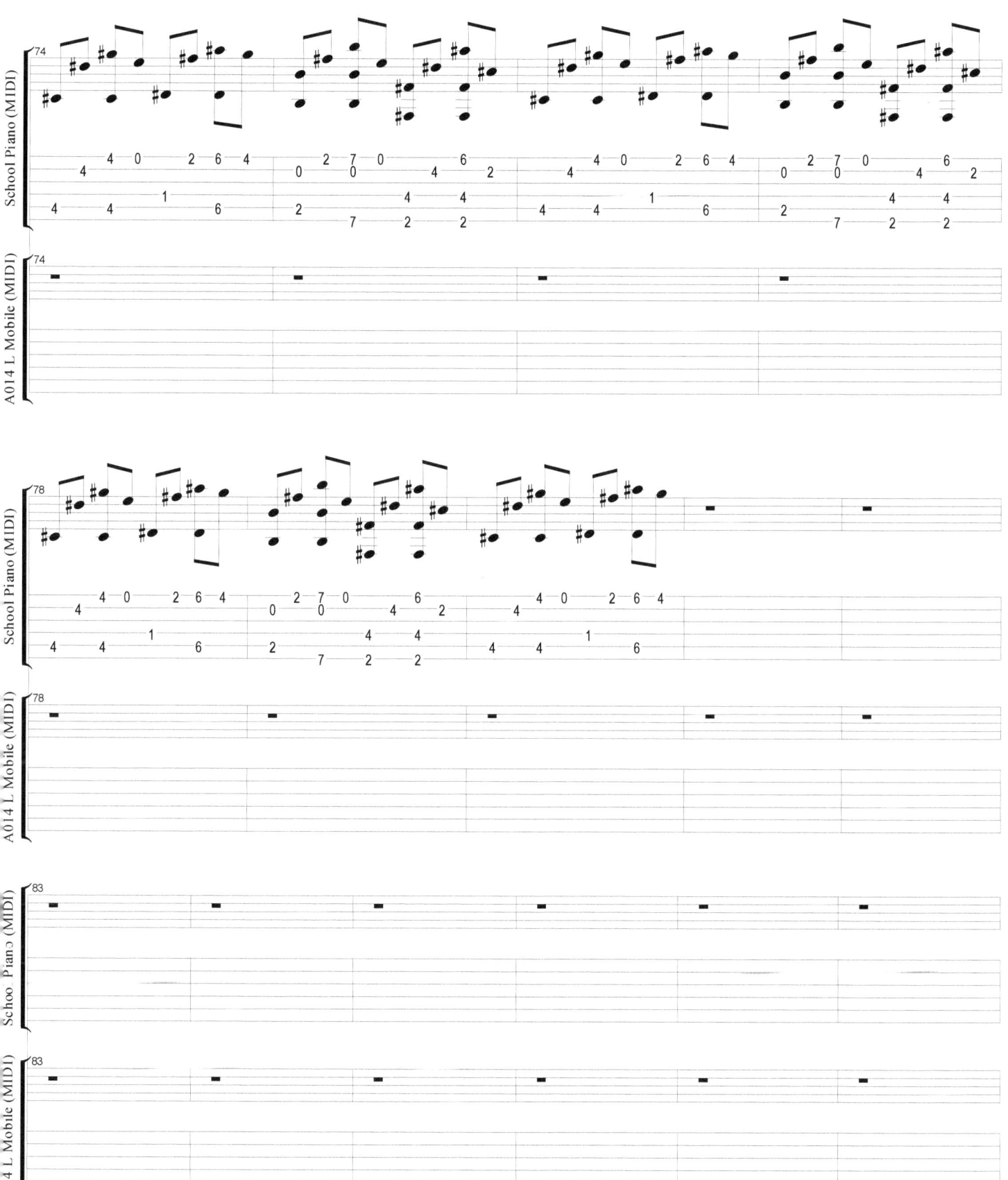

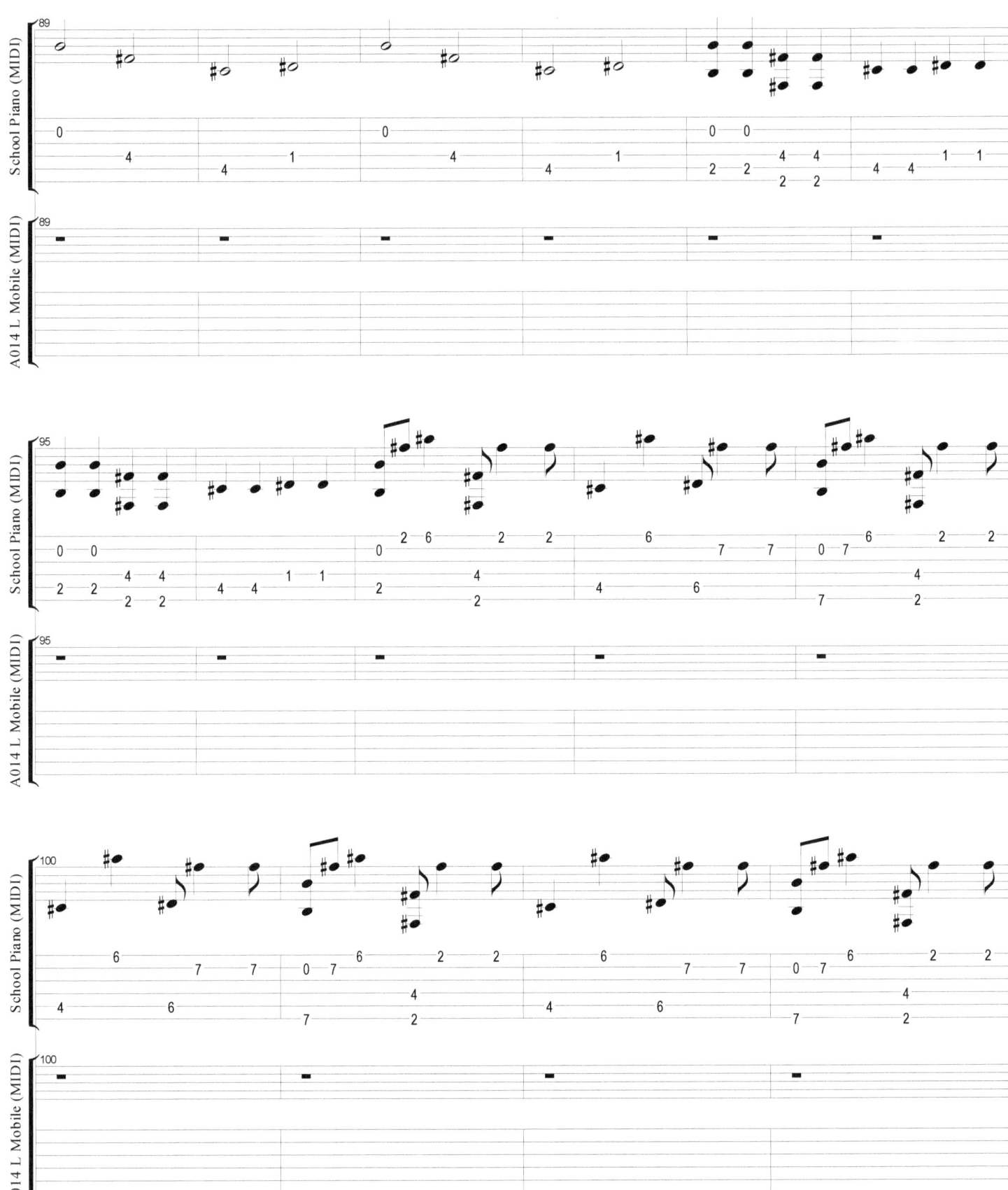

The Feeling I Get

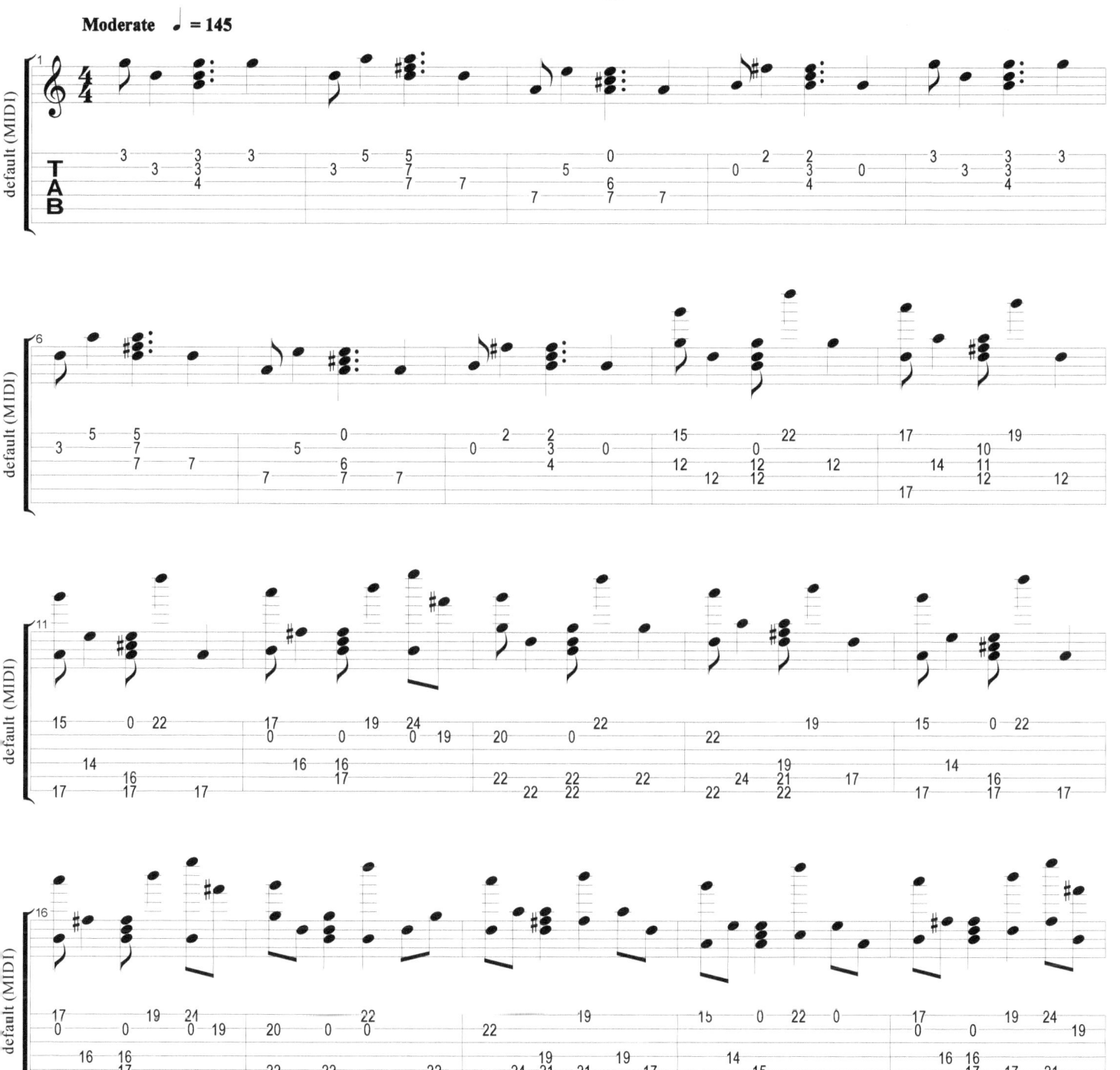

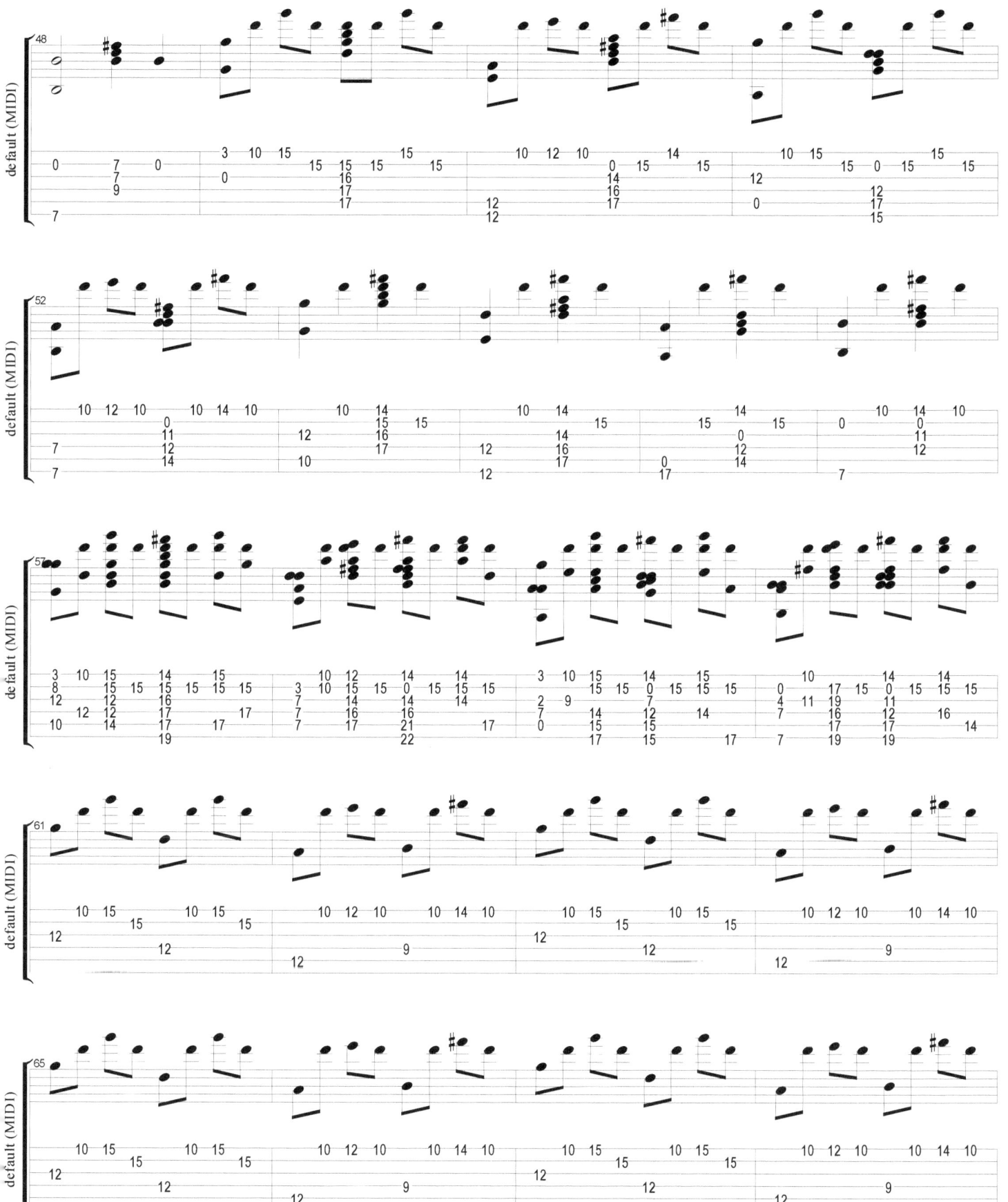

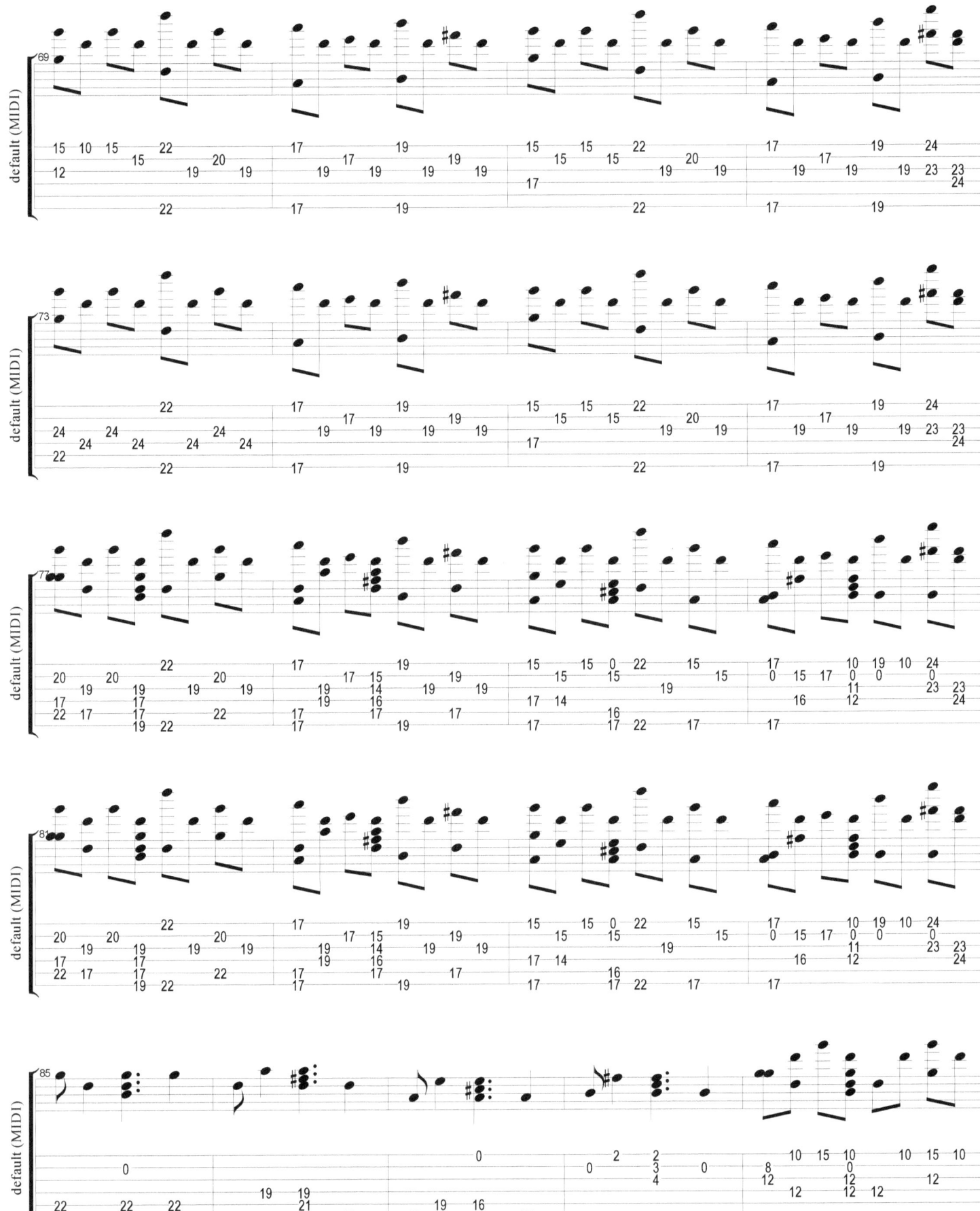

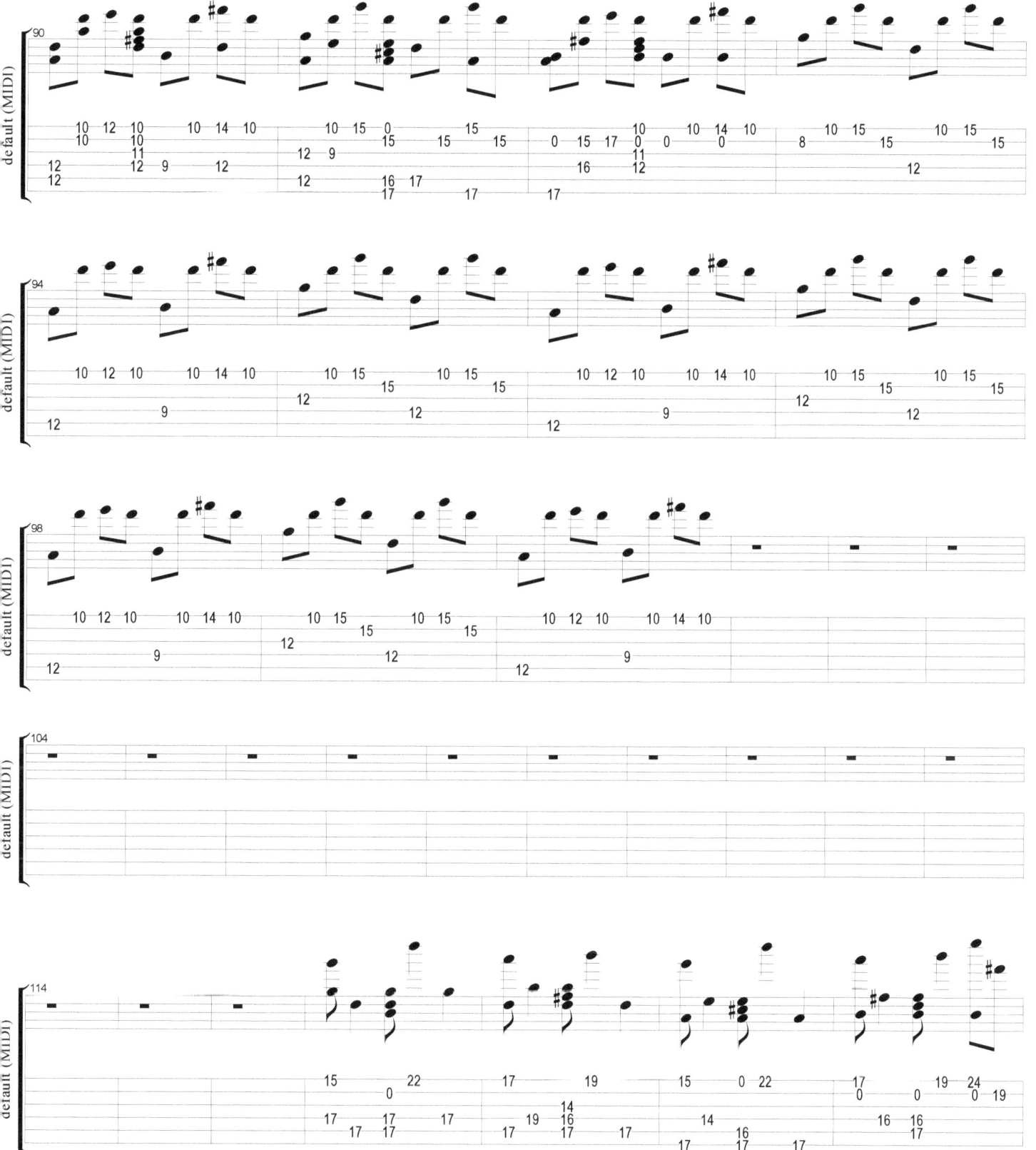

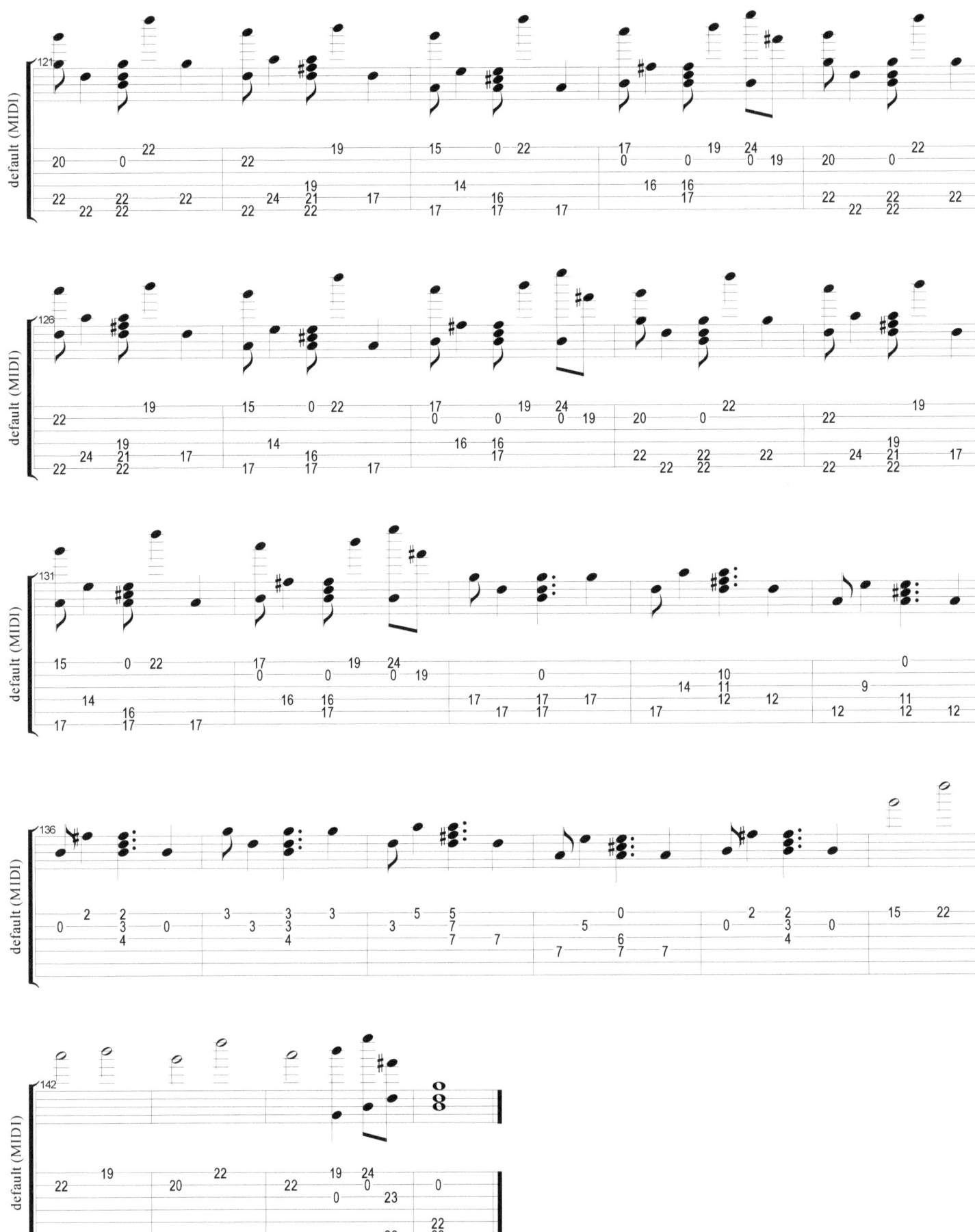

Tonight's The Night

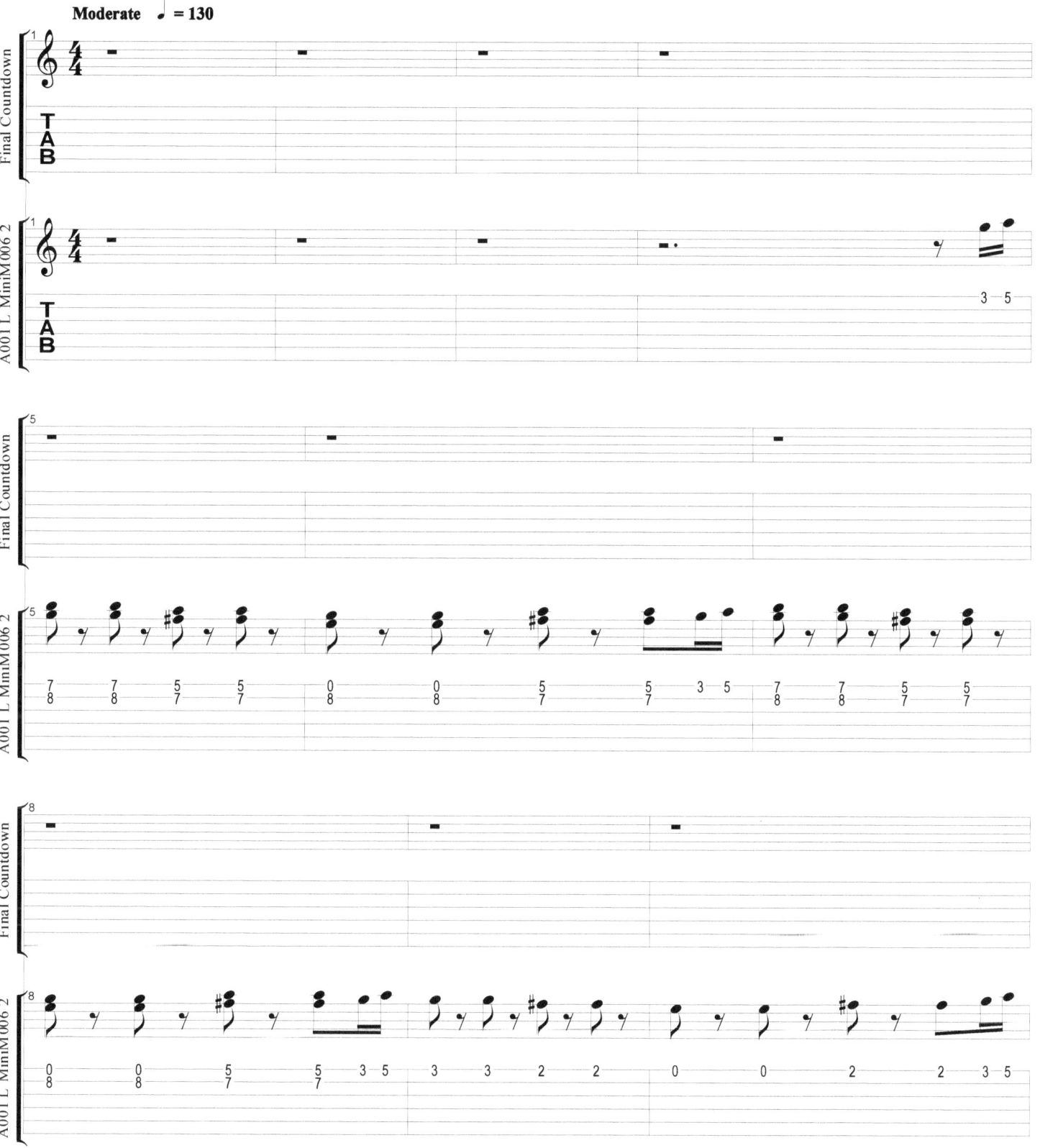

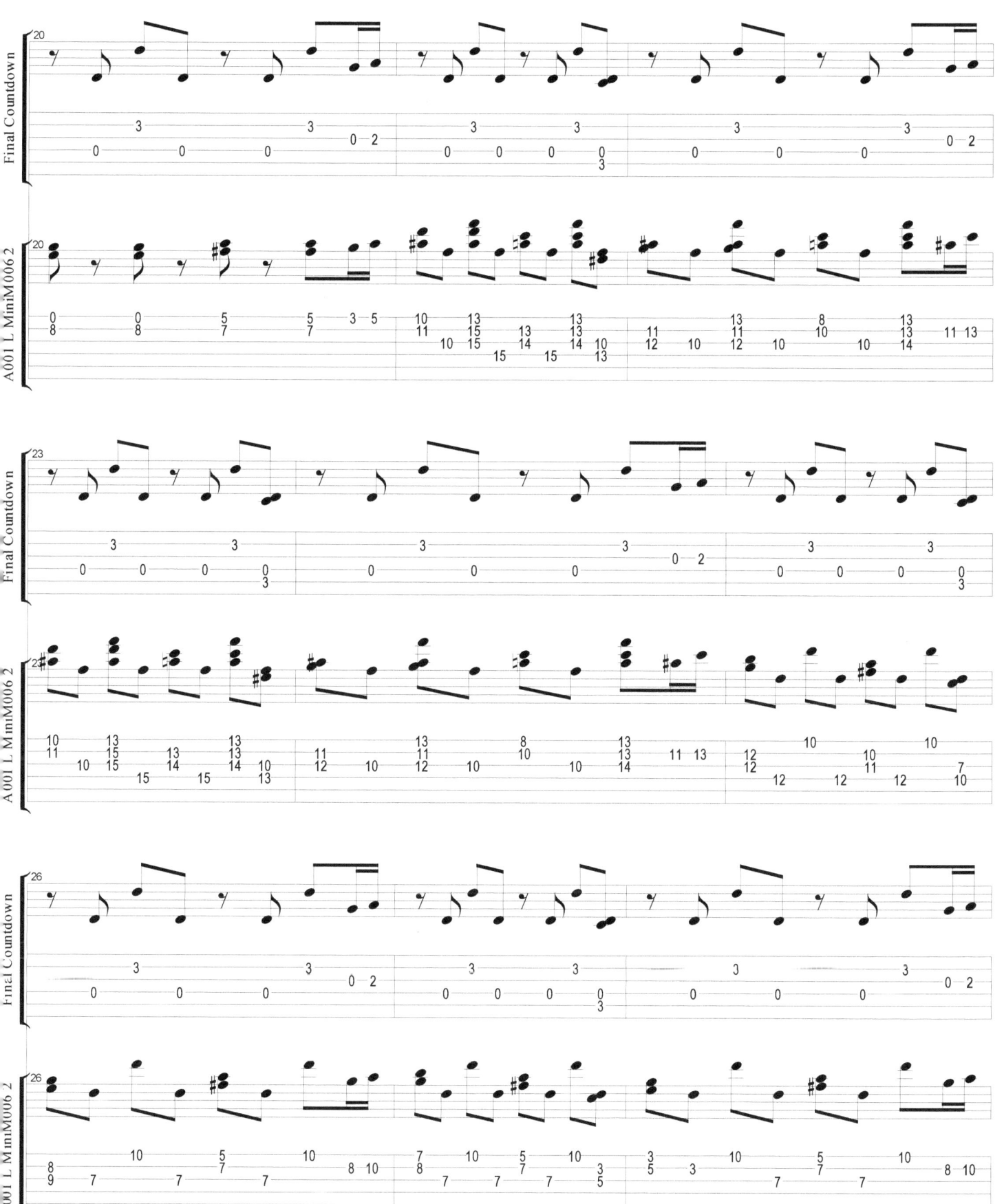

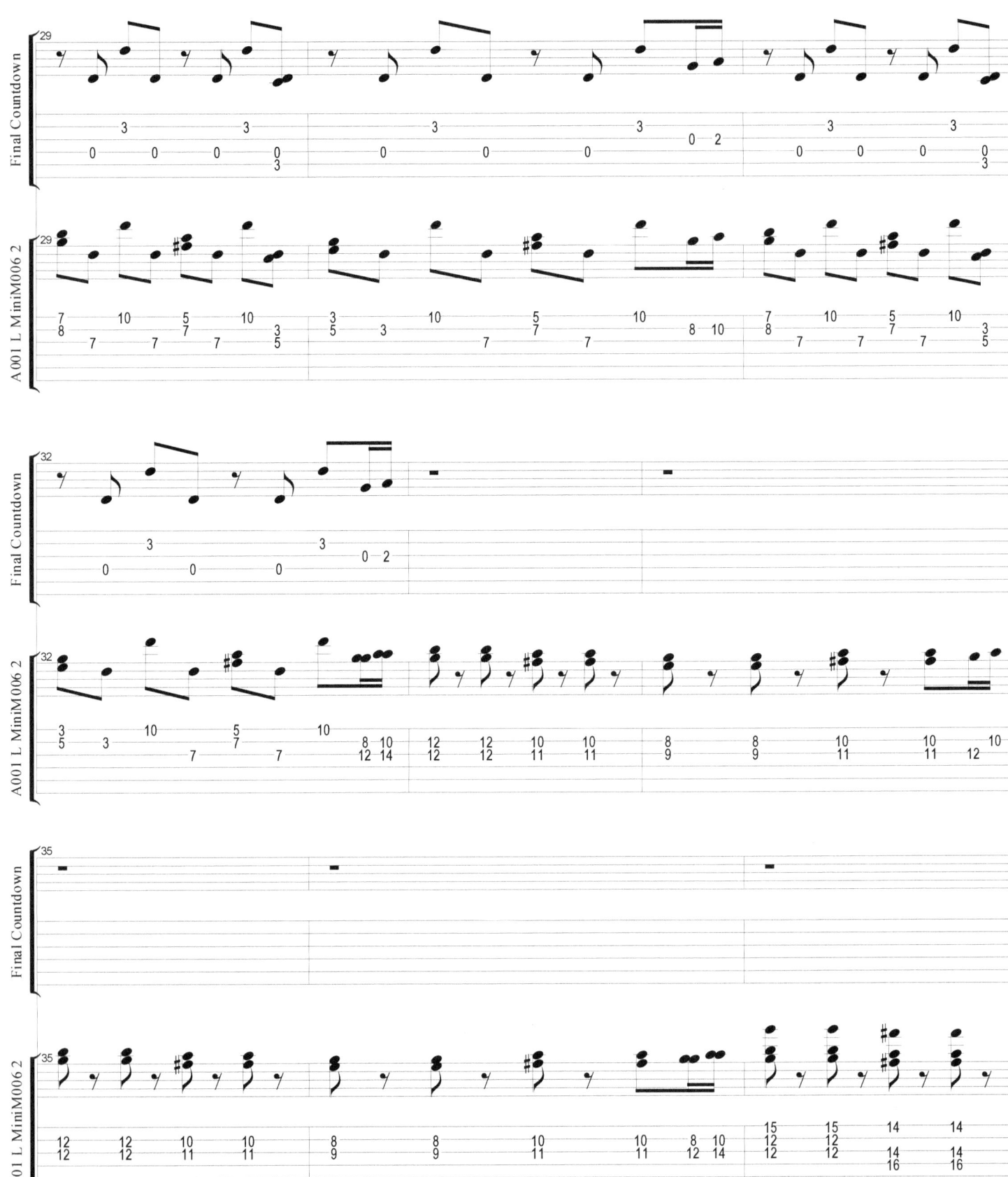

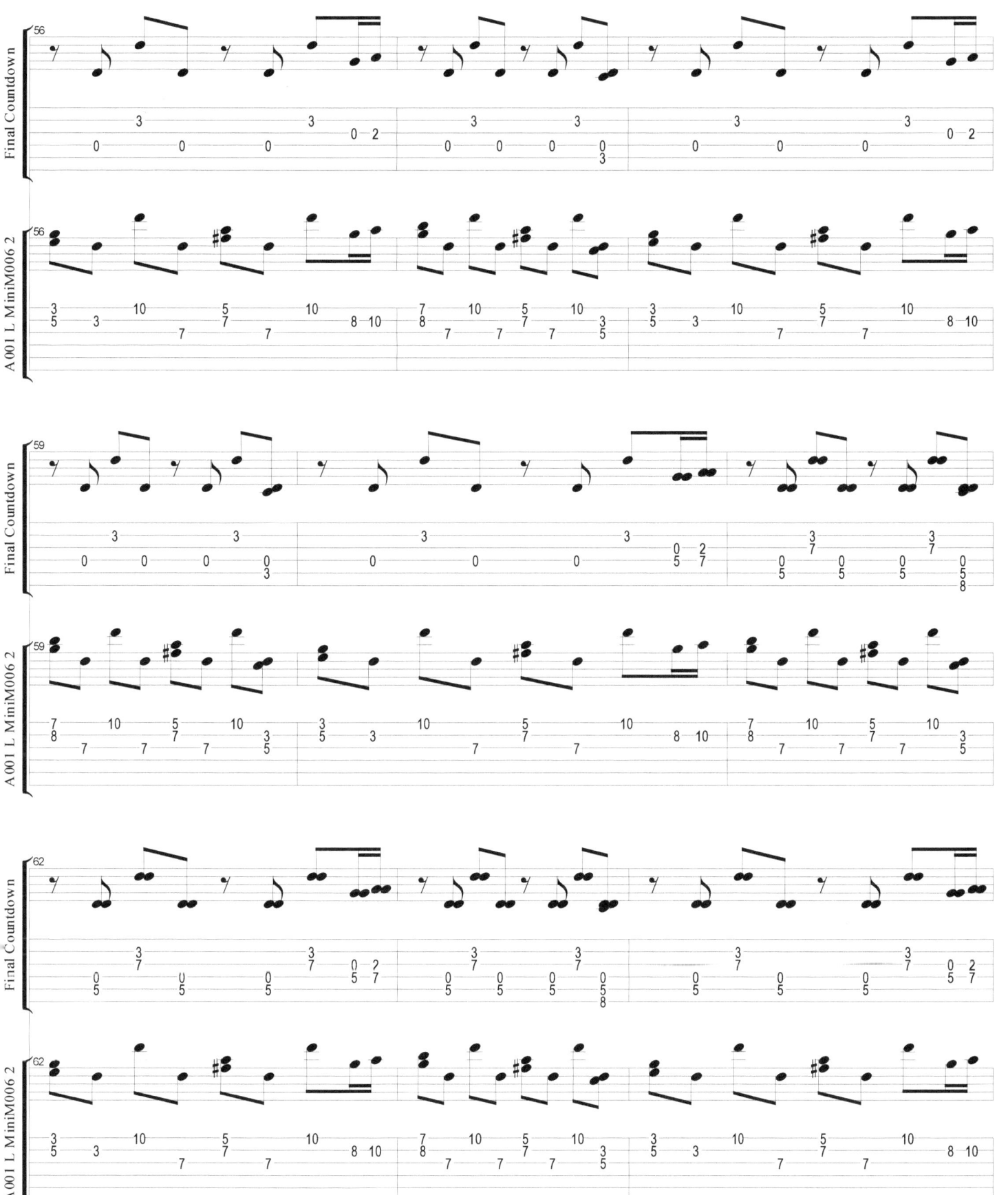

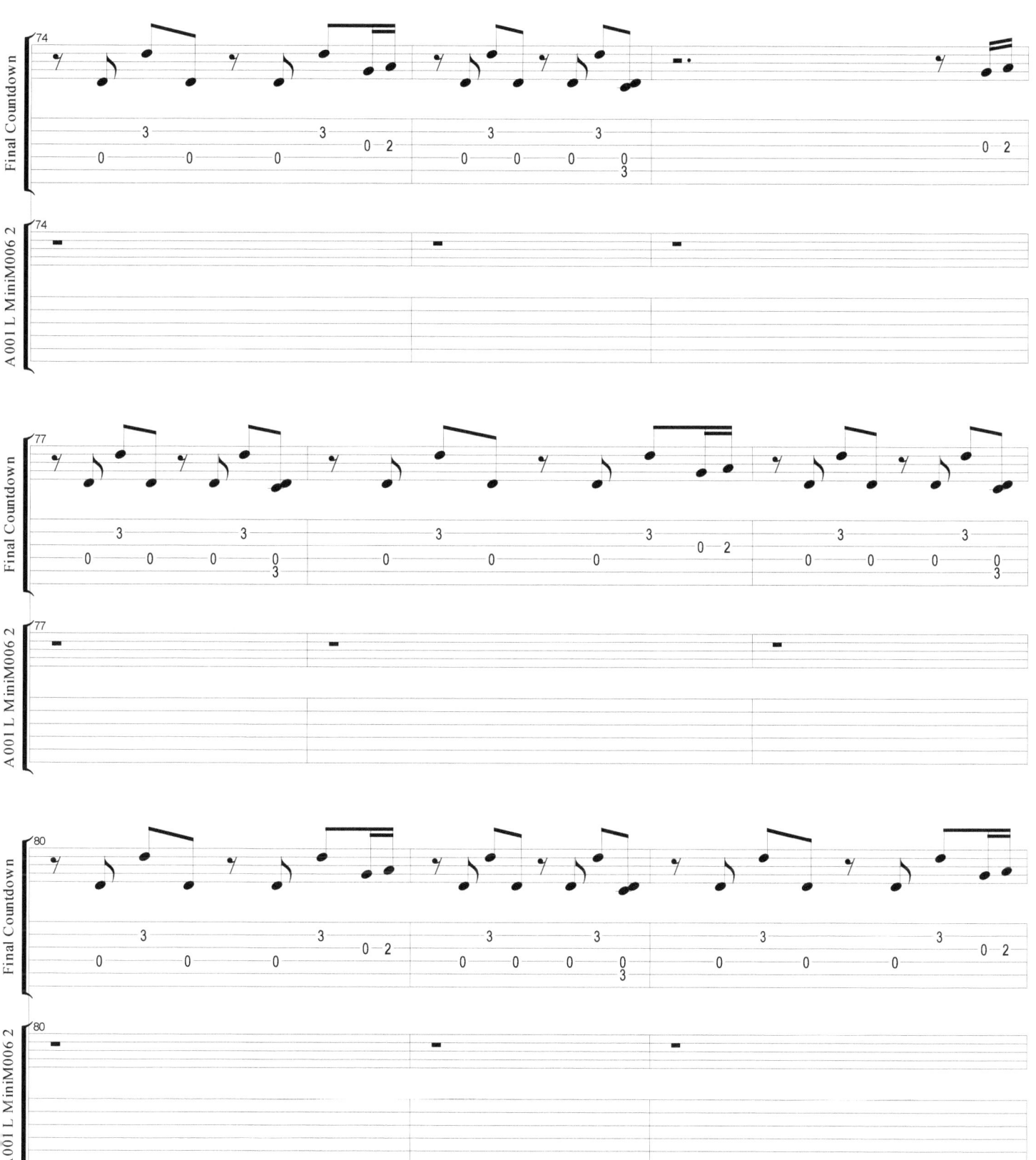

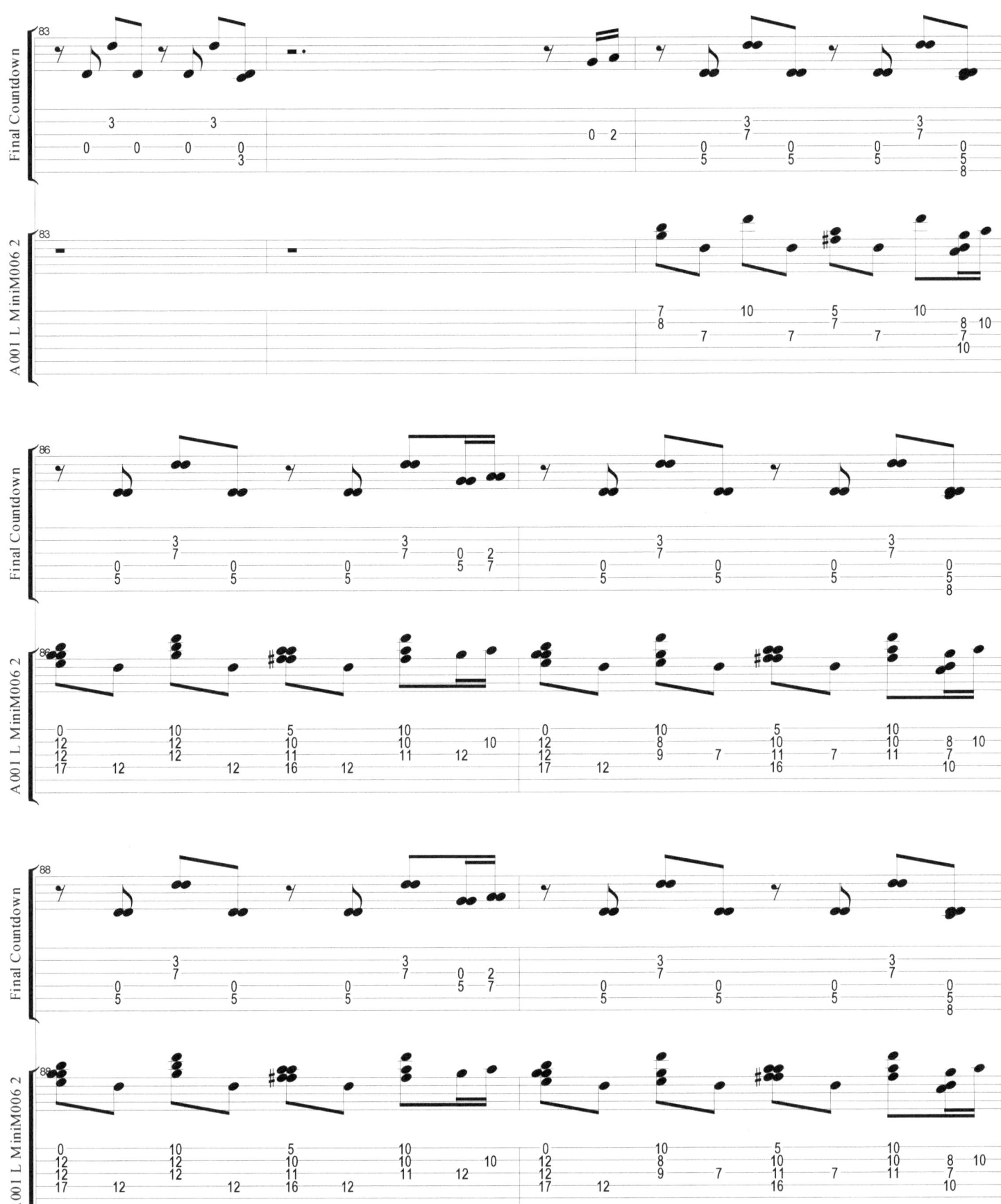

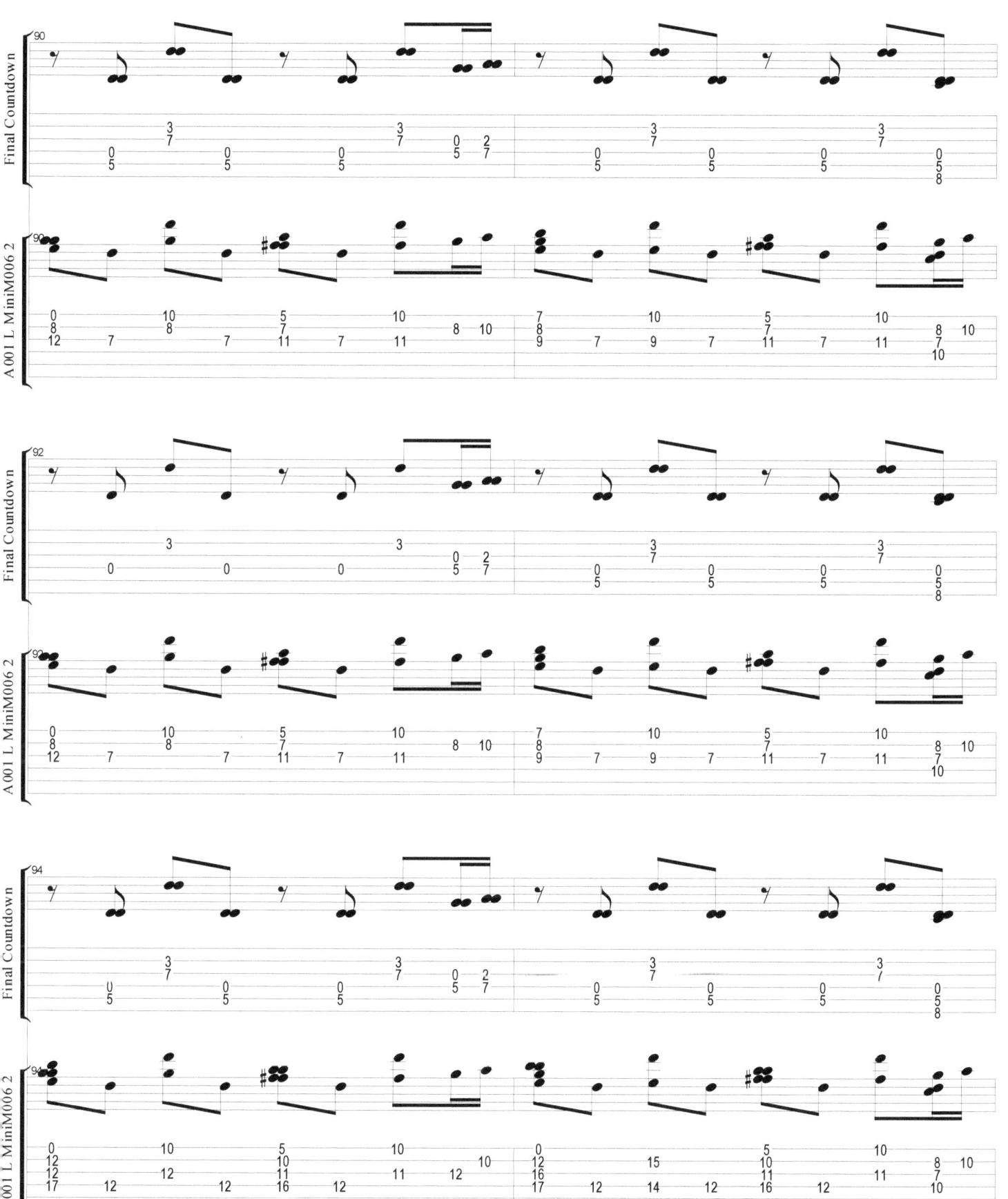

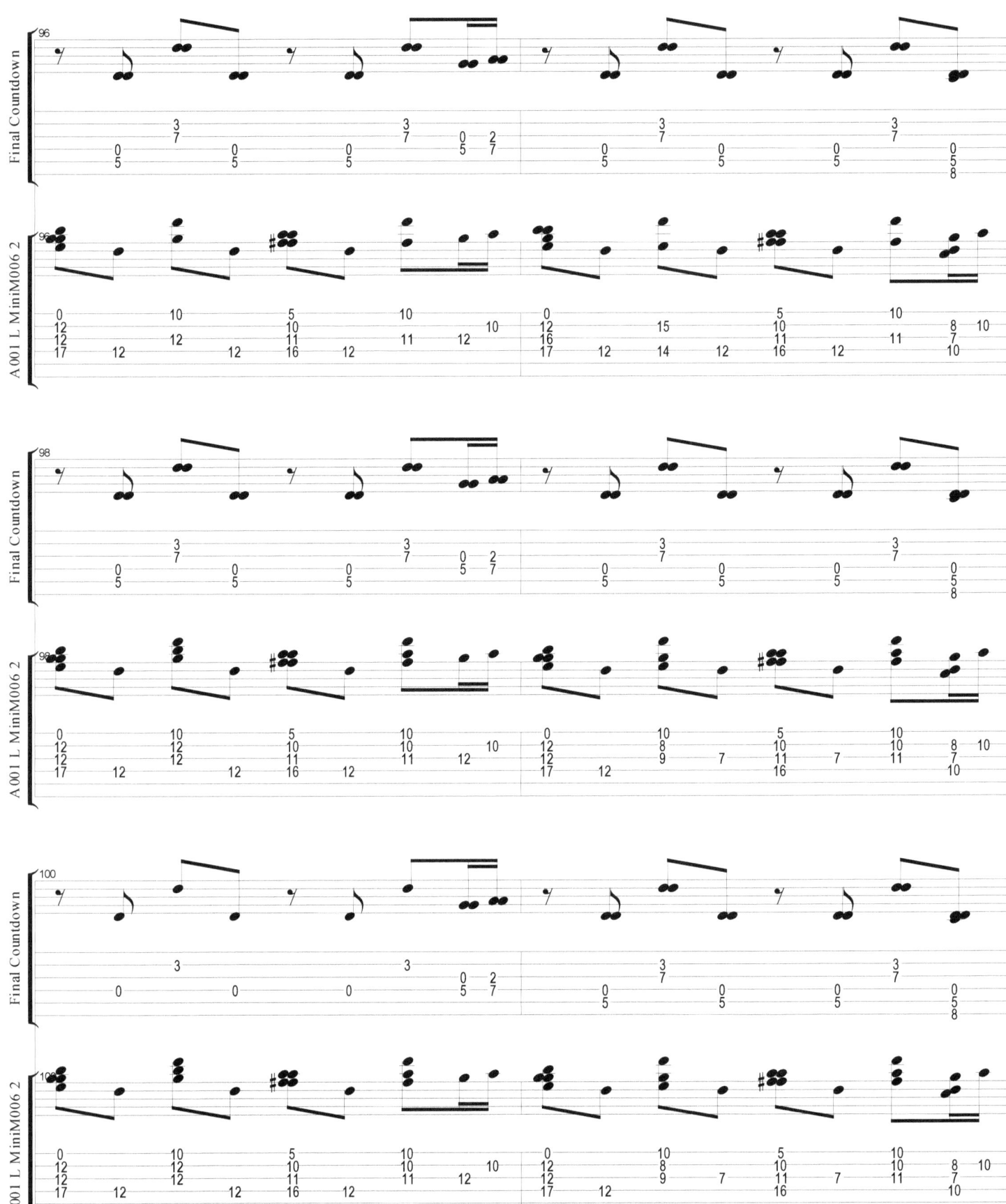

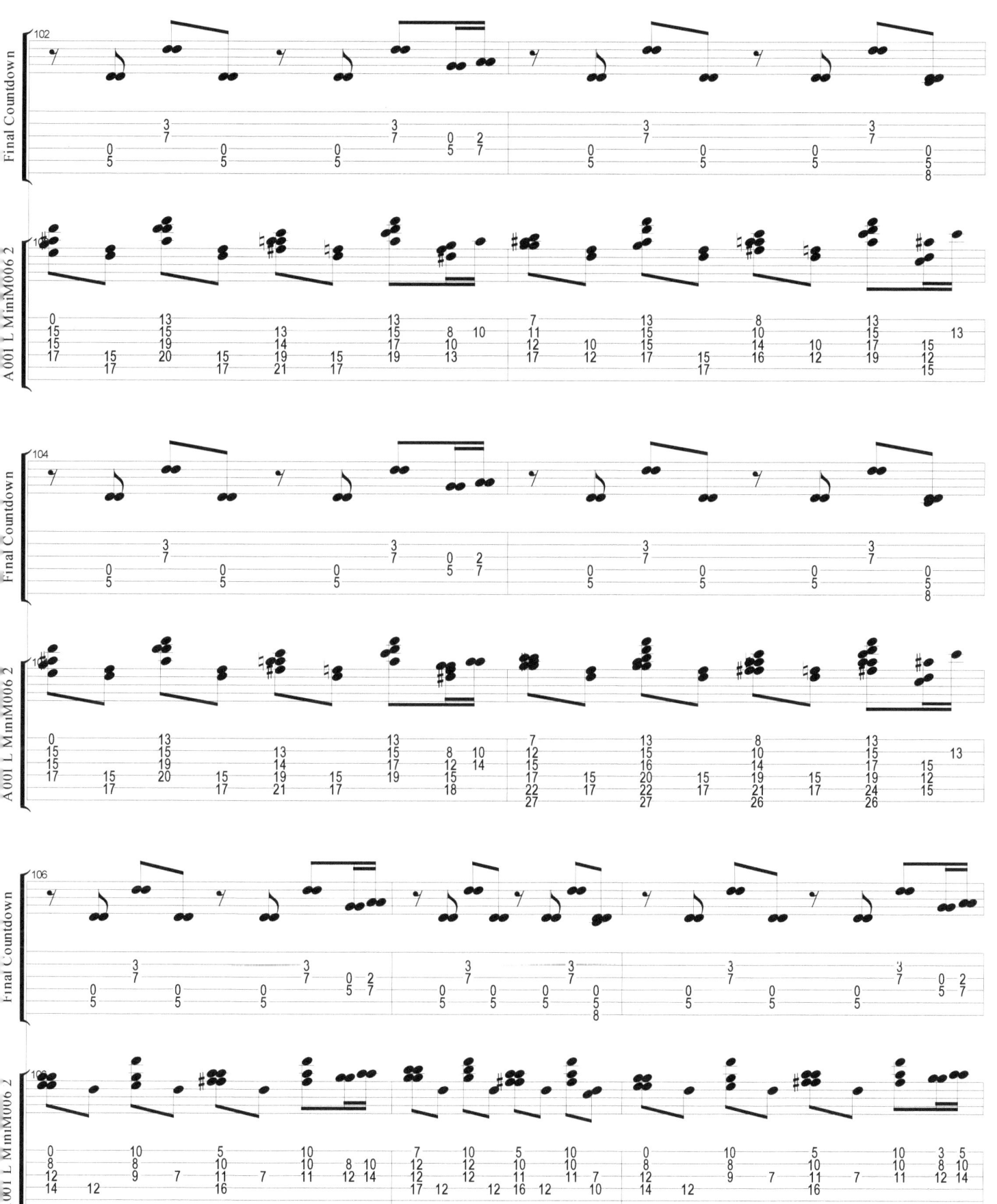

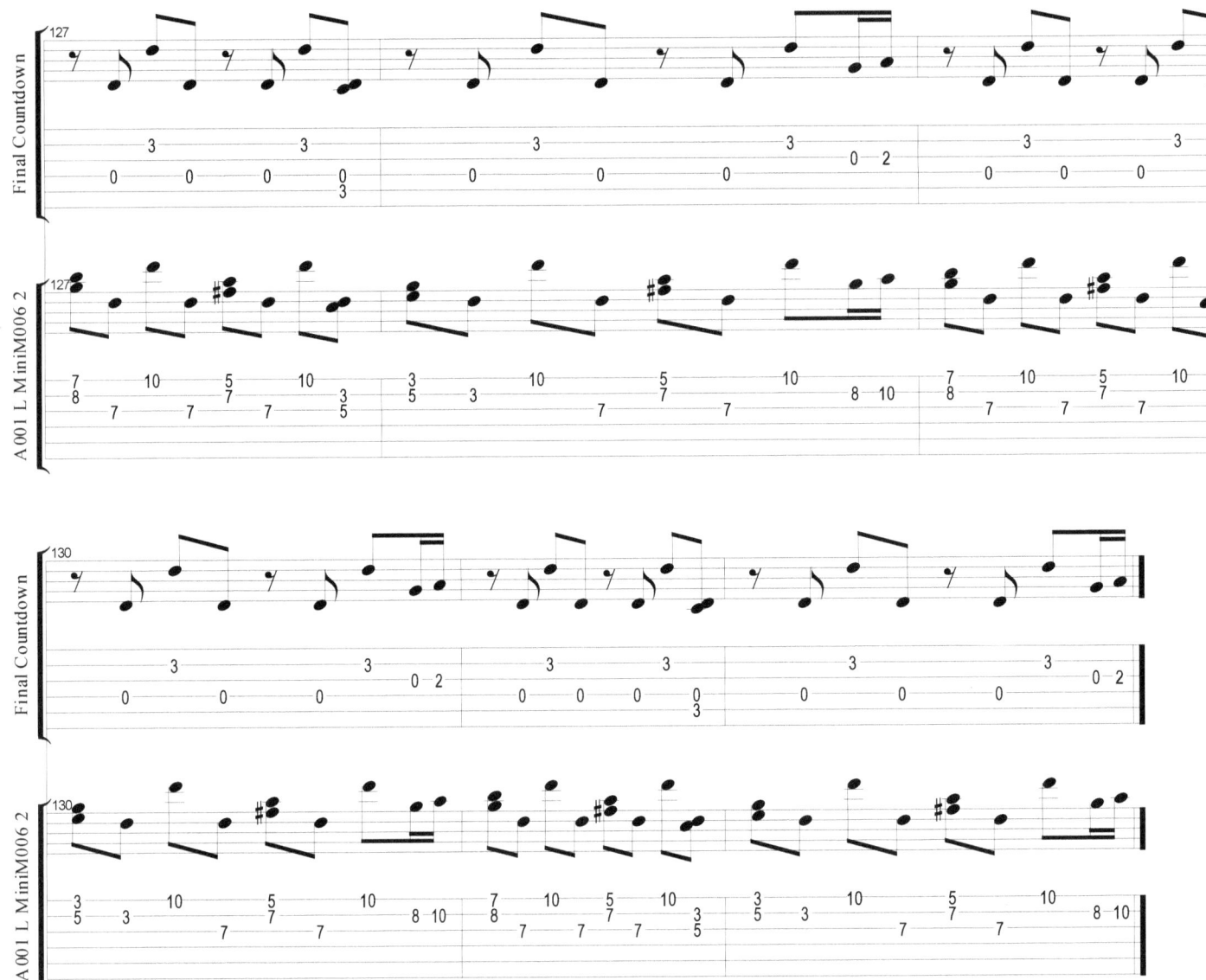

www.ingramcontent.com/pod-product-compliance
Lightning Source LLC
LaVergne TN
LVHW081549060526
838201LV00054B/1828

9798330231584